the juncture of architecture, environment, and digital culture. The
series looks at thematics in our age
of globalization that are shaping
the built environment in unexpected
yet radically significant ways.

—goes soft

[Soft] refers to responsive, indeterminate, flexible, and immaterial
systems that operate through feedback, organization and resilience.
These complex systems transform
through time to acknowledge shifting
and indeterminate situations—
characteristics that are evident both
in the dynamics of contemporary
society and the natural environment.

bracket —— goes soft —— almanac 2

www.brkt.org

editors ——
Neeraj Bhatia
Lola Sheppard

editorial board ——
Neeraj Bhatia
Benjamin Bratton
Julia Czerniak
Jeffrey Inaba
Geoff Manaugh
Philippe Rahm
Charles Renfro
Lola Sheppard

collaborators ——
InfraNet Lab
www.infranetlab.org
Archinect
www.archinect.com

sponsor ——
Graham Foundation for Advanced Studies in the Fine Arts
www.grahamfoundation.org

designer ——
Thumb
www.thumbprojects.com

published by ——
Actar
Barcelona — New York
info@actar.com
www.actar.com

distributed by ——
ActarD
Barcelona — New York
www.actar-d.com

Roca i Batlle 2
E-08023 Barcelona
T +34 93 417 49 93
F +34 93 418 67 07
salesbarcelona@actar.com

151 Grand Street, 5th floor
New York, NY 10013, USA
T +1 212 966 2207
F +1 212 966 2214
salesnewyork@actar.com

isbn ——
978-84-15391-02-9

DL: B-7933-2012

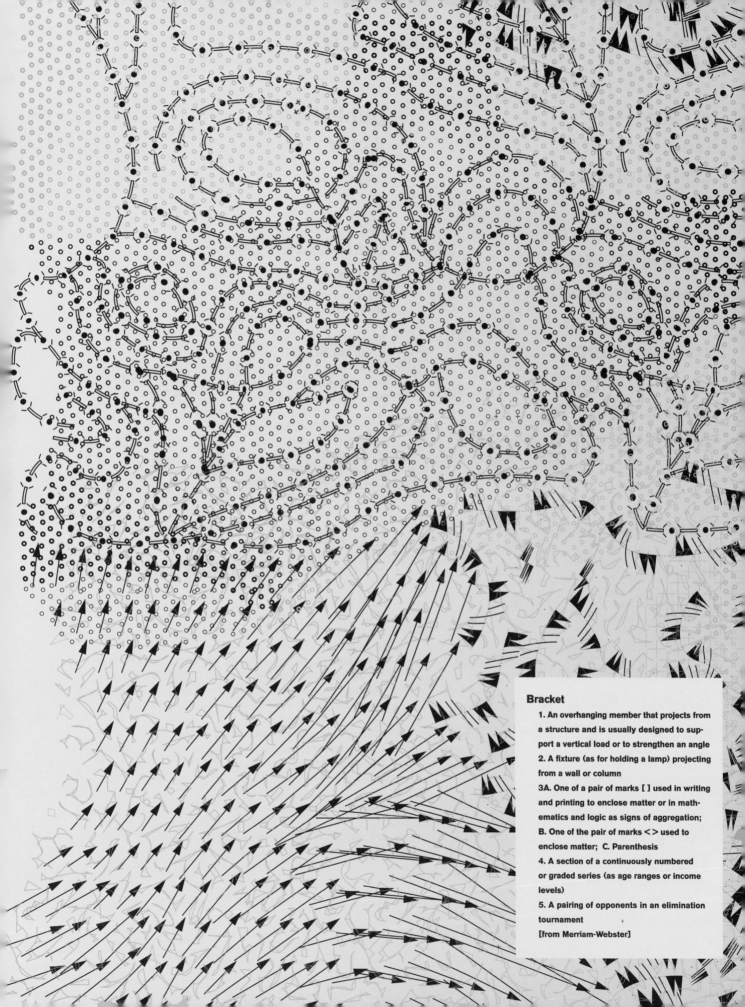

Bracket

1. An overhanging member that projects from a structure and is usually designed to support a vertical load or to strengthen an angle

2. A fixture (as for holding a lamp) projecting from a wall or column

3A. One of a pair of marks [ ] used in writing and printing to enclose matter or in mathematics and logic as signs of aggregation; B. One of the pair of marks < > used to enclose matter; C. Parenthesis

4. A section of a continuously numbered or graded series (as age ranges or income levels)

5. A pairing of opponents in an elimination tournament

[from Merriam-Webster]

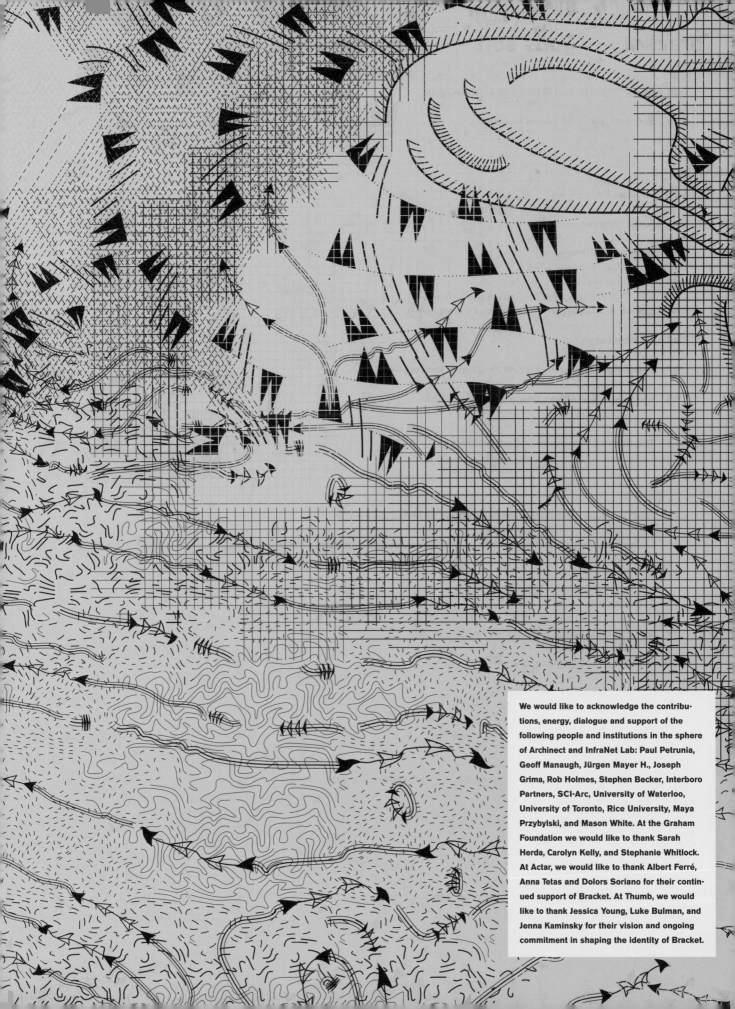

We would like to acknowledge the contributions, energy, dialogue and support of the following people and institutions in the sphere of Archinect and InfraNet Lab: Paul Petrunia, Geoff Manaugh, Jürgen Mayer H., Joseph Grima, Rob Holmes, Stephen Becker, Interboro Partners, SCI-Arc, University of Waterloo, University of Toronto, Rice University, Maya Przybylski, and Mason White. At the Graham Foundation we would like to thank Sarah Herda, Carolyn Kelly, and Stephanie Whitlock. At Actar, we would like to thank Albert Ferré, Anna Tetas and Dolors Soriano for their continued support of Bracket. At Thumb, we would like to thank Jessica Young, Luke Bulman, and Jenna Kaminsky for their vision and ongoing commitment in shaping the identity of Bracket.

bracket —— goes soft —— almanac 2

formatting/distributing

contingency/resilience

diffusing/generating

GOING SOFT

NEERAJ BHATIA & LOLA SHEPPARD

The term *soft* is expansive in its meanings—it describes material qualities, evokes character traits, defines strategies of persuasion, models of systems thinking and problem-solving, and new approaches to design. This said, the most obvious associations with soft have been material characteristics—yielding readily to touch or pressure, smooth, pliable, malleable or plastic. These definitions position soft as an *adjective* often tied to a physical thing or noun. Such characterizations of soft aligned with several design motives during the 1960s and 70s that were entrenched in a skepticism of modernism—soft was deemed to enable individualism, responsiveness, nomadism, and anarchy.

Many architects of the 1960s can be seen as forerunners in a soft campaign. Archigram's investigations into pods, Price's inflatable roof structures or Fuller's research into lightness were all literally soft, and often scaled to the material properties of human occupation. However, larger urban visions such as *Plug-In City, Ville Spatiale*, or *Potteries Thinkbelt* can equally be understood as soft. What unites these projects was their attempt to develop design strategies that shifted from the malleability of a material to the flexibility of a *system*. In so doing they developed new characteristics of soft that aligned the term as a *verb*.

The development of soft architecture strategies in the 1960s corresponded to an era of upheaval—the emerging awareness of environmental issues, radical transformations in social structures in Europe and North America and technological innovations, not least with the expansion of computing, cybernetics, aeronautics and biology. We find ourselves in yet another era of far-reaching transformation—economic, ecological, political and climatic amongst others—prompting the repositioning of the role and performance of architecture, infrastructure, and technology. Soft has reemerged and

gained increasing traction as a counterpoint to permanent, static and hard systems that are no longer viewed as suitable to address contemporary urban complexities and their continual transformations.

Bracket [goes Soft] examines the use and implications of soft today—from the scale of material innovation to territorial networks. While the projects in *Bracket 2* are diverse in deployment and in the issues they engage, they share several key characteristics—proposing systems, networks and technologies that are responsive, adaptable, scalable, non-linear, and multivalent. Certain projects reveal how soft systems rely on engagement with their larger environment, collecting and sensing atmospheric information, and through feedback, adapting the system to augment performance. Other projects propose soft systems which can function as interfaces with the environment—whether mitigating or harnessing it—operating at the scale of a wall, a building, or a landscape. Another strand of projects presented in *Bracket 2* are tactical and strategic in nature; enabling them to operate, often covertly, within existing organizational structures. They opportunistically subvert rules and limitations, to support new ecologies—whether natural, economic or political. Other proposals embed intelligence in the organization and format of the system, accommodating transformation by altering the system or process itself. Several speculations test resilience by expanding their capacity to adapt to extrinsic as well as intrinsic factors, enabling them to anticipate, recover and transform in unexpected situations. Lastly, a series of projects expose how the networking of smaller units or interventions, diffused across a larger territory, can generate, collect, or respond at a vast scale. Agile, these tentacular networks can expand or retract as resources or needs change.

Nicholas Negroponte proposed in his book, *Soft Architecture Machines* (1975), a software application which

∧   Julie Mehretu, *Black City*, 2007, ink and acrylic on canvas, 120 x 192 in. (Image © the artist/White Cube, photo by Tim Thayer)

facilitated user participation in design in order to augment the number of variables and contingencies taken into consideration in the design process, while simultaneously reducing the sole authorship of the architect.[1] More recently, Sanford Kwinter, in his essay 'Soft Systems' discusses a paradigm shift, which was sparked by the first image of the earth transmitted by the Apollo astronauts in 1968. In that moment, Kwinter argues, we understood the earth (and its systems) to be dynamic, "driven by its very 'softness,' its capacity to move, to differentiate internally, to absorb, transform, and exchange information with its surroundings, to develop complex interdependent sub and super systems."[2] Not only does Kwinter posit that the stability of the system is rooted in its very dynamism, he draws examples from the XXL (the earth) to the XS (genetics) to reveal the diversity, non-linearity and scalar indifference of various soft systems. The projects included in *Bracket [goes Soft]* offer a productive evolution to Negroponte's 'soft architecture machines.' While they embrace his ambition of architecture engaging its environmental and programmatic complexity, the projects that follow rely both on architecture's traditional and expanded parameters—materiality, spatial organization, program, as well as economics, politics, and ecology—while resolutely leveraging the design of the system, the protocol, and the organization. Akin to Kwinter's assessment of the planetary dynamics, the projects herein oscillate between a capacity for flux and indeterminacy, and conditions of stasis in which their environments are organized and reorganized temporally, programmatically, politically and socially. While rooted in such

origins, the projects and articles of *Bracket 2* expand and build on the meaning of soft.

As soft reemerges and expands its territory once again, it simultaneously risks futility by the dilution of its meaning and its associated criticality. The intention of this year's almanac is to unpack the issue of soft in order to embrace both its breadth and depth. For *Bracket [goes Soft]* we invited Benjamin Bratton, Julia Czerniak, Jeffrey Inaba, Geoff Manaugh, Philippe Rahm, and Charles Renfro to mine the renewed depth and breadth of soft systems. The projects of *Bracket [goes Soft]* expand the role of the architect, proposing an architecture which engages its wider context. In a moment of emerging crises, soft systems are particularly well-suited to operate within the increasingly dynamic complexity of our environment.

1. Nicholas Negroponte, *Soft Architecture Machines* (Cambridge: MIT Press, 1975), 360.

2. Sanford Kwinter, "Soft Systems," in *Culture Lab*, ed. Brian Boigon (New York: Princeton Architecture Press, 1993), 210.

SOFT SERVE SPACE

GEOFF MANAUGH

If soft systems, as the editors of *Bracket* maintain, serve as "a counterpoint to permanent, static and hard systems," then we should ask ourselves what spatial benefits such systems might bring, under what circumstances they will function best, and what they might actually look like (if they can be seen at all). Will we recognize soft when we see it?

Soft, in the context of this essay, is the reconfigurable, the instant, the apparently immaterial, the cloudlike, the on-demand. Soft is that which responds with flexibility. Soft is the hidden. The behind-the-scenes. The just-in-time. The hack. The quick fix. Soft is duct tape, wire, and string. Soft is always the wind and sometimes the sail. Soft can be camouflage, the near-copy, the well-intended counterfeit, the clone. Soft can be dissimulation. Soft is that which invades not by entering but by enveloping. Soft surrounds. Soft seeps up from below. Soft permeates and infests. Soft arrives without announcing itself. Soft erupts. Soft is not the crack but the caulking. Soft is not the house but the haunting.

The following examples are offered as nothing more than a short catalog of soft systems—some explicitly architectural, others geological, others entirely metaphorical. In all cases, these examples explore how the notion of going soft can be iterated across professions, disciplines, and fields of research—an accumulative approach searching for the elusive quality of what it means to be soft. These examples also all re-articulate a handful of themes, both major and minor, that can be found in the projects and essays that appear in the rest of this publication.

Soft Urbanism

What is a soft city? Taken in its most literal—and, as we'll see, least interesting—sense, the soft metropolis is a tent city, a refugee camp, a forward-operating base, a caravan park. The soft metropolis is instant and on-demand—if there is not a city here today, there will be one tomorrow. Portable, reconfigurable, and often soft on the level of tensile materials, the tent city is there when you need it. It is easily deployed, perhaps even air-dropped by helicopter or emergency airplane. Duffel bag urbanism, we might also describe it, treats the infrastructure of the city like a form of luggage, unpacked in a kit of parts at the scene of natural disasters, acts of war, and terrorist attacks.

Examples are by no means hard to find. From a "modular air-transportable field camp" that has been "tested at the Arctic Circle" by its manufacturer, Kärcher Futuretech[1] to the "first-responder architecture" of Reeves EMS[2]—which includes such "turn key" options as Casualty Collection Points, Medical Surge Facilities, a Mobile Vaccination System, and even Incident Command Posts for use in remote warzones—architectural and infrastructural networks are often pushed in new design directions by extreme events.

The "softness" of the systems referred to here is often just a metaphor; when we look at the construction and delivery systems that allow for these particular spatial formats to be implemented, we see that they can be very far from materially malleable. For instance, "soft" medical infrastructure—although, on occasion, literally inflatable, as with a 2010 Doctors Without Borders post-earthquake field hospital in Haiti[3]—takes the form of rapidly deployed medical facilities operated by organizations such as the Red Cross and the UN, and they are frequently "containerized." In other words, hard-shell freight shipping containers are simply repurposed as operating theaters, quarantine facilities, and triage wards, and then bolted together in situ to form functional micro-metropolises. Their notional softness comes simply from their ease of transport, installation, inhabitation, and dismantling, not from any material property of which they consist.

In any case, while this vision of a city in a suitcase harks back to such nostalgic avant-gardes as Archigram, it is a very real vision being implemented today by military contractors, emergency aid foundations, and even the planners of rock concert infrastructure. The soft city is alive and well, functioning with or without the design help of architects.

Soft Data

Of course, there is another kind of softness at play in this discussion, and that is the softness of data—the soft networks of demographic information, retail tracking, consumer profiling, and the state surveillance of citizenry.

As many writers elsewhere have already made clear—with concepts such as Mark Shepard's "sentient city"[4] and Dan Hill's "street as platform,"[5] or the recent work on urban software ensembles by Rob Kitchin and Martin Dodge[6]—the continuous production of information is now inseparable from many lived aspects of contemporary urbanism. The "soft city" in this formulation is not instantly delivered by military cargo plane, but instead is generated, in literal bits and pieces, every time you make a purchase, phone a loved one, log-in to a social networking site, or enter a workplace with your personal security pass.

1. Kärcher Futuretech GmbH, "Systems for Peacekeepers," http://www.karcher-futuretech.com/

2. Reeves EMS, "First Response and Paramedic EMS Equipment," http://www.reevesems.com/

3. Doctors without Borders, "Haiti: MSF Treats More than 1,000 Patients; Inflatable Hospital on the Way," http://www.doctorswithoutborders.org/news/article.cfm?cat=field-news&id=4155

4. Towards the Sentient City, http://www.sentientcity.net/

5. City of Sound, "The Street as Platform," http://www.cityofsound.com/blog/2008/02/the-street-as-p.html

6. Rob Kitchin and Martin Dodge, *Code/Space: Software and Everyday Life* (Cambridge: MIT Press, 2011).

∧   Soldiers of the Louisiana Army National Guard's 844th Engineer Company dump sand on a geotextile fabric to reinforce a rockwall on Elmers Island in Grand Isle, LA, in support of the Deep Horizon oil spill cleanup efforts. A geotextile fabric is a permeable textile material used to increase soil stability, provide erosion control or aid in drainage. (Photo by Staff Sgt. Jeffrey Barone)

∧   Tent wards at Campbell Hospital, Washington, D.C in the 1860s. (Library of Congress Prints and Photographs Division Washington, D.C. 20540 USA)

∧ **Debris Basin, Los Angeles, 2011. (Photo by Geoff Manaugh)**

These data streams come with their own quite obvious potentials for abuse. Efforts to critique the complicity of customer loyalty programs, data mining, social networking sites such as Facebook, and even iPhone tracking, maps an ongoing surrender of private information to corporate access and state regulation which deserves far more attention in the context of the soft metropolis. In an admittedly off-the-cuff but nonetheless rhetorically compelling summary of these risks, anonymous Dutch blogger Wilfried Hou Je Bek ("Wilfried Shut Your Trap") dismisses the very idea of ubiquitous computing, describing it as "short-sighted techno-fetish careerism and arty fartsy surveillance chic in ludic preparation for the aggregating police state."[7]

In any case, the hard city of streets and buildings can be supplemented and experientially complicated by the otherwise nonvisual presence of a parallel city of data flows. It is a kind of unseen digital tide with profound effects in physical space—where a new shop might open, where social-ites might gather for an evening drink, where the police will choose to increase their patrols in your city tomorrow night—to an extent that architects themselves are only beginning to work with and appreciate.

Soft Geography

However, the revelation of a soft city existing in parallel to the one you believe you currently live in is by no means limited to the present historical context. The town of Wroxeter, England,

for instance, stands atop a Roman city. Famously though, this parallel metropolis beneath Wroxeter's streets is not being dug up and studied through the use of shovels and spades; it is being mapped without moving the earth at all, through the use of magnetic resistivity and ground-penetrating radar. These tools of soft excavation do not require brute inva-sion of the rock and soil with the standard tools of today's archaeological repertoire. Indeed, performing archaeology in Wroxeter seems more like watching a strangely lo-fi, local television channel: one without plot or characterization, and broadcast from within the surface of the earth by means of handheld scanning equipment.

This Roman shadow city exists in tandem with today's Wroxeter, on the same ground—its streets intersecting with Wroxeter's streets, its houses underlying Wroxeter's founda-tions—but otherwise avoiding a physical manifestation. The traces of this city are mere bleeps on screens, anomalous readings on monitors. One might even conspiratorially sug-gest, tongue planted firmly in cheek, that this ancient Roman city is not really there at all: rather, it has been invented by bored archaeologists who never need to clean up and display material artifacts. They are thus able to tell tall tales of this soft presence beneath everyone's feet, offering digital tours of a city everyone paradoxically lives in without ever actually seeing.[8] Because soft can operate on the non-visual, it allows fiction to exist adjacent to reality.

7. Cryptoforestry, "The Sentient City [locative media again & again & again…]," http://cryp-toforest.blogspot.com/2011/05/sentient-city-locative-media-again.html

8. See, for instance, http://dissertations.ub.rug.nl/FILES/faculties/arts/2002/p.m.van.leusen/ch3.pdf

∧   **Debris Basin, Los Angeles, 2011. (Photo by Geoff Manaugh)**

∧ *Grounding: Landslide Mitigation Housing* **by Jared Winchester.**

Wroxeter is only one, particularly useful example of the techniques of soft archaeology. LiDAR, muon-detection equipment, ground-penetrating radar, and infrared spectroscopy are all used widely and to great success in the detection of archaeological remains. Literally as I write this essay, a story has appeared on the BBC that a previously unknown cluster of pyramids buried in the sands of Egypt, has been discovered through the use of infrared imaging techniques; the evidence was gathered by University of Alabama professor Sarah Parcak, using satellites in orbit "700km above the earth, equipped with cameras so powerful they can pin-point objects less than one meter in diameter on the earth's surface."[9]

In fact, technologically similar discoveries are made on a near continual basis in the rain forests of Central and South America and in the southwestern desert of the United States. In the latter case, traces of ancient canals and Native American campsites are increasingly "excavated" without invasive disturbance of the earth.

This detection of a soft geography, by means of specialty instrumentation, is not unique to archaeology. All such sensing equipment projects its own stratigraphies, we might say: its own laminations and overlays on the landscape. Wind speed, air pressure, temperature, seismicity, radiation, disease, pollen, pollution, humidity: instrumentation uncovers layers of data that can often seem, in retrospect, always to have been there; as much a part of the landscape as the bedrock our cities are built upon.

These evanescent terrains, both meteorological and digital, have already been explored at great length and there would be very little reason to repeat those analyses here. What is important in the present context is that we maintain focus on all that is soft in the environments around us.

Softslide

Protecting against catastrophic movements of the earth doesn't always have to occur within the ground, or infra-terrestrially. In his project *Grounding: Landslide Mitigation Housing*, seen on page 94, Jared Winchester proposes an architecturally unlikely but tectonically thought-provoking project, looking at how housing might be dynamically and simultaneously anchored and de-anchored from the ground in the event of landslides or earthquakes. The houses would thus act more like cable cars, roped and webbed together by way of giant hinges, thus resisting integration into the landslide they have surfed to safety. Their project brings to mind a similar work called "Retreating Village" by Smout Allen. Smout Allen's English coastal village is similarly operational in its evasion of terrestrial collapse. In their case, this is accomplished through a deliberate misuse of tactical sailing gear, which the architects have poetically renamed as "rope gardens" and other "devices of haulage," used literally to pull these homes to safety as the cliffs crumble around them.[10]

However, locations of terrestrial instability are not uncommon. In his essay "Los Angeles Against the Mountains," republished in *The Control of Nature*[11], author John McPhee

9. BBC News World, "Egyptian Pyramids found by Infra-red Satellite Images," http://www.bbc.co.uk/news/world-13522957

10. Smout Allen, "Retreating Village," http://www.smoutallen.com/index.php?/projects/retreating-village/

11. John McPhee, *The Control of Nature* (New York: Farrar, Straus & Giroux, 1989).

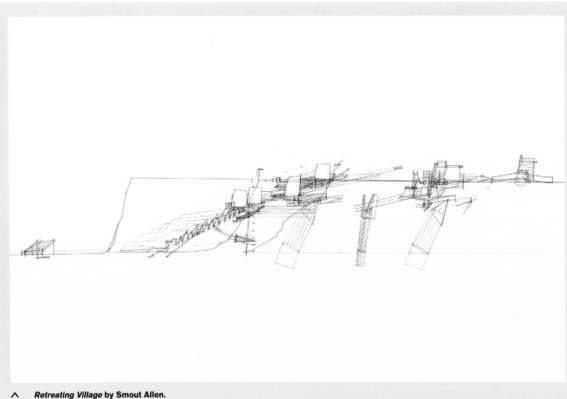

∧ *Retreating Village* by Smout Allen.

introduces us to the rockslides and debris flows of greater Los Angeles, including the often bizarre spatial defenses through which buildings try to survive in the fallout paths of "debris slugs" and other forms of geologic mass wasting. The outermost suburbs of L.A. have reached what McPhee calls the "real-estate line of maximum advance" against the dark bulk of the San Gabriels—a mountain range "divided by faults, defined by faults, and framed by them," and therefore "disintegrating at a rate that is among the fastest in the world." In the process, those mountains produce extraordinary rockslides, events of slippage that often crash right through people's houses. In the face of "this heaving violence of wet cement," as McPhee describes it, new architectural techniques have become urgently necessary. "At least one family," for instance, "has experienced so many debris flows coming through their back yard that they long ago installed overhead doors in the rear end of their built-in garage. To guide the flows, they put deflection walls in their back yard. Now when the boulders come they open both ends of their garage, and the debris goes through to the street." The house becomes a soft mechanism through which itinerant geology can flow.

Deflection walls, overhead doors, feeder channels, concrete crib structures—these emerging defensive typologies are not limited to the domestic world. As a means of protecting itself, the whole of Los Angeles County has embarked on a campaign to construct and maintain debris basins on the soft, mountainous edge of the city; these are truly massive pits into which hillside debris can be collected. The city has surrounded itself with a necklace of voids in order to counteract an earth that moves.

These soft defenses—or passive infrastructures—are the flipside of both Winchester's and Smout Allen's respective projects. In other words, in Los Angeles, the houses remain stationary while the landscape around them is revised and edited for safety; in the other case, the houses themselves move, forming mobile constellations of domestic space that slide back and forth on the earth's surface like a skater on ice. They are examples, we might say, of soft planning.

Soft Machine

It is not always the case, as some of these examples might otherwise imply, that soft can only be used for beneficent purposes. Soft can also be a strategy of invasion, surveillance, and war.

DARPA's ChemBots program, for example, aims to create "soft robots."[12] On the project's website, ChemBots' project director, Gill Pratt, explains that each robot will be able to pass through an "opening much smaller than the largest characteristic of the robot itself," squeezing through cracks, similar to a cockroach. To accomplish this, the program "merges materials chemistry and robotics," using techniques such as "gel-solid transitions, electro-and magneto-rheological materials, geometric transitions, and reversible chemical and particle association and dissociation." DARPA explains these robots' ultimately aggressive purpose: "During military

12. Defense Advanced Research Projects Agency, "Chemical Robots (Chembots)" http://www.darpa.mil/Our_Work/DSO/Programs/Chemical_Robots_(ChemBots).aspx

operations it can be important to gain covert access to denied or hostile space. Unmanned platforms such as mechanical robots are of limited effectiveness if the only available points of entry are small openings." Soon, though, soft robots "will help warfighters gain access to denied spaces and effectively perform covert tasks."

Removing these devices from their military context, however, yields extraordinary possibilities for terrestrial exploration—possibilities, we should hope, less amenable to abuse by those in positions of power. These could include what we might describe as the swarm-mapping of otherwise inaccessible cave systems, as well as tasks such as searching post-disaster ruins for survivors.

Briefly, I'll mention that Gill Pratt is also project director for, among other things, a program called Programmable Matter.[13] Programmable Matter "represents the convergence of chemistry, information theory and control into a new materials design paradigm—'InfoChemistry'—that focuses on building information directly into materials." The resulting, highly malleable material networks, able to "reversibly assemble into complex 3D objects," will thus be transformable, intelligent, potentially self-improving, and semi-autonomous. Put briefly, they will be soft.

Soft Futures

As this book's speculative projects and essays make clear, the subject of soft has only barely been broached. From non-invasive soft surgery to soft seismic engineering, strategies of resilience, flexibility, spatial auto-correction, and transformability have become a vibrant sub-stream within the larger context of today's technical practices.

The examples included both in this essay and in this edition of *Bracket* are only the beginning of a soft catalog, or soft glossary—a field of research that, by necessity, will cross disciplines, call on whole new forms of spatial investigation, and instigate shifts in the very idea of what it means to practice design.

13. Defense Advanced Research Projects Agency, "Programmable Matter," http://www. darpa.mil/Our_Work/DSO/Programs/ Programmable_Matter.aspx

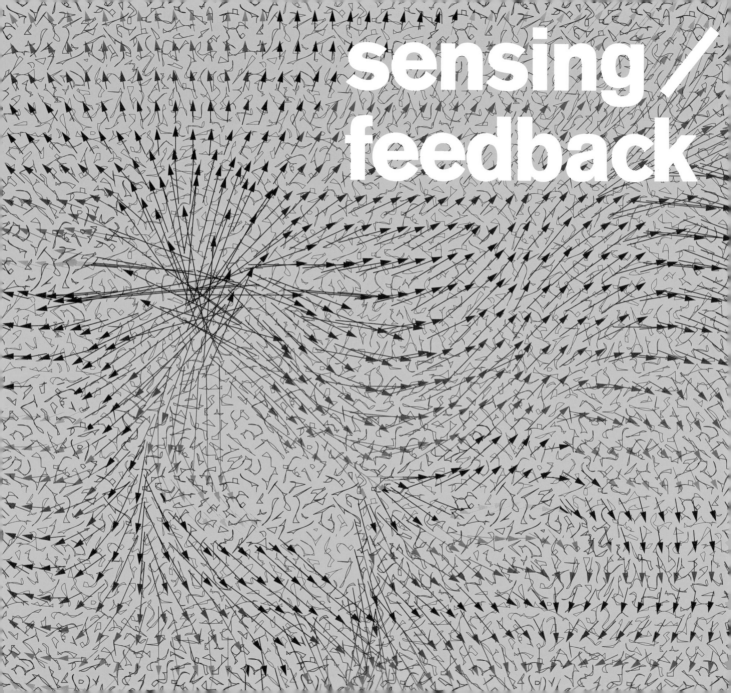

sensing/
feedback

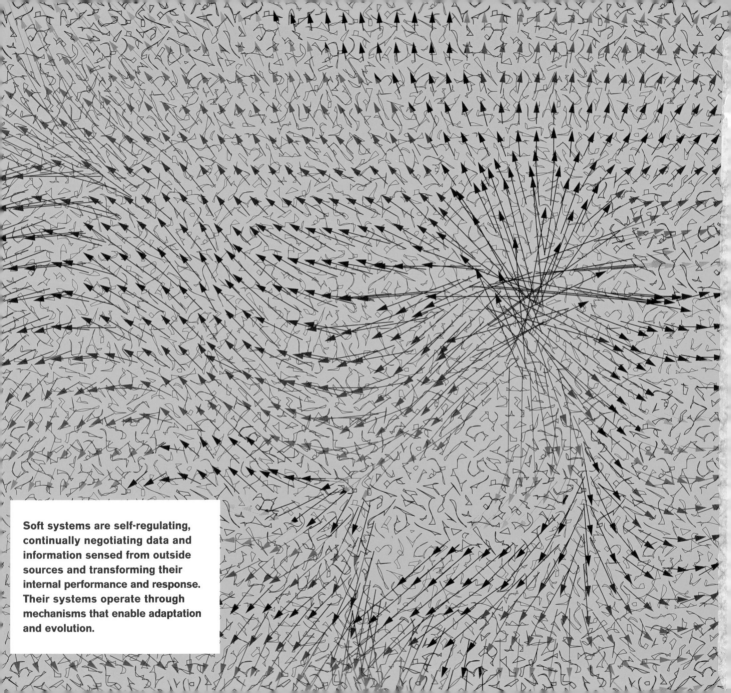

Soft systems are self-regulating,
continually negotiating data and
information sensed from outside
sources and transforming their
internal performance and response.
Their systems operate through
mechanisms that enable adaptation
and evolution.

BUOYANT LIGHT

CLAIRE LUBELL & VIRGINIA FERNANDEZ

∧   **View of Igloolik at night, illuminated
on land and water by a distributed series of
buoyant lights.**

The Canadian Arctic is a vast landscape, dotted with remote communities whose lives depend on natural cycles for subsistence. While imagining widespread distribution, *Buoyant Light* is sited in Igloolik, an Inuit community of 1600 inhabitants. Like much of the Arctic, Igloolik is witness to acute changes to permafrost, sea levels and ice depths. As an island, it is particularly vulnerable to unreliable freeze-thaw cycles of the sea, which directly affects safe hunting and traveling.

Buoyant Light frames light as a constant in the rapidly changing Canadian Arctic climate where the solar path has become a datum against which to track changes in other seasonal cycles. Recognizing that in this fragile environment, any physical changes can have powerful implications, the project proposes an ethereal intervention that would improve the life of the Inuit through light. *Buoyant Light* consists of a balloon and a buoy, which serve a dual function: to harvest solar energy, providing Igloolik with light in the long winter; and to make data visually accessible to the community. The proposal leverages the needs of global researchers with those of the Inuit by providing an interface between the information collected and the people most directly affected by it. Furthermore, this interface introduces color as part of the seasonal cycle of the Arctic and scatters light in the landscape.

Solar balloons are paired with buoys and used by researchers to gather data on tides, currents, temperature, salinity, sedimentation, and ice profile. Surplus harvested energy is kept in portable batteries in the buoy while a small portion of the energy is used to power the buoy's mechanisms and the LEDs in the balloon. Information regarding sea ice profile, already color-coded according to an international standard, is transmitted to the balloon via fiber optics and communicated through the corresponding color.

Buoyant Light addresses three different needs: the largest balloons are closest to the shore and provide the community with immediate visual access to information. Acting as a traditional lighthouse, they mark the location of the town for approaching travelers and vessels. Lowered in the winter to avoid high winds and storms, the balloons cast light onto the ice, forming a space for meetings, celebrations or performances. The balloons further out in the open waters act as way-finding devices for hunters and travelers. Once distributed throughout Arctic waters, they act as a soft network, creating points of connection between remote communities, while also providing widespread data collection points for international researchers. Finally, the balloons on land delineate gathering spaces around key buildings in the town. A few clusters measure the change in permafrost detrimental to the structural stability of buildings. Over

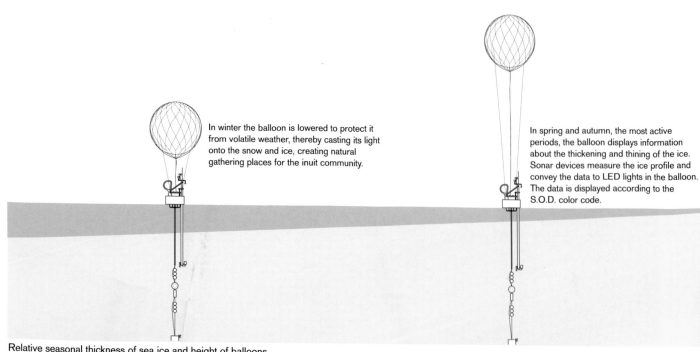

In winter the balloon is lowered to protect it from volatile weather, thereby casting its light onto the snow and ice, creating natural gathering places for the inuit community.

In spring and autumn, the most active periods, the balloon displays information about the thickening and thining of the ice. Sonar devices measure the ice profile and convey the data to LED lights in the balloon. The data is displayed according to the S.O.D. color code.

Relative seasonal thickness of sea ice and height of balloons

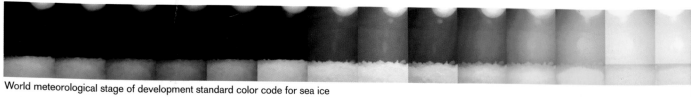

World meteorological stage of development standard color code for sea ice

24 hour daylight cycle for 70° north

Seasonal break up and freeze up of sea ice around Igloolik

| January | February | March | April | May | June |

∧   **Relationship of *Buoyant Light* to seasonal cycles. (Information compiled from: Natural Resources Canada, "Sea Ice," http://atlas. nrcan.gc.ca/site/english/maps/environment/ seaice/freeze-up, http://atlas.nrcan.gc.ca/site/ english/maps/environment/seaice/break-up)**

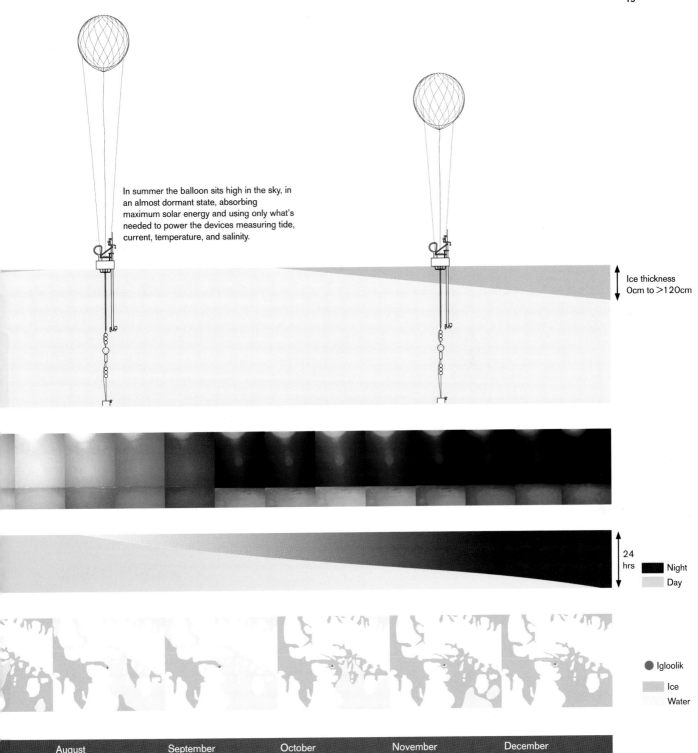

In summer the balloon sits high in the sky, in an almost dormant state, absorbing maximum solar energy and using only what's needed to power the devices measuring tide, current, temperature, and salinity.

Ice thickness
0cm to >120cm

24 hrs

Night
Day

Igloolik
Ice
Water

August   September   October   November   December

∧∧ **Lowered in the winter, balloons near the shore provide places for the community to gather, in this case to watch the youth of Igloolik's *Artcirq* perform.**

∧ **A cluster activates the space outside the Northern Store while measuring permafrost around the building's foundations. New street lighting strengthens urban framework and improves safety at night.**

time, smaller solar balloons could be used to provide a new sustainable lighting solution for Arctic communities, improving energy consumption costs and the safety of inhabitants.

The effect of the lack of daylight on individual emotional well-being has been widely studied by experts; however more difficult to study, is the effect of lack of light on the community as a collective. Due to the high cost of electricity and large-scaled constructions, communities are usually forced to gather in cramped interior spaces during the dark months. As such, beyond its role as an instrument to transmit data, energy and light, *Buoyant Light* also questions the need for, and the nature of, outdoor public space in northern towns. These towns have little urban framework or strategy for growth and development, so the provision of outdoor lighting can also begin to demarcate spaces of gathering and suggest routes or nodes of activity. *Buoyant Light* proposes to define public space in the north as ephemeral, thereby adopting an identity that is as transient as light itself.

• • • **Claire Lubell and Virginia Fernandez recently completed their undergraduate studies at the University of Waterloo, School of Architecture.**

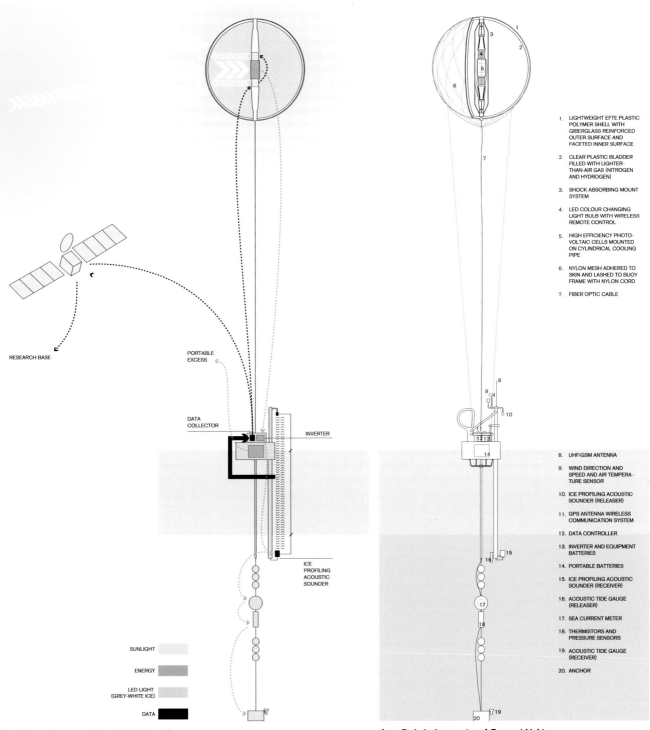

SUNLIGHT

ENERGY

LED LIGHT
(GREY-WHITE ICE)

DATA

∧ Flow of energy, data, and light through
Buoyant Light.

∧ Technical apparatus of *Buoyant Light.*

1. LIGHTWEIGHT EFTE PLASTIC POLYMER SHELL WITH GIBERGLASS REINFORCED OUTER SURFACE AND FACETED INNER SURFACE

2. CLEAR PLASTIC BLADDER FILLED WITH LIGHTER-THAN-AIR GAS (NITROGEN AND HYDROGEN)

3. SHOCK ABSORBING MOUNT SYSTEM

4. LED COLOUR CHANGING LIGHT BULB WITH WIRELESS REMOTE CONTROL

5. HIGH EFFICIENCY PHOTO-VOLTAIC CELLS MOUNTED ON CYLINDRICAL COOLING PIPE

6. NYLON MESH ADHERED TO SKIN AND LASHED TO BUOY FRAME WITH NYLON CORD

7. FIBER OPTIC CABLE

8. UHF/GSM ANTENNA

9. WIND DIRECTION AND SPEED AND AIR TEMPERATURE SENSOR

10. ICE PROFILING ACOUSTIC SOUNDER (RELEASER)

11. GPS ANTENNA WIRELESS COMMUNICATION SYSTEM

12. DATA CONTROLLER

13. INVERTER AND EQUIPMENT BATTERIES

14. PORTABLE BATTERIES

15. ICE PROFILING ACOUSTIC SOUNDER (RECEIVER)

16. ACOUSTIC TIDE GAUGE (RELEASER)

17. SEA CURRENT METER

18. THERMISTORS AND PRESSURE SENSORS

19. ACOUSTIC TIDE GAUGE (RECEIVER)

20. ANCHOR

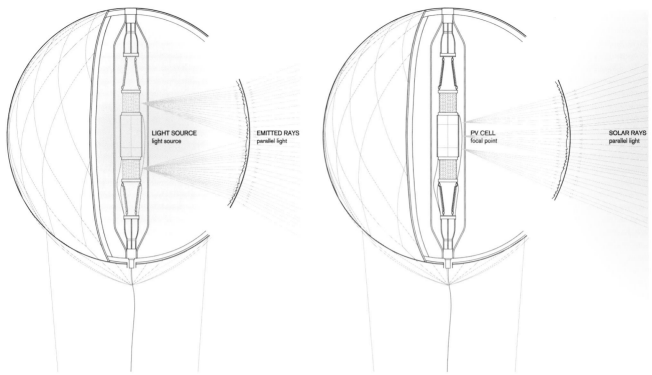

LIGHT SOURCE
light source

EMITTED RAYS
parallel light

PV CELL
focal point

SOLAR RAYS
parallel light

∧   **Light as forming a collective; Light as a**
productive source of energy.

TECHNICAL SPECIFICATIONS

Buoyant Light combines various existing technologies: research buoys, lighting balloons and
photovoltaics to create a more intelligent
monitoring and communication instrument in
the Arctic.

A multipurpose research buoy is supplemented with an additional battery and a
remote controller for the LEDs. Information
collected by the ice profiling sonar device in
the buoy is conveyed via a fiber optic cable to
the LEDs, programmed according the international ice development color-coding standards.
The LEDs and PV cells are mounted on a shock
absorption frame to counter any deformation
due to movement, pressure or temperature
fluctuation.

The standard dimensions of the buoy
range between one and a half meters to three
meters in diameter. Whereas the solar balloon
varies from half a meter diameter for those
used as street lighting, to three meters for
those close to the shore, to five meters for
those distributed along hunting paths and
throughout arctic waters. The balloon is lashed
to the buoy in the same manner that hot air
balloons are to their basket. A nylon mesh is
adhered to the balloon's skin and tied to multiple high strength nylon cords attached to
the buoy.

The balloon consists of two layers, an inner transparent plastic bladder filled with a
lighter-than-air gas, and a pre-moulded three
millimeter thick shell made of ETFE polymer
plastic with fiberglass reinforcing to provide
some rigidity and greater durability. The outer
surface is smooth while the inner is ribbed. The
ribbing creates facets, which replicate the
effects of a fresnel lens, focusing incoming
light to increase solar absorption, and dis-
persing outgoing light to maximize the emitted
color light from the LEDs. The Fresnel Lens was
developed in the late 1800s to improve the
visibility of lighthouses.

All the components would be manufactured
off site to ensure quality control and cost
effectiveness, but given the remoteness of
northern communities the equipment must allow
assembly and repair on location. Furthermore,
specific knowledge would need to be developed
within the community for general and seasonal
maintenance.

∧   The balloons fade into the sky in
the spring and local fisherman access the
equipment for maintenance after the long
winter.

〉   Following pages: Balloons along
traditional hunting and traveling routes act
as wayfinding devices and create a network
of connection points between remote
communities. They collect widespread data
throughout the Arctic region.

ARCTIC OPENING
FABRIC | CH

∧　Arctic Mediterranean, creolized
territories and remote polar nocturnal day on
the Frioul islands close to Marseille, France.

Arctic Opening is an installation that illuminates a location at nightfall with a remote sunlight transmitted from regions north of the Arctic Circle. This artificial "second day" lasts until sunrise, creating a poetic, variable landscape made of local and distant information. *Arctic Opening* was first installed on the Frioul archipelago, off the Mediterranean coast of France, in July 2010.

Each day, when night falls on our urban environments, a second artificial day begins, which is illuminated by sodium, mercury, or fluorescent glows. It marks night-time activities that remained invisible to us only two centuries ago, and which we rarely consider today. This fabricated light allows for an artificial extension of the day, transforming our relationship to time, space and landscape.[1] This second day has remained mostly functional, providing monotonous urban lighting, evoking nothing beyond its artificial nature. When it does vary, it typically stays in a preset comfort zone, unlike meteorological climates which change constantly, creating different uses and perceptions of an environment over time.

Arctic Opening does not deny this 'second day', but seeks to amplify its uncanny qualities, to develop its imaginary potential while integrating intelligent lighting cycles of low energy consumption, using a wide horizontal LED display. *Arctic Opening* proposes another kind of 'day,' a variable artificial day that rises at nightfall to illuminate a site on the Mediterranean islands of the Frioul.

In a world where new forms of mobility, temporalities, and social behaviors have emerged at the crossings of time zones, *Arctic Opening* creates a "mediated connection" with distant countries. It transplants a remote atmosphere through the transmission of climatic data compiled from locations north of the Arctic Circle including Hammerfest, Murmansk,

1. In one of his seminal books, *The Architecture of the Well-Tempered Environment*, published in 1969, writer Reyner Banham explores the relationships between technology and architecture. He is particularly interested in artificial heating and lighting, air conditioning, and energy use. He calls for the full integration of these parameters into the architectural project. See: Reyner Banham, *The Architecture of the Well Tempered Environment*, Second Edition (Chicago: The University of Chicago Press, 1984).

2. Architectural software concepts and sketches by fabric | ch, development by Computed-By.

Prudhoe Bay, Tuktoyaktuk, Igloolik, Clyde River, and Scoresby. It reveals geographic, luminous and meteorological patterns, and in so doing, builds tangible connections between remote geographies through satellite imagery, climate sensors, and networks of data. The combination of this distant light on Frioul islands' landscape produces a place that is the product of location interferences, a moiré-space: Mediterranean Arctic, remote nocturnal day.

Composed of hundreds of light emitting diodes, the eighteen meter long opening illuminates a rocky, wind-swept area. Erected near the vicinity of a military and industrial relic of the twentieth century, a tent hosting the instruments of control suggests a possible scientific expedition in a "hostile" zone. Monitored by a custom architectural software, the light source of the installation is taken at the 69° 25' N latitude. The software continuously analyzes the public data of more than one hundred meteorological stations dispatched along the selected latitude. The synthesis of this data mining is displayed by two interfaces.[2] They reveal how the light is captured, computed and redesigned for transmission to the LED interface.

Arctic Opening suggests that this temporary place near Marseille, illuminated by a transported Arctic light, could become the distant, catastrophic and fictitious future of these northern territories. Equally, the shores of the Far North could begin to resemble those of the Mediterranean Sea. This environment would hybridize itself, in a way similar to people becoming increasingly mobile over time: combinations of here and elsewhere, future and present, material and immaterial.

· · · **Combining experimentation and production, fabric|ch formulates new architectural proposals and produces singular livable spaces that mingle territories, programs, atmospheres and technologies. The founding members of fabric|ch are Christian Babski, Stéphane Carion, Christophe Guignard and Patrick Keller. Their works have been presented and exhibited internationally. www.fabric.ch**

∧   *Arctic Opening* at midnight with the
shores of Marseille and Notre-Dame de la
Garde in the far background.

∧   Close up from the illuminated landscape.

^ **Monitor in the expedition tent**
displays interface I: real time monitoring of
the arctic illumination conditions that are
transmitted to the LED lighting "opening."

^ ***Arctic Opening*'s expedition tent, flag,**
computers and monitors at night under the
remote arctic daylight.

^   **Far view of *Arctic Opening*. Variations
of a cloudy daylight at nightfall.**

WEATHER STATION
ANCA MATYIKU

∧   **Summer.**

The act of space-making finds itself in a world in which environments—whether biological, technological, or political—reconfigure themselves at increasing speeds. Entropy, as an active force within bodies, systems, and networks, has become increasingly perceptible. As a result, inherent living processes that were previously neglected have gained greater relevance in our understanding of context. It has become apparent that architecture is not a static object that exists in isolation and against its environment, but is a living organism, which affects, and is affected by, material and immaterial circumstances.

The *Weather Station* is part of an ongoing investigation on the role of weather as an active agent in the experience of space. It attempts to transform the seeming ephemerality of a building's environment into a physical experience, which is engaged with, rather than resistant to, weather and weathering. Predicting weather is based on an interpretation of real time phenomena, combined with weather data trends collected over time. The *Weather Station* attempts to investigate physical manifestations of both components.

Located high above the city of Winnipeg, the station is reminiscent of a floating vessel that is transformed by weather through physical reaction. An observation deck slides up and down inside a concrete nest, which serves as the frugal dwelling for the weather-person. Resembling mechanical petals, crane-like thermometers are operated by hydraulic pumps. As the hydraulic fluid expands with the rising outside temperature, the cranes open, lifting the observation deck and raising the ceiling

of the dwelling. The roof of the observation deck reflects Winnipeg's wind patterns, such that in the winter the snow might drift into its deepest recesses. Like a hibernating creature, the cranes envelope the weather tower and the station compresses under the insulating weight of the snow. During the warm seasons, the cauldron releases the melted snow and rain onto the concrete core of the dwelling.

At the scale of inhabitation, a large south-facing greenhouse provides passive relief from inclement weather. In the winter, it allows the thermal mass of the concrete to absorb solar heat; in the summer, its windows open so that air can cool the inside. A skin of photovoltaic-operated umbrellas opens up to register the amount of sunlight and provide shade. When temperatures sink to painfully cold degrees, the furnace breathes its steam onto an outdoor lattice. The icy crystals form patterns in which the weather-person can read tales inscribed by temperature and humidity.

The *Weather Station* re-interprets space-making as an act shaped by the changing nature of its environment. It seeks to register and respond to the living processes, which affect its material physicality and its natural context.

⋅ ⋅ ⋅ **Anca Matyiku is a Montreal-based designer and maker. She holds a Bachelor of Architectural Studies from University of Waterloo and a Masters of Architecture from University of Manitoba, in Canada.**

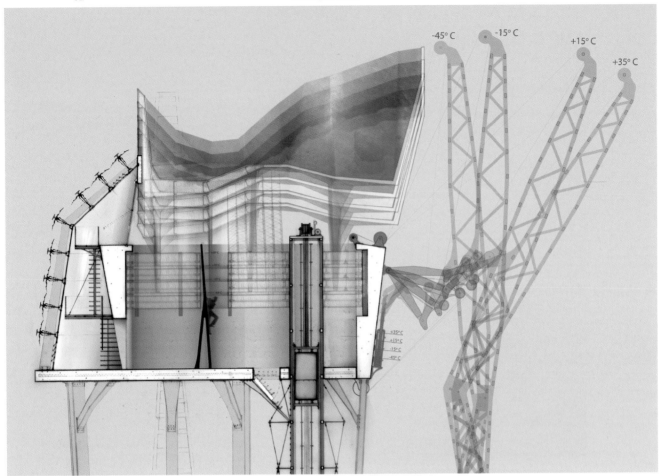

-45° C   -15° C   +15° C   +35° C

∧   **Responding to Temperature—** Hydraulic cranes respond to temperature much like a thermometer. As the hydraulic fluid expands with the rising outside temperature, the cranes open, lifting the observation deck and raising the ceiling of the bottom dwelling. Outside temperature can be read from a distance based on the position of the cranes in relation to the weather station. At the scale of human inhabitation this knowledge is inscribed in the simple relationship between the floor level of the upper storey and the ladder connecting the two storeys.

∧   **Summer.**

∧   **Winter.**

Matyiku   Weather Station

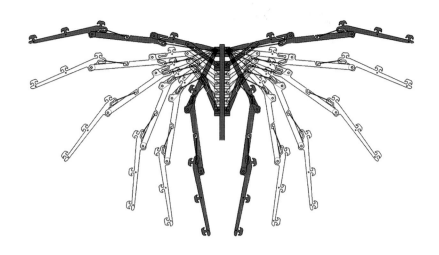

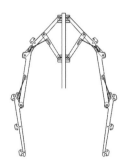

∧ **Responding to Sunlight—**
Photovoltaic-operated umbrella shading
devices passively heat and cool the building
through the south-facing double-skin facade.
When activated in the summer, they respond
directly to the amount of sunlight by an
equivalent level of "open-ness" and shading.

GOES SOFT

bracket—

SOFT GOES HARD

COLIN RIPLEY, GEOFFREY THÜN, KATHY VELIKOV

Atmospheres (Soft)

Finally, what is important, is the spiritual principle itself for using new material for a dynamic architecture. Air, gas, fire, sound, odors, magnetic forces, electricity, electronics are materials.
—Yves Klein[1]

With the transition from the 20th century to the 21st, the subject of the cultural sciences thus becomes: making the air conditions explicit.
—Peter Sloterdijk[2]

In the late 1950s and early 1960s, Yves Klein, working with architects Werner Ruhnau and Claude Parent, produced a number of designs for air architectures: projects of an architectural or urban scale that mobilized control over atmospheric conditions and were intended to produce a new human sensitivity. Klein imagined that under the protection of the air roof, a utopian civilization would come into being—doors would be unnecessary, the concept of secrecy would disappear, and inhabitants would live naked in a "new atmosphere of human intimacy."[3] Klein was of course not alone to consider the primary the role of atmosphere in architectural design. Projects on the radical edge of architectural discourse during the sixties and seventies, such as Buckminster Fuller and Shoji Sadao's *Dome over Manhattan*, Reyner Banham and Francois Dallegret's *Environment Bubble*, Cedric Price's experiments into inflatable structures, Archigram's *Living Pods*, the inflatables of Ant Farm and Coop Himmelb(l)au's *Pneumatic Living Unit*, *Heart Space* and *Cloud*, were all examining the significance and creative potential of the air-based environment.

In our modern world, as Peter Sloterdijk points out, the air is no longer something that can be taken for granted.[4] In an era of poison gas, radioactivity and germ warfare, not to mention smoke, pollen, exhaust, dust, volatile organic compounds as well as radio frequency waves, wireless signals, and noise, the right to breathe is no longer inalienable. The gaseous atmosphere on which each of us depends for survival has ceased to be simply a natural environment, and has become instead a monstrous hybrid.[5]

While the goals of the architectural projects in question vary—for some, the impetus seems to be fear of contamination from an unreliable air; for others, the desire for a fuller aesthetic and human experience—they do have some important characteristics in common. Most importantly, at least for our purposes here, the atmospheres produced by these projects remain hard systems, in the terms laid out by MIT Media Lab founder Nicholas Negroponte[6]—from the point of view of the breather, the atmospheres remain static, unresponsive and predetermined. Even Banham, while lauding the variation in atmospheric conditions afforded by his design, allows the inhabitant control only over his or her location within a varied thermal environment.[7] In other words, most of this work imagines the breather as subject, situated within an unresponsive atmosphere. But what if we imagine a more reciprocal relationship? Can we consider a relationship in which the atmosphere responds, in real-time, to the needs and actions of the breather; a relationship in which we consider the human subject and the gaseous environment as parts of a single system? As Cary Wolfe puts it in his discussion of posthumanism,[8] we would need to reconsider our fundamental approach to the question of the culture/nature—or, by extension, breather/atmosphere—relationship, posing the question not in terms of substance, but in terms of strategies, and asking questions of *how* rather than *what*. Such a consideration may occasion a re-thinking of the role of architecture, which we can begin to see not as form or product, but as interface and process. While Klein sought to produce a new soft human sensibility by repressing all technological and functional—in other words, hard—requirements by literally placing them underground, we ask instead what strategic potentials can be gleaned from these necessities? How can the literal hard parts of a building—envelopes, components, surfaces—be reconsidered in service of the softest of architectural materials: air?

Envelopes (Hard)

It is all too easy to dematerialize the building envelope when working with air. The history of construction technology in the twentieth century can be seen in part, as Banham points out in his 1965 text, "A Home is not a House," as the history of the dissolution of the building envelope. If one continues to read Banham,[9] it is possible to make the case that the widespread domestication of air conditioning after the 1930's may have had as profound an

1. Yves Klein, "The Evolution of Art Towards the Immaterial," in Peter Noever and Francois Perrin ed., *Air Architecture: Yves Klein* (Ostfildern-Ruit: Hatje Cantz, 2004), 44.

2. Peter Sloterdijk, *Terror from the Air*, trans. Amy Patton and Steve Corcoran (Los Angeles: Semiotext(e), 2009), 84.

3. Yves Klein and Werner Ruhnau, "Project of an Air Architecture," in Noevner, *Air Architecture*, 77.

4. Peter Sloterdijk, *Terror from the Air*, trans.

Amy Patton and Steve Corcoran (Los Angeles: Semiotext(e), 2009), 6.

5. In Bruno Latour's terms. Or, if you read Agamben, it is a piece of an apparatus of control and destruction. For further discussion see: Bruno Latour, *We Have Never Been Modern*, trans. Catherine Porter (Cambridge: Harvard University Press, 1993), 1-3; Giorgio Agamben, *What is an Apparatus?: and Other Essays* (Stanford, Calif: Stanford University Press, 2009), 19-24.

6. Nicholas Negroponte, *Soft Architecture Machines* (Cambridge Mass: MIT press, 1975), 131-151.

7. Reyner Banham, "A Home Is Not A House," *Art in America* 53, no. 2 (1965), 71.

8. Cary Wolfe, *What is Posthumanism?* (Minneapolis: University of Minnesota Press, 2010), 206.

9. Reyner Banham, *Architecture of the Well-Tempered Environment* (Chicago, University of Chicago Press, 1969).

∧ **Reyner Banham and Francois
Dallegret,** *Environment Bubble*, **1965.
(© 2011 Artists Rights Society (ARS),
New York / SODRAC, Montréal)**

effect on architectural development and form as had the elevator. Mechanical air conditioning meant that the role of providing interior comfort no longer depended on the performance of the building envelope. Once the envelope was freed from its traditional role of environmental mediator, its very presence and necessity was fundamentally questioned. In works that prioritize atmospheric conditions, if the envelope is present at all, it is rendered as the thinnest possible membrane, a simple separator preventing leakage between two adjacent atmospheres. In 1955, Buckminster Fuller proposed a home made entirely of prefabricated interior components, the "Standard of Living Package," and placed it under a glass dome that he claimed would provide all of the necessary environmental conditioning, while maintaining minimal visual obstruction to the exterior. Five years later, he audaciously proposed placing all of midtown Manhattan under a single, two-mile diameter air-conditioned dome, producing a continually temperate climate within. Fuller argued that the structure would pay for itself in saved heating costs within ten years.[10] Banham and Dallegret placed all weight for controlling the interior environment on mechanical equipment, drawing the envelope as the most minimal possible line. Although this line represents a material reality—the plastic bubble—it remains, nonetheless, conceptually as close to nothing as one could imagine. In some cases, no envelope is present at all. Klein envisions an "air roof and fire walls," an envelope made entirely of air and energy. The vast amounts of mechanical equipment that would be needed to maintain this air condition(ing) are placed underground, suppressed and unseen—although, Klein mentions that he is anxious about the noise.[11]

When one begins to work with the soft, it becomes incredibly tempting to erase to the largest extent possible the solid, the immobile, the hard. Henri Lefebvre, in *The Production of Space*, makes this proposition clear:

> "Now, a critical analysis would doubtless destroy the appearance of solidity of this house, stripping it, as it were, of its concrete slabs and its thin non-loadbearing walls, which are really glorified screens, and uncovering a very different picture. In the light of this imaginary analysis, our house would emerge—permeated from every direction by streams of energy which run in and out of it..."[12]

Once the condition of the "body without organs"[13] becomes apparent and of primary concern for the designer, what might be the basis for the material construction of space? As contemporary discourse once again focuses its attention on *system* over *object* and on the *mediated environment* over *form*, the question remains: how do soft systems interact spatially and aesthetically with their hard counterparts, or, how is the hard not entirely sublimated

(shrouded, blurred or buried) or presented merely as an assemblage of apparatus?

Our approach is to take advantage of the hard in service of the soft: to make use of a building's envelope and interior surfaces—the hard—to engender a responsive (and not simply manipulable) atmospheric environment—the soft. As Negroponte points out in his discussion of inflatables, it is much more difficult to render the hard parts of a building responsive than it is the soft parts; it is, literally, a hard task, and it requires a hard technology.[14] In other words, to get soft, we go hard.

These two words—hard and soft—become immediately problematic when discussing material constructions, on the one hand, and reflexive systems on the other. Negroponte previously alluded to the confusion that these terms can cause in his discussion of Brodey's Soft Architecture, and we have already seen how, paradoxically the softest of materials can be a hard system.[15] Following Wolfe again, our strategy has been to de-ontologize these terms.[16] Rather than considering the soft and the hard as polarized concepts, systems or structures, we seek instead to understand the two as aspects of a single system, teasing out potential synergies and complementarities, locating the soft in the hard and—less frequently—the hard in the soft.

Might we re-consider spatial envelopes as neither solid nor gas, not mute but active, as constitutive infrastructural elements of atmospheric design, in constant interplay with informational, sensing and energetic envelopes and spheres? Building envelopes have become more complex in recent decades as functionalities have been separated into discrete layers, but it is possible to imagine a more complex envelope still, one that is seemingly alive with sensors and intelligence, able to reconfigure itself according to its sensory input, not for the sake of its own formal play, but to affect the atmosphere it helps to produces. Such an envelope could also become much more intimately connected to the senses and actions of the body, even acting as a prosthetic for its post-human inhabitants, and allowing seamless synergy between breather and atmosphere while also rendering legible the politics of indoor air.

The Stratus Project
The word *stratus* is the past participle of the Latin verb *sternere* meaning "to spread out." Stratus clouds are horizontal, layered volumes comprised of tiny droplets of water and ice that stretch out across the sky. Stratus clouds form at the boundary when warm, moist air passes over a cool layer of air. If the warm air is cooled below its dew point, the excess water vapor condenses to form a blanket-like layer of vapor. Stratus renders legible the layered atmospheric conditions of aerial space.

10. Michael John Gorman, *Buckminster Fuller: Designing for Mobility* (Milan: Skira, 2006), 188-189.

11. Yves Klein, "The Evolution of Art Towards the Immaterial," in Peter Noever and Francois Perrin ed., *Air Architecture: Yves Klein* (Ostfildern-Ruit: Hatje Cantz, 2004), 28.

12. Henri Lefebvre, *The Production of Space*, trans. Donald Nicholson-Smith (Malden, Mass: Blackwell, 2004), 93.

13. Gilles Deleuze and Felix Guattari, *A Thousand Plateaus*, trans. Brian Massumi (Minneapolis: University of Minnesota Press, 1987), 506-508.

14. Nicholas Negroponte, *Soft Architecture Machines* (Cambridge Mass: MIT press, 1975), 150.

15. Ibid, 134.

16. Cary Wolfe, *What is Posthumanism?* (Minneapolis: University of Minnesota Press, 2010), 206.

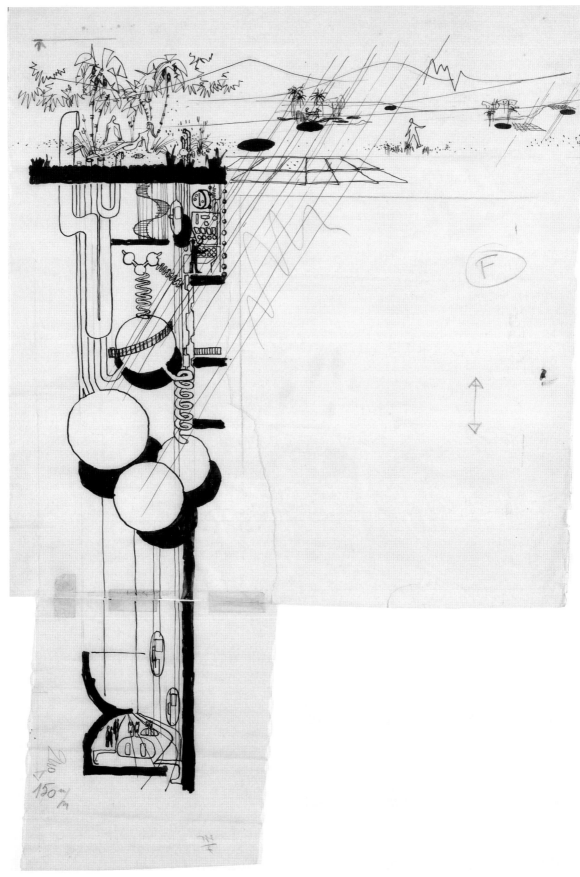

∧   Yves Klein with Claude Parent,
*Sous-sol d'une cité climatisée (Climatization
de l'espace)*, 1956. (© 2011 Artists Rights
Society (ARS), New York / ADAGP, Paris)

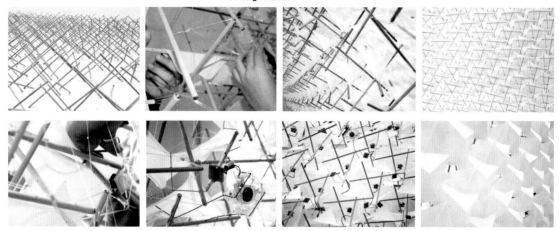

∧   **Component assembly and installation
of the *Stratus Project* v1.0 prototype: (r-l)
tensegrity weave, heat and light diffusing
membranes, sensing and actuation components, breathing cells.**

The *Stratus Project* is the name of a prototype system being developed by the authors that mobilizes the hard surfaces and technologies of building envelopes into responsive "second skins" that develop continual information and material exchange, and eventually dialogue, between breather and atmosphere. The goal of the project and the research that surrounds it is to attune attention to the immediate air-based environment and to the physical conditions that produce it. The first prototype deploys smart surfaces and responsive technologies in the development of a thick suspended ceiling that produces a light and air-based architectural environment using distributed technologies and systems to sense energy and movement flows, and, tempered by occupant-responsive feedback, to define envelopes of intimate and collective space.

The project pursues distributed, demand-driven gradient control of environmental space and atmospheric conditions through a set of material arrays that take their point of departure from the logics and spatial characteristics of the stratus cloud. The fully realized system will develop a series of immersive layers, from a sensing, breathing and energy scavenging ground plane to a thick enveloping soffit, which considers the material design of both that which is sensed (surfaces, atmospheres, thermal gradients, light) and that which lies beyond our sensory capabilities (aerosols, energies, transmission and radiation waves). The *Stratus Project* is therefore developed through multiple envelopes, which render legible the layered atmospheric and technological conditions of architectural space while also producing a kinetic, light and air-based environment that might respond directly to occupant desire, presence and bodily state.

Stratus v1.0 prototype is comprised of a thickly arrayed, suspended textile consisting of a three-dimensional structure that organizes and supports operational components. The structural foundation is a cable-strut tensegrity weave which is lightweight and stable, yet elastic and capable of deformation, allowing for controlled gross movement across all dimensions without failing or disturbing the attached components. Woven into the tensegrity mat is a distributed array of sensors, actuators, lights, micro-fans and diffusing, thermally absorptive fabric panels. On the underside of the structure are the "breathing cells": individually actuated translucent cells that form a light-diffusing skin and that, like gills, allow localized thermal conditioning and air extraction. Physical presence of the breather, as well as environmental conditions such as temperature, light, carbon dioxide and airborne pollutants, are measured through a distributed network of sensors that communicate with actuators to trigger fans to locally supply or extract air, and lights to illuminate occupied space. The next generation of the project will incorporate distributed wireless sensing networks, energy harvested from thermal gradients at the building envelope via distributed thermal electric generators and control through multi-agent systems. Custom software controls the spatial deformation of the structure, allowing it to alter the volume of the enclosed space, either based on thermal regimes or on programmatic requirements. The next stage of explorations will attempt closer material and geometric integration between the cell and support/actuation mechanism, as well as investigations into materiality and performance of the cells. Of particular interest is to develop further ways to affect the 'design' of gaseous agents, especially in response to airborne pollutants, such as investigating further ways in which the structure itself might be able to register and communicate air quality information—haptically, biologically or electronically—providing to the breather a consciousness of their own agency within the air environment.

The term "responsive" has often been used interchangeably with interactive and adaptive. Most simply, it has been described as "how natural and artificial systems can interact and adapt,"[17] yet it is related to second-order cybernetic systems where both system and user learn

17. Philip Beesley, Sachiko Hirosue, and Jim Ruxton, "Responsive Architectures." *Subtle Technologies* 06 (Cambridge: Riverside Architectural Press, 2006), 3.

⌄ *Stratus Project* rendering illustrating
gradient operation of die-cast translucent
diffuser cells relative to sensor actuation.

⌄ *Stratus Project* v1.0 prototype as
installed, with breathing cells actuated for
sensible cooling from micro-fans above.

∧   The *Stratus Project* v1.0 prototype as
installed; Occupant actuation of atmospheric
response: light and air.

over time.[18] In a responsive milieu, user and system would
be able to shape an unlimited set of outcomes. Rather
than the designer predetermining appropriate responses
to user inputs, the system could measure reactions to
its outputs and continually modify its actions according
to these responses. In the most extreme visions of this
possibility, buildings and environments might evolve
and transform based on cognitive and biological models.
The work on the *Stratus Project* includes the development of a computational script that utilizes evolutionary
algorithms to allow the system to self-adjust and learn
over time, both relative to environmental variable conditions and to occupancy patterns, preferences and habits,
as well as how the system might communicate with
the breather, allowing them to also gain cognition of the
impact of actions on the air-based environment.

Air Rights
The possibility of user-controlled responsive atmo-
spherics is of course simultaneously exhilarating and
terrifying. Although the *Stratus Project* approaches the
question inferred by Sloterdijk—who designs the air? —it
is in fact only deferred, removed only as far as the hard
equipment, the devices, the apparatus. It appears that
in the context of a responsive environment the air is not
"designed" by anyone; instead, it evolves out of the decisions and actions of many different actors. The agency
of the individual within the collective environment is
difficult to discern, and participates in the prickly arena
of biopolitics.

Indeed, it is fair to say that one effect of soft systems
in general is to make questions of agency less readily resolved, politics more nuanced, and ethics more

complicated. Breathers who exist as part of larger
breather/atmosphere/infrastructure systems must
consider their edge conditions, and may be surprised to
find that those edges will, in turn, have softened. The act
of breathing then becomes a political action—not in the
sense of resistance, but in the agonistic sense developed
by Chantal Mouffe[19]—an agonism that will take place,
more and more, distant from our breathing bodies,
defined by the actions and interests of our virtual selves.
Latour perhaps puts it best, in a discussion of Sloterdijk,

> "You are on life support, it's fragile, it's technical, it's public, it's
> political, it could break down—it is breaking down—it's being
> fixed, you are not too confident of those who fix it. Our current
> condition merely relies on our more explicit understanding that
> this tentative technological system, this "life support," entails
> the whole planet—even its atmosphere."[20]

Acknowledgements
The *Stratus Project* is funded through a University of Michigan
Taubman College of Architecture and Urban Planning 2010 Research
Through Making Grant, University of Michigan Office of the Vice
President for Research 2010 Small Projects Grant and a Social Science
and Humanities Research Council of Canada 2011 Research Creation
Grant. The authors wish to acknowledge the following individu-
als for their contribution to the ongoing research and development:
Zain AbuSeir, Mary O'Malley, Matt Peddie, F. Parke MacDowell,
James Christian, Christopher Parker, Jason Prasad, Sara Dean, Jessica
Mattson, Dan McTavish, Christopher Niswander, Lisa Sauvé, Adam
Smith, Dr. Aline Cotel, Dr. Jerome Lynch.

· · · **Colin Ripley is Graduate Program
Director of Ryerson University's Master of
Architecture and principal of the research-
based practice RVTR.**

· · · **Geoffrey Thün is Associate Professor at
the University of Michigan Taubman College of
Architecture and Urban Planning and principal
of the research-based practice RVTR.**

· · · **Kathy Velikov is Assistant Professor at
the University of Michigan Taubman College of
Architecture and Urban Planning and principal
of the research-based practice RVTR.**

18. Hugh Dubberly, Usman Haque, and Paul
Pangaro, "What is Interaction? Are There
Different Types?", *Interactions*, Volume 16
Issue 1 (2009).

19. Chantal Mouffe, *On the Political* (New
York: Routledge, 2005), 20-21.

20. Bruno Latour, "Air," in Caroline A. Jones
and Bill Arning ed., *Sensorium: Embodied
Experience, Technology, and Contemporary
Art* (Cambridge: MIT Press, 2006), 106.

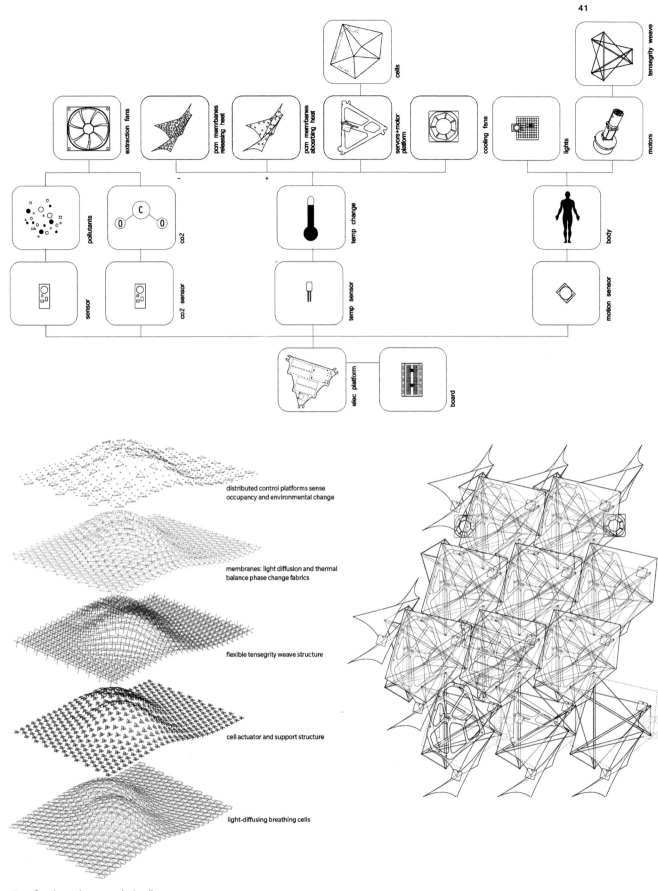

∧ **Sensing and response logics diagram;**
Performative component layers: Plan view
of layered sensing and breathing array
components.

∧   Above: Section at sensing/breathing
cell array; Below: Soffit deformation shapes
the volume of conditioned air in response to
occupant presence/demand.

Ripley, Thün, Velikov   Soft Goes Hard

GOES SOFT

bracket—

SURVEILLER ET DIVERTIR: DISCIPLINE AND ENTERTAIN

PIETRO PEZZANI

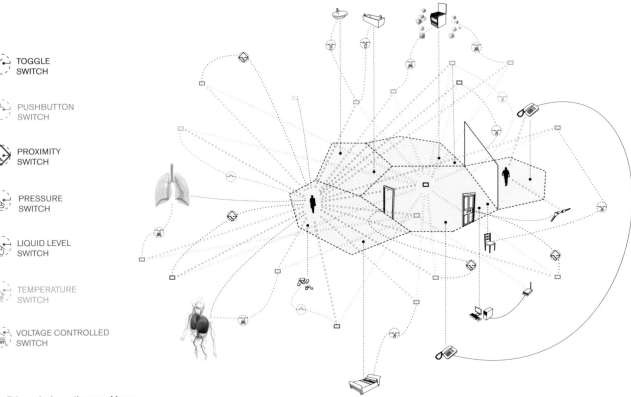

TOGGLE SWITCH

PUSHBUTTON SWITCH

PROXIMITY SWITCH

PRESSURE SWITCH

LIQUID LEVEL SWITCH

TEMPERATURE SWITCH

VOLTAGE CONTROLLED SWITCH

∧ Telecare's domestic assemblage: sensors as parasites.

Suveiller et Divertir examines the transformation of the Foucauldian model of disciplinary institutions. In his well-known book *Discipline & Punish: The Birth of the Prison*, Michel Foucault identified in Jeremy Bentham's panopticon the diagram of a technology of discipline in which building and institution coincide.[1] As anticipated by Gilles Deleuze, we are currently witnessing a shift from a disciplinary society to a society of control,[2] entailing a new relationship between building and institution.

This project aims to test the depth of this current transformation by investigating the opportunities, risks, and implications of this new scenario. To do so, Telecare is adopted as a case study. As an example of a system based on the dematerializations of former disciplinary institutions (such as hospitals, schools, barracks, etc...), Telecare is interpreted as a system that shapes various forms of spatialities. The topological definition of these spatialities sets the conceptual frame of the project. As John Law posits, "Topoi are political choices... Because they make objects, make subjects, of particular shapes... Because they set limits to the conditions of object—and subject—possibility. Because they generate forbidden spatial alterities. And because... they delete those alterities."[3] As such, defining the topological nature of the project allows one to state its political position toward the resistance of alterity in our contemporary control society.

Networks and Information

In his writings on disciplinary institutions, Foucault described a model in which discipline was exerted on human bodies via two processes: the geometric fragmentation of space and the adoption of the technological gaze. In this model, the organization of space—the walls of the institution—had the task of establishing precise relations of hierarchy, control, and subjugation. Telecare operates differently by providing non-hospitalized elderly or sick people control, assistance and aid from a distance. To do so, it relies on two main practices[4]—objects and information. The first consists of what Bruno Latour called "immutable mobiles": objects that, by maintaining a set of stable relations

1. Michael Foucault, *Discipline & Punish: The Birth of the Prison* (New York: Vintage Books, 1995).

2. Gilles Deleuze, *Negotiations, 1972-1990* (New York: Columbia University Press, 1995), 177-182.

3. John Law, "Objects, Spaces and Others," Centre for Science Studies, Lancaster University, www.comp.lancs.ac.uk/sociology/papers/Law-Objects-Spaces-Others.pdf

4. Daniel Lòpez Gomez, "Aplicaciòn de la teorìa del Actor-Red al anàlisis especial de un servicio de Teleasistencia Domiciliaria," AIBR. Revista de Antropología Iberoamericana, Ed. Electrónica Núm. Especial. Noviembre-Diciembre 2005, www.aibr.org/antropologia/44nov/articulos/nov0508.pdf

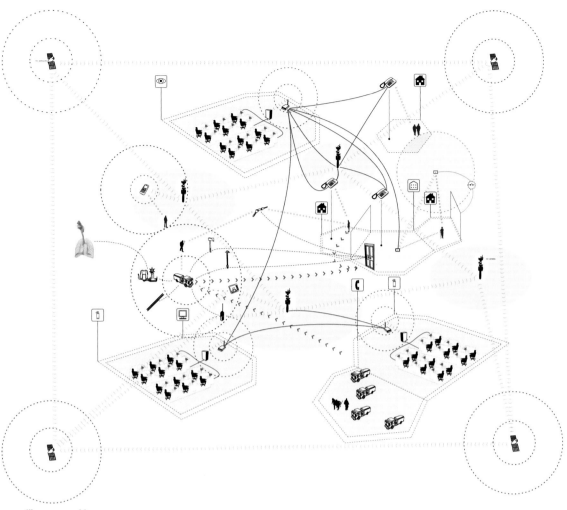

∧ Telecare's surveillance assemblage: calculation centers.

with a multitude of heterogeneous entities and places, are capable of weaving a whole with the articulation of their movement.[5] These objects, from ambulances to application forms, produce a spatiality that can be topologically understood as a network: a model that is characterized by the stability of semiotic relations between distant and seemingly scattered entities. This model reflects a strategy of control based on the colonization of heterogeneity and the accumulation of knowledge in strategic points.[6] The second practice concerns the shift from a discipline over bodies within space to discipline over information. While disciplinary institutions worked through lines of division for the confinement of bodies and the production

of individuals, Telecare exerts control over a multiplicity of overlapping information collectives that share singular parameters ranging from consumer habits to pathologies. These parameters are defined through the transformation of reality into abstract information. This work is carried out through uninterrupted chains of what Bruno Latour has termed "systems of translation"[7]: starting from the multitudes of objects that act like sensors inside and outside the domestic realm, and ending in the databases where the ever-changing "immobile mutable" mass of information is accumulated and later analyzed, classified and interpreted by Telecare's monitoring centers.

In addition to generating networks and instituting control over information, Telecare presents features that can be interpreted as topologically fluid.[8] In a fluid topology, form remains stable within a dynamic field. This can be caused by reconfiguration of pre-existing internal relations, or by the emergence of new links with entities that formerly were excluded; in any case, the occurrence of change does not imply the loss of shape. Therefore, in a fluid topology, the stability of form is defined in a way that is related to time and process; changes must occur in a gradual way, without violent breaks. Fluid topology reflects an organizational dispersion that opposes the institution of 'obligatory points of passage' that provided the network

5. Bruno Latour, *Science in Action: How to Follow Scientists and Engineers through Society* (Cambridge: Harvard University Press, 1987).
6. John Law, "Objects, Spaces and Others," Centre for Science Studies, Lancaster University, www.comp.lancs.ac.uk/sociology/papers/Law-Objects-Spaces-Others.pdf
7. Bruno Latour, *Science in Action: How to Follow Scientists and Engineers through Society* (Cambridge: Harvard University Press, 1987).
8. Marianne de Laet and Annemarie Mol, "The Zimbabwe Bush Pump: Mechanics of a Fluid Technology," *Social Studies of Science* 30/2 (April 2000).

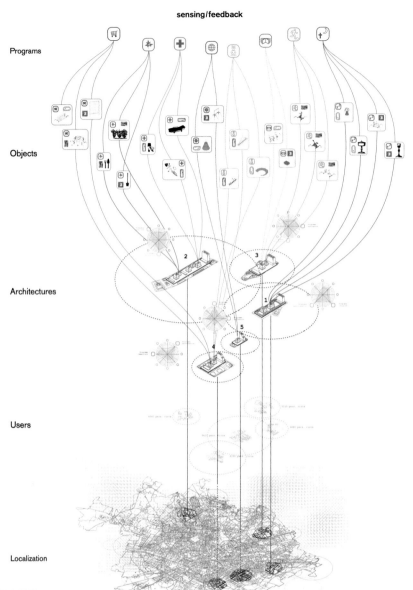

Programs

Objects

Architectures

Users

Localization

∧   The project: new programs, new
objects, and new architectures.

model with much of its power and efficacy.[9] It is based on identity through difference, on flexibility and adaptability, and on the local and specific declination of a general configuration of relations. Its definition of stability does not imply the determinations of centralities, the insistence on syntactical stability, or the accumulation of knowledge and power in strategic places.

Open Topography

While disciplinary institutions trace boundaries between "inside" and "outside," Telecare provides a surface on which many agents may connect with one another. We shift from a territory fragmented by borders to an open plane generated by lines which aggregate heterogeneous entities.[10] *Suveiller et Divertir* intercepts new programs and new categories of users with soft control technologies, such as fidelity cards, social networks, collaborative filtering, etc… The use of the surface marks a shift to a functionally undetermined typology that is no longer based on the discipline of space but rather the devices capable of mediating between different topologies and the respective "political choices" they perform.[11]

New buildings within Telecare's system are merely characterized in terms of structure, topology, and climatic behavior. They consist of an artificial, blank topography on the ground floor—an enclosed climate— awaiting informal colonization by objects and activities. The topography is covered by a roof that contains the infrastructure to allow for openness. A system of modular hanging mobiles is provided to connect to the plugs and to distribute water and electricity into the space below. The ground floor is surrounded by multi-storey constructions that host organized, temporary activities. It also

9. John Law, "Objects, Spaces and Others," Centre for Science Studies, Lancaster University, www.comp.lancs.ac.uk/sociology/ papers/Law-Objects-Spaces-Others.pdf

10. Daniel Lòpez Gomez and Francisco Tirado, "La norma digital y la extituciòn. El caso de la Tele-Asistencia Domiciliaria," Atenea Digital 5 (2004), http://antalya.uab. es/athenea/num5/lopez.pdf

11. John Law, "Objects, Spaces and Others," Centre for Science Studies, Lancaster University, www.comp.lancs.ac.uk/sociology/ papers/Law-Objects-Spaces-Others.pdf

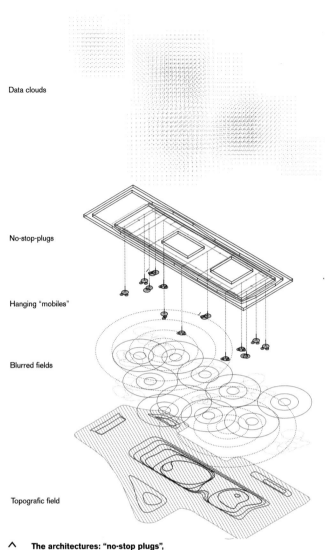

Data clouds

No-stop-plugs

Hanging "mobiles"

Blurred fields

Topografic field

∧ **The architectures: "no-stop plugs",
hanging "mobiles", blurred fields, and
topographies.**

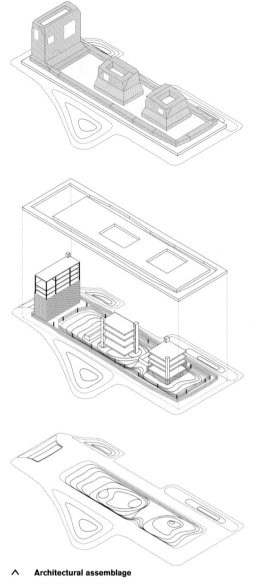

∧ **Architectural assemblage**

is ringed by a greenhouse corridor, which provides a buffer zone for a first degree of passive climate control. Both this corridor and the enclosed space form topologically continuous figures with the environmental double skin of the multi-storey buildings.

Any functional definition of the topography is the result of informal and ever-changing interaction among the objects collected and immaterial, blurred fields activated inside. Whether visual, electromagnetic, climatic, olfactory, sonic, or sacred, fields may be produced by movable, pluggable objects (like lamps, ventilators, loudspeakers, water atomizers, etc.), and may interact with other objects. By doing so, they produce continually changing, hybrid programs in a manner that is both highly informal and strictly ruled by the discipline of information.

The occupation of the open topography by people, fields, and objects directly reflects the evolution of the multilayered, transforming mass of information collected in the database. Traditional functions lose their borders and are ultimately replaced by informal groups of people interacting with objects and other people; establishing collective configurations that are positioned in relation to optimal sensory and immaterial fields. By making the content of the database visible to users, a new transparency of information is afforded. Architecture becomes a tool to spatialize information; the new buildings allow and encourage creative crossbreeding of programs and collectives, spontaneous forms of re-appropriation of public space, and innovative systems for sharing objects and information. Architecture is conceived here as a set for self-organized strategies of redistribution of knowledge and for practice

of everyday resistance and empowerment. It is the field of battle where forms of negotiation—between the need to feel safe as users and the necessity to be controlled as consumers—take place. It is conceived to incorporate the possibility of change and failure. It is, in other words, open to fluid configurations.

• • • **Pietro Pezzani is a Milan-based architect and researcher.**

∧   **Interior, open platform.**

Scenario 1

Mobile gym apparatus is installed in the same area as the hydroponic cultivations. By swiping their Fidelity Card through the mobile rfid identifier, users can access their personalized exercise regime. Hanging misting ventilators ensure a pleasant atmosphere and temperature in which users exercise amongst the plants. An echo of Ambient music can be heard from the relaxation area, where an aroma of flower emanates from the hanging diffusers. A group of New Age enthusiasts have requested a hanging hamock. We can see them lying on it, discussing the seminar on meditation that just finished on the second floor, volume 1. Another user, sat nearby, can access the wi-fi network to check his e-mail and the online program of future activities in the center.

Scenario 2

A covered market sells organic products partly produced in loco from the hydroponic cultivations. Not far off, a pop-up pavillion has been set up for a concert. A videocamera and two directional microphones record the event, which is transmitted live to another center and on the radio. Overhanging acoustic panels reduce reverb and ensure high quality of sound.

Scenario 3

Display and retail of assistive technology products. Pop-up stalls for online retail platforms (eg: Amazon are installed outside the center.

∧   **Three scenarios of blurred programs.**

BE ALARMED
LEIGHA DENNIS

The communities that are located close to the chemical industries in Louisiana's industrial corridor are afflicted by forces that transcend human perception. While the presence of harmful dust, noise and the subjugation of space are apparent at many levels, and leave these communities vulnerable, it is the power of the unseen and the unknown that are the subject of this investigation.

The industries' intent to withhold information that is necessary for the public safety has left an overriding sense of uncertainty and anxiety. Chemicals are released into community environments and nearby ecologies, rendering the consumption of air, food and water toxic. Deposited deep below the homes of many communities lie containers for dormant toxic waste whose shelf lives and stability are unforeseeable. Similarly, underground, geological salt caverns are often used for the storage of chemicals and crude oil, leaving ground water at the risk of contamination. While the air above the ground is subject to invisible, harmful pollutants, the ground below equally conceals the existence of a corresponding precariousness.

Attempts at providing systems of security and alarm for nearby communities have been benign and otherwise unsuccessful, resulting in moments of panic and confusion. Alarm speakers, functional or not, dot the landscape, while intercoms have been installed in homes—asserting a latent paranoia of surveillance and potential disaster. As the chemical companies have grown, acquired farmland and sometimes entire communities, their expansions has subsumed the landscape—leaving homes within unsafe proximities from toxic sites sometimes only feet away. Industries build directly up to property lines as a not-so-passive warnings to leave, yet some homes remain—either in resistance, or simply because there is nowhere else to go. For those homes that are bought out, swaths of pastoral green-scape are left in their place—a visual illusion that everything is fine.

In many ways, these attempts have both succeeded and failed in achieving illusions of safety. The security systems that are implemented often act to secure the plants themselves, rather than the vulnerable residents in close proximity. Alarms are sounded when danger is eminent, leaving the final and only option of fleeing. The events that are alerted are extreme, such as explosions or massive spills. However, communities are exposed to varying levels of toxins in the air, water, food, and ground on a daily basis. These quantities of contamination are equally alarming, yet go unknown and unnoticed.

For the communities that remain, this project aims to provide methods for monitoring, revealing and alerting the daily conditions of toxicity. Designed as a type of public service announcement and kit-of-parts, it provides a transparency of information that does not currently exist for the public. Through a network of devices dedicated to seeing the unseen, this alarm system will reveal levels of ground water, river water, and air contamination through recognizable and decipherable forms of display: a new kind of public utility. Personal kits to test vinyl chloride levels within homes, in drinking water, and in the body enable the residents to actively improve and keep their communities safe. By establishing trending in data, concentrations of contamination can be identified. The subterranean will be mapped above, while the air will be inscribed. The aesthetic of infrastructure is transformed into an active response system. Through the use of phyto- and sensor-technology, passive and active systems will alert to latent and harmful toxic levels, as well as provide the infrastructure for improvement in an altered and augmented landscape. Over time, the devices will improve contamination through remediation and awareness, resulting in their own optimistic obsolescence.

· · · **Leigha Dennis is a New York-based designer and architect interested in the intersection of technology, infrastructure and buildings.**

> **Following pages, left side: Poster describing the harmful effects of vinyl chloride. Following pages, right side: The geological section of Louisiana's underground oil reserves, injection wells, and the proximity of housing to the chemical industry.**

Nervous System
Nerve damage can be linked to vinyl chloride exposure.

Exposure to high levels of vinyl chloride will result in dizziness, sleepiness, as well as fainting.

Lungs
The most common way for vinyl chloride to enter the body is through breathing contaminated air.

Lung damage can be linked to vinyl chloride exposure.

Liver
The liver processes vinyl chloride, creating secondary substances, which pass through the body as well as through the blood.

Some of the new substances are more harmful than vinyl chloride. They react with other chemicals inside the body, interfering with normal chemical reactions. Some of these substances react in the liver and, depending on the amount of vinyl chloride breathed in, may produce damage there.

Skin
Only tiny amounts of vinyl chloride may pass through the skin and enter the body. It is not easily absorbed.

Evaporation
Vinyl chloride is easily released from water into the air.

Drinking Water
One of the most common ways for vinyl chloride to enter the body is through drinking contaminated water.

Hands
In cases of repeated exposure, blood flow to the hands has reduced resulting in bone and skin damage.

Kidneys
Once vinyl chloride and any secondary substances reach the kidneys, they leave the body through urine.

Most vinyl chloride is expelled from the body within 24 hours of contamination.

Kidney damage can be linked to vinyl chloride exposure.

Cancer
Studies of workers who have breathed vinyl chloride over many years showed an increased risk for cancer of the liver. Brain cancer, lung cancer, and some cancers of the blood also may be connected with breathing vinyl chloride over long periods of time.

VINYL CHLORIDE @ HOME

**VINYL CHLORIDE
TROVIDUR
CHLORETHENE
CHLORETHYLENE
MONOCHLOROETHENE
MONOVINYL CHLORIDE**

Vinyl chloride is a colorless, flammable gas that has a mild, sweet odor. It is a manufactured substance, used largely in the production of polyvinyl chloride (PVC) plastic products. Vinyl chloride can enter the air, soil and groundwater as a result of improper disposal of chemical wastes.

Household Activities
Showering, bathing, cooking or laundering with contaminated water releases vinyl chloride into the air where it can be breathed in.

Other Chemicals in Air
Vinyl chloride in the air breaks down within a few days, resulting in the formation of several other chemicals including hydrochloric acid, formaldehyde, and carbon dioxide.

There is no MCL regulation for levels of vinyl chloride in air. If an odor is noticeable, then levels are too high.

Contamination Levels
The vinyl chloride Maximum Contamination Level (MCL) for water has been set at 2 parts per billion (ppb) by the EPA. The non-enforceable Maximum Contamination Goal is set to zero.

Significant quantities of vinyl chloride are not normally found in ambient air. However, it has been detected near vinyl chloride manufacturing and processing plants, hazardous waste sites, and landfills. The amount of vinyl chloride in the air near these places ranges from trace amounts to over 1 ppm. Levels as high as 44 ppm have been recorded.

Contamination in Soil
Vinyl chloride released to soil will either quickly evaporate, be broken down by microbes or may leach to the groundwater. It also rapidly evaporates from water, but does not degrade there. It will not accumulate in aquatic life.

Vinyl chloride is unlikely to build up in plants or animals that might be eaten.

Myrtle Grove

OUT OF SIGHT

Bayou Choctaw
(Strategic Petroleum
Reserves)

Community

Agricultural

Shintec

Dow Chemical

Morrisonville

Miss.
River

Injection/
Waste Wells

Salt Dome

Strategic Petroleum Reserve

SPR is an emergency fuel store of crude oil maintained by the United States Department of Energy, with a current total capacity of 727 million barrels.

The reserve is stored at 4 sites on the Gulf of Mexico, each located near a major center of petrochemical refining and processing. Each site contains a number of artificial caverns created in salt domes below the surface.

Bayou Choctaw

Current capacity of 76 million barrels. Plans to expand to 109 million barrels.

Weeks Island, LA: retired oil reserve In 1993, a sinkhole formed on the site, allowing fresh water to enter the mine, eroding and degrading the salt structure as well as releasing oil to the ground water aquifer.

Salt Dome Storage

Very large geological salt structures formed below the surface of the earth. They can reside near the surface or thousands of feet below.

Solution Mining is used to extract a brine solution for salt or for further chemical processing. Brine can be used in the production of many chemicals, including ammonia, chlorine, hydrogen and bauxite.

In solution mining, fresh water is injected into salt domes in order extract brine. The resulting cavern in the salt structure can be used as storage for chemicals and crude oil. Saturated brine is pumped in and out in order to control pressure in the cavern, which is never left empty.

Dense, hard rock salt is mostly impermeable and will not contaminate petroleum.

Contamination in Soil

Vinyl chloride near the surface of the ground will either quickly evaporate, be broken down by microbes or may leach to the groundwater below. It also rapidly evaporates from water, but does not degrade there. It will not accumulate in aquatic life.

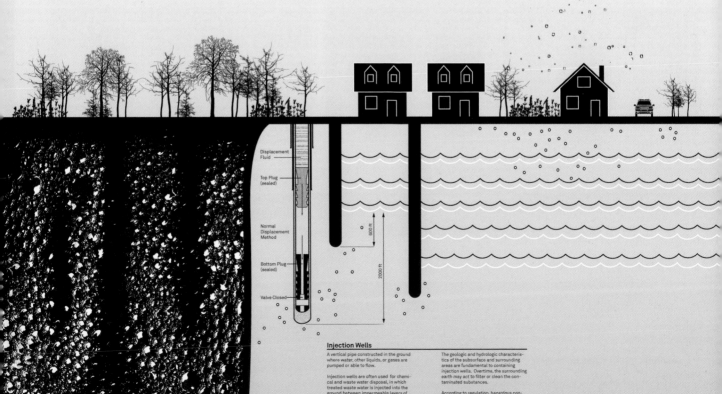

Displacement
Fluid

Top Plug
(sealed)

Normal
Displacement
Method

Bottom Plug
(sealed)

Valve Closed

600 ft

2000 ft

Injection Wells

A vertical pipe constructed in the ground where water, other liquids, or gases are pumped or able to flow.

Injection wells are often used for chemical and waste water disposal, in which treated waste water is injected into the ground between impermeable layers of rock. Solid walled, pressurized pipe at a deep elevation are used in order to prevent contamination with the surrounding environment.

The geologic and hydrologic characteristics of the subsurface and surrounding areas are fundamental to containing injection wells. Overtime, the surrounding earth may act to filter or clean the contaminated substances.

According to regulation, hazardous constituents in the injected fluids cannot migrate from the injection zone for as long as they remain hazardous, or 10,000 years. Beyond this time, there are no standards for regulation.

PHYTO-INDICATOR

Marking the landscape.

Transgenic plants: Genetically modified plants are to be developed in order to produce phyto-transformations, modifying vinyl chloride through plant metabolism. In the event of high levels of contamination, the resulting effect would produce displays of discoloration, allowing the plant to act as an alarm interface.

By absorbing vinyl chloride in soil, the plants actively reduce the contamination of air.

∧   **Strategies for community intervention
and action.**

Dennis   Be Alarmed

PSEUDO-COLOR

Enforcing the use of artificially colored vinyl chloride could reduce the risks of high-dosage contamination. By applying small amounts of color, with larger quantities of vinyl chloride, the effects would be noticeable and disturbing.

∧   **Strategies for community intervention and action.**

MARKING THE LANDSCAPE

Devices for display will mark the landscape indicating zones with
concentrations of underground injection wells, as well as the locations of drinking water aquifers. These devices will indicate the levels
of vinyl chloride contamination, allowing that which is below ground
to be made visible.

While these devices are to be located ubiquitously across the industrial corridor, larger installations of fresh water injection wells will be
located strategically and permanently. These devices will similarly
display contamination levels, but will also actively attempt to improve
the quality of the drinking water.

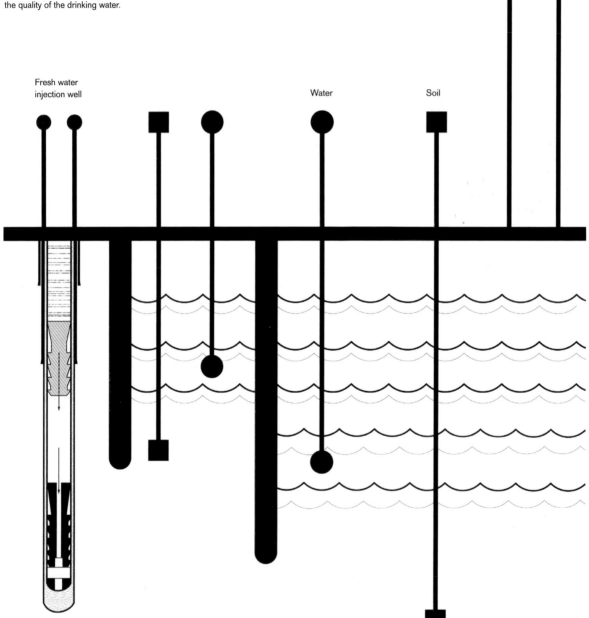

**∧   The types of devices for community
intervention and action.**

Dennis   Be Alarmed

MARKING TIME & DISTANCE

Marking the landscape through display devices enables residents to, at a glance, understand trending information according to distance as well as time.

While these devices may display infavorable information, over time through changes in behavior and policy, these same devices might be the very indicators of improvement.

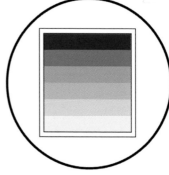

Graphic indicators are used to display trending information over time.

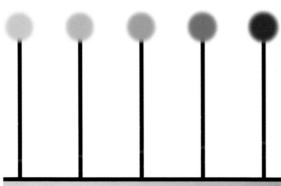

∧   **The types of devices for community intervention and action.**

∧   **Optimistic obsolescence: life after contamination.**

Phyto-color
Grass as indication

Monitoring lights

Street signage

Tree tags
Attachments to existing non-phyto trees

Phyto-color
Poplar as remediaton

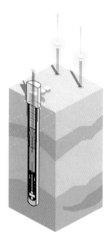

Monitoring wells
Remediaton

Capture domes
For resale vinyl chloride

∧   **The types of natural and man-made devices
to be implemented across the landscape. These
devices range from items that visualize the levels
of toxicity to those that actually remediate.**

Dennis   Be Alarmed

SIGNAL SPACE: NEW YORK'S SOFT FREQUENCY TERRAINS

MICHAEL CHEN

Antenna Iconography

While erected primarily as a mooring for airships, the top of the Empire State Building has housed a broadcasting tenant from the very beginning. RCA and its subsidiary, NBC, took possession of the interior of the mast upon completion of the building in 1931 and began experimental television broadcasts that year.[1] The mast was an obvious site for broadcasting equipment, given it's location on the tallest building on the globe at the time, enabling RCA to blanket the region with test signals. The building was the site of a number of subsequent refinements and developments to broadcast technology. NBC produced the first serial television broadcast with its coverage of the 1939 World's Fair Opening, and it enjoyed exclusive use of the top of the Empire State Building until 1950. At this time, the Federal Communications Commission (FCC) determined that a common broadcast location for all seven New York stations was essential to reduce the otherwise constant readjusting of receiving antennas. Accordingly, they ordered that an exclusive deal be established for a permanent antenna atop the building in 1950.[2]

Following the destruction of the World Trade Center, the broadcast infrastructure of the city was reconstructed at the Empire State Building, making it the primary broadcasting site for the metropolitan New York region. The current antenna extends 254 feet above the mooring mast and is leased to fifty-four different broadcasting tenants, including FM radio stations, analog and digital television stations, and telecommunications entities.

Rem Koolhaas has noted how media entities and technologies were essential to the development of new spatialities in the modern metropolis, notably in the collapsing of technical and spatial dimensions at RCA's headquarters at 30 Rockefeller Center. The massively deep podium of the building was converted for theatrical studio spaces and equipment, serving as an electronic arena that could transmit itself via the airwaves to any home on the globe, and become "the nerve center of an electronic community that would congregate at Rockefeller Center without actually being there."[3] While for Koolhaas, Rockefeller Center is the first architecture that could be broadcast; the concentration of recording and processing at RCA and the broadcasting at the Empire State Building also makes New York the first city whose iconographic form is literally an antenna.

Consolidation and centralization are the operative modes of traditional broadcast technology, and they inform broadcast's relationship to architecture. The

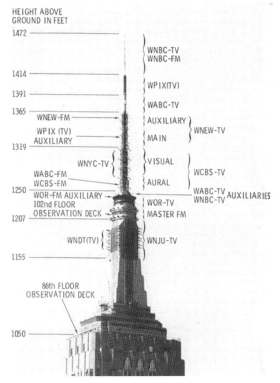

∧ A detailed view of broadcast tenants and their transmitting equipment on the Empire State Building's antenna from 1967.
(Used with permission, *Broadcast Engineering* magazine, copyright, 2011)

unobstructed line of sight between transmitter and receiver is still the surest measure of signal quality, particularly in contexts where the natural or architectural morphology present unavoidable obstructions. The primacy of the Empire State Building on the skyline establishes its iconicity, but also ensures its technical performance as an antenna, In fact, transmission problems caused by the construction of the original World Trade Center towers were the reason why most antennas were relocated to them once they were complete. The Empire State Building's owners have cited both its iconic status on the skyline and its role as an antenna in opposing the construction of nearby skyscrapers. Nevertheless, the building will likely loose its status as the primary antenna of New York upon the completion of One World Trade Center, whose antenna is to reach an iconic 1,776 feet.

1. Thomas R. Haskett, "Broadcast Antennas on the Empire State Building." *Broadcast Engineering*, (August 1967), 24.
2. The Empire State Building, "Broadcasting," The Empire State Building Official Internet Site, www.esbnyc.com/broadcasting.asp.
3. Rem Koolhaas, *Delirious New York: A Retroactive Manifesto for Manhattan* (New York: Monacelli, 1994), 201.

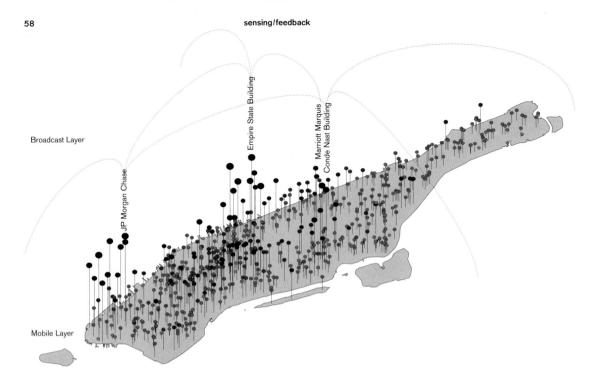

Broadcast Layer

Empire State Building

Marriott Marquis
Conde Nast Building

JP Morgan Chase

Mobile Layer

∧   **Manhattan mobile network base stations—
distributed according to address and building
height—in relation to major broadcast infrastructure locations.
(Sources: New York City Department of Buildings
Permit Filings (08/10/2005-02/10/2011); New
York City Planning Commission PLUTO Dataset
(2010). Michael Chen and Justin Snider, 2011)**

New Strata

With the advent of cable, fiber optics, internet radio, and online sources for television programming and movies, large antennas are no longer the sole mechanisms of broadcast content. Heterogeneity, rather than centralization characterizes *signal space*, a terrain that is increasingly the site of multiple networks and their infrastructures.

The shift from conventional broadcast-based to mobile-based platforms is re-contouring virtually all aspects of communication. Issues related to mobile are now the central preoccupation of the FCC, a position that was once occupied by radio and television. The Chair of the Commission recently noted that, "no sector of the communications industry holds greater potential to enhance America's economic competitiveness, spur job creation, and improve the quality of our lives."[4] Mobile networks are at once invisible, and also the systems most associated with the soft dimensions of infrastructure and its potential to act as an engine for large-scale social, economic, and technological change. For example, mobile data is central to the broader goal of making broadband Internet service available throughout the United States. The future of digital infrastructure is moving towards hybrid models involving cabled networks to deliver data efficiently over great distances and mobile networks to provide "last mile" connectivity where wired connections would be too expensive. The decentralized and pliable nature of these networks makes them more durable and robust. For instance, local telephone service was one of the systems affected on September 11, 2001, when a major centralized switching station was destroyed. In contrast, many digital infrastructures were able to fall back on alternative routing and were largely unaffected[5] suggesting that the variable organizational topology and distribution of a network system offer resilience and are as important as the physical elements.

Global network-scale communication technologies are re-scripting the fundamental spatial and informational relationships that define urbanism. The model of broadcast involving a single elevated point, blanketing the city with transmission, has given way to one where multiple, simultaneous strata—including the built environment, transmission infrastructure points, technical constraints, regulatory environments, and political resistance—are negotiated against one another to produce, transmit, and parse the amalgamation of signals that comprise an airborne network that is then absorbed into the city and its occupants.

4. Julius Genachowski, "America's Mobile Broadband Future." (Official remarks by FCC Chairman Julius Genachowski, presented at International CTIA Wireless I.T. & Entertainment, San Diego, California, October 7, 2009).

5. Anthony M. Townsend, *Wired/Unwired: The Urban Geography of Digital Networks*, (PhD Dissertation, MIT, 2003), 100.

This emulsion of transmission comprises an important third space of the city, and one that has yet to be thoroughly explored and theorized. Much of the recent interest in mobile networks has centered on applications for mobile data and communications, rather than the underlying infrastructure and its relationship to the city. Signal space is precisely this territory of negotiation between the city and its electromagnetic environment. It is the site of new forms of intelligence and information that are reflected in and made possible through the tactical distribution of antennas throughout the city, but also in the spatial processing, signal architecture, and social and political maneuvering that make that distribution a reality. While these protocols are generally the protected domain of the corporate entities that control signal space, unpacking their logics and tracking their signatures in urban space are ways to render these systems visible and available for action.

Semi Soft

The structure of mobile networks is generally based on the aggregation of individual cells describing the physical space between three antenna arrays, or base stations, that share a set of frequencies. Cells are tiled together to produce continuous coverage. A base station's processing unit and a mobile phone coordinate the connection, which is transmitted between the phone and the nearest base station, and then to a wire-office/wire-center where the network interfaces with the cabled phone system. The signal zones of each base station overlap in order to hand over the signal when a mobile phone user moves from one cell sector to another. The phone picks up the strongest of the overlapping signals and when it switches stations, it informs the network, which tracks the movement of the signal from sector to sector.

The shift from broadcast to mobile is at once technical, material, and topological. As a distributed system, the placement of base station antennas and other infrastructural components is paramount to service coverage and strength. Installations are calibrated to specific strata within the city—principally midrise building rooftops and dedicated towers. While one-way broadcast signals benefit from large-scale, projective transmission patterns, two-way communication systems must limit their range out of functional necessity. Proximity to users on the street and in buildings is important, as is limiting the number of users with access to any one tower, and minimizing the interference in an obstruction-rich environment. The necessary ubiquity of mobile antennas is such that their sites and technologies eschew and resist iconography or even visibility. While in many contexts they engage tactics

of camouflage as palm trees and the like, in a city like New York, they are simply incorporated into the visual noise of existing rooftop terrains.

The physical attributes of wireless antennas are generic, resulting in a system that is at once highly articulated and pliable, mediated against many additional computational, physical, and bureaucratic constraints. In a dense environment, two important factors determine the viability of the network: the volume of users and the obstructions that are presented by the form of the city. So, while the familiar pointillist map may be the most prevalent representation of coverage, a network's logistics and capacity are not reducible to binaries of on and off, or even to the gradients of fast and slow, strong and weak. More accurately, signal is attributable to durations of coordination and fidelity, and the directness with which transmissions move from point to point.

Can You Hear Me Now?

In recent years, the FCC has authorized a three-fold increase within the commercial spectrum. However, given that a thirty-fold increase in wireless traffic is expected,[6] antenna systems are both proliferating at greater intensity and are also developing spatial senses. Instead of providing an even and continuous blanket of coverage, antennas now tailor themselves to the signal environment to ensure the availability of a connection.

In signal space, coverage is anticipated rather than determined, involving wrangling the unpredictable and ever-changing effects of obstruction and negotiation with the terrain of the city against the placement and calibration of individual antenna arrays. Probabilistic modeling and multiple feedback mechanisms drive the actual implementation and calibration of the system. These spatial algorithms reconstitute the form of the city by correlation, reassembling it in an emergent fashion from interference patterns. The gap between signal space and urban space is not resolved by collapsing or conflating one against another, but is instead infilled through computation and systems that map urban space, a soft mode of representation, that drives both the physical and energetic manifestation of the network.

Unsurprisingly, on a physical level, the antenna strata and the mobile strata in particular tend to elude representation and documentation. New York, for instance, maintains no complete record of all of the antenna locations and related networks[7] within the city. This is certainly due to the fact that the infrastructure is entirely privately owned and that it is constantly upgraded and subject to reorganization. In 2002, the federal government began mapping the telecommunications infrastructure in

6. Julius Genachowski, "America's Mobile Broadband Future." (Official remarks by FCC Chairman Julius Genachowski, presented at International CTIA Wireless I.T. & Entertainment, San Diego, California, October 7, 2009).

7. "(City)council members said Wednesday that it was important to begin paying closer attention to the placement of equipment that until recently was installed with little public awareness. The city does not have a complete record of where antennas are, Councilman Peter F. Vallone Jr. said, and the number of antennas is unknown. 'Nobody has any idea of what's going on,' Mr. Vallone said at the beginning of the hearing. 'It's like the Wild West out there.'" Colin Moynihan, "Council Considers Rules on Phone Antennas," *The New York Times*, Dec 01, 2010.

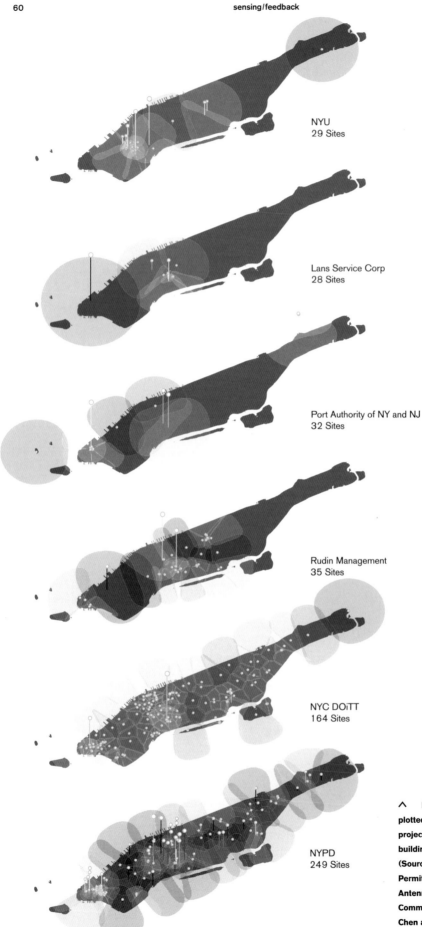

NYU
29 Sites

Lans Service Corp
28 Sites

Port Authority of NY and NJ
32 Sites

Rudin Management
35 Sites

NYC DOiTT
164 Sites

NYPD
249 Sites

∧   Manhattan mobile network base stations,
plotted individually and scaled according to
projected service volume as a function of total
building height within a fixed service radius.
(Sources: New York City Department of Buildings
Permit Filings (08/10/2005-02/10/2011); FCC
Antenna Registrations; New York City Planning
Commission PLUTO Dataset (2010). Michael
Chen and Justin Snider, 2011)

order to understand the vulnerability of such a system to terrorist attack.[8] Importantly, the physical infrastructure of signal space directly indexes the soft space of negotiation.

While only the FCC has the authority to thoroughly regulate broadcast infrastructure, local agencies such as the New York City Department of Buildings and Landmarks Commission have authority in related areas—requiring building permits for the erection of antenna arrays, for instance. In aggregate, this registration data (FCC, Permit, etc.) affords one of the clearest views of the extent of the antenna infrastructure.

The city itself is also the site of related registrations. Concerns over the potential health effects of electromagnetic radiation and the efforts to restrict the placement of base stations near schools in New York and San Francisco reflect public resistance to signal infrastructure. The emerging characteristics of political resistance are such that they manifest in small ways, as in the recent development of smart phone applications to monitor radiation levels associated with mobile phone use, and also in larger scale expressions, as in the recent protests in Manhattan over the placement of towers on residential buildings.[9] Paranoia surrounding mobile infrastructure is generally grounded in fears of over exposure to radiation. But the evolving sensitivities of the network are such that in the near future, concern over the actual data acquired by the network and the network's emerging spatial and temporal senses will inevitably converge in new applications and urban effects, as well as new modes of resistance. In this context, efforts to visualize antenna infrastructures against the representational and analytical protocols of spatial processing algorithms reveal the grading of the city and its form in tactical and technological terms.

Demands on existing infrastructure and the evolution of technology, such as the emergence of 4G technologies, are such that antenna installations will also greatly increase their density. This increases both the durability and flexibility of the network, as well as greatly augmenting the spatial senses and data capacity of the infrastructure. Already, the ability to algorithmically map the spatial and topographical dimensions of the city's physical form, as well as the recently publicized capacity of phones and base stations to store information on user activities and GPS coordinates, suggests how mobile infrastructure compiles the most complete representational account of the city, its inhabitants, and their activities in signal space and in physical space. The ubiquity of mobile devices, and of base stations in the city can be imagined to support a broad range of new infrastructures and urban practices. This also suggest that the infrastructure will migrate from the discretion of rooftops, to other spaces where it must maneuver through a broader set of urban sites within the public and street-level spaces of the city. To the extent that signal space can be understood to constitute an important public space of the city itself, the implications of this migration are of particular interest.

Proposals to harness the data gathered by sensors in mobile phones, and to embed additional sensors for biological agents and nuclear radiation outline the capacity of this infrastructure to function as a distributed and ubiquitous form of passive surveillance. The capacity of the infrastructure to "remember" the activities of users is already a reality and the ability to detect and identify an individual from electromagnetic interference patterns cross referenced with user data is not far off. This may require new degrees of protection and security, but may also prove to support new and inventive ways of negotiating urban space. Any such developments would certainly straddle public and corporate spheres. More importantly though, just as the ubiquitous and new form of public space that is signal space resists the iconography and singular nature of earlier broadcast models, its optimal expression is linked to duration, temporality, incremental time, and memory, rather than singular objects. These are important dimensions of the city itself, made potent and available in this new space. To the extent that that space and its particular characteristics are visualized, secured, negotiated, and resisted, the form of signal space is also the form of the softening city.

▪ ▪ ▪ **Michael Chen is principal of Normal Projects, an architecture and design firm based in New York, and a faculty member at Pratt Institute School of Architecture.**

8. Anthony M. Townsend, *Wired/Unwired: The Urban Geography of Digital Networks*, (PhD Dissertation, MIT, 2003), 118.

9. The residents of Salem House, a condo building on the Upper East Side, for instance, recently staged a demonstration on their rooftop, which had been made available to T-Mobile for the placement of a base station—purportedly arranged in a clandestine agreement between the condo board and the mobile carrier—effectively selecting to reduce their exposure to antenna radiation over any benefits in signal strength or transmission speed that accrue form close proximity to mobile infrastructure "NYC Tenants Fight Against Rooftop Cell Phone Tower," CBS News New York, (http://newyork.cbslocal.com/2010/11/21/nyc-tenants-fight-against-rooftop-cell-phone-tower).

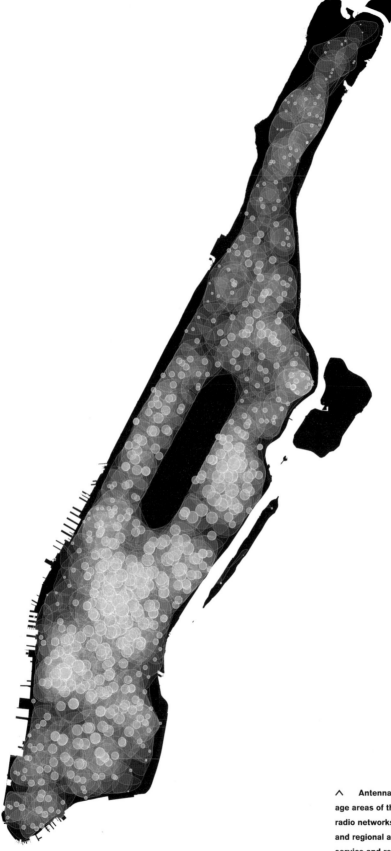

∧   Antenna distribution, heights, and coverage areas of the six largest private land mobile
radio networks in Manhattan, a mixture of city
and regional agencies, institutions, and private
service and real estate empires.
(Sources: Federal Communications Commission
Structure Registrations; New York City Planning
Commission PLUTO Dataset (2010). Michael
Chen and Justin Snider, 2011)

SHANNON WERLE

So, now, that we've reached historical height in environmental noise, are we entering an aural hell? Do we have no choice but to cover our ears and run away from all human-made and mechanical sounds?[1]
—Dajuin Yao, "To What Do We Open Our Ears?"

Listening to a city is like adjusting your ear to simultaneous strands in your music library. With headphones, we can respond to noise autonomously. Unfortunately, these digital earlids offer the creativity of an on-off switch: active noise control or a higher volume. Considering the extreme elasticity with which music is produced, and the pace with which each release spawns an infinite supply of remixes, cutups, mash-ups, etc., the autonomy of personal sound creates a bleak situation. "Sounds can be sliced and diced up into thousands of extremely short morsels and then superimposed according to statistical principles," explains Robert Henke, co-founder of the popular music software Ableton Live. "[They] can be placed in natural or convincing virtual spaces that no architect could ever construct."[2] Sound is soft and there is yet to be a copyright claim on an urban soundscape. Why then, do we tolerate it as if it were a commercial broadcast, only sporadically drawing our attention with a scream or siren, if it can be scratched like a vinyl? Over the past year, raw sounds from Linz, Hanoi, Ho Chi Minh City, Cairo, and Tokyo have been recycled into a single-track release, three albums and a concert performance. Blurring boundaries between noise, music and sound art, these artists use the urban soundscape as a springing board for sonic fiction and bring soft sounds to the foreground.

Hotspots

Invisible and amorphous, the soundscape is a vague terrain. Noise maps are crude elucidations, usually lacking data on specific sound types and our perception of them. They do, however, successfully pinpoint areas in which sound becomes a health hazard. What if it were possible to radically alter sound specifically at these points? These border conditions, although not as crisp as the map's colorful contours would suggest, could mark transitions between real and fictive sound. While stepping into a hotspot—a train station or crosswalk, for example—how would we perceive the shift?

If one could cut-and-paste Richard Eigner's compositions in-situ, stepping into a noisy area of Linz would trigger a steep volume drop. The city's library may as well expand its reading halls to include each bus stop along Main Street. Field recordings of noisy areas in and around the city—streets, public transport systems, church bells and swimming halls—provided base material for the

Austrian composer's album *Denoising Field Recordings*. Denoisers, usually applied in order to remove sounds such as the hiss of a low-grade microphone or the crackling of a vinyl, were used as a compositional tool. But how can the denoisification of noisy field recordings produce anything but blank tracks? The album is undeniably minimalist (also hinted by the transparent vinyl and colorless sleeve) and for the most part, tracks are processed beyond recognition. But similar to the remnants of ink and crayon dotting of Robert Rauschenberg's *Erased de Kooning Drawing*, bits of original sound—denoised into delicate melodies of high-pitched squeaks—infrequently surface throughout the near-silent tracks. Human voices are immediately recognizable, albeit indecipherable, in *People Denoised* and *Westbahn Denoised*'s rhythmic rise and fall in volume suggests incoming and outgoing trains. Eigner explains, "In most cases, the noisier and less melodic and harmonic a composition is, the less traces of original material emerge."[3] This also holds true for early twentieth century noise art by the futurist Luigi Russolo, Iannis Xenakis' *Concret PH*, and Lou Reed's *Metal Machine Music* of the American rock band Velvet Underground—all of which have been denoised in the composers' oeuvre. Prior to the album's release, Eigner performed a denoising set at *Acoustic City*, a 2009 initiative designed to transform Linz into Europe's model city for acoustics. Stickers with the word 'Beschallungsfrei' (free of imposed noise and background music) were pasted on buildings and campaign slogans included: "An end to the misuse of our ears! A stop to constant background music from the sausage stand to the toilet! Publicly accessible quiet zones!"[4] Denoisification failed to produce this silent utopia, but the tiny fragments of noise it left behind suggest a beautiful alternative.

Intersection, by Berlin-based Robert Henke (aka Monolake), exists on the border. Sounds of honking and revving motorbikes (there's about one motorbike for every two inhabitants in the Hanoi) seem, at first, untouched. Horns of varying pitches and duration are increasingly collaged until one eventually morphs into a brass-like sound. "Reality is step by step replaced by more abstract sounding events," explains Henke, "a dramatic escape from the ongoing city noise, where the metallic rattle from the bridge morphs into sonic mist."[5] Although recognizable sounds intermittently surface throughout the track—the Long Bien Bridge, chiming bells at St. Joseph Cathedral, trains at the Hanoi Railway Station—they've been rearranged into an intricate musical structure. Departing trains, for example, are woven into a "complex polyrhythmical entity that slowly fades away" towards the end, "leaving room for the long reverberation of the combined colors of sonic Hanoi."[6] This fifteen-minute-long

1. Dajuin Yao, "To What Do We Open Our Ears?" in *Around*, ed. Yeung Yang (Hong Kong: Soundpocket, 2010), 361.
2. Robert Henke, "Intersection," Monolake, www.monolake.de/concerts/intersection.html.
3. "Im Elektroakustischen Kraftraum," *SpotsZ*, October 2009, 18.
4. Akustikon Society of Hearing, "Gegen Zwangsbeschallung," Acoustic City, www.hoerstadt.at.
5. Robert Henke, "Intersection," Monolake, www.monolake.de/concerts/intersection.html.
6. Ibid.

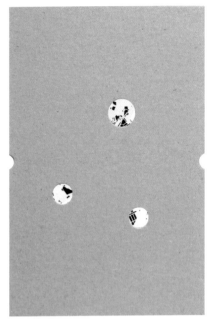  

∧ *les écoutes le caire* by Gilles Aubry (sound)
and Stéphane Montavon (text) released 2010 on
Gruenrekorder. Graphic design by Gilles Lepore.

∧ *Denoising Field Recordings* by Richard
Eigner released 2009 on Wald Entertainment.
Translucent sleeve and 12" vinyl designed by
Hans Renzler.

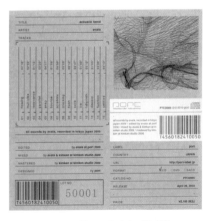 

∧ *Acoustic Bend* by evala (a.k.a Hirohito
Ebara) released 2010 on port, a label directed by
evala. Graphic design also by port.

composition can be stretched into lengthier live performances, allowing Henke ample room for improvisation. *Intersection* is not Henke's first time working urban sounds. *Hongkong* (which also includes field recordings from Guangzhou), is an album that hovers between minimal techno and ambient, and was produced together with Monolake co-founder Gerhard Behles in 1997, followed by a remastered version in 2008. Henke's multidisciplinary practice—a composer, sound designer, software developer, installation artist, and multimedia performer—resonates in this radical morphology of an otherwise ordinary traffic junction.

Sampling Cities

Sound requires space—its existence depends on movement resulting from variations in air pressure. Frozen music—as architecture was famously defined[7]—is an impossible solidification. But "if the movement of ambient air is defined as music, noise or sound art," noted Austrian composer Bernhard Gál, "it ultimately depends on the intention of the perceiving individual."[8] What if a device, sensitive to variations in these movements throughout a city, could recommend routes with interesting rhythms? Would one be able to navigate cities by shuffling through their soft sounds?

In order to compose *Phố* (Street), Vũ Nhật Tân used phở (a Vietnamese noodle soup) food stands as sound monitoring stations throughout Vietnam. Whereas the "buzz of conversation and the traffic noise drown out the clink of bowls" in Ho Chi Minh City, the clink of bowls is more distinct in Hanoi.[9] These analyses provide the framework for *Phố*'s musical structure: "I want to paint the crowded and very noisy streets in all Vietnamese cities in a piece of music and sound."[10] His ten-minute-long performance, which premiered at Hanoi's Opera House followed by a U.S. debut in Los Angeles one month later, uses a piano and traditional wind and string instruments including the Vietnamese đàn bầu. The original cacophony, however, isn't lost in translation. *Los Angeles Times* reporter Richard Ginell once described a violin and cello duo by the composer as "gliding microtonal gestures that sometimes sounded like sirens interrupted by shooting wars of snapped and plucked strings."[11] Urban field recordings are frequently included in his compositions,

most recently in collaboration with Henke and Vietnamese composer Trí Minh for the live performance *Soundscape Hanoi*. But much of the time, he does not have a choice: "Noise even penetrates my studio's windows... as a result, it's included in my recordings."[12] His acceptance is somewhat akin to John Cage's refusal to install double glazing at his New York City loft: "I wouldn't dream of getting double glass because I love all the sounds. The traffic never stops, night and day. Every now and then there is a horn, siren, screeching brakes, extremely interesting and always unpredictable."[13] Since Hanoi "is full of noise and we cannot escape from it," the Vietnamese composer employs it as a muse.[14]

From a megacity which is louder than a freight train,[15] you would expect an album of piercingly loud tracks. But *Les Écoutis Le Caire* (The Listeners of Cairo) captures the persistent blend of car horns, street music, voices and alarms through varied lenses. Swiss sound artist Gilles Aubry curated a selection of empty spaces throughout the city based on their resonant qualities—a market hall, basilica, courtyard, refrigerator and parking house—which were used as impromptu recording studios. The ability to identify sounds throughout the album's two lengthy tracks is somewhat halted by a rich palette of 'effects' generated by each of the spaces—ranging from frail, wind-like drones to the pounding beats of machinery. As a result, it seems to cast a constant state of confusion, unable to draw data from the sounds because they're either entangled in dense structures of grating sounds or melted into soothing blends. Headlined as "the city where you can't hear yourself scream" by the *New York Times*, even the call to prayer succumbs to cacophony in Cairo.[16] The most recent noise abatement attempt (six years in the making) involves broadcasting a single call to prayer from a downtown studio, which is then transmitted to receivers at mosques throughout the city. Although cities in Syria, Turkey and the UAE have implemented similar programs, Cairo—previously the setting for a "chaotic affair of wildly different voices ringing out at different times"—was deterred by thousands of unregistered mosques.[17] *Les Écoutis Le Caire* is accompanied by a 'wordmap' authored by Swiss artist Stéphane Montavon, who collaborated with Aubry on the project during a residency in Cairo. Using text to "render the rhythmical confrontations of diverse urban situations,"[18]

7. The notion of architecture as frozen music has been attributed to a range of sources, but perhaps most famously to the German philosophers Johann Wolfgang von Goethe and Friedrich Wilhelm Joseph von Schelling. Schelling originally wrote "architecture in general is frozen music" in the 1809 publication *Philosophie der Kunst* (Fred R. Shapiro, ed., *The Yale Book of Quotations* (New Haven: Yale University Press, 2006), 670) while Goethe's statement "I call architecture frozen music" appeared later in his published conversations with the German author Johann Peter Eckermann (S.M. Fuller, trans., *Conversations with Goethe in the Last Years of His Life* (Boston: Hilliard, Gray, and Company, 1839), 282). See also: Khaled

Saleh Pascha, "Gefrorene Musik" PhD diss., Technische Universität Berlin, 2004.

8. Bernhard Gál, "Klang Architektur Raum Zeit," *Positionen* 54 (2003), 15-16.

9. Diem Thu, "The Sound of Noise," *Look at Vietnam*, October 27, 2008, www.lookatviet-nam.com/2008/10/the-sound-of-noise.html.

10. Vũ Nhật Tân, "Phố" (Program for Ascending Dragon Music Festival, Los Angeles, California, April 17, 2010).

11. Richard S. Ginell, "Southeast Asia, from the Southwest," *Los Angeles Times*, April 1, 2008, Entertainment Section, http://articles.latimes.com/2008/apr/01/entertainment/et-southwest1.

12. Vũ Nhật Tân, email message to author, July 11, 2010.

13. Stephen Montague, "John Cage at Seventy: An Interview," *American Music* Vol. 3, No. 2 (1985), 205-216, www.jstor.org/stable/3051637.

14. Vũ Nhật Tân, email message to author, July 11, 2010.

15. Michael Slackman and Mona El-Naggar, "A City Where You Can't Hear Yourself Scream," *New York Times*, April 14, 2008, www.nytimes.com/2008/04/14/world/middleeast/14cairo.html.

16. Ibid.

17. Hadeel Al Shalchi, "Cairo Mosques Begin Unified Call to Prayer," *The Jordan Times*, August 13, 2010, www.jordantimes.com/index.php?news=29156.

∧   Traffic in Hanoi photographed by Robert
Henke, 2010.

∧   Vu Nhat Tan performing at the 2010 Green
Space Festival in Hanoi. Photo courtesy of the Vu
Nhat Tan Group.

the open-ended layout of multilingual phrases (conceived as a map, without end or beginning) complements the field recordings. Although the disc is stamped with a site plan, neither the Montavon's words nor Aubry's sounds offer a sense of orientation—an omission that, quite convincingly, reflects the city itself.

Toppling the Hierarchy of Sound

Canadian composer R. Murray Schafer, who coined the word 'soundscape' in the 1960s, developed a relaxation exercise in which music students were asked to sing a tone that seemed to naturally emerge from the center of their being. For students in North America, this tone resembled B natural and for students in Europe, a G sharp. "B natural is 60 cycles and G sharp is about 50 cycles," Schafer explained. "They are memory traces of the electrical frequencies of two continents."[19] What if subliminal frequencies, faint murmurs, and drowned ripples could be raised to the surface of audibility? Strolling past a fountain, would it be possible to dissect the discord into a minimal beat of individual drops?

Acoustic Bend by Tokyo-based Evala (aka Hirohito Ebara) zooms in on, and oftentimes isolates, an array of Tokyo's sonic curiosities. Evala seems to embrace scientific methodologies, and in fact his previous release, The Third Term Music Project, was developed as part of a research collaboration with the University of Tokyo, which sought to produce music based on "applications of evolutionary algorithms, chaos, nonlinear physics and complex systems."[20] Most of the sonic specimens used to create Acoustic Bend are posted alongside a snapshot of respective source on Evala's blog and podcast Hacking Tone. This archive of crisp recordings encompasses both large (Tokyo's Shibuya Station) and small (the click of an automatic lock) scales. Within everyday settings, many of his extractions would go otherwise unnoticed, such as a grating vending machine hum and the metallic squeaks of connection plates linking passenger cars along a commuter rail line. In addition to his position as a lecturer at the University of Tokyo, Evala operates parallel practices in sound design and composition. His sensitivity to sound is manifested in careful juxtapositions of natural and industrial sounds, such as a cricket chirping beneath an asphalt plate or the sound of water as it filters through a drainage trench, pounds an awning during a rainfall, spurts out of a fountain pump, and splashes along the pavement. Each song is labeled with a single word, sometimes onomatopoeic—snap, cracking, hush—or carrying a strong sonic association—flowing, resonance, bounce, cave and fuzzbox. The first track—flowing—begins with a sound resembling soft rain, transforms into a downpour, morphs into pure static and finally culminates in a simple buzz. Untitled renders a similar morphology, beginning with a dense layering of voices and ending with flowing water. These slow transformations of everyday audio extracts into processed, electronic sounds draw

fascinating, albeit far-fetched, relationships. Oftentimes Evala's field recordings anchor Tokyo's urban drone with 'found pulses' throughout the city—a beeping crosswalk, keyboard tapping or a rhythmic chime for directing blind pedestrians and even the 'found music' of street artists, rummaged out of the soundscape.

The Possibility of a Real-Time Mix

All of these individuals share a penchant for challenging predefined systems. Sounds off the street are whittled down to silent skeletons, mutated into "impossible to build" abstractions, forged with a score, sampled into colorful spectrums, collaged to form new juxtapositions and hacked. Already labeled 'experimental' by sound art and music circles, they have eroded the common perceptions of how we can react to sound in cities, raising new issues with relevancy beyond the fringe on which they operate. And the aforementioned single-track release, three albums and concert performance barely skims the surface— well over a hundred albums have included audio extractions from cities across the globe in the last decade alone. But would it be naïve to foster discussions on their work in the context of noise abatement, projecting an idea of the urban commute as a platform for live-sets? Real-time manipulation of sounds in cities has been experimented with by a variety of sound artists, musicians, and acousticians (Tramjam by Mumbai Streaming Attack, Box 30/70 by O+A, Les Voûtes by Michael Gendreau and _habitus by Cédric Maridet, to cite a few) and even a headphone set capable of amplifying surprisingly rhythmic real-time electrical charges emitted by lighting systems, ATMs, WLAN, etc. was developed by the German musician Christina Kubisch. Without doubt, these works offer a refreshing alternative to our otherwise spatial engagements with urban soundscapes, something historian Karin Bijsterveld credits toward its unhindered persistence: "It is remarkable that sound, crossing the borders between neighbors, cities and nations so easily, has often been handled spatially, for instance, by imposing zones, canalizing traffic, and drawing noise maps. We have been trying to create islands of silence, yet have left a sea of sound to be fiercely discussed."[21] In cities, construction and transportation top the pyramid, rendering the rustling of leaves, chirping birds and flowing water mute. Perhaps a well-constructed mash-up instead of pure abatement is the best solution. "Mash-ups are the sonic equivalent of the kind of flipped out mixed world we live in," states Paul D. Miller (aka DJ Spooky). "Once things get digital, anything goes. Mix John Holt with Bjork, why not? Flip Ravi Shankar into a track with Lee "Scratch" Perry, sure…"[22] We may not be able to cut a perfect track for everyone, but at least we will have material to pass along for another remix.

· · · Shannon Werle currently researches the relationship between noise, music and cities as a fellow of the Berlin House of Representatives.

18. "Les écoutis Le Caire," Gruenrekorder, www.gruenrekorder.de/?page_id=2301.

19. R. Murray Schafer, "I've Never Seen a Sound," (lecture presented at Hochschule Darmstadt, Dieburg, December 7, 2010).

20. Takashi Ikegami, "Third Term Music," Ikegami Lab, http://sacral.c.u-tokyo.ac.jp/ index.php?Third Term Music.

21. Karin Bijsterveld, Mechanical Sound: Technology, Culture, and Public Problems of

Noise in the Twentieth Century (Cambridge: MIT, 2008), 4.

22. Piers Fawkes, "Interview with DJ Spooky," PSFK, www.psfk.com/2006/05/ interview_with_.html.

THE URBAN CONSPIRACY

JEFFREY INABA

A covert organization has been plotting to take over mankind. The number involved is not entirely known, but estimates are in the millions. They are present throughout the Middle East, Africa, Asia, the Americas, and in greatest concentration in Europe. They are typically in their 60s, 70s, and 80s and claim to be 'retired,' 'part-time volunteers,' or 'mostly spending time with grandchildren.'

Having been raised in the aftermath of WW2 and coming of age during the paranoia of the Cold War, these so-called senior citizens reacted to the treacherous battles for power by banding together behind a mission that is only now beginning to surface. The anguish of growing up amid political upheaval motivated this organization to form a world where discord ceases to exist. The immediate experience of witnessing extensive damage to urban areas has provoked this group of seniors to work through back door soft channels, in an attempt to make cities places of harmony. Their efforts are visible today in the form of parks, plazas, waterfronts, sustainable greenbelts, reclaimed infrastructure, farmers markets, bike paths, streetscapes, and communal gardens. It is no coincidence that we are experiencing an aging society at the same time as we are seeing an abundance of well-groomed parks.

This population of seniors is regarded by some political leaders as "the greediest generation," hell-bent on bankrupting the developed world's social safety nets. But in actuality they have been posturing as self-centered baby boomers to conceal their efforts toward an unselfish social end. In fact, their counterculture rebellion as youths was a test to see if they could operate together in large numbers in the name of a single cause. It is likely that their frenetic consumerism later in life was also a smokescreen. They were plagued with an anxiety that more things would be destroyed and taken from them—a feeling that stemmed from the profound trauma they experienced as youths. This first manifested in an unresolved desire to acquire consumer goods, but over time, they realized that hiding behind an aura of self-absorbed spending helped to divert unwanted attention from their humanistic intentions. Cleverly, they espoused a rhetoric of individualism to mask their true power in multitude.

Who would have thought that this band of elderly—part of an age group often thought to be removed from decision-making processes—are trying to shape cities? Reports suggest the graying confederates have been waiting for this moment to make one final overwhelming push. They are using their advanced appearances to appeal for public spaces that benefit the elderly in order to achieve their ultimate objective of assuring the abundant proliferation of friendlier urban environments. Several observers indeed believe the expressed interest by some elderly in current popular notions of growing old is parallel in motive. Movements such as 'Aging in Place,' 'Age Friendly Cities,' 'Multi-generational Living,' 'Active Aging,' 'Longevity,' 'Life Course,' 'Third Age,' etc, serve as elaborate alibi that further cover their tracks as they develop urban land for general public benefit.

The Urban Conspiracy (which has yet to be disproved) reveals that seniors are not a passive segment of society that lacks agency. It also suggests that inasmuch as this group is motivated to remain vital and engaged, they aren't entirely sold on personal fulfillment 'baby boomer values'. As the following events already indicate, they have taken sweeping actions in the interest of the public far beyond anyone's expectation, let alone suspicion.

First Europe, Then the World

Most of Europe's oldest neighborhoods (those with the highest number of retirees to people of working age) were severely damaged during WW2. Living at the epicenter of cities in ruin and growing up in a deformed urban fabric left such a psychic wound on these impressionable children, it paralyzed them from leaving. It was the fear that their urban surroundings might suddenly evaporate that inspired the invention of public space, which was specifically modeled to secure land ownership in perpetuity. Experts warn that these neighborhoods are likely senior strongholds with command centers that transmit plans to take over urban properties globally.

Recruitment

Improvements in medical care, diet, and environment are cited as the reasons for the rise in the number of elderly in recent decades. But the greatest headway in recruitment today has come about with the decrease in age at which one regards oneself old. Thirty and forty-year-olds are reacting against their parents by opting out of their forbearers'—sixty is the new forty-year-old's worldview. They choose to act with extreme prevention in mind, convinced that living a maximum number of years requires acknowledging being old at a younger age. Certain that every slight physiological change in their bodies is a sign of aging, they have decided to start a longevity regime early on by living low-key lives of managed risk and even-balanced performance. The disinterest in wild youth-oriented living is boosting the number of people who consider themselves old ominously higher than birth year statistics indicate, fueling speculation that this organization is more insidious than previously thought.

Resilience and Support

In her informative model of aging, epidemiology and geriatric expert Linda Fried illustrates that as we grow older, we become less resilient to external forces. As a result, we rely increasingly on our physical environment to support our needs. Architects and industrial designers are attempting to create hospitable environments and keep up with the growing demand for senior-oriented products. But their efforts are overshadowed by unconfirmed reports that the elderly have been secretly supporting major architectural projects. Applying their knowledge of the financing models and real estate laws that they helped implement, seniors have been raising capital to acquire land

∧　**Two historic shifts are taking place. As is often stated, more than half the world's population now lives in cities. Also for the first time ever, the elderly outnumber the children on the planet. Are these events unrelated, or do they signal the final stage of an unfolding plan?** (Photo © Naho Kubota, 2011)

using public-private partnerships, BIDs, conservancies, and public trusts. By securing ownership of large land areas, legal entities to maintain them, and seed operation funding, they have quietly organized commissions in their effort to accumulate more public space in cities. Such activity suggests that despite the decline in their personal resilience, seniors have been plotting to make cities resistant to neglect and decay.

Posing

Because architects peak in the later years of life, they feel professional pressure to appear youthful in order for their work to be viewed as informed and contemporary. Bowing to this expectation, they avoid associating with whomever could suggest they are old and out of touch, such as the elderly. Seniors, on the other hand, compassionately understand this impulse and also recognize that architects of all ages are premature seniors at heart. As much as designers obsess about the timeliness of their work, their real concerns are maturation and longevity: they want to prolong their lives and make as many enduring buildings as possible.

All the while, the elderly happily pretend to be uninformed about architecture because their feigned ignorance gives them

∧   **The public influence and personal wealth of the elderly are on the rise. What will they do with their accumulating power?**
(Photo © Naho Kubota, 2011)

wide berth to move about undetected. They know very well that contemporary architecture, figurative and atmospheric alike, offer formal means to redistribute the area of a given program to allocate greater space for public use. Thousands of uploaded photos of grandparents posing in front of contemporary architecture contribute to a database cataloging building configurations that can be used in the future to aid their cause.

Storytelling and Soft Power
As a storytelling device, a conspiracy theory can create an alternative set of facts that challenge what is currently believed about a given situation. It can portray the group of conspirators as possessing more power than they are given credit for, and, as a result, it can elevate the perception of the conspirators' ability and effect. These mechanisms of storytelling can provide soft power to a group that enables real change. A conspiracy theory can also call attention to real circumstances. For example, the discourse on 'the city' is growing and has become one of the principle objects of global policy. In the past year alone, the UN has launched The World Urban Campaign and The 100 Cities Initiative. Central to these urbanization efforts is the role of public space, reflected in the international body's

∧   There is reason to believe the elderly are plotting to establish social harmony. In the last century, great faith was placed on the nation state as the most effective means to prevent human conflict. Today, possibly as part of a coordinated effort, seniors and major international organizations have turned to the city as the form for interventions to serve their cause. (Photo © Naho Kubota, 2011)

first-ever 'Public Spaces' resolution. The belief that aging should first and foremost be addressed at the level of the city is demonstrated by WHO's recent introduction of the Global Network of Age-Friendly Cities, whose requisite set of commitments have already been adopted by dozens of municipalities. Softly alerting readers to these realities will prompt the question of how we as architects will respond to the emerging concerns revolving around urbanism.

∧   Stemming from the trauma of urban devastation they experienced as children, they believe the proliferation of public space will help to bring about global political stability. (Photo © Naho Kubota, 2011)

interfacing/
enveloping

Soft systems operate at a multiplicity of scales by embracing incremental interventions that are strategically positioned to have widespread impact. They act as interfaces with the environment—whether mitigating or harnessing it—at the scale of a surface, a building, or a landscape.

FAST COMPANY: ARCHITECTURE AND THE SPEED OF TECHNOLOGY

CHRIS PERRY

The future of the past is in the future. The future of the present is in the past. The future of the future is in the present.
—John McHale, "The Future of the Future"

The instrumental and aesthetic implications of architecture's engagement with science and technology has a long history, part of which includes the period following the Second World War when the rapid technological advances of the Industrial Revolution merged with a general cultural mindset characterized by themes of progress and futurism. The Industrial Revolution, and with it the emergence of machine technology, contributed to an even larger philosophical shift from a Newtonian physics of certainty to one of increasing contingency and probability.[1] As a result, architecture was re-imagined not only in terms of its formal and aesthetic appearance, but more profoundly in terms of a transition from a logic of stasis to one of temporality, and by extension from a preoccupation with form and space to one concerning time.

Given the equally revolutionary advances in computing technology in the last twenty years, our contemporary moment can be seen in similar terms. Not unlike the postwar generation of architects and thinkers, contemporary designers are inevitably faced with the challenge of engaging new technological advances and their implications for the discipline of architecture. While computing technology has been addressed quite extensively in recent architectural discourse, the predominant focus has been on modeling software and its potential as a design tool for producing new formal languages. The result has been to limit architecture to a static representation of dynamic processes and thus reinforce the perception that architecture remains first and foremost a formal discipline.

What has been less apparent in recent years is an exploration of how computers introduce qualities of temporality, contingency, and feedback into the very performance of the architecture itself, shifting the discipline away from a preoccupation with form, space, and meaning, towards an exploration of temporality and instrumentality. This would suggest the incorporation of digital technologies into buildings from fields as diverse and pervasive as computing, interaction design, environmental science, and robotics, as a means of expanding their capacity to adjust and respond to changing programmatic and environmental forces. Furthermore, the explicit interdisciplinarity of this approach, in which

Architectural Design, February 1967, price 5s.

∧   Cover of **AD: 2000+**, John McHale, ed., 1967. (Photo by courtesy of Cutler-Hammer (Milwaukee, Wisconsin), originally used in one of their advertisements)

architects probe peripheral technological disciplines as a means of challenging and ultimately rethinking their own discipline's creative and technological limits, necessarily suggests a re-positioning of the traditional role and identity of the architect. As opposed to the more familiar heroic role of the architect as 'form-giver', or what Reyner Banham once dubbed the "fashion-master", the architect is positioned instead as a synthesizer of technological systems and peripheral areas of disciplinary expertise.[2]

Postwar Futurism

The postwar period of the 1950's and 60's brought with it enthusiastic and at times contentious debate over the impact of machine technology on architecture. Critical of the largely symbolic use of 'the machine' by many modern architects and what was interpreted by many critics as

1. Norbert Weiner, *The Human Use of Human Beings: Cybernetics and Society*, (Da Capo Press, 1954), 8.

2. For a discussion of the disciplinary definition of 'the architect' as modeled after 'the artist,' see Reyner Banham, "The Last Formgiver," in *Architectural Review* (1966).

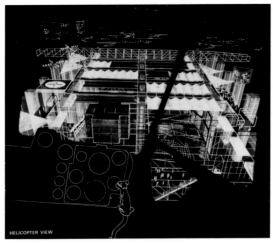

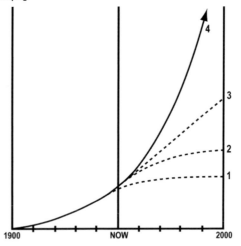

∧   Cedric Price, *Fun Palace*: helicopter view, ca.
1964. Photoreproduction laid down on hardboard
(Masonite board). 102 x 122 cm. (Cedric Price
fonds Collection Centre Canadien d'Architecture/
Canadian Centre for Architecture, Montréal)

∧   W. I. Van Der Poel III, Robert A. Heinlein's
trajectory of the future, *Galaxy Science Fiction*,
1952. (Diagram re-drawn by Chris Perry (public
domain)

a betrayal of the modern movement's promise of challenging the orthodoxy of style and formal representation in architecture, Reyner Banham, John McHale and other postwar thinkers called for a restored interest in technology in terms of instrumentality.[3] As a means of identifying this renewed architecture of instrumentality, Banham and others developed the concept of "anticipatory design," which had two connotations for the discipline of architecture. The first addressed the potential of a building to incorporate flexible and adaptable technologies as a means of anticipating and responding to changing programmatic and environmental conditions. The second addressed an implicit futurism and an approach to design rooted less in architectural precedent than technological extrapolation.[4] Banham's concept of extrapolation encouraged architects to look beyond the limits of their own discipline as a means of discovering new forms of knowledge and expertise.[5] For postwar architects like Cedric Price, this included an engagement with the emerging field of cybernetics. His collaborations with the cybernetician Gordon Pask were instrumental in conceiving buildings that incorporated

principles of feedback, specifically in terms of their capacity to respond and adjust to changing programmatic and environmental conditions.[6] For Buckminster Fuller, his familiarity with the military's use of systems engineering as a means of synthesizing a variety of technologies and forms of disciplinary expertise in the design of sophisticated hybrid weaponry led to a more technologically and materially integrated approach to the design of buildings, referred to playfully as "livingry."[7] Archigram, meanwhile, engaged in a broad multi-media experiment. Their speculative proposals operated at a variety of scales and incorporated new technologies which, similar to the work of Price, demonstrated a conception of architecture that went beyond static formal and spatial effects to capture the dynamic forces of an age increasingly defined by electronics and audio-visual media.[8]

The concept of extrapolation itself was borrowed largely from the field of science fiction, specifically the work of extrapolative writers like Jules Verne, whose projective fictions were informed by emerging scientific and technological advancements.[9] Verne's 1865 novel *From*

3. Reyner Banham, "The Machine Aesthetic," *Architectural Review* (April 1955), 227.

4. Reyner Banham, "The History of the Immediate Future," *Journal of the Royal Institute of British Architects* 68, no. 7 (May 1961), 252.

5. Ibid., 257.

6. For a discussion of Cedric Price's collaboration with Gordon Pask, see Mary Louise Lobsinger, "Cybernetic Theory and the Architecture of Performance: Cedric Price's Fun Palace," *Anxious Modernisms: Experimentation in Postwar Architectural Culture*, ed., Sarah Williams Goldhagen and Rejean Legault (CCA/MIT Press, 2000).

7. For a discussion of systems engineering and its implications for architecture, see A.C. Brothers, M.E. Drummand, and R.

Llewelyn-Davies, "The Science Side: Weapons Systems, Computers, Human Sciences," *Architectural Review* 127, no. 757 (March 1960), 188-190 as well as "The Future of Universal Man Symposium with Anthony Cox, Gordon Graham, Lawrence Alloway," *Architectural Review* 127, no 758 (April 1960), 253-260. For a detailed overview of systems engineering in the context of Buckminster Fuller's Dymaxion House, see Buckminster Fuller, "Dymaxion House: Meeting Architectural League," New York (1929), *Your Private Sky: Discourse*, ed., Joachim Krausse and Claude Lichtenstein, Lars Muller Publishers.

8. Anthony Vidler, "Toward a Theory of the Architectural Program," in *October* 106 (Cambridge, Mass: MIT Press, 2003), 69.

9. Jonathan Farnham, "Pure Pop for Now People: Reyner Banham, Science Fiction, and History," *Lotus* 104 (2000), 121. As Farnham observes, science fiction generally falls into the two categories of extrapolative fiction and speculative fiction. While the latter is driven less by science and more by fantasy, as characterized by the idealism of early twentieth century writers such as H.G. Wells, the former approach utilizes rigorous research of emerging technological advancements as a way of projecting potential scenarios for the future application of those technologies and, more significantly, their impact on society as a whole.

the Earth to the Moon, which preceded the Space Race by almost exactly one hundred years, was based on detailed scientific and technological research allowing Verne to anticipate the future with remarkable accuracy. For Banham, extrapolative fiction presented a new and potentially useful model of practice for architects and historians alike, suggesting that they might do well to investigate scientific and technological innovation as a means of anticipating a set of possible futures for the discipline:

> History is to the future as the observed results of an experiment are to the plotted graph—that is, you plot on the graph the results of which you are sure, you seek for a line that connects them convincingly and you produce it beyond the last certain point to see where it will lead – so too with all major works of historical philosophy; they extrapolate present trends into the future condition of men.[10]

The scientific and technological fields that Banham encouraged architects to consult included cybernetics, environmental studies, and disciplines focused on human behavioral systems.[11] While operating outside the immediate disciplinary envelope of architecture, these fields were of potential relevance to designers in that each explores the nature of systems or environments characterized by feedback and exchange.[12] The first implication for architects, then, was to think of a building as a reflexive system or environment, one capable of responding to a variety of internal as well as external pressures. The second implication addressed the larger question of architecture's very definition as a discipline, distinguishing between a conventional conception of architecture as a discipline concerned principally with issues of form, space, and meaning, and one that conceived buildings as carefully choreographed environments for programmatic interaction and exchange.

Cedric Price's 1964 *Potteries Thinkbelt* proposal provides one such example of a postwar architectural project informed by principles of technological extrapolation. Envisioned as a large-scale, multi-disciplinary learning institution, Price's *Thinkbelt* proposal incorporates a variety of new technologies from peripheral disciplines and industries, including gantry cranes, railway infrastructure, portable shipping containers, closed circuit TV, and lightweight industrial construction methods. Utilizing an existing network of railway tracks to facilitate the organization and distribution of portable architectural elements, Price proposed a reconfigurable campus for 22,000 occupants.[13] These portable elements include classrooms, laboratories, and residential units dispersed along the existing railway system which itself operates as a programmatic distribution network. In terms of instrumentality, then, the *Potteries Thinkbelt*

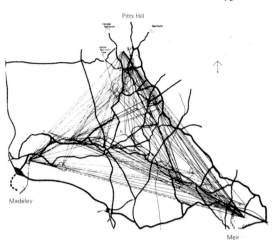

∧ **Cedric Price, overall plan showing primary road and desire line for the *Potteries Thinkbelt*, 1964. Diazotype, 59.5 x 84.4 cm. (Cedric Price fonds Collection Centre Canadien d'Architecture/ Canadian Centre for Architecture, Montréal)**

could be viewed as a temporal and reflexive planning machine. Indeed, Price referred to the project as a "socio-economic instrument," a carefully coordinated and yet open network of architectural elements, the purpose of which was to provide an infrastructural vehicle for programmatic distribution, mixture, and by extension, economic and social expansion over time.[14] Thus, one witnesses the traditional architectural and institutional identity of fixity and stability exchanged for one of dispersion, fluidity, and mixture in which architecture never takes a stable form or configuration but drifts instead in a perpetual state of temporal flux.[15]

Contemporary Futurism
In our current age of digital, biological, and environmental technologies, the contemporary experience can be seen as one increasingly characterized by temporal flux. Norbert Weiner, a pioneer of cybernetics in the 1950s and 60s, anticipated this technological and cultural shift, describing the future of human experience as one increasingly defined by the dynamism and contingency of information networks. In our contemporary technological milieu of bioengineering, man-machine interfaces, and communication networks, architecture is reconceived to take the form of a reflexive network of shifting participants, programmatic and environmental conditions, and knowledge flows. Indeed both Weiner and Banham were engaged in taking stock of the technological advances particular to their time while simultaneously anticipating the implication of such advancements for the future.

10. Reyner Banham, "The History of the Immediate Future," *Journal of the Royal Institute of British Architects* 68, no. 7 (May 1961), 252.

11. Reyner Banham, "The History of the Immediate Future," *Journal of the Royal Institute of British Architects* 68, no. 7 (May 1961), 256-57.

12. Anthony Vidler, "Futurist Modernism: Reyner Banham," in *Histories of the Immediate Present: Inventing Architectural Modernism* (MIT Press, 2008), 124-25.

13. For a detailed description of the *Potteries Thinkbelt*, see Stanley Mathews, "The Potteries Thinkbelt," in *From Agit-Prop to Free Space: The Architecture of Cedric Price*,

(Black Dog Publishing, 2007).

14. Cedric Price, "Life Conditioning," *Architectural Design* 36 (October 1966), 483-94.

15. Mark Wigley, "The Architectural Brain," in *Network Practices: New Strategies in Architecture and Design* (Princeton Architectural Press, 2007), 32.

∧   R&Sie, *Olzweg*, 2006. (Image courtesy of the architect)

∧   Howeler + Yoon and Squared Design, *Filene's Eco Pods*, 2009. (Image courtesy of the architect)

∧   Future Cities Lab (Johnson / Gattegno), *Xeromax Envelope*, 2010. Detail photograph of the back of the membrane showing robotic actuators and wiring. (Image courtesy of the architect)

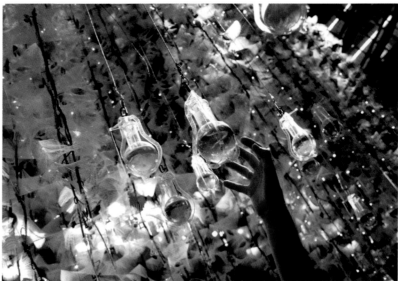

∧   Philip Beesley, *Aurora*, 2010. Detail photograph of the installation's fluid storage system. (Image courtesy of the architect)

In the same way that the postwar generation endeavored to harness the qualities of temporality and instrumentality characteristic of the Machine Age, contemporary architects and designers struggle to engage the technologies of an age characterized by even greater mobility. And just as the architects of the 1950s and 60s resisted the trappings of a disciplinary stubbornness limited to the traditional characteristics of architecture, a new generation of anticipatory designers seem focused on engaging the computing technologies of our time not merely for their capacity to generate new and increasingly seductive formal languages representative of a biological age, but in terms of their instrumental potential to produce buildings increasingly responsive to programmatic and environmental flux; buildings that, like the most rudimentary of biological specimen, exhibit flexibility, adaptability, and basic intelligence.

Both R&Sie and Howeler + Yoon, for example, have proposed the employment of large-scale robots as a means of producing architecture that is in a perpetual state of flux. This work recalls Cedric Price's use of gantry cranes in both his *Fun Palace* and *Potteries Thinkbelt* proposals from the mid-1960's, as well as Archigram's iconic *Plug-in City* proposal from 1964 in which large-scale cranes were a dominant architectural feature. Similarly, Future Cities Lab and Philip Beesley have investigated the application of robotic technologies at smaller scales, producing full-scale installations, which serve as working prototypes for the study of responsive skins and dynamic structures. One example is Future Cities Lab's recent installation of their *Xeromax Envelope*, which utilizes motion-sensing and lightweight robotic equipment to produce a dynamic membrane capable of responding to external stimuli. Comprised of flexible panels which expand and contract

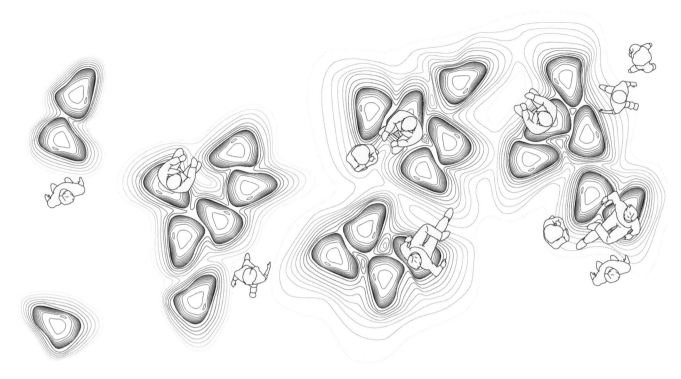

∧ **Weathers, *Wanderings*, 2008-10. (Image courtesy of the architect)**

based on user interaction, this dilating skin produces a variety of formal, organizational, and visual effects remarkably similar to Buckminster Fuller's design for a computer-controlled responsive skin to provide flexible shading for the US pavilion at the Montreal Expo in 1967. Meanwhile, in addition to experimenting with robotics and interaction technology, Philip Beesley's recent work has ventured into the realm of fluid systems. Working with Rachel Armstrong, a designer and technologist with a background in medical science, Beesley's 2010 installation in Toronto, titled *Aurora*, includes a soft infrastructure of plastic tubes and containers for the cyclical distribution and storage of fluids throughout the installation environment. Increasingly biological—both in terms of its aesthetic effects as well as its organizational mechanics—this installation work incorporates a wide range of technologies, materials, and forms of expertise

from fields as diverse as robotics, interaction design, and chemical engineering.

The architecture and design practice Weathers takes an approach similar, in some respects, to Beesley's recent interest in fluid technologies. Shifting emphasis away from the physical mechanics of robotic technology, Weathers focuses its design work on the development of intricate environmental control systems as a means of conditioning space. In this way, programmatic use is influenced less by the physical or spatial properties of the building than by the way in which it distributes and calibrates the quantity as well as quality of light, heat, and ventilation. In the 1960 article "Stocktaking," Banham suggests an alternative to 'the cave' or 'primitive hut' as a model of enclosure for the discipline of architecture.[16] The campfire, unlike the cave, Banham argues, provides enclosure through light and heat and does so in a way

∧   pneumastudio, *Spirabilis*, 2011. (Image
courtesy of the architect)

∧   Terreform ONE, *Smart DOTS + Soft MOBS:
NY 2028 Environmental Mobility*, 2008. (Image
courtesy of the architect)

that is inherently flexible and thus responsive to its user's changing needs and desires. The suggestion is that rather than limit the concept of enclosure and by extension architecture to a static surface envelope, architects might do well to consider the conditioning of space through such flexible environmental media as light and heat. Weathers seems to be doing precisely that; campfire architecture enabled by the technologies of the twenty-first century.

pneumastudio, an interdisciplinary design practice situated between the fields of architecture and landscape architecture, explores both the human and non-human application of twenty-first century technologies. In addition to robotics and interaction design, pneumastudio incorporates technological innovation from the environmental sciences, thereby envisioning architectural and landscape systems that are responsive to environmental as well as programmatic forces. The *Spirabilis* proposal, for example, takes the form of a large-scale technological respiratory machine for the collection, distribution, and perpetual regulation of natural and artificial resources. The machine cum-leisure environment is comprised of an assemblage of environmental technologies and architectural elements, including six 'phytotrons', or solariums, for the cultivation of hydroponic vegetation and oxygen-producing algae, a field of columnar funnels that in addition to providing structural support collect rainwater, and a system of architectural appliances for a broad range of programmatic activities.

This kind of interdisciplinarity can also be found in the work of Terreform ONE, a group of architects, designers, artists, and scientists exploring the application of new

technologies across a broad spectrum of scales and fields of study. And while the work often appears to be quite fantastical, serving to provoke larger questions related to architecture, science, and technology, it is also grounded in rigorous research and hard science. The group's members come from a wide range of disciplines with advanced degrees in architecture, urbanism, landscape, industrial design, and ecology. As a result, the work can be seen as futuristic and inherently provocative while also grounded in a disciplined study and evaluation of emerging scientific trends and technological advancements.

Conclusion

In thinking about the architecture of the present, specifically an architecture of technological futurism driven by the rapid and far-reaching advances of twenty-first century technologies, it is useful to reflect on the past, in part because one inevitably discovers that while the work of the present may seem novel in many respects, it is inextricably linked to the issues, challenges, debates, and ambitions of previous generations. It is in this sense that the implications of John McHale's meditation on the future which begins this article, a framing of the future within the context of the past as well as the present, provides a useful thematic lens through which to evaluate contemporary architectural discourse.

The work of Howeler + Yoon, R&Sie, Terreform ONE, Future Cities Lab, Philip Beesley, pneumastudio, and Weathers are unique in that they offer an alternative to the current trend of bio-formalism so characteristic of contemporary 'digital architecture.'[17] The particular approach

16. Reyner Banham, "Stocktaking," *Architectural Review* 127, no. 756 (February 1960), 93-94

17. The term 'bio-formalism' is used to identify the current generation of digital formalists, many of whom were students of Greg Lynn and/or Jesse Reiser at Columbia University in the 1990's when computer modeling, animation, and fabrication technology intersected with an interest in capturing the aesthetic novelty of biological processes to produce a new brand of American formalism. While this particular brand of formalism has evolved into an architectural language unique from that of The New York Five, distinguished by complex curvature and various biological referents, its allegiance to the general position that architecture is first and foremost a formal discipline concerned with the distribution of meaning through geometry can be seen as ideologically consistent with the work of Peter Eisenman, Michael Graves, John Hejduk, and others from that generation.

of bio-formalism has its origins in a very different aspect of postwar discourse, when Banham's ideological nemesis Colin Rowe laid the groundwork for the formal indulgences of the 1970's through his influential formal analysis of Le Corbusier and subsequent patronage of the The New York Five. In keeping with that particular history, the current generation of formalists seems inclined to limit architecture to a static representation of dynamic processes, with biology operating as a metaphor for the work. It has reinforced the perception, or perhaps conviction, that buildings are first and foremost cultural artifacts whose primary purpose is the distribution of meaning.[18]

What distinguishes the work of the design practices discussed in this article, and aligns them with the culture of 'anticipatory design' in the 1960's, is a fundamentally extrapolative approach to design that looks to the technological advancements of the twenty-first century as a means of providing new trajectories for the future of architecture. For these practices, the digital revolution is viewed as much more than just a catalyst for new formal languages. Rather, it suggests the introduction of contingency, responsivity, and feedback into the very performance of the architecture itself, shifting the discipline away from an exclusive preoccupation with form, space, and meaning and towards an exploration of temporality and instrumentality as well. And to the extent that these designers are attempting to strike a productive balance between instrumentality and aesthetics as they explore the potential of the technological advances of the information age, acknowledging that buildings are at once cultural and industrial artifacts, Banham's plea for a serious approach to technology, with which he concluded his seminal book *Theory and Design in the First Machine Age* in 1960, and with it a daring reconception of 'the architect' as a disciplinary figure in society, seems as relevant to the architects of that time as it does to our own:

> In the upshot, a historian must find that they [the modernists] produced a Machine Age architecture only in the sense that its monuments were built in the Machine Age, and expressed an attitude to machinery – in the sense that one might stand on French soil and discuss French politics, and still be speaking English. It may well be that what we have hitherto understood as architecture, and what we are beginning to understand of technology are incompatible disciplines. The architect who proposes to run with technology knows now that he will be in fast company, and that, in order to keep up, he may have to emulate the Futurists and discard his whole cultural load, including the professional garments by which he is recognized as an architect.

Chris Perry is a co-principal of *pneumastudio* and an Assistant Professor and the Director of the Post-Professional Program at the Rensselaer School of Architecture. Prior to joining the faculty at Rensselaer he was the Louis Kahn Visiting Assistant Professor at the Yale School of Architecture.

18. This postwar debate between the Banham and Rowe camps as to whether buildings are principally cultural or industrial artifacts becomes evident in the following two quotes. A devout member of The New York Five, Richard Meier said the following in an interview published in *A+U* in 1976: "The primary idea that concerns me and underlies my work is that high art is not necessarily a repressive art: this means that there can be an intellectual attitude about architecture which is not in and of itself elitist—that formal ideas are not a priori antisocial. In fact it is only formal ideas which elevate architecture from mere building, and make it, whether one likes it or not, a cultural artifact—a work of art." *A+U*, no. 4, 1976. Meanwhile, Peter Cook, a protégé of Reyner Banham and Cedric Price and founding member of Archigram, argued the following in the introduction to his 1970 book *Experimental Architecture*: "A fascinating shift in recent years is the rise of the 'boffin'-designer at the expense of the 'artist'-designer. The boffin works methodically, accruing and inventing when necessary, and by almost myopic devotion he frequently arrives at his objective. His is the tradition of Invention or, more precisely, of the attitude of mind that solves problems by inventing ways out of them." Peter Cook, *Experimental Architecture* (New York: Universe Books, 1970), 11. (Note, 'Boffin' is British slang for those involved in scientific or technological research)

SHAPESHIFT: SOFT DIELECTRIC ELECTROACTIVE POLYMERS AND ARCHITECTURAL SURFACES

MANUEL KRETZER

Soft Surfaces

With modest beginnings, it was plant fibers and animal wool that formed some of the earliest tensile fences in Palaeolithic camps. Since then, however, the range of textiles and their application in architecture has expanded to be nearly endless.[1] Yet, while most tensile structures would be classified as either temporary or ornamental additions, few have been able to transcend into permanence, a classical characteristic of Architecture. Moreover, few have acted as organic kinetic skins that synthesize structure within the envelope itself.

In 1802, the French architect J. B. Rondelet argued that architecture was not an art but a *science*, and its primary goals were to create solidity and comfort.[2] Solidity was argued to anchor, offer security, strength, and warmth, and symbolically express our understanding of wealth and power.[3] Comfort is, arguably, what shifted architecture into form of science. Surprisingly, the formal outcome of architecture is often at odds with the objects and surfaces of 'comfort' such as beds, couches, clothes, carpets, curtains, etc. In the last century, both the notions of solidity and comfort has been questioned, often through the emergence of new technology, forecasting the soft synthesis of surface, structure, and comfort.

The sudden rise of technology in the sixties and seventies lead to several experiments on biomorphic forms and new materials.[4] A remarkable pioneer, Friedrich Kiesler (1890- 1965), was determined to go beyond formalism to find a spatial symbiosis between man, nature and technology.[5] Further, artistic collectives such as E.A.T., Haus Rucker Co., Archigram and Coop Himmelb(l)au evolved such notions into larger spatial experiments aimed at social, political and environmental issues. Simultaneously, computer science and cybernetics were introduced into architecture and sparked new concepts for kinetic, flexible, and interactive spaces. John Frazer, who collaborated with Gordon Pask and Cedric Price, extended their ideas of responsiveness towards an architecture that would become a truly "living and evolving" organism.[6] For instance, in Price's project 'Generator' (which Frazer worked on as well), mobile cubes were designed that could be rearranged by a crane. The retreat and activity centre was constantly in a state of flux through a reconfiguration of its components. While presently our computational resources are more powerful, faster, and can be controlled remotely, kinetic principles have predominately remained the same. Avant-garde examples of so-called 'kinetic architectures' are typically no more than a blown-up replica of long established machinery and the prevalent materials are once again reduced to surface and cladding.

Smart Material Approach

ShapeShift proposes a new possibility of architectural materialization and 'organic' kinetics through the application of electroactive polymers (EAP) at an architectural scale. EAPs are polymer-based actuators that convert electrical power into kinetic force and change their shape accordingly. In the field of 'active materials', electroactive polymers are distinct due to their large active deformation potential, high response speed, low density and improved resilience. They are capable of strains up to three hundred and eighty percent their original size and can be tailored to any shape or size.[7] In *ShapeShift* these unique material properties are used beyond conventional actuator replacement and become orchestrated for their aesthetic and performative qualities. The thin responsive film functions as a potential alternative for the traditional building skin.

The component-based form results from the material's desire to return into its original shape combined with specially designed structural frames that are developed to allow an appropriate degree of flexibility. This minimum energy structure retains a variable stiffness, which allows for a variety of deformations within a given range. Each element consists of a thin layer of highly elastic, elastomeric film that is attached to a supportive acrylic frame and sandwiched between two compliant electrodes. This is achieved through coating both sides of the film with conductive powder and insulating them with a thin layer of liquid silicon. Once a high DC voltage in the range of several kilovolts is applied, electrical charges move from one electrode to another, and while doing so, squeeze a polymer film along one axis, while expanding the plane on another.[8] After actuation, the film becomes thinner and its surface area increases. As the membranes are attached

1. Sylvie Krüger, *Textile Architecture* (Berlin: Jovis, 2009). 142-144.

2. Paul-Alan Johnson, *The Theory of Architecture: Concepts, Themes and Practices*, (New York: John Wiley and Sons, 1994). 184.

3. Jonathan Hill, *Immaterial Architecture* (Abingdon: Routledge, 2006). 2, 21.

4. Kenneth Frampton, *Modern Architecture*, 4th Ed. (London: Thames & Hudson Ltd, 2007), 280.

5. *Friedrich Kiesler: Endless House 1947–1961*, exhibition catalog (Ostfildern: Hatje Cantz, 2003), 11.

6. John Frazer, *An Evolutionary Architecture* (London: Architectural Association Publications, 1995), 20-21.

7. Axel Ritter, *Smart Materials* (Basel: Birkhäuser, 2007), 66-69.

8. Patrick Lochmatter, "Development of a Shell-like Electroactive Polymer (EAP) Actuator," (PhD thesis, Swiss Federal Institute of Technology (ETH), Zurich (Switzerland), 2007), 11.

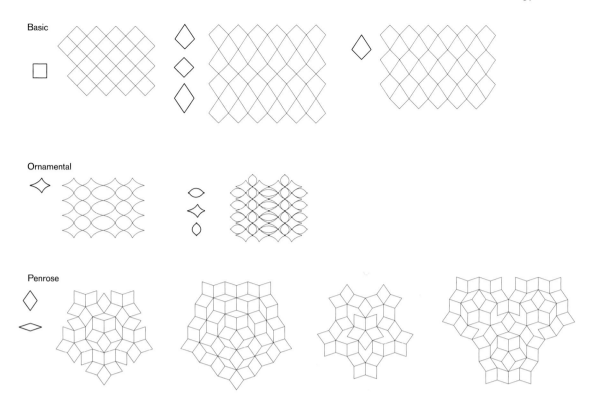

Basic

Ornamental

Penrose

∧ **Various tiling options during development.**
(Edyta Augustynowicz)

to 1.5mm flexible acrylic frames, due to the initial pre-stretching of the polymer film, the rhombic frame bends when the material is in its relaxed state. After a higher voltage is applied, the material expands, and the components flatten out.

Parallel to the design of a single element, efforts in structural arrangements and tessellations were performed. Early investigations focused on static supporting structures, but after a number of experiments the interest moved towards developing dynamic structural configurations. No static backbones are necessary in these dynamic systems as individual components are connected to each other to produce self-supporting forms. As with the single units, the dynamic structures achieve their final shape from the relationship of the pre-stretched EAP to the flexible frame and their interdependent connections. Through direct component-to-component linkages, an added layer of complexity is achieved. Each entity has an influence on the form and movement of its neighbors, and therefore, on the structure as a whole.

This concept of networked devices can easily be merged with computational approaches to collaborative intelligence and self-organization. In combination with other transformational materials, sensors and embedded control units, the creation of complex and responsive environments can dynamically adapt to external influences and physically respond to human input.[9]

The development of lightweight constructions and flexible skins allows for complex geometries, reduced transportation costs, and ease and speed of contemporary construction. This shift towards a biologically inspired model that extends formal and structural adaption into a new understanding of materiality might lead to the "end of mechanics" and the start of a revolutionary transformation of soft skins.[10]

Project done in collaboration with Edyta Augustynowicz, Sofia Georgakopulou, Dino Rossi, Stefanie Sixt, research associated with ETH Zürich.

· · · **Manuel Kretzer is an architect from Germany and co-founder of 'responsive design studio' who is currently working at the Chair for CAAD, ETH Zurich.**

9. J. G. Ballard, *Vermilion Sands* (London: Vintage Random House, 1971), 185-208.
10. Michael Fox and Miles Kemp, *Interactive Architecture* (New York: Princeton Architectural Press, 2009), 226.

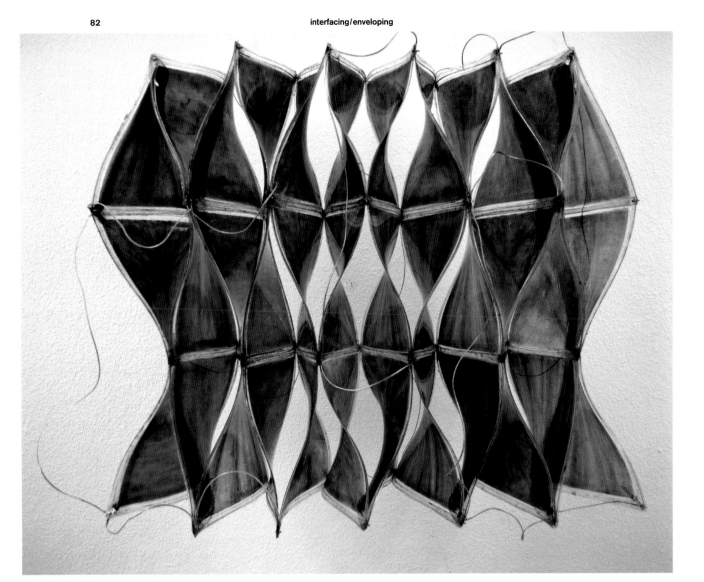

∧   **Final installation of ShapeShift.**

(Manuel Kretzer)

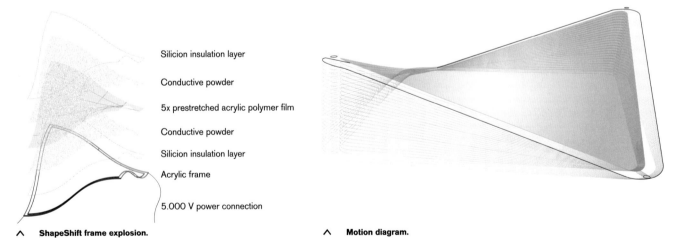

Silicion insulation layer

Conductive powder

5x prestretched acrylic polymer film

Conductive powder

Silicion insulation layer

Acrylic frame

5.000 V power connection

∧   **ShapeShift frame explosion.**   ∧   **Motion diagram.**

(Manuel Kretzer)   **(Dino Rossi)**

GOES SOFT

bracket—

A FLOATING ROOM

STUDIOGRUBER

∧ **Present day interior view of Frits
Peutz's Glaspaleis housing Schunck.**
(© SCHUNCK)

"We are apathetic people, if we do not now attempt to make a new art of living, instead of escaping from living
into rather dreary art. As a temporary measure the proposal has been put forward that every town should have
a space at its disposal where the latest discoveries of engineering and science can provide an environment for
pleasure and discovery, a place to look at the stars, to eat, stroll, meet and play."
—Cedric Price (*Pensées*, 1963)[1]

A Floating Room is the winning competition entry for a mobile event and exhibition space for
SCHUNCK, a multidisciplinary cultural center and museum in Heerlen, Netherlands. Presently,
the center is housed in the Glaspaleis, one of the first Modernist concrete structures with a
curtain wall façade, and a building noted in the UIA index as one of most significant of the
twentieth century.

In 1934, Peter Schunck asked Frits Peutz to design a seven-story department store as a covered market—one flooded with daylight so that his fabrics were seemingly sold under an open
sky. Peutz's response was a radical structure stripped of load-bearing walls and supported by
lily-pad columns. This so-called Glaspaleis offered an open floor plan and utmost flexibility. Its
dematerialized architecture also brought the spectacle of crowds and consumption to the fore.
The *Floating Room* pavilion revives the essential features of the Glaspaleis, yet takes its demateri-
alization and flexibility to the extreme. Its impact is one of a real building (measuring 15m x 25m
x 25m) however its materiality is soft and paper-thin. Architecture's new substance is one of
gas, reflections and events. The *Floating Room* is a catalyst for social interaction and sensational
experience—the space Cedric Price argued for having in every town, if only temporarily.

The project is essentially a floating roof—a room buoyed by air, and large enough to shelter
visitors from the elements while exposing them to the sky above. Its slanted cube is transparent
on the top and bottom, while its sides are mirrored. Together these surfaces frame and capture
the sky, clouds and weather movements in a kaleidoscopic game of reflections. Occupants and

. . . .

**1. Cedric Price, 1963. *Pensées* as quoted
in Stanley Mathews, *From Agit-Prop to Free
Space: The Architecture of Cedric Price*
(London: Black Dog Publishing, 2007) 66.**

∧   **View through *Floating Room*.**

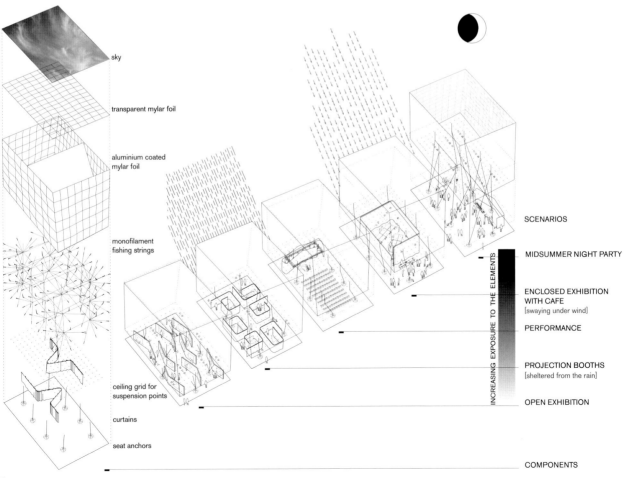

sky

transparent mylar foil

aluminium coated
mylar foil

monofilament
fishing strings

ceiling grid for
suspension points

curtains

seat anchors

SCENARIOS

MIDSUMMER NIGHT PARTY

ENCLOSED EXHIBITION
WITH CAFE
[swaying under wind]

PERFORMANCE

PROJECTION BOOTHS
[sheltered from the rain]

OPEN EXHIBITION

INCREASING EXPOSURE TO THE ELEMENTS

COMPONENTS

∧   **Scenarios of multiple events.**

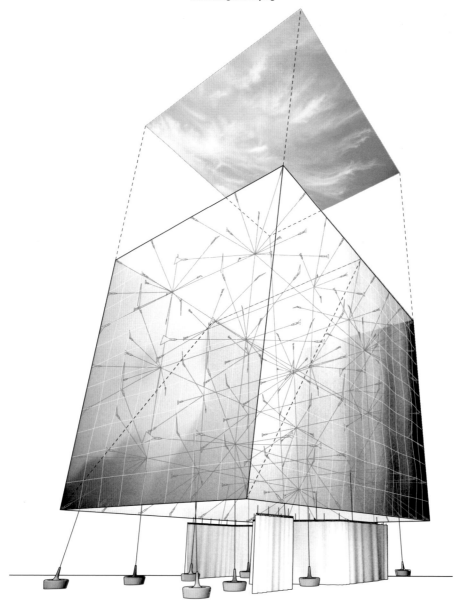

∧   **Dematerialized architecture.**

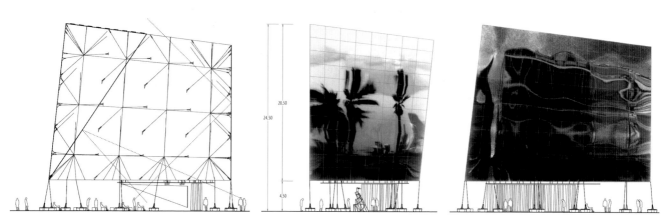

∧   **Elevations of *Floating Room* in various locations.**

STUDIOGRUBER   **A Floating Room**

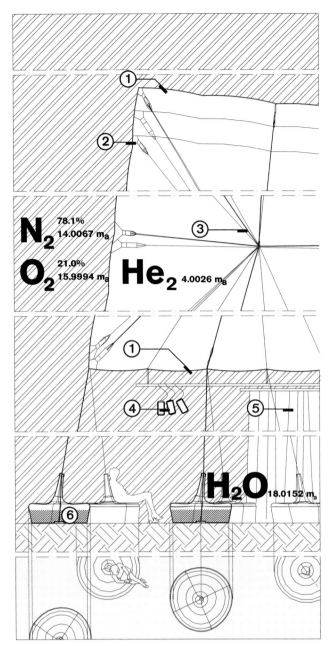

∧   **Detailed section.**

1. Transparent mylar foil
2. Aluminum coated mylar foil
3. Monofilament fishing strings
4. Track lights
5. Curtains
6. Seat anchors

artworks are literally suspended and melded in an affective environment; the collapsed and distorted images heighten and slow the perception of immediate events and time.

While the pavilion is a place of pleasure, it is driven by economic necessity and material frugality. Thus permanent components are flexible. The space outlined by the floating roof provides an open platform for variable activities, spontaneous appropriation, and endless reconfigurations. Lightweight space-defining elements such as curtains, which slide on tracks, are suspended from a 1.25 meter grid. Anchoring the pavilion to the ground are water-filled seats, allowing its independence from topography, soil conditions or specific location. Water and helium are supplied on site. When deflated, the pavilion and its components fit into a small van.

The mobile pavilion will appear in cities on the occasion of biennales, festivals or fairs. Though its presence is short lived, the pavilion engages its context by softly reflecting its surroundings while creating a sheltered gathering place in direct contact with the city. Here, temporality is conceived of to produce maximum effect with minimal means.

· · · **Stefan Gruber is principal of STUDIOGRUBER and professor for Geography, Landscape and Cities at the Academy of Fine Arts Vienna.**

∧ **Within the *Floating Room.***

SOFT HOUSE

KVA MATX & MIT SOFT CITIES RESEARCH

∧ **Cross sections of façade system in use: summer day, summer night, winter day, winter night.**

In 2010, the IBA (Internationale Bauaustellung) Building Exhibition in Hamburg announced a call for architecture proposals to address sustainable development in Wilhelmsburg, Europe's largest river island. The site's estuary ecology escapes classification. Neither 'farmland', 'urbanization' nor 'industrial', it encompasses aspects of each with maritime enterprises, working-class neighborhoods, and small farming polders distributed among waterways and fields of thatch.

The *SOFT HOUSE* is a winning proposal that examines how soft and dynamic skins can produce a more flexible and ecologically sound housing typology. The site is known for its low-latitude luminosity and the dynamic atmospheric qualities of the Hamburg sky. Extensively documented by twentieth-century Impressionist painters, the ephemeral cloud formations, animated by strong winds, are created by the collision of cool air from North Sea with the warmer inland air. The *SOFT HOUSE* responds to the site's fluid geography and atmospheric indeterminacy, as well as the legal mandate to comply with ENEV 2012, the rigorous German Energy Conservation Code.

The *SOFT HOUSE* locates itself conceptually as a reflection on two seemingly polarized visions of domestic life and architectural materiality, Michael Webb's *Cushicle* of 1968 and the Passivhaus construction typology popularized (and heavily subsidized) by the German Federal Republic in the last two decades. Webb's *Cushicle* is an inflatable personal capsule for nomadic modern life. In its packaged form it is an "armature or spinal system" that fits on a person's back.[1] In its deployed form, it is both an architectural enclosure and soft media screen, its structure formed by a clear inflated plastic envelope. As Webb intended, the *Cushicle's* lightweight, transportable packaging and soft malleable form opens up a flexible conceptual space that destabilizes modern distinctions of architecture and infrastructure, fixity and mobility, body and enclosure, and material and media.

As a material proposition that is both architecture and infrastructure, the *Cushicle* suggests for the *SOFT HOUSE* a double agency for domestic space that encompasses and conjoins two distinct scales of architectural endeavor. The *SOFT HOUSE* proposes that the architect operate as designer of the operative object/space systems that acquire their defining life and changeable formal attributes through the actions of their inhabitants in ways that cannot be determined or fully described by the architect. Yet at the same time, since the object/space systems of the *SOFT HOUSE* function in ways that are inextricably material and mutable, the conceptual task of the architect engages specific material knowledge to explore the effectual range of soft materiality for the domestic landscape and the life of the house.

Although the soft space of the *Cushicle* successfully undermines the modern ethos of an inherent, immutable relationship between domestic form and function, the reduction of its envelope to a single, thin transparent surface remains tethered to modern notions of totality and utopian universality, reducing the political agency that Webb had proposed. Banham describes the *Cushicle* in its actualized material state as an overly friendly "bubble of innocence" reliant on soft technology that fails to meet its conceptual

potentials.[2] The *SOFT HOUSE* suggests a renewed agency for architecture in light of contemporary environmental concerns and a recovery of architecture's reflective and affective capacities, where the envelope is acknowledged as a paradoxical thick void space—a flexible slippage zone between domestic form and program.

The Passivhaus is predicated on the maintenance of a domestic interior as a consistent environment that meets defined comfort standards, without heat gain or loss. The singular internal thermal 'body' of the Passivhaus is to be produced with zero or near zero operational energy inputs. Localized control over different interior zones is limited. Like the *Cushicle*, the Passivhaus invests in, and totalizes its exterior envelope. While the *Cushicle*, as a concept, is deft, deployable and capable of a range of formal transformations, the Passivhaus' legal standards typically produce a singular, rigid, highly insulated, and mostly opaque exterior shell. The 'gray' energy required in the manufacturing, demolition and disposal of the shell is significant. Within the shell, heat recovery equipment recirculates interior air, creating once again a "bubble of innocence" built around the modern premise of the domestic interior as an 'autonomous' volume that is conceptually distinct from the exterior environment.

The *SOFT HOUSE* explores how the thickened architectural envelope and calcified domestic space of the Passivhaus typology can become more supple—engaging a reallocation and new cross-pollination of 'hard' and 'soft' materiality with a spatial reframing of the architecture and infrastructure of domestic space. The *SOFT HOUSE* returns

1. Michael Webb, "Cushicle & Suitaloon," in *Archigram*, ed. Peter Cook, Warren Chalk, Dennis Crompton, David Greene, Ron Herron & Mike Webb, 1972 (reprinted New York: Princeton Architectural Press, 1999).

2. Banham, Reyner, "Triumph of Software", page 109 reprinted in *The Plastics Age: from Bakelite to Beanbags and Beyond*, ed. Penny Sparke (New York: 1993).

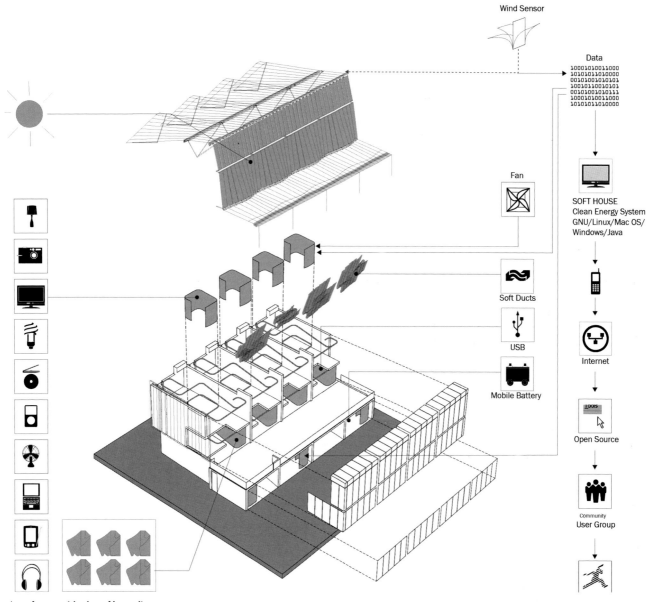

Wind Sensor

Data

Fan

Soft Ducts

USB

Mobile Battery

SOFT HOUSE
Clean Energy System
GNU/Linux/Mac OS/
Windows/Java

Internet

Open Source

Community
User Group

∧ **Axonometric view of low-voltage
building systems.**

to a pre-modern thatch insulation—thick, hairy and light. The structural envelope utilizes local Brettstapel panels—a dowel jointed wood construction system that is temporally 'soft,' as it sequesters carbon and with no glues or welds, is fully demountable. The responsive house façade twists to create views, protect privacy, and harvest energy locally, for illumination, digital electronics, and radiant heating. Infrastructure and envelope are woven together in a palette of optically differentiated material properties: translucency, reflectivity and absorption/energy generation. The redistribution of historically 'hard' energy infrastructure (photovolatics, sun tracking machinery) into an operative, soft optical filter, transforms the façade into a light organ that, as it twists, animates the interior domestic space with optical, luminous effects

as it mediates and augments the dynamics of natural light. With multiple, mobile soft layers, the *SOFT HOUSE* unpacks the singular perimeter of the Passivehaus typology creating a set of changeable thermal zones and re-configurable domestic spaces that are conceptually allied with the decentralization of domestic energy and information.

The energy harvesting *SOFT HOUSE* façade is complimented in the interior dwelling with a simple system of adjustable tracks and movable smart curtains, which distribute and integrate renewable power and solid-state lighting. Rechargeable, mobile batteries adopted from the automobile industry store the harvested energy. Complimenting the horizontal movement of the curtains, a vertically moving textile soft 'duct' can be lowered or raised to modulate heat loss in winter

and shading in summer. Radiant floor zones and movable curtains with programmable lighting allow residents to shape domestic space, direct localized lighting, and configure personal thermal micro-climates. The 'Visual Breeze' is one of several network modalities, which animate this domestic landscape with solid-state illumination. Integrated in the textile, light moves along a curtain surface in relation to exterior wind levels—creating a material and visual experience of weather that engages software that acknowledges the thermal boundaries of the architectural envelope.

The *SOFT HOUSE* smart building system software senses and monitors invisible aspects of the local climate, recording real-time changeable patterns of wind, air quality and domestic energetic expenditures, and establishing connectivity between 'domestic' and

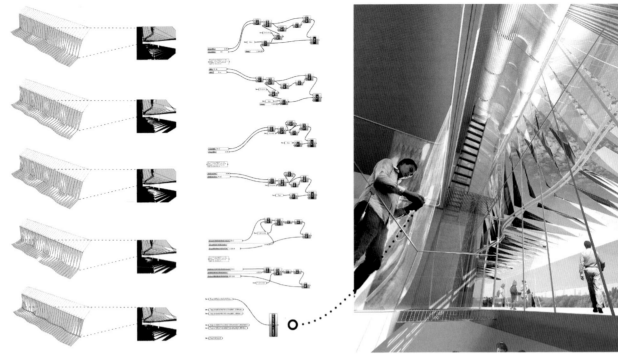

∧   **Dynamic solar harvesting positions, customized by parametric scripting
language. This allows users to adjust the
building components for personal comfort
and views.**

'natural' environments. The software drives
the dynamic changeable form of the project's
energy harvesting textile canopy, creating
unexpected local distortions that disturb
the reading of a singular expression of the
building. Light, decentralized, and adaptable,
the *SOFT HOUSE* reveals an inherent relationship between domesticity and environment:
exposing both moments of disjuncture and
alignment between the body of the house and
its enclosure.

Project done in collaboration with Jan Knippers/
Knippers Helbig Advanced Engineering, ITLEK
Stuttgart, Buro Happold, and a consortium of
European building industry partners.

· · · **SOFT HOUSE Leadership: IBA Hamburg
International Competition.**

· · · **Dirk Mangold is a Mechanical Engineer
and Partner of Solites, a firm which special-
izes in innovative climate design and thermal
storage.**

· · · **Sheila Kennedy is a Principal of KVA
MATx, an interdisciplinary practice of architecture and design and Professor in Practice at
MIT. Kennedy directs KVA's material research
division MATx which works collaboratively with
industry leaders, cultural institutions and public
agencies to realize designs that advance sustainable resources, materials and technologies.
www.kvarch.net.**

· · · **Jan Knippers is a structural engineer
and partner of Knippers Helbig-Advanced
Engineering. Dr. Knippers is professor and
director of ITLEK at the University of Stuttgart
where he explores bio-mimetic/kinetic efficient
materials and structures.**

· · · **Viet Kugel is Senior Associate at KVA
MATx and directs the Soft House Construction
& Manufacturing Consortium.**

· · · **Frano Violich is a principal of KVA MATx
and Chair of DIGMA, the Design & Industry
Group of Massachusetts.**

∧ **User-controlled smart curtains**
demonstrating visual breeze.

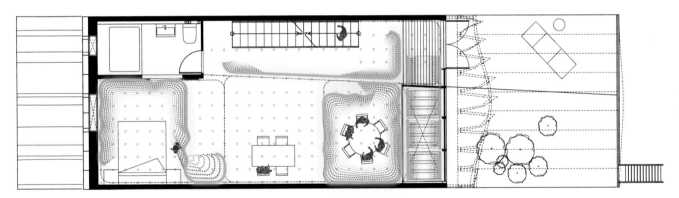

∧ **Summer curtain positions creates space.**

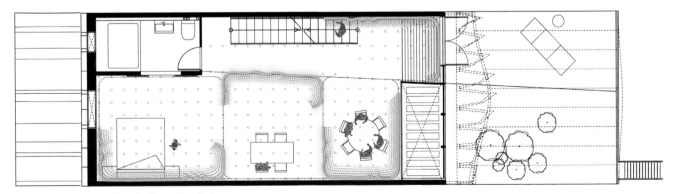

∧ **Winter curtain positions give thermal comfort.**

GROUNDING:
LANDSLIDE MITIGATION HOUSING

JARED WINCHESTER

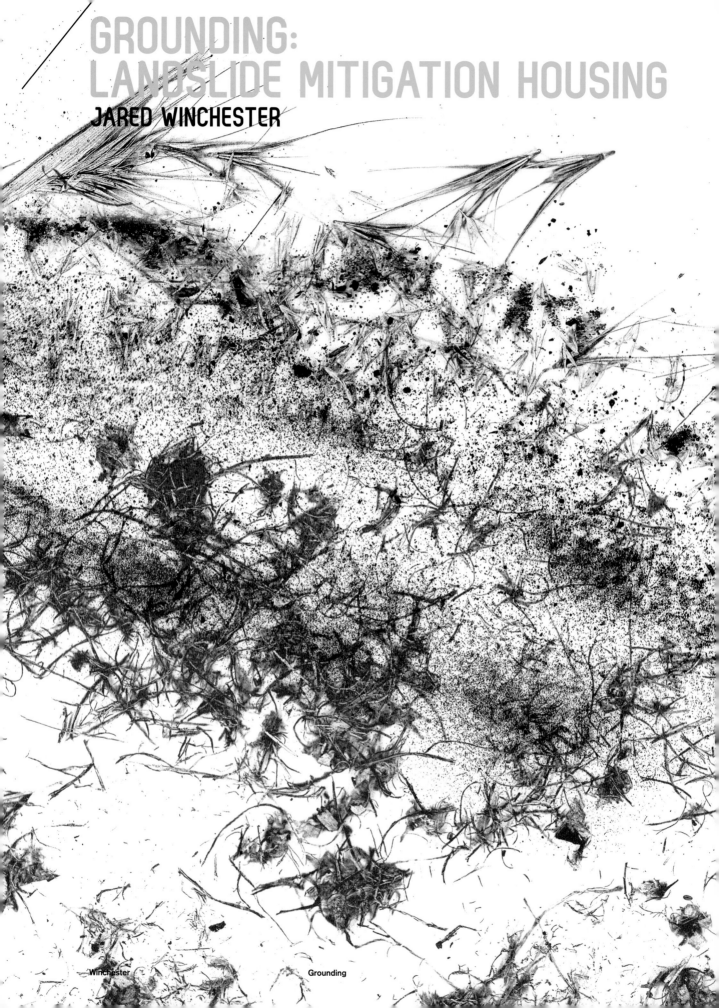

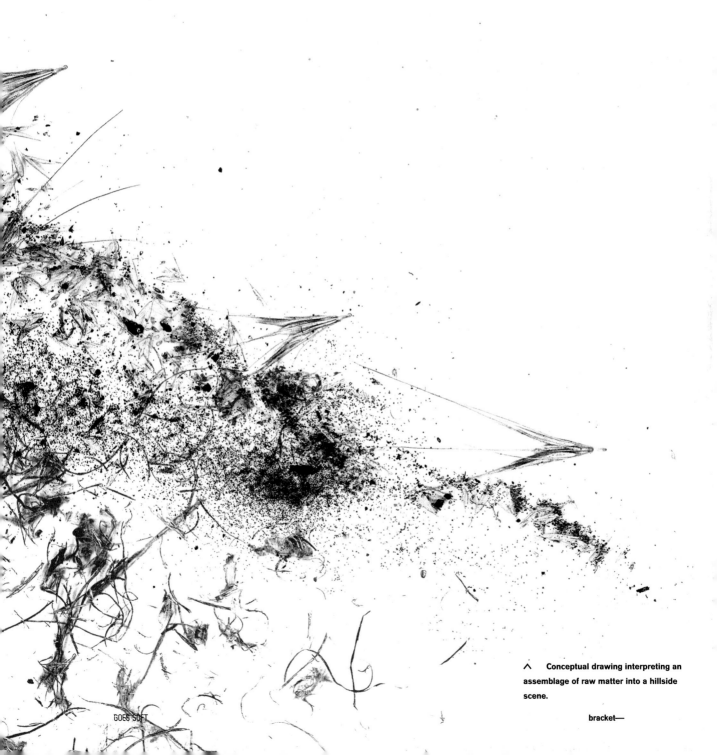

GOES SOFT

∧   **Conceptual drawing interpreting an assemblage of raw matter into a hillside scene.**

bracket—

Landslide Event Morphologies   Slope Morphologies

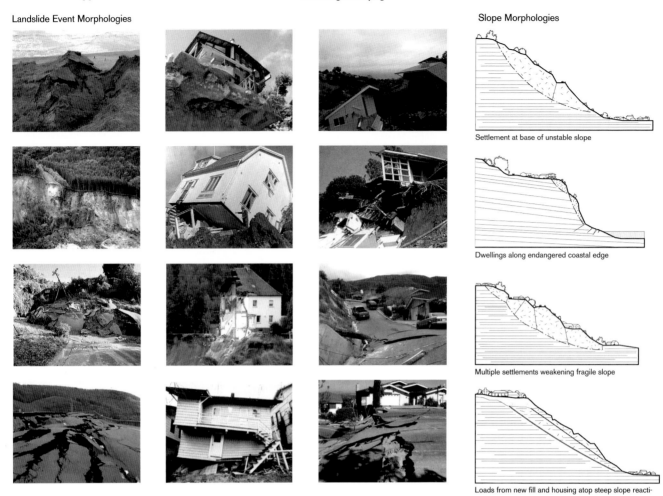

Settlement at base of unstable slope

Dwellings along endangered coastal edge

Multiple settlements weakening fragile slope

Loads from new fill and housing atop steep slope reactivates an ancient landslide feature

∧   **Landslide hazards interacting with**
statically conceived buildings reveal both a
crisis and potential for future development.

"Landslides and other 'ground failures' cost more lives and money each year than all other natural disasters combined, and their incidence appears to be rising. Nevertheless, the government devotes few resources to their study—and the foolhardy continue to build and live in places likely to be consumed one day by avalanches of mud."
—Brenda Bell, *The Atlantic Monthly* (Jan. 1999)

Precarious relationships between human occupation and geophysical metamorphism are a common occurrence along coastal areas of Los Angeles County. The architecture of this region is a perpetual game of chance between tranquil domesticity and the risk of its tragic upheaval. A network of soil stabilizing housing units is proposed within the fragile sub-strata of the Rancho de Palos Verde community. The area is the site of an ancient landslide condition that was reactivated by the development of poorly conceived housing communities in the 1950s. A new network of housing serves to mitigate future catastrophic events, salvage a currently unbuildable landscape, and evolve an architectural vernacular of dwelling within tight topographic conditions.

Grounding is a prototypical dwelling type that employs existing technologies to stabilize steep slopes, such as soil nails and helical piles, but adapts these into a "stitched" foundation system that allows a home to be tethered to its site rather than rigidly fixed to a ground condition. The new homes do not function as stand alone objects, but as above ground indicators and monitoring points for a continuous geo-textile grafted within the slope. Rather than the typical hard approach to a retaining structure in which the designed system either remains stable or fails catastrophically, this new system allows for a gradual transformation within the landscape while simultaneously slowing down and counteracting the sudden hazardous effects of soil movement.

Like lighthouses perched along the edge of a shoreline as an orientation and warning device, these new grounding devices are positioned along threatened slope contours to act as safeguards for the community. Further, they become indicative instrument that behaviorally convey information on the geological and hydrological processes occurring below grade. Since soil movement

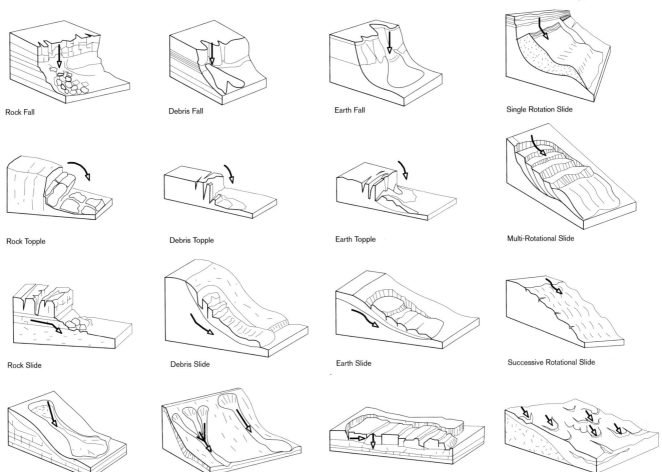

Rock Fall

Debris Fall

Earth Fall

Single Rotation Slide

Rock Topple

Debris Topple

Earth Topple

Multi-Rotational Slide

Rock Slide

Debris Slide

Earth Slide

Successive Rotational Slide

Mud Flow

Debris Flow

Earth Spread

Periglacial Debris Flow

∧   Diagrams of earth movement suggest reactive behaviors that architecture could embrace to adapt to changing slope conditions.

∧   Soil nailing and slope stabilization technologies will be utilized and adapted to a development strategy for new homes. Not simply as a civil engineering project, it serves as community revitalization for distressed areas.
(Images courtesy of Landslide Solutions, Inc. www.landslidesolutions.com)

∧   On January 10, 2005, a landslide struck the community of La Conchita in Ventura County, California, destroying or seriously damaging 36 houses and killing 10 people. This was not the first destructive landslide to damage this coastal California community, nor is it likely to be the last. This scenario of existing threatened settlements within historically active landslide geographies is the primary focus for the landslide mitigation housing deployment.
(Photo by Robert L. Schuster, courtesy of USGS. http://landslides.usgs.gov/)

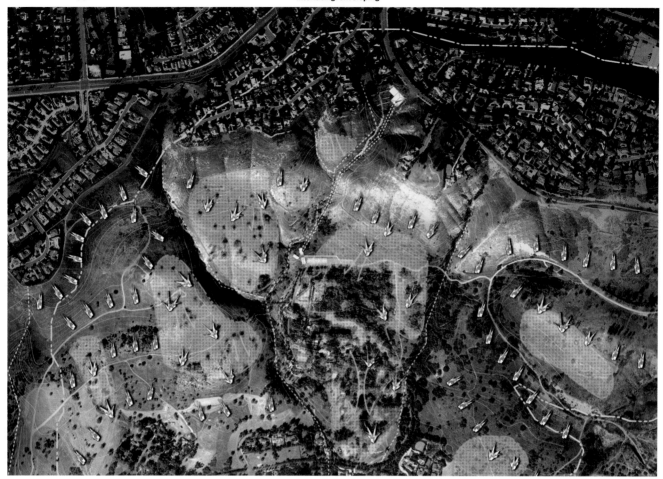

∧   Site plan for targeted community
development within Palos Verdes.

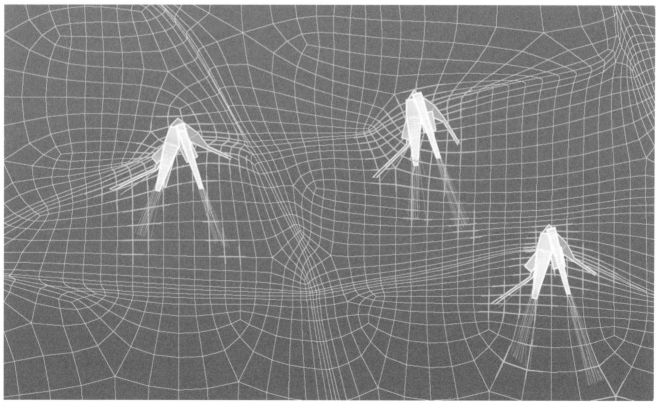

∧   Kinetic plan diagram.

Winchester   Grounding

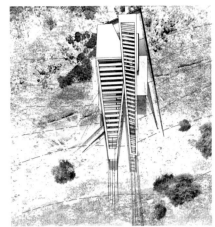

Stage One: (0-5 yrs) Minor drainage and settlement

Stage Two: (5-15 yrs) Noticeable settlement around unit, altered drainage and tension cracks.

Stage Three: (15-30 yrs) Formations of scarps around hillside, swales running through property.

Stage Four: (30+ yrs) Widening of swales, bulges and soil rupture.

∧   **Time lapse of unit/site evolution.**

is a natural, regenerative mechanism of the area's geologic procession, the homes do not eliminate earth flow, they simply slow down and make perceivable the ongoing processes beneath the ground surface. The houses predictably align themselves to the former pathways laid out by the previously abandoned development and initially follow the rhythm of a cookie-cutter suburban community. However as the inevitable subsidence in the landscape affects the position and posturing of the vessels, the development will take on a more organic composition that expresses a hybrid merger with the site's geology. These houses will bulge, grip, and position themselves to act as a drag upon the force of the advancing slope movements. In the process of slowing down and deterring landslide activity, the spatial conditions of the homes and the position of specific rooms will be altered.

The houses will have their own internalized piezometric landslide monitoring system, along with indicators for precipitation, groundwater pressure, slope settlement, and vibration. Geologists will collect data periodically; similar to the how a utility company monitors various meters in a traditional dwelling. Experientially, the owner may sense other immeasurable spatial changes in the light qualities produced by the canting of a roof plane or the torqueing of trellis louvers. A change in tension to the anchoring foundation cables will extend out to the projecting roofs, rooms, decks and catwalks of the home. In addition to the architectural elements of the house, imbedded soil fabric around the home's landscape will topologically deform in relation to specific geological conditions.

The new landslide mitigation housing development acts as a performative infrastructure—echoing its specific location's transforming slope characteristics. Spatial and architectonic information become synonymous with scientific readings of ground surface displacement, soil saturation and pressure. *Grounding* attempts to work with dynamic geological processes to form a new typology of soft architecture and infrastructure.

· · · **Jared Winchester is a designer based in Albuquerque, New Mexico. He is founder of the architectural studio, Entropic Industries.**

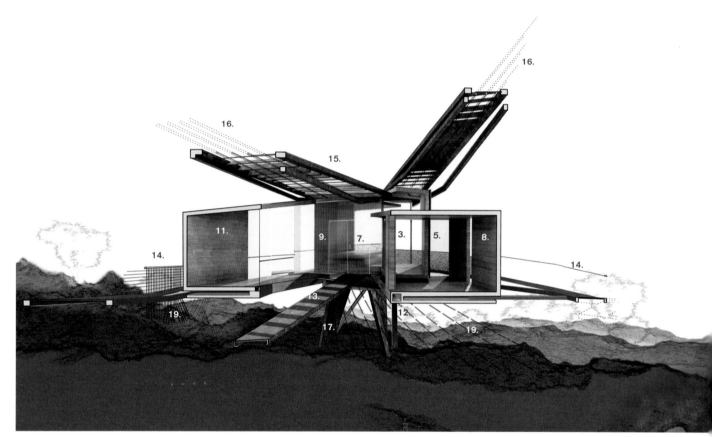

House Sections and Index of Adaptive Elements:

01. Swiveling View Deck
02. Living Room
03. Kitchen
04. Bar Counter/Coffee Table
05. Library
06. Dining Nook
07. Entry Foyer
08. Master Bedroom
09. Accordion Screen Wall
10. Bath
11. Bedroom/Studio
12. Pivoting Pier Supports
13. Entry Stair/Rampway
14. Embedded Catwalk
15. Torquing Trellis
16. Slope Cable Tethers
17. Retaining "Plow"/Shear Wall
18. Utility Crawl Space
19. Structural Soil Fabric Mesh

∧ **Displacement due to soil movement.**
> **Following pages: Hillside view.**
(Rendered in collaboration with Viktor Ramos)

OF POP AND PROSTHESES: VIENNA, 1965–72

JON CUMMINGS

"Architecture
Is in exile now
On the moon
Or at the North Pole

While people are building

HOUSES
HOUSES
HOUSES
HOUSES
HOUSES
HOUSES
HOUSES"

ARCHITECTURE IN EXILE, 1967[1]

The brief but intensely focussed design interest in pneumatics and transient environments affecting the avant-garde European scene in the late 1960s has been revisited in recent years; however, the work emerging from Vienna at the time remains, arguably the most prolific, poetic, and hermeneutically opaque. As *de facto* father figure to the Viennese scene, Hans Hollein's mission statements on environmental control perpetuated a critique of pure functionalism that had begun in Vienna with Frederick Kiesler's notion of the 'Endless City' (1959). His German-speaking avant-garde audience was exposed to this persuasive rhetoric in the pages of the Vienna-based journal *BAU* (1962-69), of which Hollein served as editor along with other local luminaries such as Günther Feuerstein and Walter Pichler. To Hollein and his compatriots, architects had been blindly plodding along as the cutting edge of environmental design was pursued by American and Soviet aeronautical engineers. The capsular environments of Cold-War era jet fighters, along with the achievements of Sputnik and Mercury had demonstrated, before the eyes of the world, the capacity for advanced technology to colonize otherwise inhospitable environments. That interest in new modes of bodily perception paralleled a pop sensibility undeniably

∧ **Hans Hollein in his Mobile Office, 1969.**
(Copyright Atelier Hollein Vienna)

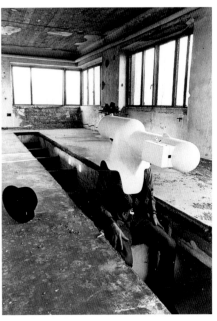

∧ **Walter Pichler, *TV-Helmet* (Portable Living Room), 1967. (Courtesy Generali Foundation ©**
Archiv Walter Pichler)

concerned with prosthetically expanding the consciousness of the architect's space-making capacity by the appropriation of aeronautical imagery.[2] Further, it was also a technologically deterministic model upon which to expand the architect's formal repertoire, a position sufficiently congruent with contemporary interests in mobile or transient environments.[3] While most scholarship on this era highlights its pop sensibility, local myths, and self-stylizations,[4] it also must be supplemented by a broader consideration of the architectural moment.

Lineage of the Soft

It is useful to begin with the prescient German model in Gottfried Semper's *Style*— the notion that clothing, as the primary means of environmental control is the original architectonic device, a position consistently at odds with the classically formalist notion of Abbé Laugier's primitive hut. A

prosthetically-based design ethos runs consistently through Viennese work in the 20th century, blossoming in conjunction with the counter-culture and sexual freedom movements of the 1960s. Simultaneous to this, a clearer distinction between 'hard' and 'soft' was being created in architectural discourse. Emblematic is Reyner Banham's dual film review *The Triumph Software* from 1968, in which he compares Stanley Kubrik's *2001: A Space Odyssey* with Roger Vadim's *Barbarella*.[5] Where the failure of the inflexible mainframe computer Hal was hailed as a sign of the limits of artificial intelligence, the cultural moment of the 1960's was in far greater favor of the bodily-responsive, animate "software" of *Barbarella*. Applying this ethos back into the world of avant-garde architecture, Banham would extend this criticism to Archigram's *Plug-In City*, which for him was fundamentally still a vision of hard urbanity. The later *Cushicle* and *Suit-a-Loon's* of Mike Webb were

1. Wolf Prix, ed. *Stadt=Form, Raum, Netz: An Exhibition at the Austrian Pavilion for the 10th International Exhibition of Architecture*, La Biennale di Venezia 2006 (Vienna: Springer, 2006).

2. Georg Schollhammer, "The Bolted Gesture," *Pichler: Prototypes 1966-69* (Vienna: Generali Foundation, 2000).

3. A notable exception is Georg Schollhammer's essay *The Bolted Gesture* in a catalogue for a retrospective on the "Prototypes" of Walter Pichler.

4. Ibid., p. 48.

5. Reyner Banham, "2.14 Triumph of Software," *Design By Choice* (London: Academy Editions, 1981), 136.

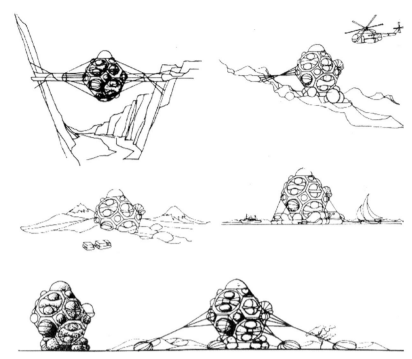

^ Utopie, *Dyodon House*, 1967, configurations in non-urban environments.

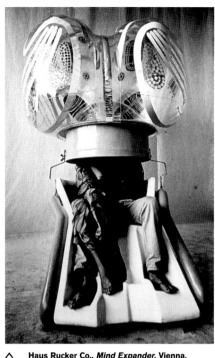

^ Haus Rucker Co., *Mind Expander*, Vienna, 1967.

by contrast seen as progressive acknowledgements of the principles of "software".

Resistance + Criticality

The pure-Pop argument further runs aground when considering the cultural influences acting on the Viennese scene from the preceding time period. Pop—at its core—was an eschatological, out-of-body yearning, yet never entered the domain of resistance. In this sense, much of the work generated by members of London's *Independent Group* articulated a wide-eyed search for new forms of communication. The pure-pop sensibility which adopted, with little criticality, the imagery of mass culture, unintentionally served to reinforce fantasies of omnipotence. As an architecture of resistance, the capsular and pneumatic environments of Hollein and Pichler, were protective vessels insulating from a potentially hostile environment. The

concerns of the avant-garde of the nuclear age and protest movements of 1968 were different from the *Independent Group*'s famed *This is Tomorrow* exhibition of 1956. We need only look at the original photo of Walter Pichler's staged performance wearing his iconic personalized TV Helmet, in which the subject is happily distracted from a barren, post-industrial, seemingly post-nuclear, environment. He is at once the fighter pilot *and* the war target. Similarly, Hollein's portable office was calculatingly photographed in a patch of disused green space at a military air force base. Coop Himmelb(l)au's *Cloud*, Haus Rucker's *Yellow Heart* environment, Quasar Khan's *pneumatic apartment*, and Ortner and Ortner's *pneumatic house* were all manifestations of a transient, nomadic, volumetrically indeterminate architecture. When coupled with the low cost of fabrication and user assembly, this portable architecture

held the potential to be constituted in any environment, free of the problem of land ownership traditionally imbricated in the architectural act, a position sympathetic to Marxist principles whose sway on young continental intellectuals at the time cannot be underestimated.[6]

Environments for Sexual Emancipation

A liberated take on sexuality was an integral component to the work of the pneumatic era. In pop film, the aforementioned *Barbarella* as well as Robert Freeman's cult film *The Touchables* from 1968 undeniably expressed a link between transparent plastics and the liberated body, characteristic of the free love culture of the late 1960s. Much of Coop Himmelb(l)au and Haus Rucker's work was no less sexually charged. The device description from Haus Rucker's *Mind Expander*

6. In fact, parallel practices working with transient inflatable environments in France would become unequivocally politicized. The work of the Parisian group Utopie, consisting of architects Jean Aubert, Jean-Paul Jungmann, and Antoine Stinco, all very recent students out of the Ecole des Beaux-Arts, as well as a host of essayists involved in the events of May 1968, including Jean Baudrillard, was an explicitly anti-establishment movement (see Rosalie Genvro and Marc Dessauce, eds. *The Inflatable Moment: Pneumatics and Protest in '68* (New York: Princeton Architectural Press, 1999)). In

a manifesto published in *AD* in June 1968 intent on reaching out to their English compatriots, Aubert and co. rallied against architectonic activities that responded to administratively controlled town planning practices and the socio-economic structure of free enterprise. Heavily influenced by the French Marxist Henri Lefebvre, Utopie designed objects along Lefebvre's slogan of "All Technics at the Service of Everyday Life." (see: Beatriz Colomina and Craig Buckley, eds. *Clip Stamp Fold: The Radical Architecture of Little Magazines 196X to 197X* (Barcelona: Actar, 2010), 194).

Even the title of the group—a reference to Thomas More's novel from 1516, referring to a society free of private property—demonstrated socialist tendencies. The etymology of More's invention of the word Utopia must have had significance for the group' a Greek pun on ou-topos (no place) related to transient environments, and eu-topos (good place), suggested liberated modalities of living that these new architectures would engender (see: "Thomas More," Wikipedia. org <http://en.wikipedia.org/wiki/Thomas_More#Utopia> (Accessed: November 29, 2008)11/29/08)).

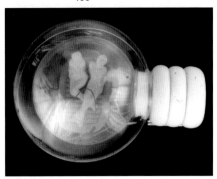

∧　Haus Rucker Co., *Yellow Heart*, Vienna, 1968.

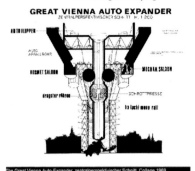

∧　Zünd-Up. *The Great Vienna Auto Expander*, 1969. Unbuilt. (Copyright Zünd-Up: Timo Huber, Bertram Mayer, W.M. Pühringer, Hermann Simböck)

∧　Zünd-Up. *Hot Tar and Level!*, 1969. Photo collage. (Copyright Zünd-Up: Timo Huber, Bertram Mayer, W.M. Pühringer, Hermann Simböck)

(1967) is demonstrative: "The seat shell fixes two persons in a certain position. The lower seat allows one person to sit with their legs slightly open. The thigh of their right leg rests against a step forming the transition to a second seat area that is higher by the thickness of a thigh."[7] Though more subdued, the iconic images of Coop Himmelb(l)au's *Hertzraum Astroballon* depicted a more or less exposed female body whose heart beat was externalized into pulsating light. Even more pronounced was the work of Zünd-Up, another group of young Viennese architects whose interest lay in human-machine conflations playing on technological perversions. In their most significant project, *The Great Vienna Auto Expander*, they approached the fetishization of automobile culture by focusing not on the design and marketing of objects of commercial desire, but through sexualized automotive imagery. This was explored through a mix of representational strategies including orthographic drawings of a drag racing track in central Vienna shaped as a phallus and testicles, combined with collaged images sourced from pornography and automobile magazines, and highlighted with poetic narratives involving nocturnally-based machinic/sculptural labor scenarios.

Georges Teyssot, writing in *The Mutant Body of Architecture*, refers to a deep current of thought amongst architects and engineers that he designates as "partisans of the building-machine... resulting from the mechanical conception that considers the body as a machine."[8] He traces a lineage from Dr. Tenon's "healing-machine" (late 18th century) through to architect Adolphe Lance's

"house-machine" (1853); to Henry Provensal's 1908 building conceived as a "human thoracic cage" reproducing the respiration of the lungs; to the "dwelling-machine" launched by Le Corbusier in L'Esprit Nouveau in 1921. In both Haus Rucker Co.'s *Yellow Heart* and Coop Himmelb(l)au's *Villa Rosa*, the sole programmatic element is a revolving bed. If pneumatics for the Viennese architects of the late 1960s was at least partially seen as a hygienic container for voyeuristic sexual encounters, then we might add to this lineage 'the pneumatic building-sex-machine'.

Performance + Ritual

Another factor contributing to the emergence of such prosthetic environments was the rise of the body and performance art emerging in the preceding decade. By the late 1960s the consideration of the body as a prime site of artistic activity began to coagulate with social and cultural protest movements, witnessed not least in the resistance movement of the Situationist International. This was an urbanism that saw the existing bourgeois city re-positioned through the movement of the body in their detournement mapping practices. In Vienna itself, there was also the influence of the Aktionists, Günther Brus, Otto Mühl, Hermann Nitsch, and Rudolf Schwartzkogler. Combining a local heritage of Catholic procession and ritual with the same general tendencies of other body art, the Aktionists would carry out extreme transgressions on their own as well as female bodies, in order to violate high art notions of the perfect Venus.[9] Locally the performative impact would find its closest relative in the

body performance *aktionen* of the architect's of Zünd-Up, and the actions of Coop Himmelb(l)au in which spectators would follow pneumatic spheres propelled by the architects suspended in them through the streets in a play on both the *détournement* and Catholic procession.

Autonomy

"Cities that beat like a heart. Cities that fly like a breath! The cloud is an organism for living" proclaimed Coop Himmelb(l)au in 1968, when Prix and Swiczinsky were still students, referring to their now well-published un-built pneumatic house project.[10] Mobility meant expanding volumes, dynamic bases without foundations, and the possibility that, by virtue of environmental control, the whole apparatus could be reconstituted anywhere on the planet. For Coop Himmelb(l)au, Haus Rucker Co, as well as Hans Hollein in the *Aircraft Carrier City* project, preference for living in the traditional city was replaced with the autonomy of the vessel. What enabled the autonomy of the vessel, and the individual within, was an emergent and multitudinous capacity for technologically-enabled communication and global connectivity.

Prostheses + Bodily Transformation

The concept of architecture as communication would necessarily give way to notions of man-machine symbiosis. For Freud, all technology was understood to be a supplement, either motor or sensory.[11] Marshall McLuhan echoed these thoughts in his contemporaneous work, *Understanding Media: The Extensions of Man* where he argued that in amplifying and

7. "Mind Expander: Vienna, 1967." Haus Rucker Co. <http://www.ortner.at/hr_mi1e.html> (10/24/08)

8. George Teyssot, "The Mutant Body of Architecture," in *Flesh: Architectural Probes*, ed. Elizabeth Diller and Ricardo Scofidio (New York: Princeton Architectural Press, 1994), 24.

9. Stefan Beyst, "Paradise Regained." The Vienna Actionists: The Essential Viennese Aktionism Resource. http://www.freewebs.com/vienna-actionists/ottomuehl.htm (10/05/08)

10. Wolf Prix, Helmut Swiczinsky, *Coop Himmelblau, architecture is now: Projects,* *(un)buildings, actions, statements, sketches, commentaries, 1968-1983* (New York: Rizzoli, 1983).

11. Giuliana Bruno, "Mind Works: Rebecca Horn's Interior Art," in *Public Intimacy: Architecture and the Visual Arts* (Cambridge: MIT Press, 2007), 140.

∧   Coop Himmelb(l)au, *Basel Event*, 1969.
(Image copyright Katharina Vonow)

∨   Coop Himmelb(l)au, *Villa Rosa*, Vienna,
1968. (Coyright Coop Himmelb(l)au)

extending our capacities through technology, we amputate our senses in order for our nervous system to bear the shock.[12] Motor supplements manifested themselves in Walter Pichler's *Finger Extensions* and also the *Small Room*, essentially a helmet with a microphone. In Coop Himmelb(l)au's *Hertzraum Astroballon*, the human heart beat was translated and extended into pulsing, streaming electric light. Haus Rucker's aforementioned Mind Expander and their Environment Transformer were both meant to isolate and draw out auditory and visual senses. Perhaps most extreme was Hans Hollein's image for the *non-physical environment* pill, a gesture toward a spatial augmentation of absolutely minimal means in a dual evocation of drug culture and pharmaceutical treatment for mental-spatial disorders such as agoraphobia.[13]

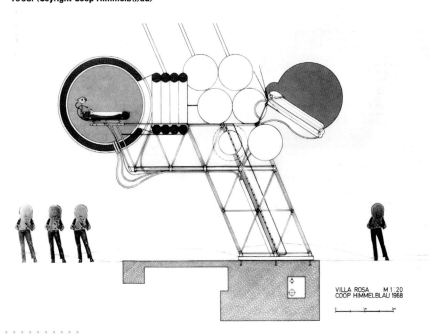

VILLA ROSA   M 1:20
COOP HIMMELBLAU 1968

12. McLuhan, Marshall, *Understanding Media: The Extensions of Man*, 1964 (Cambridge: The MIT Press, 1994).
13. Beatriz Colomina and Craig Buckley, Ed. *Clip Stamp Fold: The Radical Architecture of Little Magazines 196X to 197X* (Barcelona: Actar, 2010), 380.

PLASTIC MOVES UPTOWN

This man is hearing great stereo sound, enjoying a sense of isolation, and seeing pleasant green scenes. His helmet, which produces these effects, was designed by three architects, Laurids, Pinter, and Zamp, of the Haus-Rucker-Company of Vienna. It is made of plastic – to other material would do as well. For years, plastic has ersatz wool, bogus leather, fake hats china – ever for aircraft hangars and motel rooms but not fit for the discriminating kind of household. But a growing movement of designers now recognizes that plastic is wonderful as long as it's being itself and not imitating anything. A glimpse of your plastic future, not in every case available on the market as yet, follows.

∧   **Haus Rucker Co.,** *Environment Transformer,*
1968.

Return to Bare Nature

Central to Reyner Banham's article *A Home is Not of House* (1969) are themes of nature; how service systems enable us to control its effect on our bodies, and how a mobile architecture allows a unique symbiotic relationship with nature. These notions were explored in Haus Rucker Co.'s *Oasis No 7*, which involved the suspension of a transparent pneumatic sphere from the side of Kassel's Fridericianum. The PVC sphere emerged symbolically as a growth from the façade, at the centre of which was a space for two palm trees, clearly, an edenic lair, yet extroverted so that the garden remained exterior to an Enlightenment institution corrupted by a National Socialist past. The subject being raised is clearly the individual in a state of nature, but a nature understood as an often hostile entity to be feared and tempered. Pneumatic devices enabled man to segregate himself, in pleasure, from a corrupt society. Banham equally took on this lineage, when he spoke about the spatial freedom of the nomad who lacked the encumbrances of permanent dwelling. New in the work of Hollein and others however, was this kind of urban thinking at the height of an age of

nuclear anxiety, coupled with the architect's newfound technical capacity to respond to that desire.

Soft Technologies & Ecologies

Banham also equated the emergence of new fabrication methods with a paradigm shift in the broader public. In *Monumental Windbags* published in New Society in 1968 he noted "a confluence between changing taste and advances in plastic technology."[14] Of further significance was the degree to which publishing as an act of discourse linked together similar preoccupations in the Viennese scene with their counterparts in Paris, London, and beyond. Seen in this light, the Viennese groups, represented through *BAU*, were in part a regional constituent of a vaster architectural network responding to common and salient technical fascinations. Whole issues were devoted to developments in pneumatics in *Domus* (Dec 1967) and *AD* (June 1968). Particularly fascinating about the *AD* issue on pneumatics is the emphasis placed on the accessibility of the technology, making the issue read more as a user manual with ties to industrial manufacturers. In this way we can see the trajectory of a certain form of modernist critique coming to a built fruition through technologies available to students no less than to practitioners. Further, there was an explicit imperative communicated here for architecture's appropriation of research from the related military and industrial fields generating this new technology, a position paralleled now with calls in certain areas of the architectural discourse for an engagement in infrastructural systems.

Present Concerns

While some thematic underpinnings of this historical moment will remain concerns of the past, certain dormant tendencies have resurfaced. Architects are once again operating in an age of technological expansion through advanced modelling software and responsive, sensor-activated environments. Parametrics in particular would appear to extend possibilities for the volumetrically indeterminate. Projects at the extra-small scale have also re-emerged in critical spatial practices as the preferred mode for reclaiming public space through transient social

environments, in practices such as Raumlabor Berlin and Vancouver's Instant Coffee collective, although individual autonomy has most certainly been replaced in these cases by direct social engagement.

Other tendencies may yet further guide us. Oswald Wiener, an instrumental Viennese author wrote "*The Improvement of Central Europe*" (1969), describing a cyborg world in which human consciousness had been liberated from its earthly body.[15] In this fantasy, the individual, outside of the formal arrangements of society, repressed nature through consciousness, and with language created transient objects independent of the body.[16] This work has become a prescient forerunner for second-life and the digital avatars of our contemporary online gaming and social media platforms. This reveals perhaps the most pertinent significance of the Viennese scene, which is the heritage of the body supplement as the core human impetus behind the soft project. It represents a persistent searching for an otherness always just beyond the grasp of our present temporal existence and the rigidity that most often structures our built environments.

· · · **Jon Cummings is a Toronto-based designer. He received his Masters of Architecture from the University of Toronto.**

14. Reyner Banham, "Monumental Windbags," *New Society*, April 18, 1968.
15. "Remarks on Some Tendencies of the 'Vienna Group,'" Oswald Wiener, David Britt Trans. *October*, Summer 2001, No. 97, 120-130. < http://www.mitpressjournals. org/doi/abs/10.1162/octo.2001.97.1.120> (11/10/08)

16. Georg Schollhammer, "The Bolted Gesture," *Pichler: Prototypes 1966-69* (Vienna: Generali Foundation, 2000), 50.

VAPORIZED TECTONICS

PHILIPPE RAHM

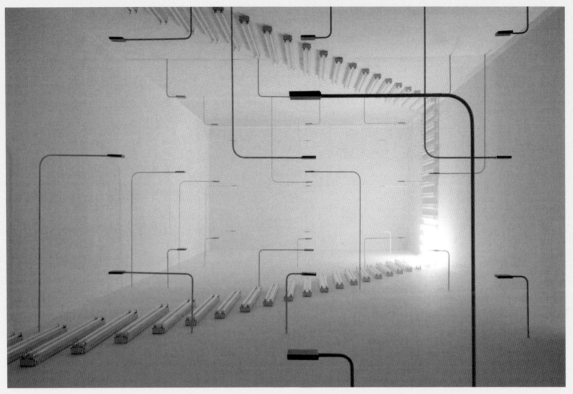

∧ *Interior Weather*. Canadian Center for Architecture, Montreal, 2006. *Interior Weather* is a study on the possibilities of introducing notions of meteorology as formal and programmatic elements for architectural design into the domestic habitat. It is a space that looks superficially neutral, but whose changes of light, humidity and temperature create a richness of situations and diversity of experiences—enabling new ways of living. (Philippe Rahm Architects with a writing collaboration by Alain Robbe-Grillet. Photo by Michel Legendre)

"Imagination is the analysis, it is the synthesis… it breaks down all creation and, with the materials collected and arranged according to rules whose origin you can find only in the depths of the soul, it creates a new world, it produces the sensation of new"
—Baudelaire, Salon 1859, in *Beyond Romanticism: Writings on Art*

The methodology of contemporary architecture is no longer to work with tectonics, but rather to decompose and disintegrate materiality into a multitude of microscopic particles of heat, vapor and light—atomized and separated from their whole. Space is no longer a visible, solid, and tactile macroscopic block; instead it expands, diffracts, and opens to the infinitely small and the invisible. Several of the key principles of soft contemporary meteorological architecture emerge from nineteenth century Impressionist painting, which

was rooted in notions of dissociation, decomposition, analysis and synthesis, in the chemical sense. These are methods and processes that are derived from the sciences—nineteenth century advances in chemistry, physics or biology—transforming the methods of imagination simultaneously. We proceed by decomposition of the whole into elements and then recomposing these elements according to other hierarchies, updated priorities, and new needs. Instead of gestalt, which opposes a holistic view by stating that "the whole is different and not reducible to the sum of its parts", we postulate that the isolated parts are more interesting than the whole.

The vaporized, atmospheric, meteorological and impressionist work of Claude Monet was influenced by the principle of colors optical mix of Charles Blanc, and the law of simultaneous contrast, theorized by Michel-Eugène Chevreul.[1] He

1. Charles Blanc, *The Grammar of Painting and Engraving* (Charleston: BiblioLife, 2009) and: Michel Eugène Chevreul, *The Principles of Harmony and Contrast of Colours and Their* *Applications to the Arts* (Charleston: Nabu Press, 2010), original edition 1839.

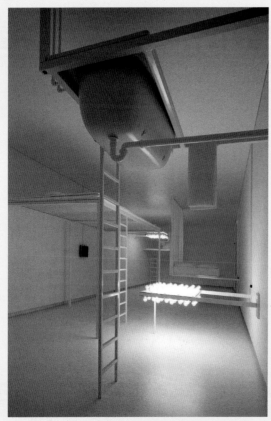

∧   *Domestic Astronomy*. Louisiana Museum, Denmark, 2009.
Philippe Rahm architectes with a graphic collaboration by Amy
O'Neill. *Domestic Astronomy* is the prototype of an apartment
where you no longer occupy a surface, but rather an atmosphere.
As they leave the floor, furnishings rise: they spread and evapo-
rate in the atmosphere of the apartment, and stabilize at certain
temperatures determined by the body, clothing and activity.
(Philippe Rahm Architectes. Photo by Brøndum & Co)

∧   *De-territorialised Milieus*. VIA carte blanche prize, France,
2009. This interior design project aims at recomposing a specific
milieu in an interior, using construction techniques to control
air-flow with cooling, heating and ventilation. Micro-regions with
chemical, electromagnetic and physical properties are set to work
in an interior—de-territorialised or a-territorial—evoking a specific
type of soil, climate, exposure to sunlight, and aromas in the air.
(Philippe Rahm Architectes. Photo by A. Dupuis / VIA)

decomposed visual reality into particles of light and what
mattered most was not the subject but the shapes that arose
from the analytical dissociation of the methods he operated
with. The same methodology of dissociation occurred in
music with Debussy or literature with Mallarmé. For these
artists, art disintegrates the "whole" into elementary particles—understanding reality in touches of color, fragments of
sounds and words. In the 1950s, in a similar deconstruction
of literary language, the "New Novel" by Alain Robbe-Grillet
and Nathalie Sarraute proposed literature in which narrative
is devoid of any psychological intention, in order to become
pure sensation; literal and objective descriptions of the world
without any globalizing and unifying subjective intention.[2]
More recently, the spectral music of Gérard Grisey or Tristan
Murail does not compose, but de-composes.[3] More simply
said, they pose sound by disintegrating the instrumental
sounds, reducing them to their essential components, and

then, recomposing or synthesizing new aggregates from
these elements. We explore the infinitely small, we analyze
the optical or sound spectra, we decompose reality into
visual, electromagnetic or thermal particles, then we recom-
pose it, but with a number of its elements, not all of them. In all
these works, there is the legacy of Enlightenment rationalism,
the whiteness of writing, independent of narrative. But from
this condition emerges something magical, a "disturbing
unreality", related to "a further realism more than a deliberate fiction" as Gerard Genette[4] wrote, describing the work
of Robbe-Grillet.

Meteorological architecture is part of this "tradition." It
processes and understands space in elementary chemical
particles—wavelengths, humidity rates, light intensities, heat
transfer coefficients; but also hormonal secretion levels,
kilocalories, nanometers, etc. The expansion of the field of
the 'real' produced by scientific knowledge modifies the

2. See Alain Robbe-Grillet, *For a New Novel:*
Essays on Fiction (Chicago: Northwestern
University Press, 1992) and Nathalie Sarraute,
Tropisms (New York: George Braziller, 1967)

3. Listen to: Tristan Murail, Désintégrations,
Audio CD, 2004, Label: Disques Montaigne
and Gérard Grisey, Les Espaces Acoustiques,
Audio CD, 2008, Label: Kairos

4. Gérard Genette, Vertige fixé, *Figure 1*
(Paris: Seuil, 1966).

∧ **Evaporated Tenement**, 2010. Office building in La Défense. While it is usually the solidity and opacity of walls, floors and ceilings which define the void of interior spaces, our ambition is to define these voids no longer with solids, but with voids. The intention is to evaporate structures, to sublimate walls and ceilings, to pass from the solid state to a gaseous state, to make an architecture of air and light; a transparent state, open, light, and broken up.

field of art, which shifts into new dimensions, slides into other phenomena, solicits other perceptions. How are forms composed together once the "whole as gestalt" ceases to be the only paradigm? How are forms dissociated, exploded into fragments of reality, into sensible particles? Our interest in the disintegration of the real and its synthesis into just two or three chemical and electromagnetic components, is not only an aesthetic project, it reveals the soft atmospheric qualities of architecture. It allows for the re-evaluation of the human landscape, architecture, urbanization, and the notion of territory.

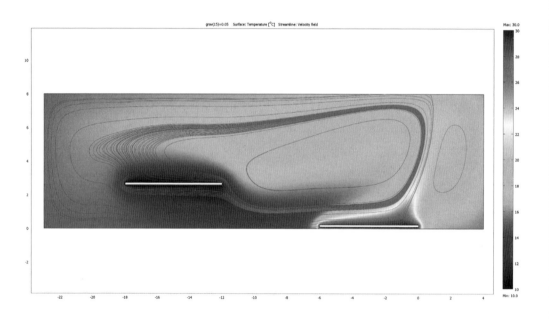

grav(15)=0.05   Surface: Temperature [°C]   Streamline: Velocity field

∧ **Digestible Gulf Stream**. Venice Architecture Biennale, 11th International Architecture Exhibition, *Out There: Architecture Beyond Building*, directed by Aaron Betsky. Two horizontal metal planes are extended at different heights. The lower plane is heated to 28°C, the upper one is cooled to 12°C. Like a miniature Gulf Stream, their position and temperature encourage a movement of air using the natural phenomenon of convection. The inhabitant may move around in this invisible landscape between 12°C and 28°C, temperatures at the two extremities of the concept of comfort, and freely choose a climate according to his or her activity, clothing, dietary, sporting or social wishes. (© Digestible Gulf Stream / Philippe Rahm architectes. Photo by Noboru Kawagishi)

subverting /
hijacking

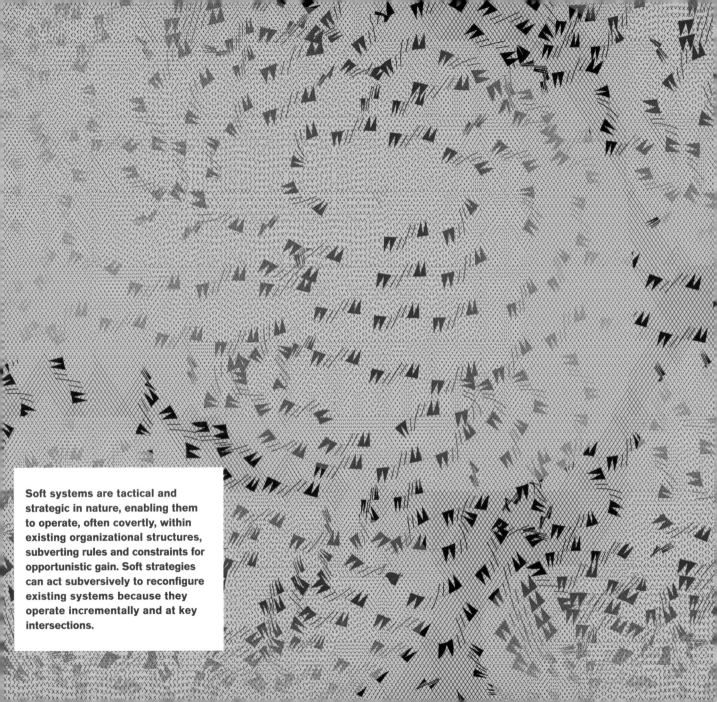

Soft systems are tactical and strategic in nature, enabling them to operate, often covertly, within existing organizational structures, subverting rules and constraints for opportunistic gain. Soft strategies can act subversively to reconfigure existing systems because they operate incrementally and at key intersections.

CONTESTING LIMITS: ARCHITECTURE AND BOUNDARY CONDITIONS IN ISRAEL/ PALESTINE

SUZANNE HARRIS BRANDTS

On November 9th, 2010 the Israeli government announced the construction of 2,100 Jewish-only housing units on occupied West Bank land.[1] This surge in proposed construction was strongly contrasted by the demolition of a Palestinian Mosque in the same area just two days earlier. More than isolated incidences pertaining to planning regulations, these events reflect a larger scheme of Israeli territorial expansion that has been taking place in the Occupied Palestinian Territories for the past four decades. The construction and destruction of architecture and landscape in the West Bank exemplifies the dialectical nature of spatial and political transformation in Israel/ Palestine. Competing territorial claims and frozen political negotiations have caused the transfer of this protracted conflict onto its landscape.

Hills, valleys, forests, and agricultural plots are now geopolitical casualties. The complex legalistic framework emanating from forty-three years of Israeli military occupation continues to scar this landscape with a multitude of boundaries, barriers, and demolitions. Each scar exposes the contested realities of a continued state of exception operating under the guise of the temporary. Prolonged political negotiations have served as a catalyst to this system. Instead of the promise of resolution embodied within negotiations, the frozen peace process has sustained the capacity for a *fait accompli* on the ground vis-à-vis the ongoing expansion of Israeli settlements on seized West Bank land. Within such a framework, the architect has become a key political player capable of constructing new realities that impact the outcome of the final negotiated solution. Yet, spatial ambiguity in the region has the potential to serve as both ally and foe to the Palestinians. By exploiting opportunities within the existing imbalanced political landscape a spatial counter-insurgency could challenge conventional notions of separation by imagining a different mode of reclamation for Palestinian space.

Contesting Limits seeks to uncover the various ways in which the architect can politically intervene in contested territories through the use of soft systems of design. A series of tactical interventions speculates on how Palestinians can generate a greater sense of economic empowerment, territorial control, and legal clarity by spatially exacerbating the underlying legal mechanisms that govern the boundary conditions dividing this landscape. Taking into account the volatility of the landscape, a design approach that is comprised of interconnected spatial tactics operating in a responsive, malleable, and indeterminate fashion has been utilized. Two such tactics are *Seizing the Temporary* and *Extraterritorial Appropriation*.

Seizing the Temporary aims to capitalize on the legal ambiguity afforded by the temporary and represents actions through which the meaning, ownership, and structure of occupied lands under Israeli-control can be temporarily suspended. Specifically, it seeks to challenge the very notions of built, un-built, and natural in areas where construction is prohibited by inscribing new collective functions and instrumentality onto the landscape. Israeli-seized "State Land" is reclaimed for the common use of all Palestinians through the processing and re-envisioning of their waste. This tactic exploits waste disposal issues existing across the West Bank by engaging waste as both an asset for development and as a tool for operating in a manner of legal ambiguity. Bags of household organic waste interspersed with plant seeds and growth matter produce a new building block that is neither fully natural nor constructed and that ultimately can only be returned to nutrient-rich soil benefitting Palestinian agricultural plots. These building blocks

. . . .

1. Sherwood, Harriet. "Israeli settlement plan sparks international outrage," *The Guardian*, November 10, 2010, World News, http://www.guardian.co.uk/world/2010/nov/10/israeli-plan-settlement-risks-us-anger (accessed on November 10, 2010).

TIMELINE

1923
BRITISH MANDATE PALESTINE

NOVEMBER **1947**
PROPOSED UN PARTITION PLAN

MAY **1948**
ISRAEL WAR OF INDEPENDENCE

APRIL **1949**
ARMISTICE AGREEMENTS

JUNE **1967**
6-DAY WAR
OCCUPATION OF TERRITORIES
ANNEXATION OF EAST JERUSALEM

NOVEMBER **1967**
UN RESOLUTION 242 CALLS FOR
ISRAELI WITHDRAWL FROM
OCCUPIED TERRITORIES

OCTOBER **1973**
YOM KIPPUR WAR

DECEMBER **1987**
FIRST PALESTINIAN INTIFADA

OCTOBER **1991**
PEACE PROCESS BEGINS WITH
THE MADRID CONFERENCE

AUGUST **1993**
OSLO DECLARATION OF PRINCIPLES

SEPTEMBER **1995**
OSLO INTERIM AGREEMENT

JULY **2000**
CAMP DAVID SUMMIT

SEPTEMBER **2000**
SECOND PALESTINIAN INTIFADA

JANUARY **2001**
TABA SUMMIT

JUNE **2002**
CONSTRUCTION OF THE WEST BANK
SEPARATION BARRIER BEGINS

APRIL **2003**
ROAD MAP FOR PEACE ANNOUNCED
BY THE'QUARTET'

JULY **2004**
INTERNATIONAL COURT OF JUSTICE
RULES THE SEPARATION BARRIER
VIOLATES INTERNATIONAL LAW

NOVEMBER **2007**
ANNAPOLIS PEACE CONFERENCE

SEPTEMBER **2010**
DIRECT PEACE TALKS RESUME

OCTOBER **2010**
PA DEMANDS SETTLEMENT FREEZE
FOR CONTINUED NEGOTIATIONS

PROTRACTED PEACE PROCESS

∧   **New construction in the West Bank Israeli settlement of Har Gilo (located south of Jerusalem, adjacent to the Palestinian**   **village of Al Walaja) where a security buffer zone is comprised of three separate vertical barriers.**

aggregate to produce an armature for temporary pavilions, which can be assembled and disassembled before Israeli demolition is possible. Used for numerous purposes including market stands and farming rest-stops, these soft pavilions are ephemeral zones of commerce and social interaction that circumvent the laws preventing the establishment of buildings in prohibited areas while simultaneously reinforcing and broadening the existing social and economic networks. The value of the temporary, here, is in its ability to function within ambiguity.

Extraterritorial Appropriation seeks to transform the meaning and functions of highly restricted areas through the exploitation of their residual character. Seemingly insignificant acts of extraterritorial wildflower propagation have the hidden capacity to re-activate Palestinian apiaries by converting large swaths of previously unusable lands as their feeding grounds. The diminishing historical practice of Palestinian apiary management can be re-invigorated in a manner that not only stimulates economic growth but also reinforces the biodiversity of the area. The once neglected residual gains its power only through a soft colonization that sparks new economic and industrial programmes.

More than isolated instances, these tactical acts of insurgency culminate with other such soft tactics to produce a unified system of spatial resistance. Ultimately, the design strategies of *Contesting Limits* aim to remain responsive to the unforeseen social, political and militaristic forces at play in the West Bank, while still giving purpose to the land in its present-day form. By instilling such tactics, design can adapt to the geographical, architectural, and political dynamics existing between the explicit governance of the built environment by humans and the implicit governance of humans through the built environment. Spatial resistance in such a contested territory can only be achieved by the complexity and responsiveness embodied in the soft project.

. . . **Suzanne Harris Brandts is a Graduate student at the University of Waterloo's School of Architecture and an Architect-in-Residence at Decolonizing Architecture, an art and architecture collective based in Beit Sahour, Palestine.**

∧ Encroaching construction of the Israeli Separation Barrier in the Palestinian village of Al Walaja, located south of Jerusalem and west of Bethlehem. (Jerusalem is in the background of the photo.) The Barrier will completely enclose the village on all sides. Approximately half of the village's land was confiscated by Israel for the construction of the settlements of Har Gilo and Gilo.

∧ Israeli 'Facts on the Ground' continue to be generated through settlement construction on land occupied by Israel in 1967. New units being built in the settlement of Har Homa encroach towards the Palestinian village of Beit Sahour.

∧ The landscape of Wadi Makhrour near the Palestinian village of Battir contains pockets of Israeli-seized State Land which Palestinians are prohibited from using.

WEST BANK JURISDICTIONAL CONTROL UNDER THE 1995 OSLO INTERIM ACCORDS

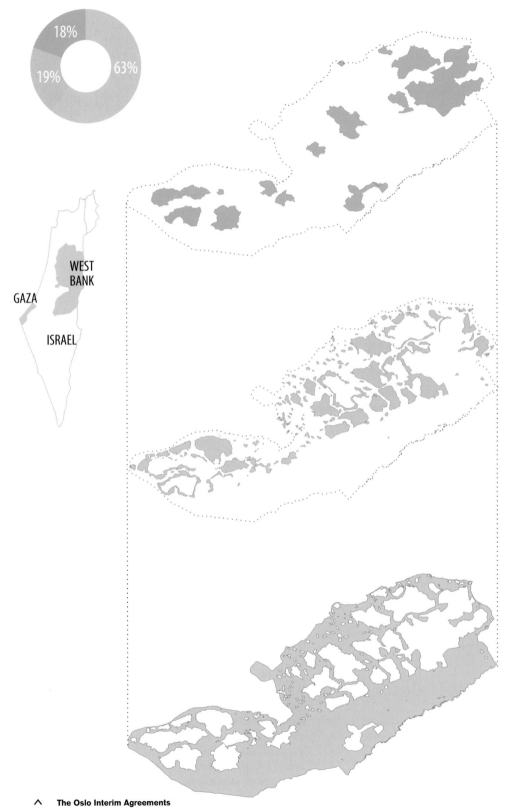

AREA A

Palestinian civil control
Palestinian military control

Land Coverage: 1,015 km^2

AREA B

Palestinian civil control
Israeli military control

Land Coverage: 1,072 km^2

AREA C

Israeli civil control
Israeli military control

Land Coverage: 3,553 km^2
Palestinian Population: 300,000

∧   **The Oslo Interim Agreements
fragmented the West Bank into a series
of land-locked islands under Palestinian
control which are surrounded by a large
contiguous area of occupied territory under
full Israeli control.**

PROHIBITED & RESTRICTED AREA FOR CONSTRUCTION IN ISRAELI CONTROLLED AREA C

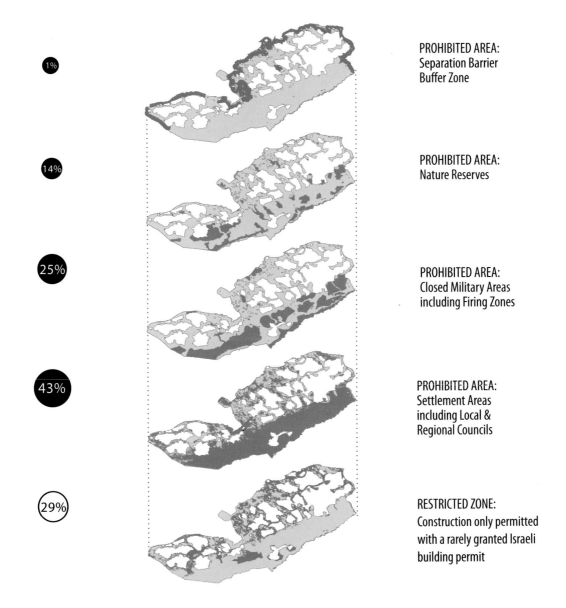

1% — PROHIBITED AREA:
Separation Barrier
Buffer Zone

14% — PROHIBITED AREA:
Nature Reserves

25% — PROHIBITED AREA:
Closed Military Areas
including Firing Zones

43% — PROHIBITED AREA:
Settlement Areas
including Local &
Regional Councils

29% — RESTRICTED ZONE:
Construction only permitted
with a rarely granted Israeli
building permit

AREAS APPROVED FOR CONSTRUCTION IN AREA C

<1% Permits are only approved for Palestinian construction conforming with an Israeli planning scheme.
These schemes cover less than 1% of West Bank land, much of which is already built-up

PERMIT REQUESTS SUBMITTED
(2000 - 2007)

94% 1,533 PERMITS DECLINED

6% 91 PERMITS APPROVED

DEMOLITION ORDERS ISSUED FOR CONSTRUCTION WITHOUT A PERMIT (2000 - 2007)

+3,000 PENDING DEMOLITION

+1,600 DEMOLISHED

 **Land within Israeli-controlled Area C
falls under numerous designations, which
restrict its access and use by Palestinians.**

TARGET GUERILLA EXTRA-TERRITORIAL PLANTING SITES IN THE WEST BANK

GROWTH SEASON ONE   GROWTH SEASON TWO   GROWTH SEASON THREE

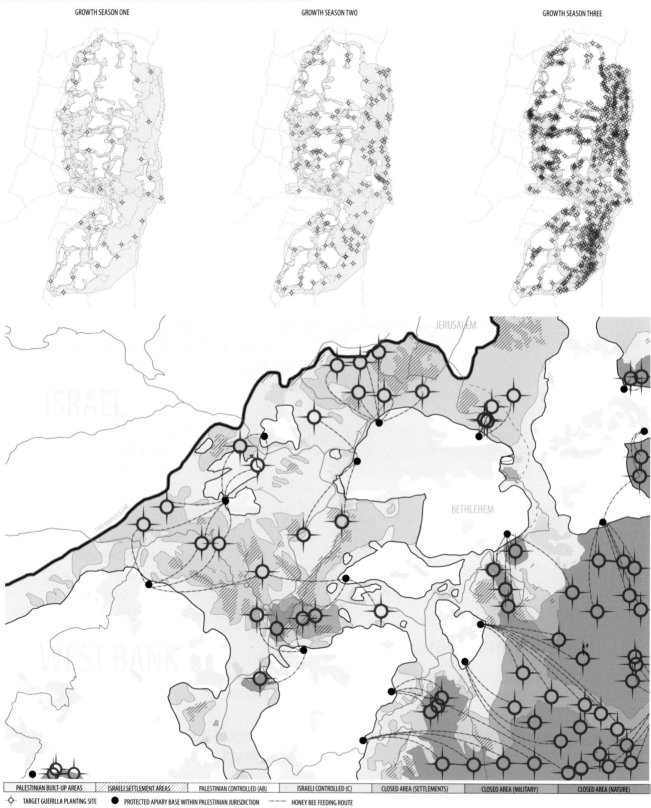

| PALESTINIAN BUILT-UP AREAS | ISRAELI SETTLEMENT AREAS | PALESTINIAN CONTROLLED (AB) | ISRAELI CONTROLLED (C) | CLOSED AREA (SETTLEMENTS) | CLOSED AREA (MILITARY) | CLOSED AREA (NATURE) |

◇ TARGET GUERILLA PLANTING SITE   ● PROTECTED APIARY BASE WITHIN PALESTINIAN JURISDICTION   ·—··— HONEY BEE FEEDING ROUTE

∧∧ **Wildflower locations begin to propa-
gate throughout the West Bank after each
growth season, converting huge swaths of
restricted territory into an integral part of
the Palestinian ecology and economy.**

∧ **Map of the Bethlehem region showing
local apiary management within Palestinian-
controlled Area A (white) and extra-territorial
apiary feeding in the closed military areas of
Israeli-controlled Area C (red).**

1] CULTIVATION CAPSULES

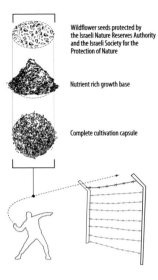

Wildflower seeds protected by the Israeli Nature Reserves Authority and the Israeli Society for the Protection of Nature

Nutrient rich growth base

Complete cultivation capsule

2] EXTRA-TERRITORIAL GROWTH & BEE POLLINATION

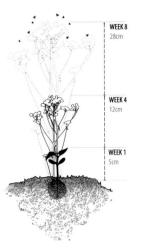
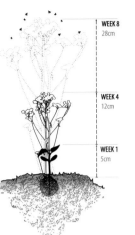

WEEK 8 — 28cm

WEEK 4 — 12cm

WEEK 1 — 5cm

Northern Mountain Region
Michauxia Campanuloides
Nigella Unguicularis
Orchis Tridentata
Ranunculus Asiaticus

Desert Region
Ixiolirion Tataricum
Periploca Aphylla
Matricaria Aurea
Anemone Coronaria

Valley Region
Grewia Villosa
Limonium Meyeri
Periploca Aphylla
Gundella Tournefortii

Desert & Dead Sea Region
Colchicum Tuviae
Coridothymus Capitatus
Anemone Coronaria
Ranunculus Asiaticus

Southern Mountain Region
Helichrysum Sanguineum
Matricaria Reoutita
Nigella Unguicularis
Matricaria Aurea

3] LOCAL APIARY MANAGEMENT

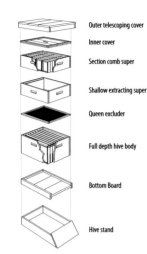

Outer telescoping cover
Inner cover
Section comb super
Shallow extracting super
Queen excluder
Full depth hive body
Bottom Board
Hive stand

∧∧ **Procedural outline for Apiary appropriation, beginning with the creation of cultivation capsules containing the seeds of protected Israeli wildflowers which are to be projected into closed military areas, and culminating in the flowers' extra-territorial growth and provision of nectar to bees.**

∧ **Bees travel unimpeded into Israeli-designated 'Closed Military Zones' in search of nectar to bring back to their hives located within areas of Palestinian jurisdiction.**

GOES SOFT

bracket—

SEIZING THE TEMPORARY: RE-ACTIVATING LAND SEIZED BY THE STATE OF ISRAEL

An occupying power may temporarily seize privately-owned land and buildings if required for essential and urgent military needs. By invoking the temporary, for 44 years Israel has been exclusively using seized land to expand its Jewish-only settlements while prohibiting the Palestinian public from using these areas for their own collective needs.

Seizing the temporary utilizes these areas in an ephemeral fashion through construction materials that are organic and evolving, enclosure systems that are portable, and programming that supports the peak usage of the adjacent areas. Reclaiming this unilaterally declared State Land will increase Palestinian economic activity and re-inforce existing farming practices so that the Palestinian public will now be able to harness the power afforded by the *temporary* and utilize it towards their own means.

ROADSIDE MARKET STATIONS CREATE COMMERCE CORRIDOR

| AM | 5 | 6 | 7 | 8 | 9 | 10 | 11 | 12 | 1 | 2 | 3 | 4 | 5 | 6 | 7 | 8 | 9 | 10 | 11 | PM |

PEAK USAGE (7 8 9 10)   PEAK USAGE (5 6 7 8)

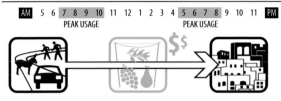

Maximize agricultural revenue potentials by capitalizing on through-site traffic. Farmers avoid checkpoints, reduce transport expenses and minimize food losses.

FIELDSIDE FARMER STATIONS CREATE CULTIVATION CORRIDOR

| AM | 5 | 6 | 7 | 8 | 9 | 10 | 11 | 12 | 1 | 2 | 3 | 4 | 5 | 6 | 7 | 8 | 9 | 10 | 11 | PM |

PEAK USAGE (11 12 1 2 3 4)

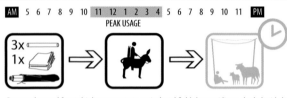

Prevent the need for multiple commutes to agricultural fields by providing a shaded mid-day resting area for farmers and their livestock.

ORGANIC WASTE CREATES NUITRIENT-RICH SOIL SOURCE FOR AGRICULTURAL LANDS

| AM | 5 | 6 | 7 | 8 | 9 | 10 | 11 | 12 | 1 | 2 | 3 | 4 | 5 | 6 | 7 | 8 | 9 | 10 | 11 | PM |

PEAK USAGE (6 7 8 9 10)   PEAK USAGE (4 5 6 7)

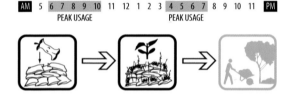

Re-inforce the growth capacity of the existing agricultural lands by providing an ongoing supply of new, nutrient-rich soil to farmers. Land that is continuously cultivated is less at risk of being seized by the Israeli military.

ISRAELI- SEIZED LAND IN THE WEST BANK

SURVEY LAND

Private property whose owner left the West Bank before, during or after the 1967 war. This land is defined as 'abandoned property.'

REGISTERED STATE LAND

Land which on June 1967 belonged to Jordan or was registered in its name, as defined by Israeli Military Order 59.

DECLARED STATE LAND

Private land declared as State Land by the Israeli government after 1979 for military purposes or for lack of cultivation for 3 consecutive years.

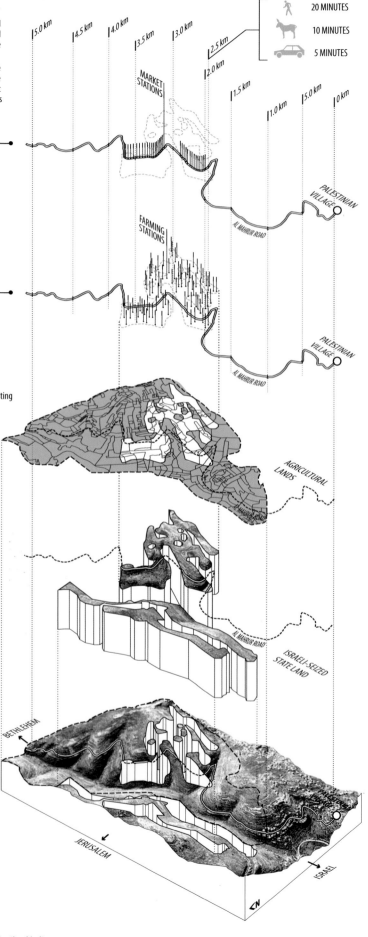

20 MINUTES
10 MINUTES
5 MINUTES

5.0 km 4.5 km 4.0 km 3.5 km 3.0 km 2.5 km 2.0 km 1.5 km 1.0 km 5.0 km 0 km

MARKET STATIONS

PALESTINIAN VILLAGE

AL MAHOUR ROAD

FARMING STATIONS

PALESTINIAN VILLAGE

AL MAHOUR ROAD

AGRICULTURAL LANDS

AL MAHOUR ROAD

ISRAELI-SEIZED STATE LAND

BETHLEHEM

JERUSALEM

ISRAEL

N

CONSTRUCTION ON STATE LAND: LAND UNILATERALLY SEIZED BY THE ISRAELI MILITARY IS RECLAIMED FOR THE COMMON USE OF PALESTINIANS

1

2

Dispose of bags on Israeli declared 'State Land' under the guise of illegal dumping.

3

4

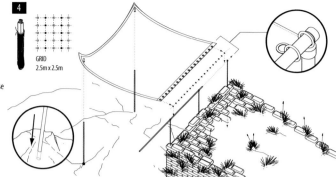

GRID
2.5m x 2.5m

Mix household organic waste with plant seeds and topsoil then store in biodegradable bags.

Bio-degrating bags will begin to sprout plant life, stabilizing areas at risk of soil erosion. Plant matter can be cultivated for animal feed.

Bags culminate to produce a new, fertile topography into which a grid of canopy supports is inserted. An organic foundation and portable enclosure components enable the installation to evade the threat of Israeli demolition through constant spatial transformation.

15 KG OF NUTRIENT RICH TOPSOIL
GENERATED PER BAG

12-30 PLANTS
GROWN PER BAG

25L OF PALESTINIAN HOUSEHOLD ORGANIC
WASTE COMPOSTED PER BAG

< **Exploded axonometric breakdown** of the use of state land in the Palestinian village of Battir to increase Palestinian economic activity and reinforce existing farming practices.

∧∧ **Procedural outline for reclaiming land** seized by the Israeli Military, beginning with the collection of organic waste and plant seeds into biodegradable sacs and culminating in an inhabitable landscape that provides an armature for temporary Palestinian pavilions.

∧ **Palestinian farmers head to their** fields by cart, bringing with them canopies to be attached to the site's hidden infrastructural grid. Beside them workers manage the development of recently 'dumped' organic sacs as they begin to grow and harvest new plant life.

OPERATION "HELLO EDEN"

FIONN BYRNE

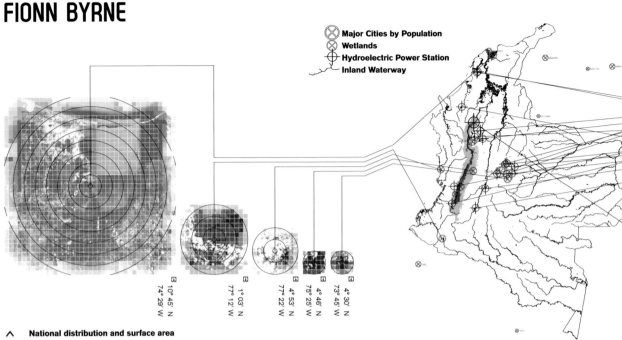

Major Cities by Population
Wetlands
Hydroelectric Power Station
Inland Waterway

10° 45' N
74° 29' W

1° 03' N
77° 12' W

4° 53' N
77° 22' W

4° 46' N
75° 25' W

4° 30' N
73° 45' W

∧ National distribution and surface area
of Internationally Protected Wetlands under
the Ramsar Convention.

Since the 1970s, our planetary environment has been characterized as being in a state of crisis so profound as to challenge our very survival. NASA's release of the Apollo's images of Earth from space galvanized fear of impending environmental doom due to nuclear warfare, overpopulation, and pollution.[1] Today, this sense of crisis has shifted away from destruction by military means towards economic causes that have instigated environmental transformations. The fear of instant destruction has been replaced with a sense of chronic environmental weakening exemplified by localized system failures. Instead of acting as protagonist, the modern military has increasingly been responsible for responding to environmental crisis.[2] This role of the military in reacting to environmental crisis is projected to increase in the future as climate change alters the predicted parameters of ecological systems, resulting in the failure of infrastructural systems upon which they are built or vice versa. If it is recognized that ecological failure will often require military intervention,[3] then it can be argued that preemptive ecological action is a legitimate military pursuit.

The increased bandwidth of the military will require new expertise. In the Canadian context, The Canadian Armed Forces Disaster Assistance Response Team (DART) is a useful organization to study, as its framework is well defined. The team consists of five distinct platoons: military engineer, medical, defense and security, logistics, and headquarters.[4] As environmental degradation applies greater pressure to global security, international military response teams like DART could be aided by incorporating the skills of an ecologist, biologist and landscape architect. In so doing the design of ecologically aware infrastructural systems is re-imagined to engage today's most financially secure and technologically advanced organization—the modern military.

Although financial security is essential to initiating projects, it is the technological sophistication of the military that is of greater importance to the design process.[5] Writing in the political and economic context of the 1970s, John McHale was keenly aware of the growing ecological crisis and the imbrication of technology with ecological systems. He more broadly defines 'soft' technology as "all systems for attaining to greater predictive understanding and expanded control of the human environ."[6] Infrastructural systems are perhaps most implicated in this definition. In his book, *The Ecological Context*,

1. Felicity D. Scott, *Architecture or Techno-Utopia: Politics After Modernism* (Cambridge: MIT Press, 2007), 213.

2. Perhaps the most telling example was the response and ensuing criticism at the lack of response of the American military following the breaching of New Orleans' hydrological infrastructure system as a result of pressure placed upon it by Hurricane Katrina. The military was called upon to repair damaged infrastructure (hydrologic, transportation, energy), provide medical aid and logistical support.

3. The CNA Corporation, *National Security and the Threat of Climate Change*, 2007, 13-18. Online PDF: http://securityandclimate. cna.org/report/SecurityandClimate_Final. pdf. (accessed: Jan. 13, 2010)

4. Additional information on the DART program can be found online at http://www. cefcom.forces.gc.ca/pa-ap/nr-sp/doc-eng. asp?id=301 (accessed: Feb 2011).

5. Consider as an example, the impact that the internet (a military invention of the late 1960s) has had on the profession of landscape architecture and the outcome of ecologically sensitive designs.

6. John McHale, *The Ecological Context* (New York: George Braziller, 1970), 86.

■ 1 mile box

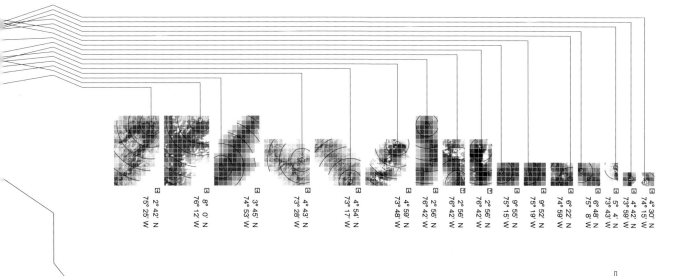

75° 25' W / 2° 42' N
76° 12' W / 8° 0' N
74° 53' W / 3° 45' N
73° 28' W / 4° 43' N
73° 17' W / 4° 54' N
73° 48' W / 4° 59' N
76° 42' W / 2° 56' N
76° 42' W / 2° 56' N
76° 42' W / 2° 56' N
75° 15' W / 9° 55' N
75° 19' W / 9° 52' N
74° 59' W / 6° 22' N
75° 8' W / 6° 48' N
73° 43' W / 5° 4' N
73° 59' W / 4° 42' N
74° 15' W / 4° 30' N

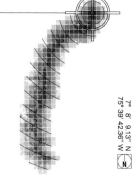

7° 8' 9.13" N
75° 39' 42.36" W

Ⓝ

ECOLOGICAL LOSS

Cauca Valley Wetlands:

"... in just 50 years nearly 90%
of the wetlands in the valley
have disappeared."

INFRASTRUCTURAL GAIN

Pescadero-Ituango Hydroelectric Project >

... this proposal will increase the National
generative capacity by 2,400 MW while
producing a reservoir 70 km long with a
volume of 2,720m^3 (3,800 Hectares).

∧   **National distribution and surface
area of Hydroelectric Dams & Constructed
Reservoirs, scaled equally to facilitate
comparison.**

McHale argues that technology is not only a means of environmental control but is also an integral component to a functional ecosystem, positing that "industrial and agricultural undertakings need to be redesigned as ecologically operating systems."[7] This refocuses energy from landscape architecture to landscape *infrastructures*.

McHale's categories of technology as *predictive understanding* versus *expanded control* are well matched with the landscape architectural terms of *analysis* versus *intervention*. With respect to landscape architecture, predictive understanding refers to all manner of tools, systems, and practices for collecting and projecting information on the past, present, and future of a site—what commonly materializes as mappings. Whereas expanded control is any process that increases, decreases or limits the flow of materials or energy to or from a site—a physical transformation of site conditions or experimentation. Although perhaps weary of technologies of predictive understanding, such as aerial imaging, this data, made available in large part by the military through advances in satellite and spy technologies, has facilitated analysis tools readily used by landscape architects, scientist, and the public. Less accepted is supporting technological interventions of expanded control into ecological systems; or experimenting

. . . .

7. Mason White, "The Productive Surface,"
in *Bracket: On Farming*, Volume 1. Ed. Mason
White and Maya Przybylski (Barcelona:
Actar, 2010), 102.

with ecology. The distinction McHale has made between technologies of predictive understanding versus expanded control is more ambiguous when applied to modern military platforms. For example, Unmanned Aerial Vehicles (UAV) operating in conflict zones are able to react with these two technology categories responding in tandem. Visual satellite observation is continuously fed to a remote operator who is able to respond near instantaneously with audio signals or an array of armaments, providing real-time situation control. Nowhere is this collective consciousness of our extended faculties (technologies) being advanced as quickly as in military research centers. The United States Air Force express their future ambitions clearly in the document *Unmanned Aircraft Systems Flight Plan 2009-2047*:

> Advances in computing speeds and capacity will change how technology affects the OODA loop [observe, orient, decide, and act]. Today the role of technology is changing from supporting to fully participating with humans in each step of the process... UAS [Unmanned Aircraft System] will be able to react at these speeds and therefore this loop moves toward becoming a "perceive and act" vector. Increasingly humans will no longer be "in the loop" but rather "on the loop"—monitoring the execution of certain decisions. Simultaneously, advances in AI will enable systems to make combat decisions and act within legal and policy constraints without necessarily requiring human input.[8]

Clearly the boundaries between observation and experimentation, predictive understanding and expanded control, between site analysis and design, are dissolving. *Operation 'Hello Eden'* acknowledges its use of military technology for site analysis and explores the potential benefits to the use of technologies of environmental control in a remote site facing significant ecological challenges. It begins to explore the possibilities of landscape architecture when the designer is liberated from responding to singular closed systems and allowed to operate across a variety of dynamic feedback loops.

As a case study, a hydroelectric dam proposed for an exceedingly remote location in Colombia was examined, given that Colombia has an ambitious plan to double its energy capacity through an expansion of its hydroelectric infrastructure. Integral to this plan is the proposed Pescadero-Ituango dam, with a projected cost of 2.29 billion dollars and an associated reservoir stretching seventy kilometers through critically endangered habitat.[9] The design of the dam accommodates changes in the area's hydraulic regime by storing enough water in the reservoir to ensure a reliable flow though the turbines even in dry seasons. This designed variability in reservoir's depth,

known as the drawdown, has a significant impact on the ecological diversity and biomass along a reservoir's edge. A drawdown of greater than 9.5 meters is said to have an inhibitory effect, reducing any ecological measures to a minimum.[10] The Pescadero-Ituango dam is projected to have a drawdown of twelve meters, creating significant inhibitory effects. Wetlands and riparian ecosystems provide ecological services towards improved dam operations by reducing sediment load while also providing regional services by supplying habitat to migratory species. At a local scale, a productive ecological system can ensure available food and clean water. Globally, Colombia has a high level of biodiversity despite having only five protected wetlands.[11] Even before increasing their generative capacity two-fold, the area of inundated lands serving as reservoirs for hydroelectric dams is greater than protected wetland habitat. This habitat type is known to be critical in protecting species diversity. Thus the local imbrications of infrastructure, energy, economy, and ecology have true global consequences. Assuming the development of the dam as a given, *Operation 'Hello Eden'* explores a means of realizing rapid and substantive topological transformation without the need for the construction of transportation infrastructure in this remote mountain valley ecosystem.[12]

· · · **Fionn Byrne (mr.Fionn.Byrne@gmail. com) is an Internet-based landscaper interested in ecology, evolution, technology and velocity. He is receptive to dialogue.**

8. USAF, *Unmanned Aircraft Systems Flight Plan: 2009-2047*. Washington, 2009, 41. Online PDF: http://www.aviationweek.com/media/pdf/UnmannedHorizons/17312080-United-States-Air-Force-Unmanned-Aircraft-Systems-Flight-Plan-20092047-Unclassified.pdf (accessed Jan. 30, 2010).

9. WWF (World Wildlife Fund), WildFinder. http://gis.wwfus.org/wildfinder/ (accessed Feb. 4, 2010). Pescadero Ituango no

nacio ayer. http://3.bp.blogspot.com/_J3EPkJAz1xY/ SLxM3sxigWI/ AAAAAAAACj0/LRbLPw2dZJY/s1600-h/ GRAFICO+PESCADERO+ITUANGO1.jpg (accessed June 13, 2011).

10. Food and Agriculture Organization of the United Nations: Fisheries and Aquaculture Department, *Dam design and operation to optimize fish production in impounded river basins* (Rome: FAO, 1984).

11. Ramsar, *The List of Wetlands of International Importance*. March 26, 2010. http://www.ramsar.org/pdf/sitelist.pdf (accessed April 4, 2010).

12. It should be noted that the intervention is compared against the requirements for international recognition of a wetland of significance under the Ramsar Convention. Meeting these criteria will ensure the continued protection and success of the project.

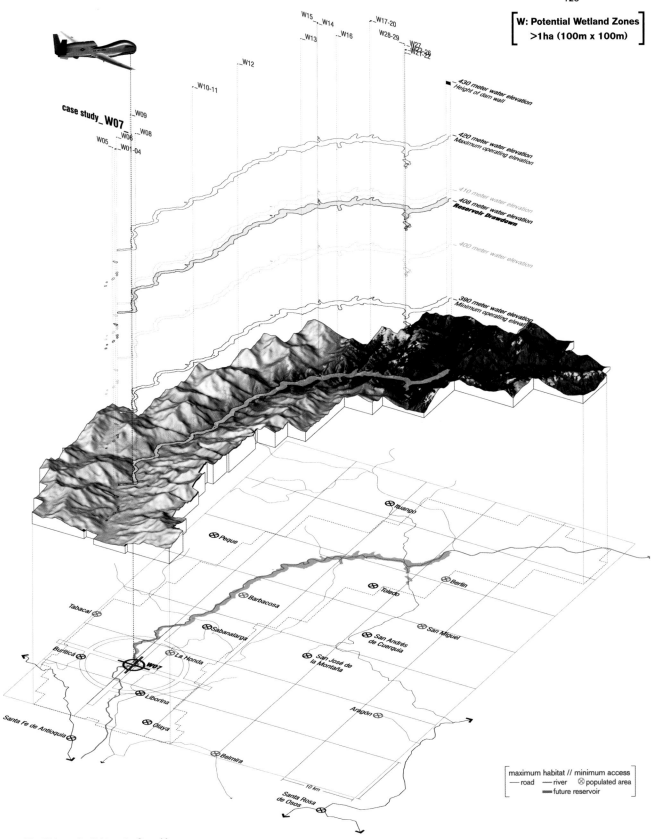

W: Potential Wetland Zones
>1ha (100m x 100m)

case study_ **W07**

430 meter water elevation
Height of dam wall

420 meter water elevation
Maximum operating elevation

410 meter water elevation

408 meter water elevation
Reservoir Drawdown

400 meter water elevation

390 meter water elevation
Minimum operating elevation

W01-04 W05 W06 W08 W09 W10-11 W12 W13 W14 W15 W16 W17-20 W21-22 W23-26 W27 W28-29

Ituango
Peque
Berlin
Toledo
Barbacosa
Tabacal
San Miguel
Sabanalarga
San Andrés de Cuerquia
Buritica
La Honda
San José de la Montaña
W07
Liborina
Aragón
Santa Fe de Antioquia
Olaya
Belmira
10 km
Santa Rosa de Osos

maximum habitat // minimum access
— road — river ⊗ populated area
━ future reservoir

∧   **Identifying potential targets. Operable**
targets are identified remotely by having a
relatively high amount of surface area pro-
jected to be inundated with water at a depth
conducive to the production of identified
wetland ecozones.

Existing Valley Edge Conditions

Projected Ecological Failure due to Reservoir Drawdown

Site W07 4x Bombing Runs

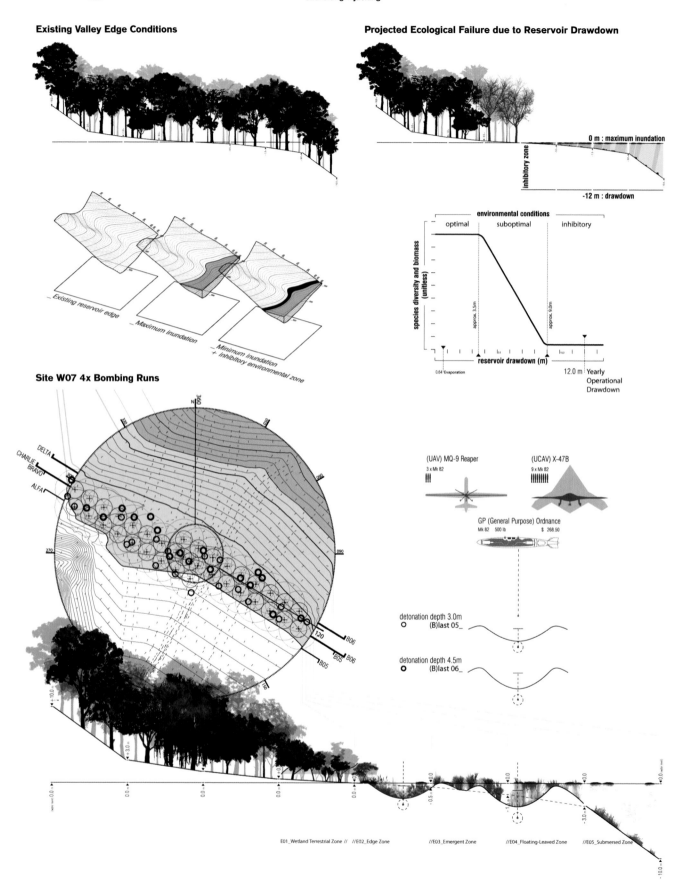

Rapid ecological differentiation by way of
tactical topographic manipulation.

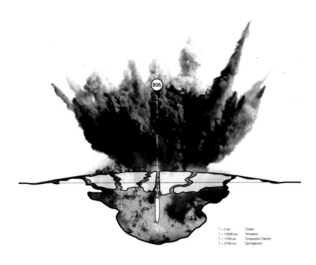

i. [Stage_02 // HAVEN]
Detonation B06 1xMk 82 500 lbs

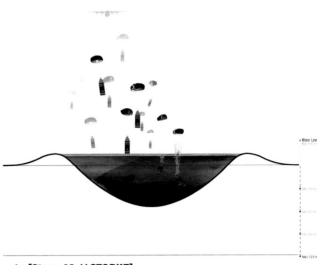

iv. [Stage_03 // STORKE]
Bombing run ECHO_biomaterial delivery

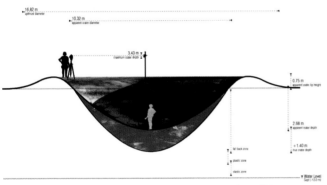

ii. Data collection: Accommodating local geological conditions

v. Reservoir at maximum inundation. Vegetal colonization

iii. Reservoir at maximum inundation

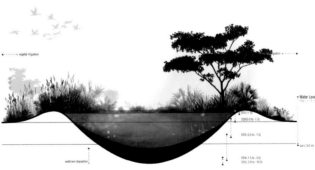

vi. Reservoir drawdown. Ecological holding pattern

∧ Phasing strategy from detonation through
to colonization.

OPERATION "HELLO EDEN"

TARGET
01

OPERATION "HELLO EDEN".

ESTUARY SERVICES PIPELINE

BIONIC/MARCEL WILSON

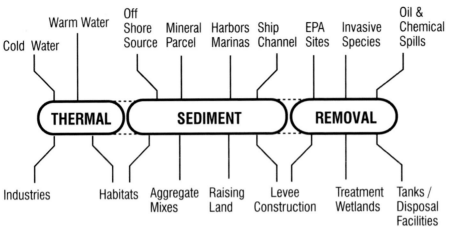

^ **ESP** diagram of material sources, end uses, and placements.

The *Estuary Services Pipeline* (ESP) is a regional utility infrastructure designed to anticipate, adapt, respond, and leverage the changes presented by sea level rise in the one hundred and seventy miles of coastline in the San Francisco Bay estuary. This century sea levels are projected to rise as much as fifty-five inches, due to global climate change. This epic disaster will unfold slowly and will threaten our most productive economies, infrastructures, cultures, and coastal ecologies. Given the history of disaster relief, the sheer magnitude of the issue promises uncoordinated efforts among governments, agencies, and the private sector. Response is likely to be slow, late, and resource intensive. The pipeline is a coordinated large-scale project for the San Francisco Bay Metropolitan Area. It develops a long-term strategy that reduces disturbance, lower costs, and copes with known and unknown challenges that sea level rise and climate change present.

The San Francisco Bay Metropolis has a population of seven million people, and a GP of $487 billion. Much of the infrastructure and industries that support its economy and population are in areas directly threatened by sea level rise. In addition, the bay itself is environmentally damaged and accident-prone. There are over seventy sites regulated by the Environmental Protection Agency at the Bay's edge. Further, there are potentially over 100,000 acres that could be restored to tidal marsh, which would serve to mitigate environmental damage, but costs, lack of sediments, and high salinity prevent progress. There have been more than ten major oil spills in the Bay since 1970. As recently as 2008, the container ship *Cosco Busan* suffered a spill and released 53,000 gallons of toxic bunker fuel.

ESP consists of components that both rigid and flexible, hard and soft. The pipeline will use conventional pipeline technology to conduct ecological flows. Financed by a new financial market for sediment materials, the *Estuary Services Pipeline* will build a biomechanical relationship with the San Francisco Bay. The *ESP* is malleable, adaptable, and generative: it can construct coastal defenses, supply industries, raise land, create habitats, clean up contamination spills, manage invasive species, and provide civic-scale waterfront spaces and programs through its four primary functions.

Material Transport

Every year, six million cubic yards of sediment is dredged from the San Francisco Bay—enough to fill the Trans America Building twenty-seven times. The *ESP* is designed to conduct these sediments and other ecological and landscape materials from places where they are burdens (such as shipping lanes and ports) to areas where they are needed to supply coastal defense, land elevation, and habitat creation projects. Any soft, loose, or liquid material can be conveyed including water, sediment, plant materials, and contaminated soils.

Thermal

To cope with the influence of climate change, thermal exchange loops mediate water temperatures. Shallow areas would support industrial ecologies such as alga biofuels, aquaculture, remediation wetlands, waste-water treatment, and native oyster beds. Thermal loops would supply the needs of these industries by exchanging warm water in shallow areas with cool water from

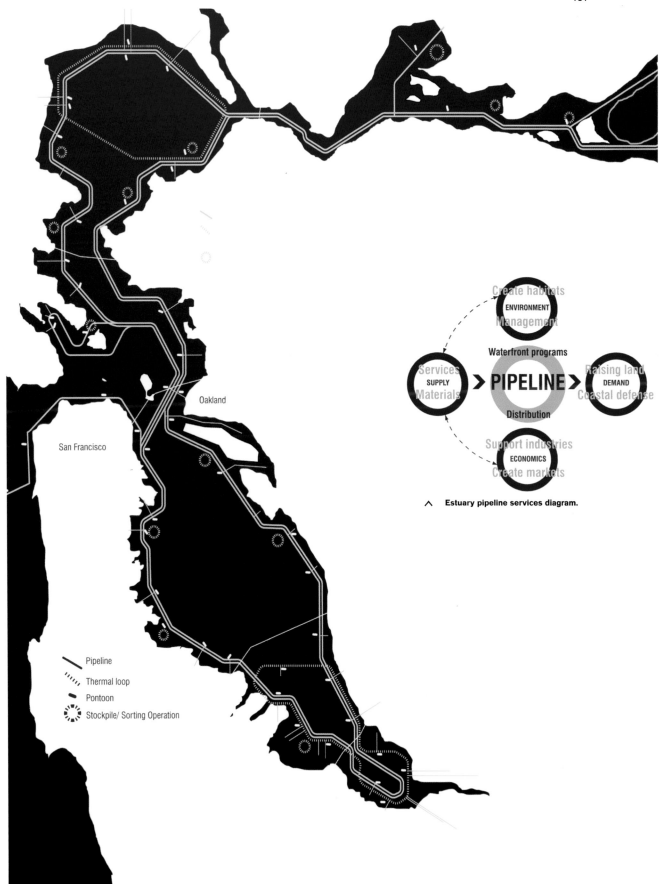

Oakland

San Francisco

Pipeline
Thermal loop
Pontoon
Stockpile/ Sorting Operation

Create habitats
ENVIRONMENT
Management

Waterfront programs

Services
SUPPLY
Materials

❯ **PIPELINE** ❯

Distribution

Raising land
DEMAND
Coastal defense

Support industries
ECONOMICS
Create markets

∧   **Estuary pipeline services diagram.**

∧   ***ESP* routing plan showing main
line routes, thermal loops, and material
stockpiles.**

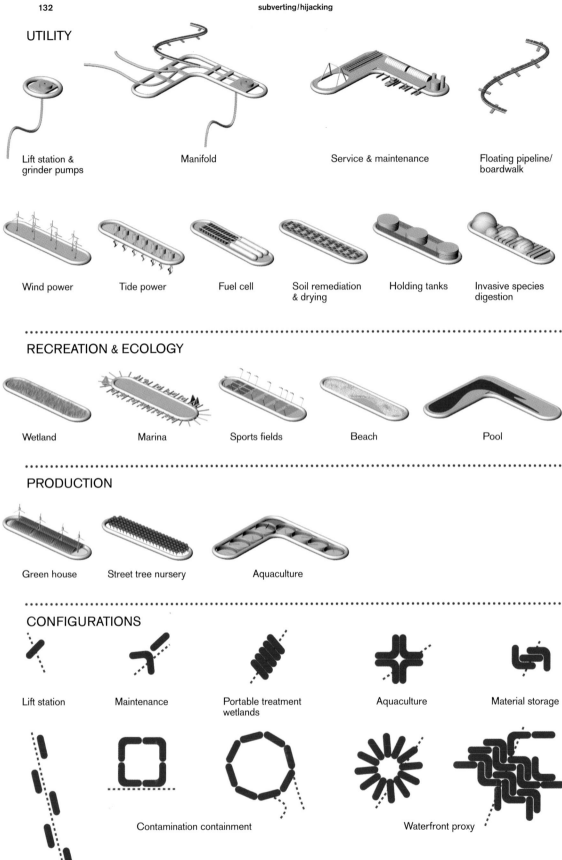

UTILITY

Lift station & grinder pumps

Manifold

Service & maintenance

Floating pipeline/ boardwalk

Wind power

Tide power

Fuel cell

Soil remediation & drying

Holding tanks

Invasive species digestion

RECREATION & ECOLOGY

Wetland

Marina

Sports fields

Beach

Pool

PRODUCTION

Green house

Street tree nursery

Aquaculture

CONFIGURATIONS

Lift station

Maintenance

Portable treatment wetlands

Aquaculture

Material storage

Contamination containment

Waterfront proxy

Power array

∧   **Typical pontoon types, and configurations based on the tasks they perform.**

Bionic   Estuary Services Pipeline

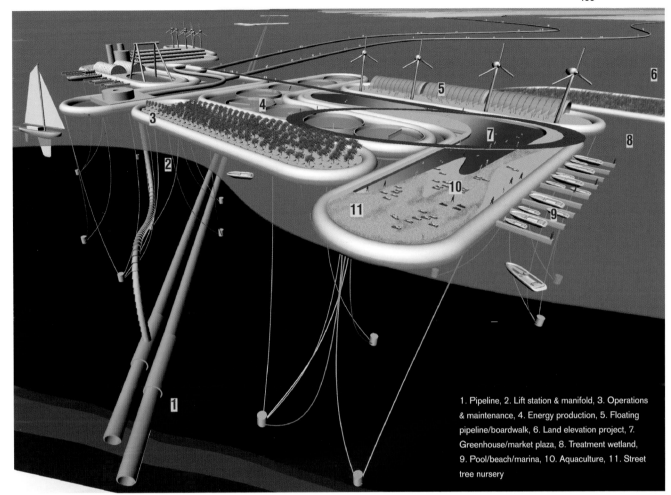

1. Pipeline, 2. Lift station & manifold, 3. Operations & maintenance, 4. Energy production, 5. Floating pipeline/boardwalk, 6. Land elevation project, 7. Greenhouse/market plaza, 8. Treatment wetland, 9. Pool/beach/marina, 10. Aquaculture, 11. Street tree nursery

∧ **Typical flotilla of pontoons hosting waterfront programs, pipeline operations, and productive industries.**

deep trenches. Cool water would also augment stream flows to facilitate fish migrations back to spawning grounds.

Invasive/Toxic

The San Francisco Bay supports over two hundred and fifty invasive species that affect its ecological health and function. Plant species such as Wakame, form dense underwater forests that harbor invasive predators, block light, and entangle boats. This pipeline and its utilities can maintain these populations and others as they migrate into the Bay over time. In moments of disaster when a rapid, large-scale response is required, the *ESP* would function as a conduit for evacuating spills and moving contaminants to holding tanks and settling ponds.

Support/Proxy

Support operations and other programs would be stationed on a fleet of pontoons that serve as new programmatic realms during the adaptive replacement of waterfronts over the next one hundred years. Forms are intentionally simple to allow for periodic relocation, maximum stability, and various configurations in flotillas. Along with support operations, pontoons would host civic-scale programs and income producing uses that are otherwise difficult to locate in urban areas such as marinas and food production. Pontoons would also replace waterfront programs displaced by coastal projects with long construction periods.

· · · **Marcel Wilson is a licensed landscape architect based in San Francisco, CA. He is the principal of Bionic, and he teaches graduate level design and urbanism studios at the University of California Berkeley.**

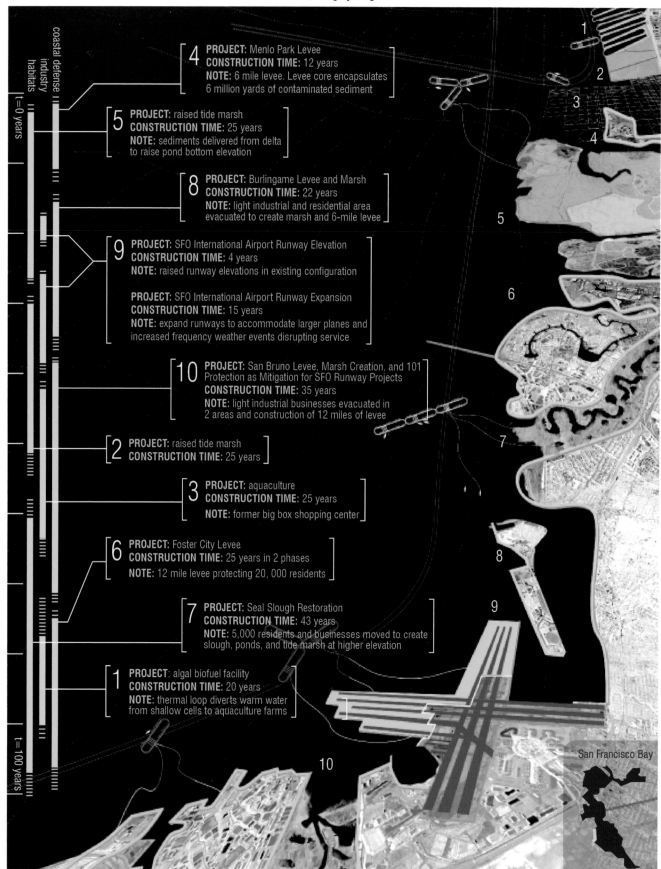

coastal defense
industry
habitats

t=0 years

4 PROJECT: Menlo Park Levee
CONSTRUCTION TIME: 12 years
NOTE: 6 mile levee. Levee core encapsulates
6 million yards of contaminated sediment

5 PROJECT: raised tide marsh
CONSTRUCTION TIME: 25 years
NOTE: sediments delivered from delta
to raise pond bottom elevation

8 PROJECT: Burlingame Levee and Marsh
CONSTRUCTION TIME: 22 years
NOTE: light industrial and residential area
evacuated to create marsh and 6-mile levee

9 PROJECT: SFO International Airport Runway Elevation
CONSTRUCTION TIME: 4 years
NOTE: raised runway elevations in existing configuration

PROJECT: SFO International Airport Runway Expansion
CONSTRUCTION TIME: 15 years
NOTE: expand runways to accommodate larger planes and
increased frequency weather events disrupting service

10 PROJECT: San Bruno Levee, Marsh Creation, and 101
Protection as Mitigation for SFO Runway Projects
CONSTRUCTION TIME: 35 years
NOTE: light industrial businesses evacuated in
2 areas and construction of 12 miles of levee

2 PROJECT: raised tide marsh
CONSTRUCTION TIME: 25 years

3 PROJECT: aquaculture
CONSTRUCTION TIME: 25 years
NOTE: former big box shopping center

6 PROJECT: Foster City Levee
CONSTRUCTION TIME: 25 years in 2 phases
NOTE: 12 mile levee protecting 20, 000 residents

7 PROJECT: Seal Slough Restoration
CONSTRUCTION TIME: 43 years
NOTE: 5,000 residents and businesses moved to create
slough, ponds, and tide marsh at higher elevation

1 PROJECT: algal biofuel facility
CONSTRUCTION TIME: 20 years
NOTE: thermal loop diverts warm water
from shallow cells to aquaculture farms

t=100 years

San Francisco Bay

∧ **Timeline depicting long-range projects
and coordinating material sources.**

∧   Aerial perspective of a managed
retreat project in Foster City, CA. Low
lying developments on fill are abandoned
for the protection of other development
areas and infrastructure. Levies aligned
with the street grid extend into the water
and provide protection of wetlands from
wave action. A flotilla of utility pontoons
and waterfront replacement programs is
stationed near shore.

〉   Maintenance crews inspect the main
pipeline routing and make repairs.

UNDAMMING THE DUTCH DELTA

KIMBERLY GARZA & SARAH THOMAS

By the end of this century, sea levels in the Netherlands may rise more than four feet, a troubling prospect in a country where seventy percent of GNP is produced in protected areas that reside below sea level.[1] To cope with the prospect of rising water, two schools of thought have evolved in the nation of vulnerable delta cities: utilizing engineering know-how to build up dikes and improve pumping technology —the hard approach—or open cities to the sea in such a way that natural systems can co-exist with human habitation—a soft system approach using "proto-ecological intervention."[2] The second strategy is the focus of this design research project for Dordrecht, a thousand year old city located on an urban island in the Rhine-Waal watershed of the delta region of the Netherlands.[3] Dordrecht's risk extends beyond rising sea levels; it faces sea surges from the west, river flooding from the east, and dramatic subsidence in "polders," the tracts of land captive within dikes.

In order to address Dordrecht's climate conundrum, the proposal highlights how strategic adoption of hydrological dynamics can act as a primary structuring device for urban form. The project proposes to open the Haringvliet Dam (a dam built as one of the Delta Works projects in 1971) in order to re-introduce the exchange of salt and freshwater for the reclamation of estuarine ecologies.[4] Together with tidal dynamics, silt, and sedimentation, the ground is transformed with the accretion of the estuary's most vital resource: mud. The mud flats host thousands of bivalve species, one of the basic building blocks of intertidal ecologies. The benthic and pelagic foodshed are allowed to thrive with plankton and bacteria, clams and crabs, smelt and salmon, beavers and seals, reeds and cattails, willows, and poplars. It is a landscape where the dichotomies of wet/dry and sweet/salt dissolve, allowing an ecological gradient to emerge. Every living species co-exists, co-operates, and co-develops across a range of hydrological zones, shoreline territories, and intertidal time-scales.

In the space of this geographic convergence and ecological systematization, a new aquatic habitat provides ground for proto-ecological processes to emerge and proto-urban conditions to spin-off. Once fertilizer-intensive dry-land agriculture gives way to farming mollusks, dikes are expanded to become places to live, patterns of development no-longer face away from the river Rhine, and Dordrecht establishes a commercial concert with the sea. The coast is a plastic entity that will flex with natural rhythms instead of defying them and the estuary represents a place of climate capitalism where closed, linear, and engineered controls make way for the flexibility of soft systems. Ecology becomes infrastructural and the future of the city becomes inseparable from the future of the estuary.

- - - **Kimberly Garza is a recent graduate of the Master of Landscape Architecture program at the Harvard Graduate School of Design and holds a Bachelor of Arts in Landscape Architecture from University of California, Berkeley.**

- - - **Sarah Thomas is an Assistant Professor of Landscape Architecture at the University of Nebraska-Lincoln. Sarah received her Master of Landscape Architecture from the Harvard Graduate School of Design where she received the Norman T. Newton Prize.**

1. V. McKinney, "Sea Level Rise and the Future of the Netherlands," *ICE Case Studies* 2, May 12, 2007. See also: Ireland, Corydon, "Rising Seas, Raising Hopes," *Harvard Gazette*, May 5, 2010.

2. Ministerie van Landbouw, Natuur en Voedselkwaliteit. "Spatial Planning Key Decision 'Room for the River'—Investing in the safety and vitality of the Dutch river basin region," Ministry of Transport, Public Works and Water Management, Rotterdam (2006), See also: PZH, "Dordrecht: The Water City of Dodrecht," *PZH* No.2 (November 2009), 12-13.

3. This following design research project is part of a collaborative studio focusing on climate change in the Netherlands sponsored by the Harvard-Netherlands Project on Climate Change, Water, Land Development, and Adaptation, in association with the Netherlands Ministry of Transport, Public Works and Water Management; the Netherlands Ministry of Housing, Spatial Planning and Environment; and the Netherlands-based Deltares Institute. The studio was led by Associate Professor of Landscape Architecture, Pierre Belanger and Associate Professor of Urban + Regional Planning, Nina-Marie Lister at the Harvard Graduate School of Design, students including: Casey Elmer, Julia Grinkng, Jianhang Gao, Eamonn Hutton, Jae Yoon Lee, Haein Lee, James Moore, Gyoung Tak Park, Richa Shukla, Abhishek Sharma, and Laci Videmsky. The point of departure for this project focused on the ecological and economic benefits of opening the Haringvliet dam to generate lost estuarine conditions in the Rhine-Meuse Delta.

4. Jongejan, R., J. Vrijling, M. Stive, and S. Jonkman, "A Comment on "Changing Estuaries, Changing Views," *Hydrobiologia* 605 (2008), no. 1: 11-15.

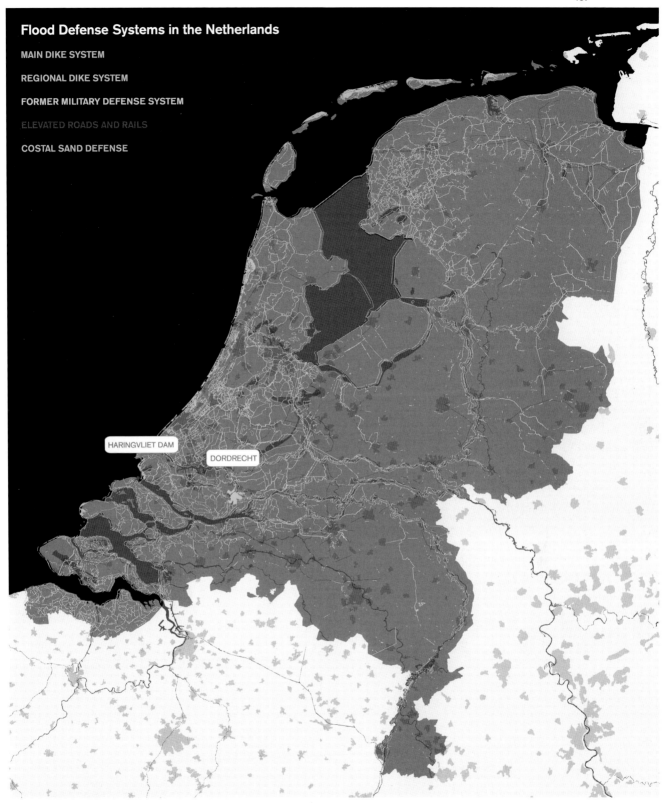

Flood Defense Systems in the Netherlands

MAIN DIKE SYSTEM

REGIONAL DIKE SYSTEM

FORMER MILITARY DEFENSE SYSTEM

ELEVATED ROADS AND RAILS

COSTAL SAND DEFENSE

HARINGVLIET DAM

DORDRECHT

∧ **Controlling the River: Despite a
history of coastal defense strategies, the
Dutch coastline has eroded five kilometers
in four centuries. Strategies ranging from
kelp dikes to Delta Works Projects and sand
nourishment represent efforts to hold a line
between the land and the sea. Specifically,
the damming of the shoreline has drastically altered the ecology of the delta.**

> Constructed Ecology: Several of the estuaries that once exchanged fresh and salt water are now transformed into fresh water basins closed by linear engineering systems. This project focuses on opening the Haringvliet Dam, constructed in 1971 as a Delta Works project, to re-establish a mixing zone of fresh and salt water.

∨ Phasing strategy for the changing land-use patterns as a result of opening the dam and allowing for fluctuating water levels.

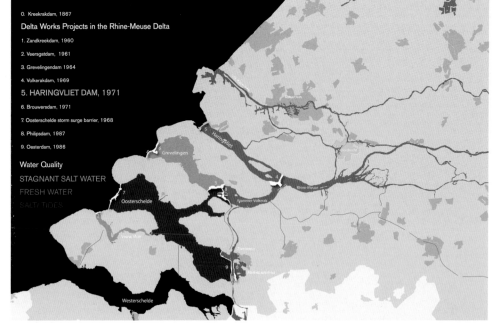

0. Kreekrakdam, 1867

Delta Works Projects in the Rhine-Meuse Delta

1. Zandkreekdam, 1960
2. Veersgatdam, 1961
3. Grevelingendam 1964
4. Volkerakdam, 1969
5. **HARINGVLIET DAM, 1971**
6. Brouwersdam, 1971
7. Oosterschelde storm surge barrier, 1968
8. Philipsdam, 1987
9. Oesterdam, 1986

Water Quality

STAGNANT SALT WATER
FRESH WATER
SALTY TIDES

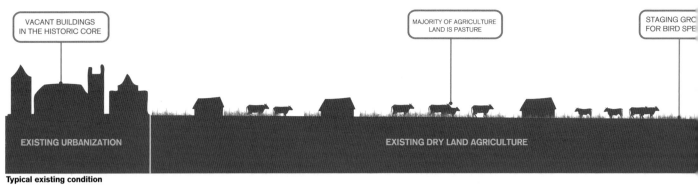

Typical existing condition

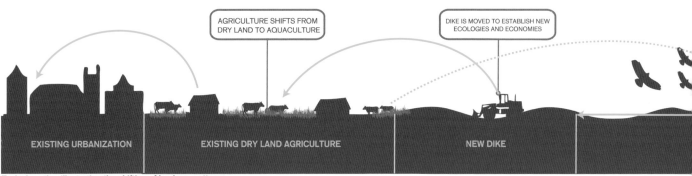

Typical section illustrating the shifting of land use patterns

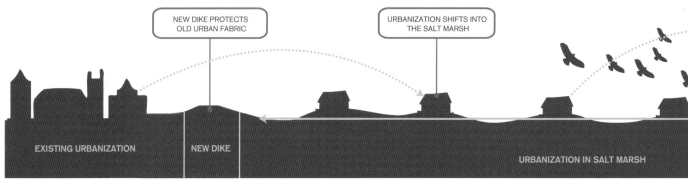

Typical section illustrating a robust ecological infrastructure

Garza, Thomas   **Undamming the Dutch Delta**

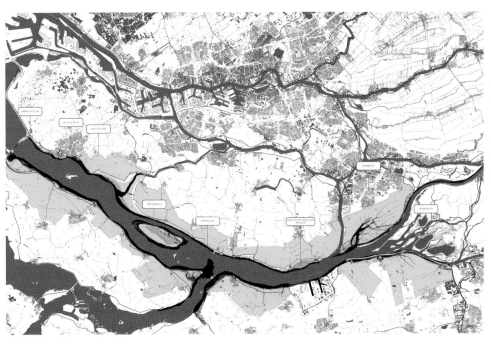

Agriculture to Aquaculture: Dry Land Agriculture is the dominant land use pattern in the Netherlands. Opening the Haringvliet Dam and moving the existing dike back (dashed line on the map) creates new land-use opportunities (shaded portion on the map): once fertilizer-intensive, dry-land agriculture gives way to farming mollusks, dikes are expanded to become places to live, and patterns of development no-longer face away from the river Rhine.

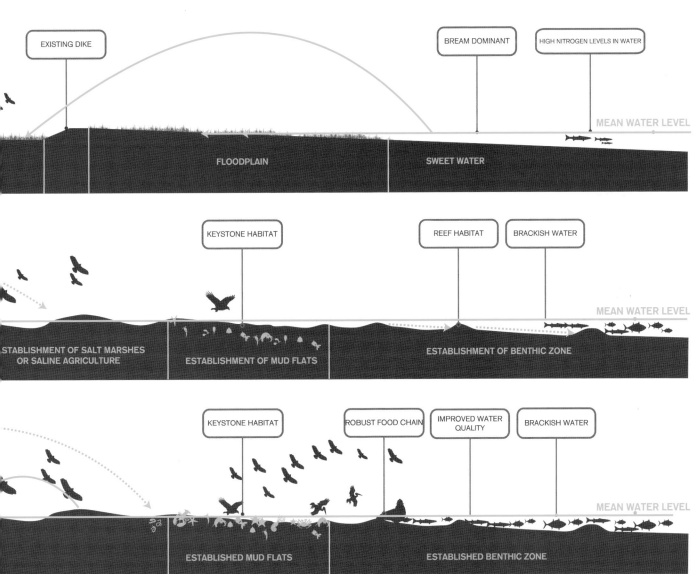

EXISTING DIKE

BREAM DOMINANT

HIGH NITROGEN LEVELS IN WATER

MEAN WATER LEVEL

FLOODPLAIN

SWEET WATER

KEYSTONE HABITAT

REEF HABITAT

BRACKISH WATER

MEAN WATER LEVEL

STABLISHMENT OF SALT MARSHES OR SALINE AGRICULTURE

ESTABLISHMENT OF MUD FLATS

ESTABLISHMENT OF BENTHIC ZONE

KEYSTONE HABITAT

ROBUST FOOD CHAIN

IMPROVED WATER QUALITY

BRACKISH WATER

MEAN WATER LEVEL

ESTABLISHED MUD FLATS

ESTABLISHED BENTHIC ZONE

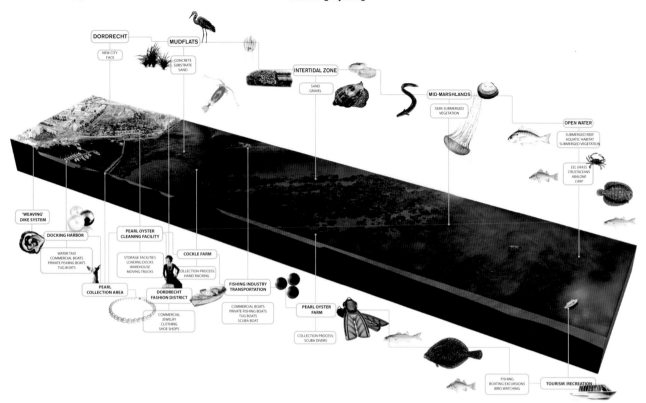

^   **Pearling and Oyster Ecologies and Economies:** New economies are established through the harvesting of pearl oysters. Dordrecht's edge, historically defined by a linear dike system, is now transformed into a meandering dike system. Corridors for pearl oysters and cockles are made available through the weaving of the dike, in and out of the cityscape, creating saltwater pockets for cultivation. The dike, historically used as a flood control barrier, serves a multitude of functions for the pearling oyster industry: commercial transportation, collection area, docking infrastructure and storage facilities. This new economy establishes a cultural identity for the city of Dordrecht.

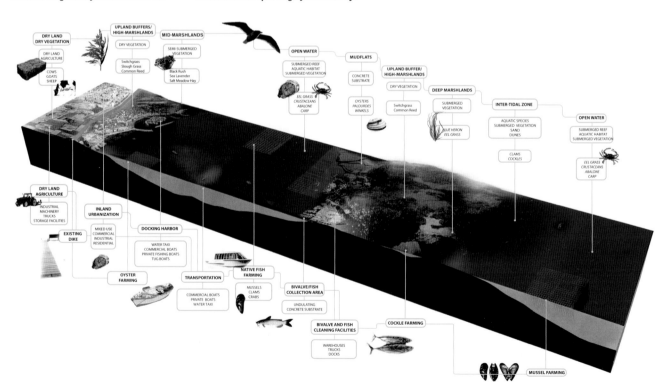

^   **Bivalve and Fish Economies and Ecologies:** New bivalve economies are established through the opening of the Haringvliet Dam. By utilizing the existing dike and island as a transportation network and storage infrastructure for bivalve and fish industries, dry land agriculture areas are transformed into robust productive landscapes. From oysters to mussels, the area is economically revitalized through robust estuarine ecology.

LANDSCAPES OF CO-OPTION: SOFT POWER AND THE ENVIRONMENTAL TURN IN CORPORATE AMERICA

DAN HANDEL

Imagine you work in a place where white noise is used to control your environment, a densely vegetated deep floor acts as a platform where your working station shifts position once every three months, and your superior sits in the adjacent workstation. Now imagine this place, where you spend many hours, demarcated by something that has no clear edges, a context that is not really a building nor outside in the strict sense of the term, which has thousands of people working in it but is positioned in the middle of a forest. As futuristic and disturbing as this image of a total working environment might be, it is in fact already existing: a materialized instance of American corporate architecture in a transformative phase of its history. And in this instance, architecture, landscape, art, interior design and forestry techniques came together under an ideology of management that was as subversive as it was precise in the delineation and maintenance of power relations and maximum efficiency. It was production through a soft environment and soft power.

In the arena of world politics, the term *soft power* was used to reason an alternative form of power, deployed by governments and organizations as a supplement to hard coercion and direct confrontation, previously used by states to force their will upon other states. Joseph Nye, who coined the term,[1] anchored its relevance in two historical processes: first, the dissolution of the nation-state model as a leading paradigm of international relations and second, the diffusion of the Soviet Union and, as a consequence, the depolarization of political ideologies that would call for new means of achieving strategic goals. Most importantly, Nye argues that in this new condition, the exercise of power becomes an environmental operation: proof of power, he says, is expressed not in the possession of resources but in an ability to alter the behavior of states. The challenge facing the United States at that moment was whether it would be able to "control the political environments... and get other countries to do what it wants." Moreover, as the balance of world power changes, new non-state actors such as multi-national banks or NGOs

are taking a part in such operations. The techniques of exercising power become in turn increasingly co-optive: rather than forcing others to do as you wish, you convince them that they want it. You might not be able to control their actions, but you will be able to direct outcomes. That end, however, can only be achieved by a thoroughly designed environment.

As timely as this concept might have seemed in world politics at the closure of the cold war, the idea of deliberately affecting an environment had existed in political thinking already two decades before. This theoretical landscape was formulated during the nineteen seventies, caught two between conceptions: first, the transfiguration of state into control apparatuses which infiltrate all structures of society, and second, the hypotheses of the human body broken down into pure substance, or dissolved into its surrounding atmosphere. With these challenges to modern conceptions of sovereignty and to its definition of social boundaries, the environment was reconstructed as a communicative organism—a system which integrates human beings and dictates their behaviors.[2] In real political terms, this integration also meant that the volatile conflicts of the previous decade could be remediated by putting different social groups in the same ecological boat and using a terminology of shared destiny.[3] Richard Nixon's environmental policies, opening the decade with the signing of the National Environmental Policy Act, sought to do just that; and by calling for a joint effort of all Americans, he implicitly imagined (and probably hoped for) a changed political sphere.

At that moment, architecture was already struggling with similar issues. As early as 1965, Reyner Banham launched an assault on the preconceptions of the discipline, suggesting that Americans rid themselves of the envelopes of architecture (really meaning European traditions) in favor of homes that would be individually controlled environments.[4] In that, he not only expressed his well-known fascination with technology and its mocking of previous conventions ("... what is the house doing except

1. Joseph Nye, "Soft Power", *Foreign Policy*, No. 80 (Autumn, 1990), 153-171, and later in his books, *Bound to Lead: The Changing Nature of American Power* (New York: Basic Books, 1990), and *Soft Power: The Means to Success in World Politics* (New York: Public Affairs, 2004).

2. For this idea, expressed for instance by

Leo Marx, as well as for a thorough account of the interrelations between the conceptualizations of the environment and cultural discourse, see Martin, "Environment, c.1973," *Grey Room* no.14 (Winter 2004), 78-101.

3. Hans Mangus Ezbensberger provided a materialist reading of the central themes of the ecological discourse, arguing that they

were used in fact to diffuse and neutralize tensions of class and race. See Hans Mangus Ezbenberger, "Critique of Political Ecology," in *Political Ecology*, ed. Cockburn and Ridgeway (New York: Times Books, 1979), 371-93.

4. Reyner Banham, "A home is not a house," *Art in America* no.2 (April 1965), 109-18.

^   The siting and architecture of the
Weyerhaeuser headquarters enforce its ambivalent reading as a building-turned-landscape and
as a total environment.

^   The landscape plan by Sasaki and Walker
demonstrates their approach to the project as a
"clearing in a forest."

concealing your mechanical pudenda from the stares of
folks in the street?"[5]), but also reasoned his proposition
in an American tradition of facing the great outdoors.
Rather than avoiding the exterior altogether by building
a shelter, which would be architecture as we know it,
the campfire posed an alternative trajectory in which
habitation was a dynamic and soft manipulation of
local meteorology, constantly forming and reforming
with the need, use, or caprice of its dwellers. The collection of these individual constructions would constitute
an environment of environments that would be, at least
for Banham, an authentic expression of an American way
of life. Less devastating perhaps to modern architecture
(and certainly lower on electric power, and all other forms
of consumption) were other propositions that followed
the environmental thread, from Christopher Alexander's
systems of architectural program, to Ian McHarg's ecologically driven landscape design principles. These excursions
circumscribed a particular framework in which building
became synonymous with an environment, and organization was pursued through softer, less confrontational
design strategies. Architecture, in this process, was not to
remain unaltered.

Back in the Pacific Northwest, and in the context
of a single project, the design of such an environment
and the redefinition of the instruments of power took
form with the headquarters of Weyerhaeuser Co., a
forestry company, outside of Tacoma, Washington. The
new building was designed by Skidmore Owings and

Merrill (SOM) with landscape architects Sasaki, Walker
and associates and completed in 1971. As a preliminary
sign of a new approach to corporate management, the
project was significantly transposed by executive order of
president George H. Weyerhaeuser by shifting the design
from the authorship of Gordon Bunshaft in the New York
office, to the management of Edward C. Bassett of the
San Francisco branch; because a Western architect was
proclaimed "more compatible" with the task.[6] It turned
out to be, for SOM San Francisco, the first major statement on the ex-urban corporate office type. The project
embodied the thematic of soft power in two central
techniques of environmental control: first, by being a
pioneering experiment in adopting the *Bürolandschaft*
system for its interior, and second, through its advanced
attempt at complete integration with its surrounding.
It was as a result described as a "building that makes its
own landscape", a dam, or a horizontal skyscraper. These
depictions, whether impressionistic or metaphorical,
expose the inherent difficulty in describing the project
through contemporary architectural terms. What is made
clear however, is its intentional ambiguity which blended
the physical and the managerial, to the point of absolute
identification. This ambiguity is pursued through the
simultaneous, relentless redesigning of internal and
external landscapes.

5. Ibid.
6. Dean, "Evaluation of an Open Space
Landscape: Weyerhaeuser Co.," *AIA Journal*
v.66, no.8 (July 1977), 40.

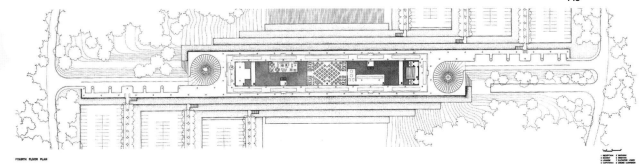

∧ **The entrance (fourth) floor plan show-ing the column diagrid and recessed building envelope.**

The architecture of the project, organized in five deep office floors, supports its ambivalent apprehension as a building-turned-landscape: recessed strips of windows amplify the extreme horizontality of its layout; the receding slabs, terraced and vegetated, neutralize its massive impact, and its location on the valley's floor, above a natural reflecting pool, consciously act as to diffuse and naturalize its presence. The siting, specifically, is not only a refined expression of the interdependency between environment and architecture, but exposes a sublimation of forestry techniques and their application through design terms. As opposed to being a building in a garden, the project is implanted within a selective forest clearing that leaves, according to Pete Walker, a "naturalistic edge to the site": figure and ground are hence reversed at the outset, only to have their tracks covered over time by the careful orchestration of foliage.[7] This radical proposition is further developed, from the inside, through a deliberate collapsing of surrounding views, planted vegetation and works of art, which amalgamate to enhance a striking effect of seamless continuity, prompted by uninterrupted glazing. The diagrid structural organization allows for deep sight lines and enables the *Bürolandschaft* system itself.

The Office Landscape system, originating in Germany, was developed by the Hamburg based Schnelle brothers as part of their work with management consultants at the end of the nineteen fifties. In the European context, the *Bürolandschaft* schemes produced in these years, in projects such as the BP prototype in Hamburg and the Osram offices in Munich, integrated the newly introduced technology (in European terms) of air-conditioning, to create deep floors of highly versatile working schemes. The system was first introduced in an American design publication in 1964,[8] soon after, it was being experimented with in individual floor plans in different parts of the country. While considered to be a European innovation, the system was in fact based on earlier American conceptions of increased communication and productivity, wrapped in the terminology of system analysis and cybernetics and presented as a smooth, designed environment. The fundamental

difference between the office organizations produced in Germany, Sweden or the Netherlands and their American counterparts is to be found in their political aspirations. While the Continental European instances implicitly proclaimed a social-democratic agenda of decentralization and cooperation,[9] American corporate structures soon internalized and appropriated the system for their own needs of increased efficiency and control, resulting in its subversive incorporation.

The Weyerhaeuser project elucidates this process and its implications, precisely when set in opposition to an immediate precedent, the 1964 John Deere Headquarters in Moline, Illinois, designed by Eero Saarinen.[10] The latter was cited by Reinhold Martin not only as a mature project of an architect whose oeuvre became synonymous with the corporate soul, but as an exemplar of an environment in which communicational flows bind humans and machines under the same imperatives only to result in curious disintegrative moments of design; the entropy nested within organization itself.[11] Advanced as the project was in articulating an organicist setting for the managerial exercise of power, it still lacked in flexibility and integration—in other words, in its softness—when seen against the Weyerhaeuser undertaking. These differences are evident both in its landscape as in its interiors. The divergence of site design lies in the strategy of diffused cultivation. While the Deere building creates its own landscape, it nevertheless adheres to the modern paradigm of the inherent antagonism of interior and exterior, which in Weyerhaeuser is transcended and transformed. In its interiority, Saarinen deployed the open plan only to a limited extent, organized rigidly around the hardware of communication and company hierarchies This compromise was annihilated by SOM in the supply of a constantly changing office configuration, taken on by a new regimen of corporate managers. Weyerhaeuser took the idea of the continual reorganization of the interior very seriously (and, one might say, very literally), employing an in-house space planner to manage the relentless change in spatial relations in accordance with corporate strategy. Curiously,

7. Not surprisingly, landscape architect Pete Walker referred to its site design as "forest management... more than landscape design." See Montgomery, "A Building that Makes its Own Landscape," *Architectural Forum* v. 136, n. 2 (March 1972), 20.

8. For the system's first introduction to American audience, see "Office Landscape: Interior Design Data," *Progressive Architecture* Vol. 45 (September 1964), 201-3

9. It was the same underlying political agenda that soon challenged the assumptions of Bürolandschaft in Continental Europe and

proposed, with the development of strict regulations prompted by workers organizations, alternatives such as Herzberger's "communal" offices in the Centraal Beheer project and the cellular office/common spaces model, which prevails to this day as a preferred organizational scheme.

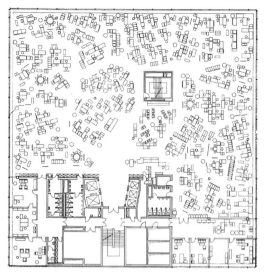

^   In the Weyerhaeuser project, the open
office scheme was turned into an environment
of executive coercion.

^   The European version of a *Bürolandschaft*
scheme, designed by Walter Henn for the Osram
Offices in Munich.

this technique of relocating a third of the work force every year was understood to be the most efficient response to changes in company structure. While the in-house planner estimated the adaptation period to be ten to fourteen days after a major change, the company's manager of corporate services calculated the costs of the changes to be substantially lower than in parallel systems of cubicle space. The employees, at least according to some reports, were happy with the system.[12] In Weyerhaeuser therefore, the environment as such—from the microscopic to the visual, the intimate to the social—becomes the medium for the exercise of soft power; its rearrangement, manipulation, camouflaging and alteration becomes the tactics of effective subordination. From the extensive deployment of vegetation, to the innovative use of "white sound," and the infiltration of top executives into open office arrangements, the design of interiors in the Weyerhaeuser headquarters projected, first and foremost, a politicized landscape in which people were co-opted to work with the corporate plan; to do as it wished and to want what it wanted.

And thus one ventures beyond the historical and conceptual boundaries of Martin's ideas. Whereas his reasoning of the *organizational complex* and its architectural register—the curtain wall—can be immediately applied in the John Deere building, it is short circuited in the doctrinal shift from Bunshaft to Bassett, from building to landscape and, one might say, from East to West. The Weyerhaeuser project invalidates the signifying role of the building envelope (by avoiding it altogether), and pursues a localized architectural strategy that is anchored in the particularities of a natural resources industry and

the functions of its advanced stage. In its working, it also changes the modern notion of modular flexibility to become an integrated biome of perpetual change. It is within this setting that design is repositioned. It is not merely a peon in the race for communication and efficiency; it is pulled off the universal grid to be redefined as the agent of ideology. Acting as everything—from an expression of values, to a representation of processes, to the analogy of power—design becomes an applied string-theory of corporate ideation, operating in a total landscape. However, while the Weyerhaeuser project stands for a short-lived promise of a reciprocal relationship between the architectural and the political, one must be careful for what one wishes. Banham's wild techno-optimism and hopes for individual freedom were eventually contained in an environment that might be considered as a softer physical construction. But it was, in fact, one in which the prospect of a liberating way of living in America was taken over and replaced by increased means of centralized control. Decades later, and in light of Nye's more recent analysis of America's decreasing soft power, this paradigm might be coming to an end.[13] However, one should question whether the presentation of more "casual" and "democratic" corporate environments in the Silicon Valley (to name the more obvious instance) is in fact an essential challenge to the logics of people management or but another illusionary moment in the larger dynamics of Taylorism in America.

. . . .   Dan Handel is an architect and writer
engaged with the intricate and ever-changing
correspondence between political thinking and
designed form.

10. Notably, the landscape schemes for both projects were designed under Hideo Sasaki and as such represent an interesting shift in his firm's approach.

11. Reinhold Martin, *The Organizational*

Complex: Architecture, Media, and Corporate Space (Cambridge, Mass.: MIT Press, 2003), 213-31.

12. Dean, "Evaluation of an Open Space Landscape: Weyerhaeuser Co.," *AIA Journal*

v.66, no.8 (July 1977), 44.

13. Joseph Nye, "The Decline of America's Soft Power: Why Washington Should Worry," *Foreign Affairs*, Vol. 83, No. 3 (May-June, 2004), 16-20.

SOFT PROGRESSIVISM IN A WASTELAND OF URBAN CODE

SCOTT COLMAN

"The integrity of its span was rigorous as the modern program itself, yet around this had grown another reality, intent upon its own agenda."
—William Gibson, *Virtual Light*, 1993

The Bridge

The central, architectural character of William Gibson's Bridge Trilogy (1993-1999)—the squatter settlement colonizing and transforming the San Francisco-Oakland Bay Bridge—first appears in "Skinner's Apartment," a short story Gibson submitted for the 1990 *Visionary San Francisco* exhibition at the San Francisco Museum of Modern Art.[1] Gibson's story follows the desperate squatters as they escape the city of San Francisco—the embodiment of American destiny—now in a state of civic decay. In a series of drawings and annotated diagrams for the exhibition, the architects Ming Fung and Craig Hodgetts felicitously rendered Gibson's San Francisco: its economy sucked pallid by Silicon Valley; its great sites of governmental occupation and public recreation subsumed by private interests; and previously vital precincts transformed into the bowels of global trade.[2] Conceiving the spontaneous annexation of the bridge by the disenfranchised, Gibson's story played out the failure of the prevailing regime to accommodate:

> The cities have their own pressing difficulties. This is not an easy century, the nation quite clearly in decline and the very concept of nation-states called increasingly into question. The squatters have been allowed to remain upon the bridge and have transformed it. There were, among their original numbers, entrepreneurs, natural politicians, artists, men and women of previously untapped energies and talents. While the world watched, and the cities secretly winced, the bridge people began to build, architecture as *art brut*.[3]

The occupation of the bridge embodies the eclipse of the modern nation state and the birth of a local, yet globally resonant, agency. The narrative of "Skinner's Room" follows the protagonist's choice to abandon her upscale apartment in the city for life on a bridge platform that is being constantly transformed by an ongoing performance of provisional assemblage—recycled wood, motors, metal, fuselage, and plastic. The story is a tale of liberation as the unfulfilled desires of a disaffected multitude search for spatial expression.

For the architecture critic Paul Goldberger, Gibson's 'vision' was an irresponsible abandonment of modern agency, and therefore an abandonment of vision as such.[4] In important ways, it is. Since the mid eighteenth century, the modern project, largely exercised in the name of the state (often the pseudonym of capital), has looked forward to a single platform that facilitates the enlightened goal of universal accommodation. Whether it's the liberal-democratic constitution, the road and rail networks, or the functionalist city, the underlying vision of modern agency foresees the institution of a frictionless, transparent system in which contingencies are absorbed and differences reconciled. The depiction of an icon of New Deal planning overrun and transformed by an alternate agenda is therefore powerfully disturbing to many.

Yet, in Gibson's diagnosis, the unaccounted detritus inevitably overwhelms and blinds this modern vision. The crisis of the modern project pervades Gibson's writing like a Bay Area fog. Nevertheless, Gibson's Western sunset evokes the dawn. His new-age settlers—the disenfranchised detritus of a systemic striving to secure the future—stake alternate, multiple, often irreconcilable, claims in the present. Seizing what is available to them, Gibson's squatters wrestle with the modern legacy, projecting it toward unforeseen ends. And just as Gibson's cyberpunk invests modern science fiction with unanticipated history, Hodgetts and Fung, in their depictions of Gibson's bridge, breathe a new, unanticipated life, into the legacy of the megastructure.

Rather than a permanent platform of modernity, Hodgetts and Fung portray a bridge fundamentally transformed by the manifold programs of its occupants. The structure undergoes a radical, unpredictable metamorphosis as the new residents transform this artificial ground for their own purposes. Rather than a fixed platform, systematically accommodating diverse and transforming programs, the constitution of the bridge is

1. Paolo Polledri, ed., *Visionary San Francisco* (Munich: San Francisco Museum of Modern Art and Prestel Verlag, 1990).

2. See the illustrations by Ming Fung and Craig Hodgetts in William Gibson, "Skinner's Room," in Polledri, *Visionary San Francisco*, 155-162.

3. Gibson, "Skinner's Room," 163.

4. Paul Goldberger, "Architecture View; In San Francisco, a Good Idea Falls With a Thud," *The New York Times*, August 12, 1990.

∧   The modernist megastructure, with an
unchanging armature, asserts the priority of
infrastructure in the infrastructure/architecture
dialectic. Le Corbusier, *Obus A Project*, Algiers,
1933. (© Fondation Le Corbusier (14345), Paris)

continuously and unpredictably altered by the power of a perpetually evolving social vision.

An ad-hoc reprogramming of hard modernism, the bridge barrio resonates with recent developments in Silicon Valley, where the emphasis has shifted from the permanence of platforms to the seductiveness of applications, or 'apps'. Today's applications make new demands on ever-more rapidly obsolescent platforms; they outlast them, migrate across them, and in large part determine their design. In its liberating, transformative occupation of modern infrastructure, Gibson's cyberpunk commune is the architectural harbinger—the application—of our time.

The Megastructure

Since the consolidation of the nation state in the late eighteenth century, architectural production and the design of infrastructure have been conceived as coincident or codependent and architecture has viewed itself as central to the modern project. So long as cities constructed infrastructure as architecture—a pure urbanism—architecture's presumption of sovereign agency made sense. But with the specialization of engineering in the nineteenth century and the development of advanced communications technology in the twentieth, architecture's role in the construction of the systems crucial to the functioning of the state has been gradually superseded.

Insofar as twentieth-century architectural practice sought to consciously reclaim this agency, however, it took up the planning of infrastructure as the basis of its speculations. One after another, modernist architects and theorists aligned the social efficacy of their visions

with architecture's capacity to constitute the enlightened state. The apotheosis of this vision, as Manfredo Tafuri has pointed out, was Le Corbusier's *Plan Obus for Algiers* (1933)—the origins of the megastructure for Reyner Banham—in which architecture became a structuring armature, wholly coincident with a regional-urban infrastructure.[5] The Algiers scheme reasserted architecture's historic connection to infrastructure and reiterated the claim of a pure urbanism. It established the ultimate promise of the megastructure: a platform upon which hitherto unaccommodated and unanticipated applications can develop. As the model was taken up in the 1950s and 60s, the megastructure remained acutely modern, conceiving architectural agency as the institution of a permanent, autonomous system that anticipates and ensures future flexibility. Even in cases where the temporal transformation or growth of the megastructure's constituting armature was conceived, these potential transformations were factored into the design of the armature itself and therefore pre-empted by the system.

The megastructure's appearance of autonomy was obtained through its structural armature's apparent indifference to the extant infrastructure on which it relied (water, power, waste, transport, etc.), even as its appearance as infrastructure was obtained by the ability of that armature to appear as found. In short, the megastructure realizes the slippage between architecture and infrastructure twice, but only to efface it, only in order to monumentally reassert architecture as infrastructure.[6] Although this reengagement with infrastructure allowed architecture to extend its claims to agency, the

5. Manfredo Tafuri, "The Crisis of Utopia: Le Corbusier at Algiers," in "Toward a Critique of Architectural Ideology," *Contropiano* 1 (January-April, 1969), Stephen Sarterelli trans. in K. Michael Hays, ed., *Architectural Theory since 1968* (Cambridge, Mass. and London: MIT Press, 1998), 25-28. Banham described

the megastructure as the apotheosis of modernism, both its fulfillment and exhaustion, "the hinge of a crisis in architectural thinking that may also prove to have been the terminal crisis of 'Modern' architecture as we have known it." Reyner Banham, *Megastructure: Urban Futures of the Recent Past* (New York: Harper & Row, 1976), 9.

6. On the slippage between architecture and infrastructure see Neyran Turan, "Editorial," *New Geographies*, no. 0 (2008): 4-5; and Neyran Turan, "Megaform," Flip Your Field: 2010 American Collegiate Schools of Architecture West Central Fall Conference, University of Illinois at Chicago, October 21-23, 2010.

∧   Hodgetts + Fung, *Untitled*, 1989; ink
and electrostatic print on paper; 5-9/16 in. x
7-3/4 in. San Francisco Museum of Modern Art.
Commissioned for the Exhibition: *Visionary San
Francisco*. (© Hodgetts + Fung)

intensification and hardening of architecture's material, financial, and disciplinary investments meant architecture became more brittle.

By contrast, Gibson's bridge, at least as rendered by Hodgetts and Fung, is unpredictably plastic. The bridge settlers transform this armature with the assumption that this platform—and the modernity it embodies—is decidedly impermanent. Without predestination, the megastructural armature becomes soft, provisionally organized material, available for creative reformation. In Hodgetts and Fung's capriccios of Gibson's bridge commune, it is not the infrastructural armature, but the architectural agency of its occupation that is emphasized. As the bridge settlers strive to construct new worlds, the architectural evidence of the manifold and changing intentions of its inhabitants piles up and the readymade armature is transformed to accommodate these ongoing, empirical investigations.

Moreover, Hodgetts and Fung's renderings of the bridge are strewn with the recognizable wreckage of the discipline's previous engagements. The spherical objects, inflatables, suspended gantries, structural props, and open scaffolds in the illustrations evoke the soft armature-less forms and arrangements—transient, instant, elastic, plastic, and pneumatic—of the 1960s and 70s. The shipping-container-like accretions echo the 'stacked-boxes' of Moshe Safdie's *Habitat* (Montreal Exposition, 1967), if not also delineating, in passing, a genre of assemblage architecture, fascinated—in its

use of corrugated iron, shipping containers, and the like—with reconstituting the material and informal refuse of the world system. An organic, sculptural form, perches precipitously in a section of the bridge that has been largely dismantled by its new inhabitants. Billowing sails, carapace-like shelters, slack Piranesian ropes, and rickety ladders lend any specific architectural character a much deeper historical context. The paddy wagon in the central foreground of one image, a symbol of authority stranded far below the active deck of this 'ship of fools', signals the political affect implicit in the collapsed temporality of the bricolage above.

In rendering Gibson's story, Hodgetts and Fung clearly embrace the soft project of the anti-establishment neo-avant-garde and its critique of modernism. Yet, many looking back to the architecture of the 1960s and 70s today, simply take this loose aggregation of objects as the evidence of architecture's incapacity, as a representational-formal model, or as a moral imperative for participatory design, when this work can be more productively conceived for its latent architectural efficacy. In this way, one might suggest Hodgetts and Fung catalogue the ongoing assertion of architecture's relative provisionality and the ability this provisionality gives architecture to denature its foundations and context. Rather than the modern vision of architecture as a hard, intransigent platform accommodating all applications, Hodgetts and Fung's renderings suggest soft, transitory architectural applications that transform their platforms.

148

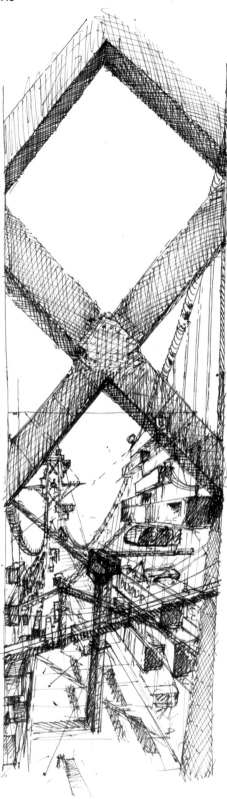

∧ Hodgetts + Fung, *Untitled*, 1989. Courtesy of the Architects. (© Hodgetts + Fung)

Platforms and Applications

Recent developments in ecological systems—from solar cells to waterless toilets to vertical farming—promise the sort of autonomy from extant infrastructures that space-age architects could only imagine. Architecture, as independent units or, more productively, in small collectives (campuses), may indeed obtain 'unearthly' self-sufficiency. This 'mobilized' architecture would be free to abandon its historical urban responsibilities. Independent of the ameliorating directives of the state, and unwed to any infrastructure, architecture has the potential to become truly projective, the collateral expression of alternate worlds and provisional associations. Nevertheless, it remains utopian to envision such free agency in a condition in which urbanism is already global and ubiquitous. In order to realize the progressive potential inherent in the dialectical slippage between architecture and infrastructure, an empirical negotiation with a socioecological landscape saturated with extant determinations is both unavoidable and imperative.

Although they now form megastructures on a vast scale, the landscapes that constitute the majority of our built legacy were formed, in fact, by a process that was the very opposite of that conceived by modern architects and theorists. Today's landscapes were determined less by the infrastructural frameworks of modernist planning than by the applications around which they were designed. Whereas in the nineteenth and early twentieth-century metropolis, infrastructure came first, awaiting application, in the late-twentieth century megalopolis, an application and its infrastructure are conceived, if not always constructed, together.[7] The suburban enclaves characteristic of this development are a testimony to architecture's seductive soft power and an indication of the potential of the discipline should it finally abandon its pretensions to act in the name of the state. Crafted to changing life style dictates, from the ranch house to the faux Tuscan villa, a ubiquitous, continental infrastructure has emerged, that, far from homogenous, has nevertheless oversaturated our available territory with a quilt of inflexible suburban patches. Each patch is specifically designed to accommodate its own built typology, infrastructural logic and dimensions, locally legislated social mores and institutions; a corporatized, suburban geopolitics largely built on the persuasive power of speculative fashion and cultural identity.[8] Globally exported, this nexus of architectural styling and attendant infrastructural armatures is rapidly becoming the normative landscape of a hegemonic economy. These settlement patterns—designed to rapidly outmoded, narrowly constructed, and commodified desires—constitute the readymade armature 'through' which any future architectural agency must be constructed.[9]

Although the development that has dominated the latter half of the twentieth century is striking testimony to the power of architectural applications to determine

7. On the differences between the metropolis and the megalopolis, see Albert Pope, *Ladders* (Houston and New York: Rice University School of Architecture and Princeton Architectural Press, 1996).

8. Albert Pope, "Blue Archipelago," *Log*, no. 5 (Spring-Summer 2005): 8-14.

9. Albert Pope, "Terminal Distribution," *Architectural Design* 78, no. 1 (January-February 2008): 20.

the design of infrastructure, the provisionality of architecture—particularly highly commodified and cheaply built architectural applications—is already beginning to leave behind an over-determined, inflexible patchwork of infrastructure without application. Faced with the irrational armatures of readymade continental megastructures, architecture today has no choice but to abandon its historical focus on the direct development of new platforms and take up the task of developing new applications for reforming old platforms.

Beyond the Readymade

The cyberpunk vision of Gibson's bridge commune and the exploration of its architectural potential by Hodgetts and Fung suggest architecture can engage the collective project at a new scale. Foregoing any statist obligation within the context of an emerging global regime, architecture can direct its agency toward developing alternate modes of social engagement.

Rather than seeking to ossify the state in its own form, a soft architecture cultivates the sovereignty of non-state actors as geographically specific and provisional acts of consent. This soft progressivism develops projective, programmatic engagements with the limitations and potentials of extant, local conditions. In this scenario, architecture obtains its socio-political efficacy through the contingent persuasiveness of designed environments.

Fully cognizant of its soft power, tactically working against the grain of today's patchwork infrastructure, the discipline might finally exercise its progressive potential. Once platform specific and dependent, we can conceive seductive architectural software that, constantly updated, migrates and proliferates, and ultimately, if only indirectly, anticipates and precipitates new platforms. Therefore, far from denying the historical role of infrastructure in the formation of our built environment and subjectivity, engaging the architecture-infrastructure dialectic realizes architecture's capacity to effect new subjectivities, directly, through the reform of extant infrastructure and the full gamut of local architectural effects, and indirectly, in the development of applications that affect the transformation of global systems. Urban systems respond to the development of architectural applications. Applications jump platforms. New platforms may be designed differently. But, most importantly, extant platforms are reformed and supplemented.

The need to engage architecture's softness, and the revolutionary capacity this softness allows, is a consequence of the brittleness of the systemic structures—both material and immaterial—that a progressive agenda seeks to abandon or reform. Successive occupation dissolves the hard logics of functional structure into a dynamic ecology.[10] Free from the State and of modernity's singular claims, a progressive architecture might realize its soft power as never before: the optimism of a disequilibrating, rather than homeostatic, social vision, ceaselessly constituting and reconstituting subjectivities and socioecologies. The seduction of an alternate program, soft progressivism leverages acquiescence. It wagers apparent weakness. The hard logics across which it plays out may appear to be reinforced, but they are inevitably questioned, reconstructed, and altered. From Detroit to Dublin infrastructure lays fallow, its complicit architectural applications abandoned or never adopted, a wasteland of urban code. Indeed, architecture's most saleable protocols are suspect in far less extreme conditions. Unstable applications undermine even the most rigorous platforms. Reprogrammed or forsaken, infrastructure only remains indelible within the history of cities. The apparently hard proves remarkably soft. Gibson's bridge is everywhere.

∙ ∙ ∙ **Scott Colman teaches architectural history, theory, and design at Rice School of Architecture.**

10. Scott Colman, "Float On: A Succession of Progressive Architectural Ecologies," in Lisa Tilder and Beth Blostein, eds., *Design Ecologies: Essays on the Nature of Design* (New York: Princeton Architectural Press, 2010), 146-163.

AMBIVALENCE AND/OR UTOPIA

BENJAMIN H. BRATTON

It is useful to begin an investigation on the troubled relationship between urbanism and futurity by citing the dictum by that famous British urbanist, J.G. Ballard, which says that "sex times technology equals the future"[1] and for our purposes modify it slightly but without changing its essential meaning to 'political theology times technology equals the integral utopia.' That is, the historical temporality of the city is, as Walter Benjamin has already argued, bound to the rhythms of theological and prophetic history and in the guise of the city, that prophetic economy takes the form of utopia and dystopia.[2] In this, Urbanism is not only the design of systems in the spatial present but for better and worse, a politico-theological projectionin which real cities always exist in some fallen simulacrum of an eventual ideal. Among these, the aspiration of security as a utopia of urban interfaces is most compelling.

Utopia is essentially both a political and an urban-geographic function and it not only depends upon futurity, it produces futurity as a space to be described and filled with peace or war. Unlike cities in the real world, utopias are bounded totalities, enveloped singularities, from the Jerusalem that was the geographic center of the world, to the island jurisdiction of Thomas More, to Theodor Adorno's insistence in conversation with Ernst Bloch that the utopian impulse is not one of positive reform but of complete transformation of the totality of what is, up to and including the apparent reality of death.[3] But what is their use today? Against disavowals that the twentieth century was a bloodbath of totalitarian utopias, Alain Badiou demands that it was the transformative spirit, despite their failure, that must inspire and inform a continuous push toward a total transformation. So is Fredric Jameson's oft-repeated line—"it is easier to imagine the end of the world than the end of capitalism"— even still true?[4] Was it less true at the end of 2008 than now in 2011, when after the storm, we have blithely resumed business-as-usual and officially wasted a good crisis?

But we are hardly lacking in utopias and utopians: capitalist, critical, green, securitarian, sacred; it is this surplus of utopias that presents the problem. First let's be clear—whatever "end of history" began in 1989 and ended in 2008,

it was in no way the eclipse of utopia as some who believe themselves dispassionate pragmatists would have it. The flat earth of digital globalization was nothing if not intensely utopian. Cities too were adorned with a new brotherhood of obelisks to this new "post-utopian" order, predicated on the cargo-cult economics of Bilbao effects and affects. And, of course, this era was punctuated by the destruction in New York City by the utopian urbanist Muhammed Atta, whose master's degree in Urban Planning described the segmentation of Aleppo, Syria into Islamic and Western zones. In Atta's account, the immunity of the former could be protected from the dangers of the later as well as his mortification at the mistreatment of the twin towers of the Gates of Al Basir. His utopian security urbanism was to sacrifice one set of twin towers to save another.[5]

What about our Urbanism? Cambrian lurches forward in design ecologies tend to occur in response to an emergency, often a war. Recently, design has been asked to choose between two meta-emergencies: 1. Ecological deterioration or 2. Securitization/the war on terror. Lines are drawn. Use cases are modeled. Budgets are allocated. And now, the financial crisis adds a third meta-emergency/ productive constraint, against which design thinking can push. The three work in combination and in competition for prioritization.

These crises are predicated on a shared set of techno-logical developments and perspectives. Urban computing, ubiquitous computing, augmented reality, and so forth, direct our attention to the interfaces between urban software and hardware as critical design points. The realities of climatic, ecological, natural and energy economies as limit conditions on urban systems focus attention on every point within that system as a interfacial transference point to be interrogated or optimized. For security, the permanent emergency of potential, exceptional violence recasts every partition, aperture, or choke point as a site of governance for the generalized interior and the immunity of the aggregate urban body. The utopia of security might even be defined as the aspirational notion that the polymorphous, polyspatial and polytemporal interfaces of the city can be known and governed in total and as a totality.

1. *J.G. Ballard: Quotes*, edited by Mike Ryan, V. Vale (San Francisco: RESearch Publications, 2004).

2. Walter Benjamin, *The Arcades Project*, edited by Rolf Tiedemann and Howard Eiland (Cambridge: Belknap Press of Harvard University, 2002).

3. "Something's Missing: A Discussion between Ernest Bloch and Theodor W. Adorno on the Contradictions of Utopian Longing, 1964," in Ernest Bloch, *The Utopian Function of Art and Literature: Selected Essays*, trans. Jack Zipes

and Frank Mecklenburg (Cambridge: The MIT Press, 1988).

4. I don't think anyone knows for certain the origin of this now famous bot mot, but it is often, and with good cause, referenced to Fredric Jameson, "Future City," *New Left Review* 21, May-June (2003). However in this article Jameson himself attributes the quote to "someone once said.."

5. This line is drawn from Roger O. Friedland, "Money, Sex and God: The Erotic Logics of Religious Nationalism," *Sociological Theory*,

Vol. 20, issue 3, November (2002): 381-425. To my mind, this essay remains the most provocative reading of Atta's motivations and the complexity of the dark utopiansm that drove his violent vision of the symbolic city.

6. "Something's Missing: A Discussion between Ernest Bloch and Theodor W. Adorno on the Contradictions of Utopian Longing, 1964," in Ernest Bloch, *The Utopian Function of Art and Literature: Selected Essays*, trans. Jack Zipes and Frank Mecklenburg (Cambridge: The MIT Press, 1988).

So then, it is not the utopian versus the realist, but the multiple utopias, open utopias and closed, fully operational at once and co-occupying the same location: totalities on top of totalities. In thinking about the futurity of urbanism, what I want to sketch is how this interlacing of utopias, one involving the other, even through the medium of a single urban form, defines the present.

Mumbai

Consider by way of parable the attacks in Mumbai on civilians by Laskar-e Taiba. The Pakistani state within a state, was armed, it is believed, with an array of sophisticated, but off-the-shelf personal locative media tools: satellite phones, stolen SIM cards, encrypted email, Google Earth and Google Maps to plan and organize the mission. Laskhar's utopian urbanism is predicated on an expansive geographical vision of Dar-es Islam, whereas the cosmopolitan logic of Google and Google Earth is a singular denuded space into which competing claims can be enveloped. I think one lesson of Mumbai is less that Jihad can fit within Google Earth but rather that Google Earth fits within Jihad. Just as fundamentalism is a function of Modernity, Modernity becomes a function of fundamentalism. The open utopia of Google Earth's cosmographic capacities are instrumentalized by fundamentalist politico-theological geographies, such that one space can interweave through the other in the same projection. And again, their interweaving and interdependency produces the space of their encounter. Whatever highly conditional equivalence or exchangeability exists is not an a priori feature, but the result of the real operations of encounter. In other words, this space of this interlacing of utopias is made and thereby entered into, or not. Again, after Adorno, "but in that we travel there, the island of utopia rises out of the sea..."[6]

USA Embassy

We are overwhelmed today by a surplus of now ubiquitous, even normative utopianisms, both of openness and closeness at once, and this is rendered in the official symbolism of the State. While the new American embassy in Berlin by Moore Ruble Yudell, constructed during the Bush-era, didn't bother to even suggest civil space or civilian purpose, others do. Consider Kieran and Timberlake's winning American Embassy in London design, which was quickly derided for its schizophrenic posture to the world, at once transparent glass and defensive bunker; an ambivalent posture for global presence in the Obama era. Or Morphosis' CalTrans where dynamic, expressionistic forms look like public sculpture but perform as martial security program: precisely decorative camouflage. Our attempts to reconcile the demands of open and closed within the same architectonic entity, whether a building or a city, means interweaving the open and closed into one—liberal cosmopolitan urbanity interlocked with control society partitions and surveillance sorting. Enlightenment transparency plus gated bunker: a typology we could call the "Glass Fort." What is the effect? This interweaving of

both into a single fabric and single body makes for densely reversible political boundaries and interiorities collapsing on themselves and, less for the vast pens of Giorgio Agamben's canonical model of "the camp" as the space of universal exception, but for soft and provisional camps, furtive moments of mundane exception, closely sandwiched between interfaces of generalized freedom and mobility.[7]

San Diego

In San Diego, the affluent Global North directly abuts the Global South. Along with Tijuana, the border towns and the maquiladoras it should be viewed as a single indissoluble urban form bifurcated by an international border into two formal jurisdictions and two socio-economic realities. The border, like any interface, activates as much energy and information as it cleaves and suppresses, and while there are persistent calls to finalize a West Bank style total wedge, from the Pacific to the Gulf of Mexico, the utopia of securitization that motivates this is not possible. The border economy is so deeply and thoroughly interdependent (money, goods, labor, people, data, water, food) that to imagine their final disentanglement (the sorting central to any security of utopia) is impossible. Instead the emergent conditions of flows and networks continually overwhelm the zombie jurisdictions of this prophylactic geopolitics. At Calit2 at the University of California at San Diego, in the core of the Golden Triangle, BANG Lab has launched the Transborder Immigrant Tool, a software running on inexpensive GPS cell phones that allows migrants attempting to cross the dangerous desert to find fresh drinking water. This is one example of how security lines produce complex interfacialities that are as productive of new modes of political subjectivity, in this case a "user" halfway between homo sacer and full citizen, beyond security's capacity to control.

Jerusalem

Jerusalem is in so many ways archetypical of this interweaving. The physical city constitutes the material signified for the sacred maps of three major religions, one layered on top of another, one woven through another. History and prophetic future are differentially activated for Jews, Muslims and Christians, constituted by the imaginary architectures of rebuilt temples, original foundations, polydimensional boundaries and land rights codes, and of course, a blunt wedge introducing an artificial canal between spaces which torture the limits of legitimate jurisdictionality. But the boundary of this camp condition is not only at the external membrane of official Israeli territory. Like the international borders held deep within landlocked airports that sit nowhere near another country, it is inside Jerusalem, with the ubiquitous checkpoints, that the political envelope of interior and exterior is repeated again and again. These checkpoints infinitely multiply the border interface while internalizing it (lots of little within big) like some self-reproducing fractal fold into the interfaces

7. Giorgio Agamben, *Homo Sacer: Sovereign Power and Bare Life* (California: Stanford University Press, 1998).

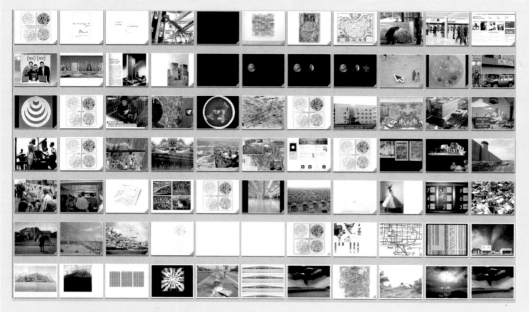

∧   Image by author

of everyday life, effectively dissolving the politico-theological imaginaires of the civil war of Abrahamaic monotheism into the symbolic realities of everyday urbanism. Finally, it is no clearer there than here—where the secular economy is predicated on military segmentation and where military segmentation is built on the secular economy—their association is concretized in the governed interfaces of mutual immunization.

Surplus of Utopias

"Imagine no lines," is the manifesto of security experts, as in no frontlines to definitely site war and no clear interior demarcated by exterior membrane. But this infinite smoothing is another name for what Paul Virilio called "Pure War" is the same thing as "imagine nothing but lines", where the infinity of smoothness proves upon more granular inspection to be infinite striation.[8] The reversibility of the line and the no line is mirrored in the reversibility of the open and the closed within the same architecture. Just as for the embassies, the paired demands of open liberal democracy and its open transparent interfaces and the western hegemon under siege from multitudinous enemies, open and closed, democratic and martial, co-occupying the same structure and the same architecture, less juxtaposed than interwoven one within the other like two solutions that won't dissolve, threads in same quilt.

No dichotomy between soft systems and hard systems can last long under such incessant inversions. Or perhaps it is the persistence of the dichotomy itself which allows for these oscillations between soft targets that become hardened and hard targets that become squishy to continue in this way, and to serve the needs of its programs so efficiently: decorative camouflage, the theater of security, the spectacle of transparency, the proscenium of public infrastructure. The hard is what gives the un-politicized flux of soft architecture its alibis, the soft is what gives the stale authority of the hard its claim on institutionality. They are complicit, the hard and the soft. For Michel Serres information and language soften up the hard things of the world.[9] But as Jean Genet plays out for us in *The Balcony*, this is a political pantomime, the soft dressing up in the cop suit of the hard, the hard escaping out the back door in the streetwalker's costume of revolution: it's a drag show.

So what then? Only more questions: is it the surplus of utopias that is preventing macrostructural political will to act on a planetary level, precisely because it sublimates too much energy into realm of the imaginary? Are these dreamworld fragments recoverable? If Romanticism is the will to lost unity, and utopia the will to potential totality, can there be an anti-romantic utopianism? A catastrophe without melancholy? For cosmopolitics can there be a true plurality of utopias, not a totality of the multiple, but like cities or as cities, a multiple of totalities?

8. Virilio's use of the term Pure War is considered in detail in the book of the same name, *Pure War*, edited by Sylvere Lotringer (Semiotext(e), 1998).

9. See the chapter, "Boxes" in Michel Serres, *The Five Senses, A Philosophy of Mingled Bodies* (Continuum Press, 2009).

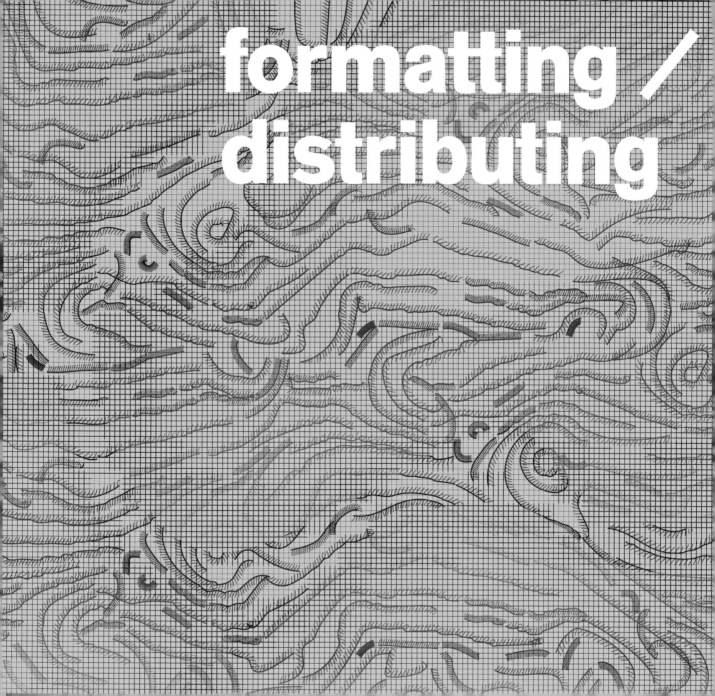

formatting /
distributing

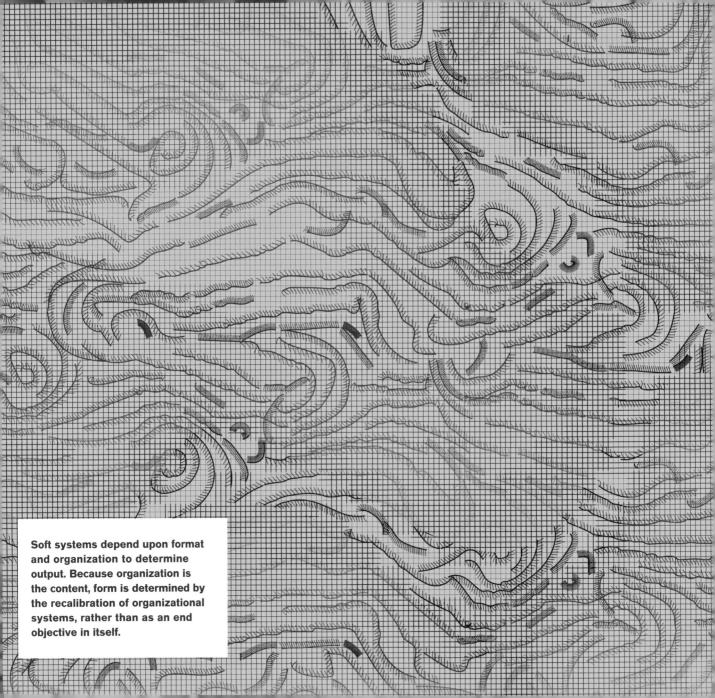

Soft systems depend upon format and organization to determine output. Because organization is the content, form is determined by the recalibration of organizational systems, rather than as an end objective in itself.

DREDGE

STEPHEN BECKER, ROB HOLMES, TIM MALY, BRETT MILLIGAN

∧ Dredging of the Port of Fremantle's Shipping
Channels, 2010, Perth, Australia. Image courtesy
of NearMap, 2011. (Permission granted under site's
standard free commercial license)

A continuous stream of shipping barges pass along the Mississippi River Delta, moving over 350 million tons a year through its three largest ports. Of those, the Port of South Louisiana alone stretches eighty-seven kilometers along the Mississippi, and annually sees some four thousand ocean-going vessels and fifty thousand barges.[1] It is the largest tonnage port in the Western Hemisphere and the fifth-largest in the world.[2] To maintain this logistical flow, channels must be kept clear; their size and depth determined by the needs of the international shipping industry.

This is no small task, given the two hundred million tons of sediment that are carried down the river every year.[3] Much of this sediment is washed out to sea or deposited inoffensively along the banks, but a significant portion of it comes to rest in industrially inconvenient places. In the Army Corps of Engineers' (USACE) "Mississippi Valley" district, around ten million tons of such sediment must be shifted each year.[4] The channels are dredged, and refilled, dredged and refilled, in a constant battle between economics and ecology.

Sisyphus Climbs the Hill

At its core, dredging is an excavation operation carried out at least partly underwater, with the purpose of gathering up bottom sediments and disposing of them at a different location. Dredging is "used to improve the navigable depths in ports, harbors and shipping channels, or to win minerals from underwater deposits. It may also be used to improve drainage, reclaim land, improve sea defense, or clean up the environment."[5] The most common purpose is to counter the

1. Robert E. Randall, "Dredging in the United States," in *Dredging in Coastal Waters*, ed. D. Eisma (London: Taylor & Francis, 2006), 157.

2. Port of South Louisiana, "Port of South Louisiana," http://portsoflouisiana.org/documents/port_profiles/South_Louisiana.pdf.

3. USGS, "Spatial Patterns of Sediment Concentration," http://co.water.usgs.gov/sediment/conc.frame.html.

4. Robert E. Randall, "Dredging in the United States," in *Dredging in Coastal Waters*, ed. D. Eisma (London: Taylor & Francis, 2006), 148.

5. Gerard H. van Raalte, "Dredging Techniques; Adaptations to Reduce Environmental Impact," in *Dredging in Coastal Waters*, ed. D. Eisma (London: Taylor & Francis, 2006), 1-2.

∧   Close up view of dredged sediment being
pumped onto a manufactured marsh platform.
Louisiana, East Timbalier Island. (Erik Zobrist,
2000, courtesy of NOAA Photo Library)

∧   USACE Passive Dredge Collectors, in
operation near Louisiana's Biloxi State Wildlife
Management Area.

forces of gravity and erosion manifested as clogged waterways or disappearing coastline.

Classic dredging operations treat dredge as a linear proposition.[6] A dredging machine —typically a barge fitted with scooping ("mechanical") or vacuuming ("hydraulic") components—arrives at the site and begins collecting sediment. That sediment is transferred off-site via pipeline, barge, conveyor belt, truck, or some combination thereof. The sediment is then disposed of at another site, either through underwater dispersal, contained land placement in fields, pits and other receptacles, or the creation of new coastline.[7]

The great irony of dredge is that dredging contributes to the acceleration of the very forces which it is intended to counter.[8] As the rivers and coastlines where dredging occurs are dynamic, unstable environments, loosening and transporting sediment tends to further destabilize these landscapes, causing more erosion and siltation. Dredging thus begets more dredging, and is situated within a wider network of anthropogenically accelerated sediment handling activities and practices.[9]

A Tour of Sisyphus' Domain
Dredge can be understood as a soft system at two levels. First, there are the techniques, technologies and tools used in the management of landscapes of dredge. This kind of softness might be described as *operational softness*. The second order of softness is defined by the contemporary shift in dredging process from linearity towards feedback and cyclicality. Whereas operational softness is concerned with discreet instances of dredging, this is *systemic softness*, encompassing

the entire set of interrelated processes and landscapes of the vast dredge cycle. At all scales—from a flimsy silt fence to regional dredge management plans—dredge is a malleable set of tactics responding to an ever-more affected terrain.

Anticipation and Flexibility
The expansion of dredge beyond barges in a river can first be seen in the proliferation of preventative techniques. Erosion control is anticipatory; for instance, planting to arrest the anticipated erosive action of water on slopes and stream banks precedes any actual threat. However, vegetation takes time to grow and many projects require a faster solution. For this reason, a variety of geotextiles have been developed.

On land, silt fences are installed prior to the commencement of new construction, anticipating the loosening of the sediment. In water, turbidity curtains are placed around an area before dredging begins, to both arrest fluid motion into the dredge zone and to reduce the movement of suspended sediment

out of the dredge zone. When flooding threatens to turn land into water, sandbags are deployed as emergency levees.

One anticipatory technology, which is directly linked to dredging, is the *Passive Dredge Collector* (PDCs). Derived from submersible barges developed for naval transportation, PDCs are deployed to ease the process of maintaining shipping lanes in places where there is rapid accumulation of sediment. The barges are placed on the riverbed where a suite of on-board sensors allows remote operators to monitor the accumulating load. When they are ready to be harvested they rise to the surface through air ballast for retrieval and transport.

Many geotextiles are produced by TenCate, an international materials technology corporation. Perhaps their most striking invention is the hulking *geotube*; massively-scaled hybrids of sandbags and silt fences designed to be filled with the slurry byproduct of a dredging operation. They have two major functions: temporary structure and material

6. Ibid., 5. Uses the term "dredge cycle", but to refer to a linear process.

7. Ibid., 7-36.

8. Dredging contributes to the acceleration of anthropogenic processes in both large-scale (loose spill layers, poorly structured sediments created in the deposition process) and small-scale ways (release of

suspended sediments, overflow, spillage). See: Ibid., 5-7.

9. In fact, some geologists argue that—in large part because of the way humans have altered sediment transport processes—we are now living in a new geologic epoch, the "Anthropocene", which is characterized by human impact on sedimentary and

geological processes. These geologists note that this human influence constitutes a distinct and noticeable new layer in the geologic record. Elizabeth Kolbert, "Enter the Anthropocene," *National Geographic Magazine*, March 2011, http://ngm.nationalgeographic.com/print/2011/03/age-of-man/kolbert-text.

Geotubes and their applications. In the background, a worker stands by a Geotube placed near Barren Island in the Chesapeake Bay, during restoration work undertaken by NOAA. (Background photo by Chris Doley, 1998, courtesy of NOAA Photo Library)

Aerial Image of Poplar Island Restoration in the Chesapeake Bay. Located in the Chesapeake Bay, Poplar Island is a flagship example of the USACE's beneficial uses of dredge. Working with state and federal organizations, the USACE has been placing dredged sediments from The Port of Baltimore's shipping channels onto the island since the mid-1990's. This practice meets the Port's immediate need for a dredge disposal site while symbiotically creates much needed habitats for fish and wildlife, at a time when such habitat is threatened due to sea level rise. Over approximately 18 years, 40 million cubic yards of dredge material will be placed here to create 1,140 acres of manufactured island. (Jane Thomas, 2006, courtesy of The University of Maryland Center for Environmental Science, Integration and Application Network Public Image Library)

containment. The best deployments exploit both functions at once.

When they are used for containment, dredged material is pumped directly into the tubes. Purified water seeps out of the porous walls while the remaining particles are processed for fill or topsoil. They are excellent for projects with limited settling areas including water treatment, aquaculture, and industrial lagoons.

Geotubes are also semi-permanent structures that can be easily inflated, deflated, and repositioned. They are made of flexible material, so they ooze and flow to conform to the topography, however, their size and mass make them very stable once deployed. Their applications include breakwaters, dams, shoreline protection, and island creation. They are highly adaptable and it is not difficult to envision treating their hulking, undulating form as an aesthetic feature to be championed.

Adaptability is similarly displayed by cellular confinement systems, also known as *geocells*. First developed by the USACE to provide a way to lay roads quickly on unreliable terrain, they are composed of strips of material which, when pulled into tension and deployed, expand into honeycombs. The cells are then packed with material, such as sand, soil, stone, or plants. They are used for a variety of stabilization purposes including roads, slopes, channels, and retaining walls. In reservoirs and landfills they are paired with impermeable geotextile membranes to isolate the contents from the wider landscape.

Recycling, and Responsiveness

One key characteristic of the transition from linear processes of dredging to more cyclical operations is the growing re-use of dredged material. Traditional dredge techniques rely on the availability of designated 'disposal' facilities (or landfills for sediment). As these facilities have quickly run out of storage capacity, creative recycling practices have emerged by necessity. The USACE has dubbed this the "Beneficial Uses of Dredge". The list of beneficial uses includes the creation of aquaculture facilities, construction materials (such as fill and topsoil), decorative landscape products (sculpture, cultured stone, etc.), beach nourishment and shore protection, berm creation, landfill capping, land creation and improvement, creation of fish and wildlife habitats, fisheries improvement and wetland restoration. Dredge is no longer approached as a problematic material to be disposed of as cheaply as possible, but as a strategic resource.[10]

Consider the *Sand Engine*, a land creation technique currently under development. The project involves the strategic deposition of 21.5 million cubic meters of sand in the shape of a large hook projecting out from the Netherland's coastline. Using existing patterns of wind, waves, and ocean currents, the formation will gradually distribute its accumulated sand along the coast. "'Building with nature' in this way will ensure natural sand suppletion, so that the coastline grows [and] will therefore help protect the coast and create new land for conservation and recreational purposes at the same time."[11] Once set in motion, engineers will no longer have to mechanically dredge sand from some other location to replenish the beaches every five years. The landscape

10. United States Army Corp of Engineers and the United States Environmental Protection Agency, "Beneficial Uses of Dredged Material," 2006, http://el.erdc.usace.army.mil/dots/budm/intro.cfm?Topic=Intro.

11. *Dredging Today*, "The Netherlands: Sand Engine Project Starts," http://www.dredgingtoday.com/2011/01/19/the-netherlands-sand-engine-project-starts/

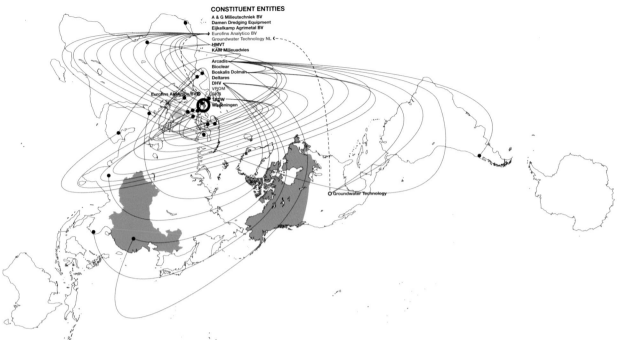

CONSTITUENT ENTITIES
A & G Milieutechniek BV
Damen Dredging Equipment
Eijkelkamp Agrimetal BV
Eurofins Analytico BV
Groundwater Technology NL
HMVT
KAM Milieuadvies

Arcadis
Bioclear
Boskalis Dolman
Deltares
DHV
VROM
JK'S
TAOW
Wageningen

Eurofins Analytico BV

Groundwater Technology

∧ Few landscaping organizations can operate at the global scale of the Netherlands Soil Partnership. The unique geographic condition of the Netherlands led the Dutch to develop world class expertise in the legislation, science, and practical tools for combating soil contamination. Key areas include soil risk assessment, remediation technology, and purity control, all of which are essential to the practice of re-use.

Success in vanquishing domestic soil contamination has led to saturation of the market. Very little local soil needs remediation, leaving companies with expertise and capital and nowhere to apply it. The Partnership is a public/private cooperative effort, which seeks to disseminate Dutch technical know-how to partner countries. In turn, new markets open for participant corporations. The result is technologies and practices—developed for a very particular need—applied to landscapes all across the globe. Whole geographies reshaped by Dutch expertise.

will do it itself. This responsive landscape is created through a combination of predictive foresight and intervention in formative processes. Responsiveness uses existing landscape forces for desired ends, rather than fighting uphill against such systems.

The process used in designing the *Sand Engine* is like forensic anthropogenic geology. The "computed morphological development" of the design is based on the integrated data of "wave fields, flow velocity fields, sediment transport fields, morphological evolution, sedimentation/erosion patterns, erosion of adjacent coastlines, necessary nourishment volumes and evolution of the dune area."[12] Yet even with this dauntingly complex foresight, the strategy still has an operational uncertainty factor of about thirty percent.[13]

Such inherent uncertainty exposes the more nebulous softness of dredge operations,

revealing the inherent lack of certainty of the effects of their own agency, even when rigorously considered. Dredge always entails guesswork and improvisation.

Embedded Intelligence and Self-Organization

The predictive foresight of the *Sand Engine* is literally and materially external to the operation. The capacity to improvise is enhanced by making dredge itself—sediments in liquid suspension—smart. Imagine embedded intelligence: predictive foresight and sentience integrally distributed within the material of dredge.

Geodetect (another geotextile by TenCate) illustrates the principle. Fiber optic sensors woven into the fabric allow it to read, with exacting sensitivity, soil structure strain and temperature changes in the terrain.[14] Given

the prevalence of geotextiles, that terrain can be virtually anywhere: from roadbeds and railways, to dikes and retaining walls, to tunnels, underground structures and pipelines. By reading signals from the intelligent fabric, operators receive early warning of dangerous geotechnical conditions, such as the imminent collapse of karst topography into underground caverns, or the destabilization of a dam. In each case, *Geodetect* renders dull and inert earth capable of reporting on its own condition, achieving a proto-integration of soil and slope. It is easy to imagine an even more extensive integration. Picture an EPA erosion-tracking program, where tiny particulate sensors are dropped into your backyard. You can watch (in cheerful timelapse) as your topsoil erodes, slides into an adjacent stream and out into the ocean, whence it is dredged to clear a channel before being deposited in a field.

12. Mulder, Jan P.M. and Tonnon, Pieter, "Sand Engine": Background and Design of a Mega-Nourishment Pilot in the Netherlands," http://journals.tdl.org/ICCE/article/viewFile/1454/pdf_357

13. Ibid.

14. TenCate Geosynthetics, "TenCate Geodetect Solution White Paper," 2010, http://www.tencate.com/TenCate/Geosynthetics/documents/Geodetect/GeoDetect%20White%20Paper%20Final%202011.pdf.

Diagram of the Dredge Cycle. Background
(Photo by Erik Zobrist, 1998, courtesy of NOAA
Photo Library. Graphics by authors)

While the original interest in soft systems in the 1970s was highly concerned with user participation, dredge systems are usually characterized by expert control and top-down command structures. This is no surprise, given that the foremost dredging organization in the United States is a branch of the Army. This structure changes in times of emergency. When soft landscapes perform their predictably unpredicted acts, the management of uncontrolled sediments becomes more spontaneous and open source.

Consider the sandbag — a vernacular technology for emergency response to natural disasters such as floods and infra-natural disasters such as levee failures. They are participatory at both a tactical and strategic scales. One of the enduring images of Midwestern floods is the chain of volunteers passing sandbags to protect the small-town levee. The sandbag is small enough, cheap enough, and simple enough that it requires little expertise. As a result, sandbag emplacements crop up around homes and businesses, at the initiation of residents, as often as at the direction of a centralized authority. With a rise in networked dredging technology, we will perhaps

see a corresponding rise in self-organizing dredge operations.

The Dredge Cycle

Most of the dredge operations and techniques outlined above are applied to single landscapes; they help prevent a neighborhood from being inundated with sediment, or reverse the erosional trend of a coastline. But as the larger and more ambitious techniques previously discussed suggest, it's the cumulative interrelationships of these landscapes that truly dictates how sediments move and come to rest. It's the co-mingled gestalt of these altered erosional trajectories that give rise to novel anthropogenic geologies. Systemic softness cannot be reduced to component characteristics, but we can nevertheless identify multiple interlocking trends within it. One of these trends is the transition from a linear process of dredge to the dredge cycle. The dredge cycle is the time-warped anthropogenic sibling to geologic and hydrologic cycles. In some places, it short-circuits or accelerates those natural cycles. In other places it puts massive reservoirs of sediment in suspended animation, resisting natural processes.

The landscapes of dredge are fundamentally indeterminate. At the same time, the dredge cycle describes a circle of emergent feedback loops. Through the forces of what might be called anthropogenic erosive entropy—the proliferation of impermeable surfaces, the intensification of storm events due to climate change, the digging of deeper and deeper shipping channels, the loosening of vast tracts of soil for development—ever more material comes under the influence of accelerated erosion. The dredge cycle is shifting away from being a closed system, where sediments are continuously shuffled and re-circulated (as water is in the hydrological cycle), and moving towards a recombinant spiral of ever-increasing girth. Indeterminacy and feedback loops together can be understood as soft systems. As we struggle to combat both of these conditions, the process of handling the material gets softer through technological advancements and the proliferation of soft methods. Indeed, the current methods by which humans maintain and shape the landscape intensifies the softness of the landscape itself. Every time Sisyphus climbs the hill, the hill shifts and is remade. This is where the architectural opportunity lies.

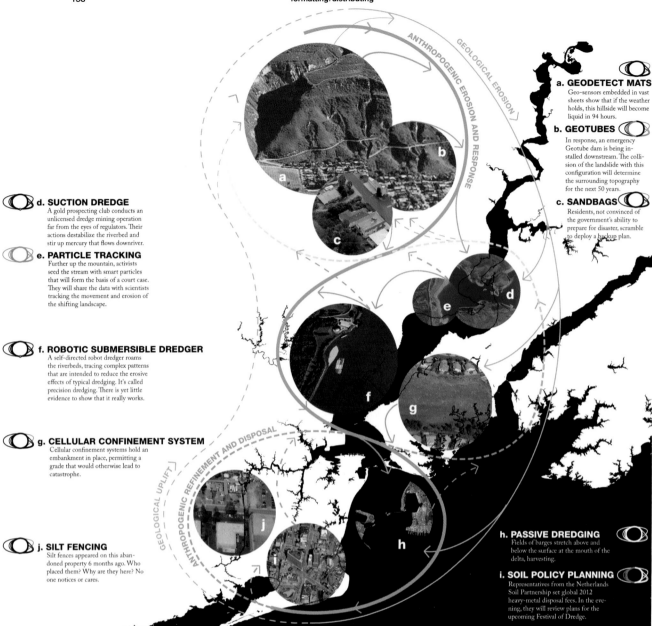

a. GEODETECT MATS
Geo-sensors embedded in vast sheets show that if the weather holds, this hillside will become liquid in 94 hours.

b. GEOTUBES
In response, an emergency Geotube dam is being installed downstream. The collision of the landslide with this configuration will determine the surrounding topography for the next 50 years.

c. SANDBAGS
Residents, not convinced of the government's ability to prepare for disaster, scramble to deploy a backup plan.

d. SUCTION DREDGE
A gold prospecting club conducts an unlicensed dredge mining operation far from the eyes of regulators. Their actions destabilize the riverbed and stir up mercury that flows downriver.

e. PARTICLE TRACKING
Further up the mountain, activists seed the stream with smart particles that will form the basis of a court case. They will share the data with scientists tracking the movement and erosion of the shifting landscape.

f. ROBOTIC SUBMERSIBLE DREDGER
A self-directed robot dredger roams the riverbeds, tracing complex patterns that are intended to reduce the erosive effects of typical dredging. It's called precision dredging. There is yet little evidence to show that it really works.

g. CELLULAR CONFINEMENT SYSTEM
Cellular confinement systems hold an embankment in place, permitting a grade that would otherwise lead to catastrophe.

j. SILT FENCING
Silt fences appeared on this abandoned property 6 months ago. Who placed them? Why are they here? No one notices or cares.

h. PASSIVE DREDGING
Fields of barges stretch above and below the surface at the mouth of the delta, harvesting.

i. SOIL POLICY PLANNING
Representatives from the Netherlands Soil Partnership set global 2012 heavy-metal disposal fees. In the evening, they will review plans for the upcoming Festival of Dredge.

∧   As the Dredge Cycle is distributed spatially and temporally in landscapes, inequalities and disequilibriums become clear. Anthropogenic uplift, for instance, operates primarily to cycle sediment at lower elevations—here, closer to the bay—producing a gradual transition of sediment from higher to lower elevations, as geological uplift occurs on far too great a time-scale to counteract anthropogenic erosion.

· · · **Stephen Becker** is co-founder of mammoth and an unlicensed architect in the Northeast.
· · · **Rob Holmes** is co-founder of mammoth and practices as a landscape architect in Virginia.
· · · **Tim Maly** is the creator of Quiet Babylon and is a writer and independent educator based in Toronto.
· · · **Brett Milligan** is the creator of Free Association Design (F.A.D) and is a landscape architect based in Portland, Oregon.

CHICAGO INSTITUTE OF LAND GENERATION

STEWART HICKS & ALLISON NEWMEYER

Chicago's Institute of Land Generation (ILG) and the Accumulation Administration, which generates and manages more salvaged land, industry, and opportunity for civil expansion than any another land manufacturer in history, had its humble beginnings in the wreckage of a ship. The night was black with new moon; thunder cracked and lightening flashed as the steamboat *The Ruetan*, captained by George W. Streeter, plowed into a sandbar hidden just below the waves of Lake Michigan. Once the storm had receded, Streeter, a seasoned circus owner, took command of the submerged sandbar and declared from the bow of his boat that the new-found land to be the sovereign United States district of Lake Michigan. Situated in the choppy waters just a few hundred feet east of the growing city of Chicago, Streeter envisioned his newly discovered land expanding into a thriving business, just as the circus had under his direction as ringmaster.

Always resourceful and ambitious, Streeter found opportunity for his recently claimed land during the tragedy of the Great Chicago Fire. Encouraging and charging contractors to dump the charred rubble remains on his claim, Streeter's empire grew wildly. Padded by donated silt from the Chicago River, the land mass was free from the regulation and rules that hindered citizens trapped within the boundaries of the city of Chicago and the state of Illinois. Soon the demands resulting from its popularity could not keep up with its growth. Streeter sold deeds to parcels at a hefty profit, maintaining his own circus inspired law. However, as Streeterville (as it is now known) grew ever closer to Chicago's shoreline, city officials ordered Streeter to turn over the land he had cultivated. A feud began as shorelines kissed. Government officials declared Streeter an illegal squatter and preparations for his removal ensued. Streeter brought in reinforcements, mooring another ship named *The Castle* and readied for battle. He guarded his claim for decades with heavy fortifications and a trained army. Streeter grew old and eventually died defending his rights and his way of life. The city, recognizing no claim to the land for any of Streeter's descendants, buried the issue. Streeterville soon became part of Chicago proper and its independent status revoked. More than a century later, as Chicago attempted to revive itself from brutal recession, the Institute for Land Generation was formed. The Institute brought new industrial economy to the shoreline, replacing the picturesque landscape with production. With the city burdened by unfinished buildings and unpaid bills, the ILG set out in the spirit of G. W. Streeter to take the wreckage of the past and rebuild with it. Headquartered in the hole of what was set to be the greatest skyscraper known, the ILG was established to produce and oversee the process of land production, and choreograph its distribution. Steered by the Accumulations Officer, materials salvaged from building demolition are transformed into P.L.O.T.s (Patties Of Land Trash). P.L.O.T.s don't reach toward the sky, but instead spread out across the horizon, redefining the role of land and urbanism in Chicago.

The distinct regional mentality of the Midwest towards the role of architecture, infrastructure, politics and the regulation of land is the pressing issue occupying the Institute. What are the possibilities afforded by newly formed P.L.O.T.'s? These land patties allow for the foundation of new political scenarios, new societies, and new relationships to land. P.L.O.T.'s provide the nutrients to grow colonies never before imagined by Chicagoans. Like bacteria, these soft colonies can multiply and grow, mutate and adapt. Each colony has the potential for a new offshore infrastructure for the mother city of Chicago. Given the exciting and unpredictable method of their growth and geopolitical situation, the city becomes a lab, experimenting with ways to make the colonies useful. Some are more successful than others.

Chicago continues to define, layer and grow land in the southwest region of Lake Michigan. Streeter's legend illustrates and typifies the cycle of conflict that results from growing land in the Midwest. From natural nuisance to debris re-distribution, the ILG generates a desirable commodity that challenges the relationship to new land that defines a particular brand of Chicago urbanism. Mistakenly, recent developments have lost sight of this uniquely Chicago tradition and the narrative presented here through text and graphics recovers, extends and ultimately exports this lineage of urban progress.

· · · **Stewart Hicks is a designer and Assistant Professor at the University of Illinois.**
· · · **Allison Newmeyer is an architectural designer, teacher and activist in Urbana, IL.**

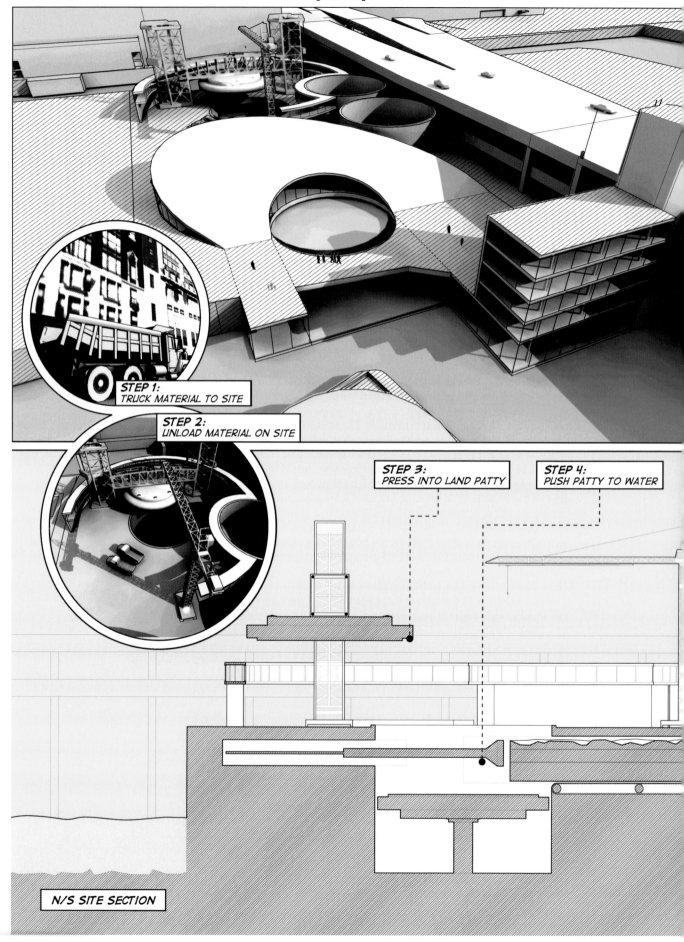

STEP 1:
TRUCK MATERIAL TO SITE

STEP 2:
UNLOAD MATERIAL ON SITE

STEP 3:
PRESS INTO LAND PATTY

STEP 4:
PUSH PATTY TO WATER

N/S SITE SECTION

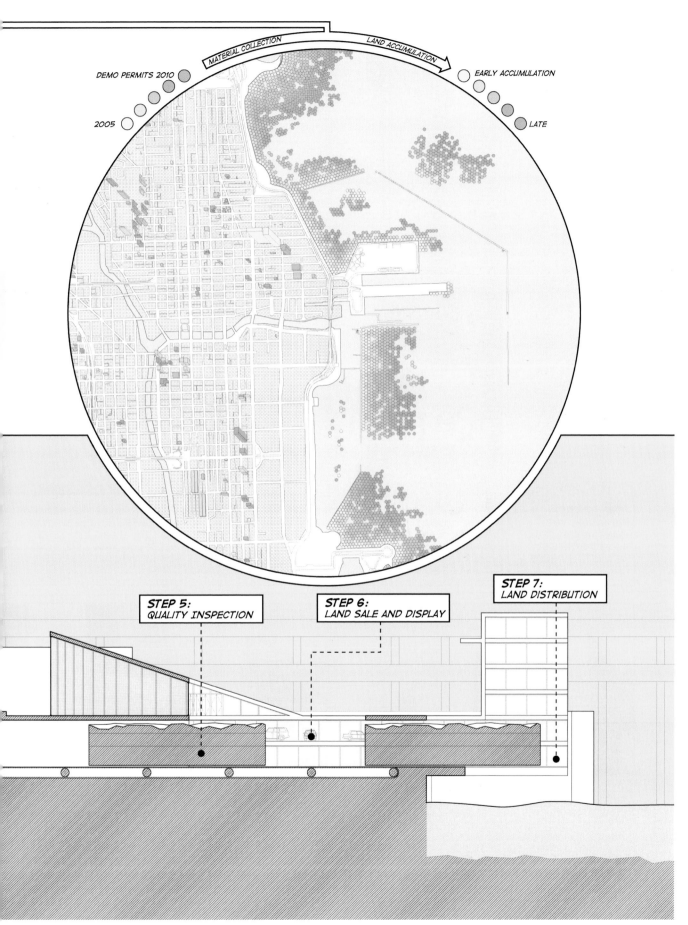

DEMO PERMITS 2010

2005

MATERIAL COLLECTION

LAND ACCUMULATION

EARLY ACCUMULATION

LATE

STEP 5:
QUALITY INSPECTION

STEP 6:
LAND SALE AND DISPLAY

STEP 7:
LAND DISTRIBUTION

A BRIEF HISTORY OF CHICAGO'S GROWING LAND

1820S

THE GRID: THE CONTINENTAL GRID WIDENED TO BECOME STREETS FOR MOVEMENT. INFINITE POSSIBILITY TO CONSUME LAND.

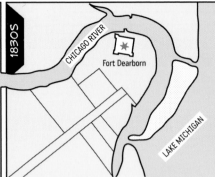

1830S — CHICAGO RIVER · Fort Dearborn · LAKE MICHIGAN

THE SANDBAR: THE CITY WAS ENGAGED IN A PERPETUAL BATTLE. THE CITY NEEDED THE MOUTH OF THE RIVER CLEAR, THE LAKE NEEDED TO DEPOSIT SAND. LAND IS WINNING.

1850S

RAISING CHICAGO: THE NEED FOR AN UNDERGROUND SEWER SYSTEM OUTWEIGHED THE LOGIC OF KEEPING BUILDINGS ON THE GROUND.

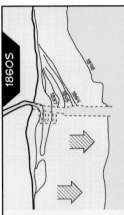

1860S

THE SANDS: REMOVING THE SANDBAR CAUSED LAND TO DEPOSIT ALONG THE SHORE LINE.

1870S

THE SANDS: THIS LAND WAS PHYSICALLY WITHIN THE CITY BUT OUTSIDE OF ITS LAWS. GAMBLING AND PROSTITUTION WAS LEGAL THERE. DURING THE GREAT FIRE, IT WAS THE ONLY LAND WITHOUT BUILDINGS AND BECAME A REFUGE FOR THE RICH AND POOR.

1871

THE GREAT FIRE: ONCE THE FIRE HAD BEEN EXTINGUISHED, THE RUBBLE WAS PUSHED INTO LAKE MICHIGAN. THE OLD CITY WAS REUSED AS NEW LAND FOR WHAT IS NOW GRANT PARK AND THE EXTENDED AREA.

1880S

SKYSCRAPER: THE FIRE CLEARED THE WAY FOR A NEW TYPOLOGY WITH A RADICALLY NEW RELATIONSHIP TO THE LAND. FINALLY THE PEOPLE OF CHICAGO WERE ABLE TO GET AWAY FROM IT TO VIEW IT ANEW.

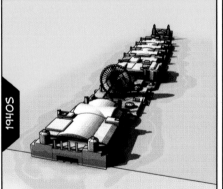

1940S

NAVY PIER: THE SHORE LINE HAS BEEN EXTENDED INTO LAKE MICHIGAN A NUMBER OF TIMES FOR DIFFERENT NEEDS. NAVY PIER WENT FROM INDUSTRY TO EDUCATION TO ENTERTAINMENT. NEW LAND IS FICKLE...

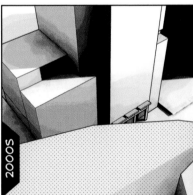

2000S

GREEN ROOFS: NEW LAND HAS BEEN LAID ON TOP OF BUILDINGS. NATURE IS TARNISHED BY OUR INTERVENTIONS AND ONLY A SEALED COVERING OF LAND CAN CONTAIN OUR MISTAKES.

INSITITUTE FOR LAND GENERATION SITE PLAN

GENERATION OFFICE
PRODUCTION OFFICES FOR LAND MANUFACTURING AND GENERATION.

OBSERVATION AND OVERSIGHT
A RAISED WALK FOR EXECUTIVES TO MONITOR OPERATIONS.

PATTY PRESS
MULTI-TON HYDRAULIC PRESS TO GENERATE SUFFICIENT PRESSURE TO FORM INSOLUBLE LAND PATTIES.

PATTY PRESS MOLD
THE FORMER FOUNDATION FOR THE SPIRE IS REPURPOSED AS A MOLD FORM FOR LAND CASTING.

RAW MATERIAL RECEIVING
DUMP TRUCKS LOADED WITH FRESH MATERIAL FROM THE CITY TO BE UNLOADED.

RAW MATERIAL STORAGE
LARGE CONCRETE HOLDING BINS FOR THE STORAGE OF BUILDING MATERIALS AND SOIL.

MATERIAL RELOCATION CRANE HAS SPECIAL MEASURING INSTRUMENTS IN ORDER TO PROVIDE THE BEST MIXTURE FOR GUARANTEED CHICAGO LAND PATTIES.

VISITOR PARKING

LAND SALES, DISTRIBUTION AND SPECULATION
HOUSES THE SALESMEN OFFICES AND MODEL LAND PATTY FOR PROSPECTIVE BUYERS TO VIEW THE PRODUCT.

NEW LAND TESTING AREA
THIS IS THE LAST STOP FOR THE LAND PATTY BEFORE IT LEAVES THE INSTI-TUTE. IT IS VISIBLE FROM THE CUSTOMER GALLERY, THE QUALITY ASSURANCE LAB, AND CAN BE EXPERI-ENCED ABOVE GROUND.

LAND BARGE DOCK
THE INSTITUTE UTILIZES THE RIVER AS A PIECE OF INFRASTRUCTURE FOR THE DISTRIBUTION OF LAND.

ACCUMULATION ADMINISTRATION AND OFFICES
THE OFFICE BUILDING HOUSES THE CITY OFFICIALS IN CHARGE OF THE ACCUMULATION ADMINISTRATION. THE ELECTED OFFICE HAS AN OFFICE ON THE TOP FLOOR WITH A BALCONY TO ADDRESS THE CITY

LAND BARGE WITH PATTIES READY FOR SHIPMENT.

DISTRIBUTION AND EXPORT

P.L.O.T. EXPORT SCENARIO
RE-SHAPING CHICAGO

SHAPING THE POSSIBILITIES

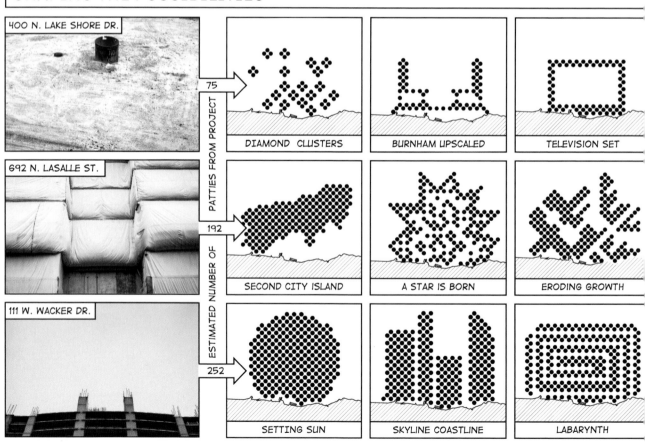

400 N. LAKE SHORE DR.

692 N. LASALLE ST.

111 W. WACKER DR.

PATTIES FROM PROJECT

ESTIMATED NUMBER OF

75

192

252

DIAMOND CLUSTERS

BURNHAM UPSCALED

TELEVISION SET

SECOND CITY ISLAND

A STAR IS BORN

ERODING GROWTH

SETTING SUN

SKYLINE COASTLINE

LABARYNTH

THE COLONIES...

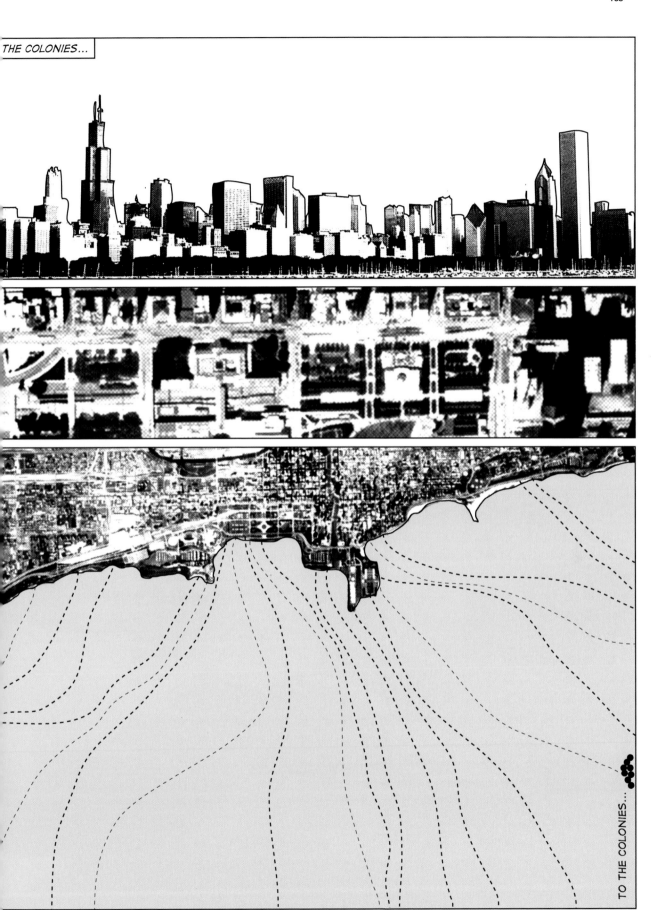

TO THE COLONIES...

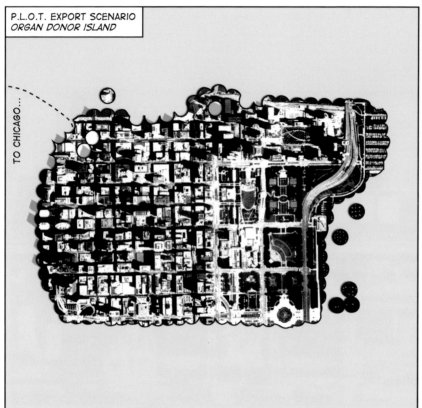

P.L.O.T. EXPORT SCENARIO
ORGAN DONOR ISLAND

TO CHICAGO...

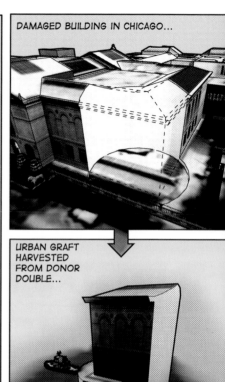

DAMAGED BUILDING IN CHICAGO...

URBAN GRAFT
HARVESTED
FROM DONOR
DOUBLE...

P.L.O.T. EXPORT SCENARIO
PRIVATE ISLAND RESORTS

CIRCLE SQUARING
ATTACHMENT

P.L.O.T. EXPORT SCENARIO
ISLAND NATION STATES

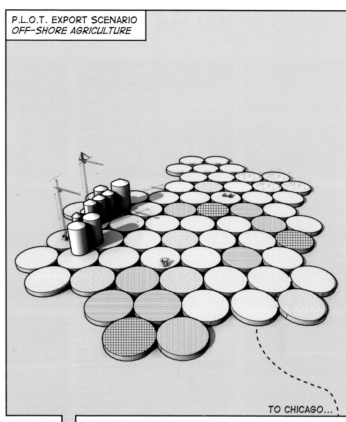

P.L.O.T. EXPORT SCENARIO
OFF-SHORE AGRICULTURE

TO CHICAGO...

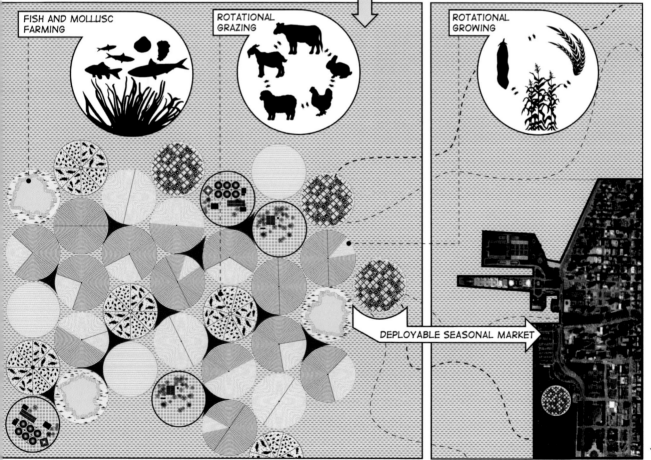

FISH AND MOLLUSC FARMING

ROTATIONAL GRAZING

ROTATIONAL GROWING

DEPLOYABLE SEASONAL MARKET

OLMSTED'S BLANK SNOW

HOLES OF MATTER / SERGIO LÓPEZ-PIÑEIRO

∧ **Chronological images of the landscape.**

Most architects and urban planners typically consider snow in terms of practical concerns such as mitigation, safety, or energy efficiency. Winter is perceived as a temporary season, while summer is portrayed as an everlasting condition. Lawn is an urban material, while snow is not. The denial embedded in this permanent "summer mindset" is no longer tenable in cities such as Buffalo. In contrast to summer's green spaces, this project demonstrates the value of winter's white spaces. *Olmsted's Blank Snow* proposes a '*whites*ward' for winter seasons, exposing how standard snow plowing practices can be considered beyond mere practical needs. This winter landscape shall be understood as a snow observation ground, encouraging the city to appreciate the accumulation of snow and how it could positively alter a city's public spaces.

Olmsted's Blank Snow is a temporary winter landscape located in the parking lot of Front Park, one of the six parks Olmsted designed in Buffalo. Due to its proximity to water and its alignment with prevailing winds, Front Park receives an abundance of lake-effect snow that is typically gathered into mounds based on the efficient relationship of surface size and location. With the ambition of transforming Front Park's parking lot into a winter garden, a snow plowing plan is implemented that locates eleven snow mounds that are the result of daily plowing—each about six to eight feet high and thirty feet in diameter—into various positions to create a winter topography. As a prototype, this project seeks to transform standard snow-plowing practices into creative tools for generating new landscapes.

When maintaining parking lots, snow-plowing crews tend to push the snow to the lot's edges to maximize usable parking stalls. Only in large parking lots—such as the ones found in American shopping malls—do crews form snow mounds in the middle of the lot. This act only becomes efficient due to the size of the snow's surface. *Olmsted's Blank Snow* gathers and consolidates the snow in Front Park as a form of design hacking. This allows for an exploitation of the spatial conditions defined by these typically overlooked snow mounds while also exposing the hidden potentials of snow removal as a winter practice that can positively transform public space. For instance, *Olmsted's Blank Snow* offers topography to an area that is otherwise flat, providing unique views to the city and its relationship to Lake Erie. This topography becomes the first public

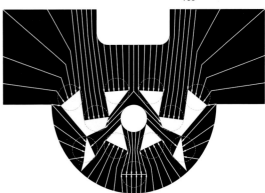

Snow plowing technique type A

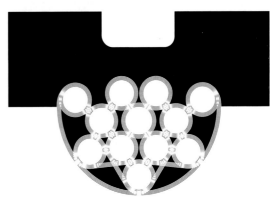

Snow plowing technique type B

∧ **Snow-plowing techniques used in the shaping of *Olmsted's Blank Snow*.**

space to welcome travellers coming into Western New York through the Peace Bridge. As such, it provides a new temporal understanding of the city, its relationship to larger climatic patterns and acts as a positive urban identifier. By opportunistically hacking the temporal, *Olmsted's Blank Snow* becomes a materialized landscape of weather.

• • • Sergio López-Piñeiro is the founder of the architectural practice Holes of Matter and an Assistant Professor at the University at Buffalo Department of Architecture.

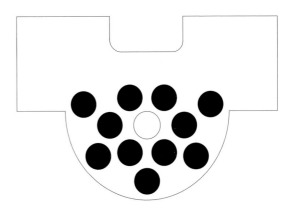

Distribution of snow mounds

∧ **Proposed distribution of the eleven snow mounds as well as the two snow-plowing techniques that would be utilized to achieve such distribution and configuration.**

January 16, 2011

February 8, 2011

∧   **Panoramic views of the winter garden.**

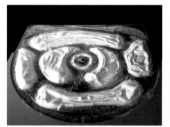

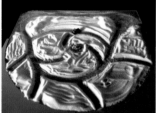

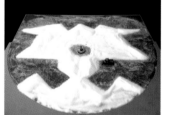

How to estimate the volume of snow that will be necessary to plow? After the snow falls on the ground, how much of it does melt, drift, compact? What is the relationship between snowfall [predicted and average] and the volume of snow to be plowed? The following figures have been used in this project:
Theoretical snow volume = 763, 720 cu. ft.
Estimated snow volume = 152, 744 cu. ft.
Attempted snow volume = 110, 490 cu. ft.

The theoretical volume of snow to be plowed is calculated based on Buffalo's snowfall annual average of 93.6".

Based on specific research [scientific publications, discussions with the park foreman, visual estimates, weather data, etc], the 'real' amount of snow to be plowed is estimated as 20% of the theoretical volume—snow melts, compacts, drifts,...

The attempted landscape is composed of 11 mounds. Weather permitting, each mound is expected to measure 42' wide and 10' tall approximately.

∧   **Several studies for different snow plowing techniques and their resulting landscapes. One of the difficulties in the design of this project was the inability to predict the amount of snowfall that Front Park would be receiving during the winter as well as the inability to estimate the resulting 'real' volume of snow that would be required to be plowed.**

Holes of Matter   Olmsted's Blank Snow

iMOBILE
OFFICE OF MOBILE DESIGN

∧ **Metamorphosis: Featuring mobile fiber connectivity and hydlar-z Kevlar panels.**

Fold-out. Plug-in. Boot-up.

The *iMobile* is an online roving business port for accessing global communication networks. Armed with the latest computer systems, peripherals, hardware and software, the *iMobile* offers building solutions for the mobile entrepreneur.

The dynamic mobile enterprise has remarkable efficiency. It is here that the workplace effortlessly evolves, enabling businesses to respond to the need for augmentation, contraction and metamorphosis. Based on an economy of movement, where form follows necessity, this adaptable and flexible structure is responsive to its immediate and shifting environment. Composed and durably constructed from a composite of Kevlar, glass and copper coated carbon fibers, this self-sufficient and relocatable structure gives shape to the metropolis of the future.

Project credits
Principal: Jennifer Siegal; Design Team: Elmer Barco, Arona Witte; Project Team: Ashley Moore, Saul Diaz, Jason Panneton; Photographer: Benny Chan

• • • Jennifer Siegal is known for her work in creating the mobile home of the twentieth century. She is founder and principal of the Los Angeles' based firm Office of Mobile Design (OMD), which is dedicated to the design and construction of modern, sustainable and precision-built structures. The winner of the inaugural 2009 USA Network "Character Approved Award" she is celebrated as a "leading innovator shaping American culture".

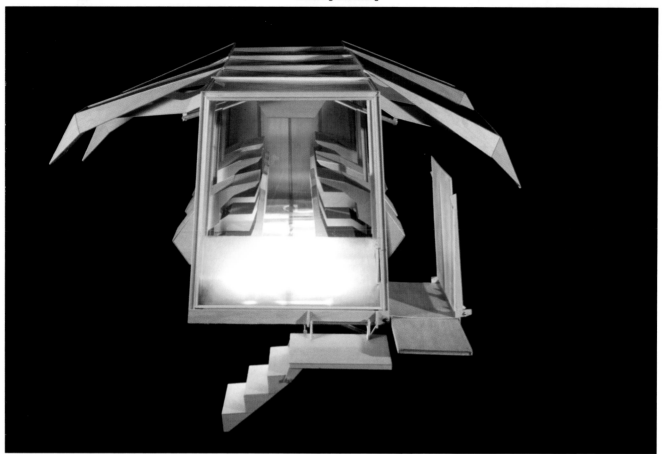

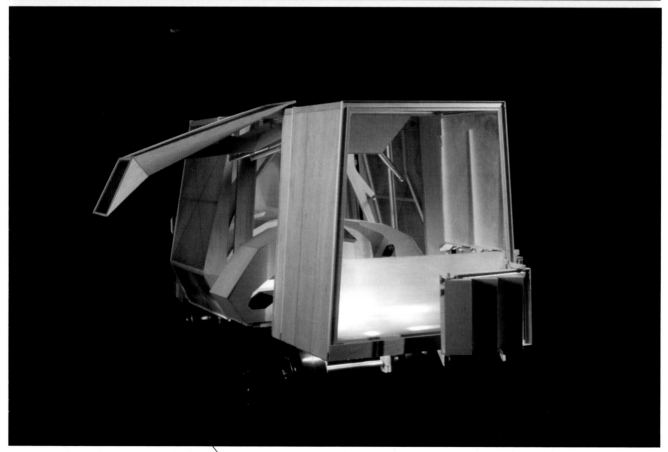

∧   **Enterprising: Featuring self-sufficient it-36 portals and retractable pneumatics.**

Office of Mobile Design   iMobile

CITY TICKETS

MAYO NISSEN

∧ Reusing existing urban infrastructure
to do more—in this case, in Copenhagen.

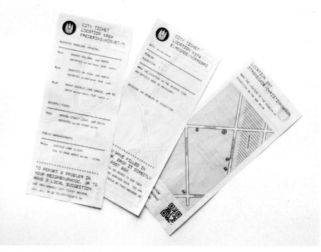

∧ Left to right: A *City Ticket* to-do list; a
City Ticket report form; the reverse, showing a hyper-local map.

∧ Each existing machine already
includes a vast array of technology. In cities
such as Copenhagen, each machine costs
about $11,000. Why not do more with it?

∧ A *City Ticket* report form being filled
out with a local non-urgent issue.

Urban infrastructure is often hidden and ignored as the technical backdrop of the city. Pay-and-display parking ticket machines are an example of an intensely technological piece of infrastructure that could be exploited to become integrated into everyday life. *City Tickets* explores how we can use these ubiquitous and expensive boxes to make cities more responsive to the needs of its inhabitants. It proposes a service by which ticket machines become a communication channel between citizens and their local authorities. Designed initially for the specific context of Copenhagen, *City Tickets* can be applied to various urban contexts, and adjusted to their unique constraints and opportunities. Copenhagen presently has two thousand suitable machines installed, while New York currently has approximately five thousand Muni-meters, which could be adapted to print *City Tickets* in addition to the parking receipts they already dispense. By taking functions otherwise found on websites or mobile devices, and physically embedding them directly into the urban fabric, *City Tickets* democratizes access and input to municipal services and brings a dialogue of the city's infrastructure to the foreground.

Citizens are empowered to report problems—whether a pothole, a damaged sign, or an awkward junction—from the bottom up. Furthermore, they can offer suggestions for local improvements that could effect discussions on various planning issues. The use of short forms

∧   A *City Ticket* to-do list, with a hyper-
local list of known issues being dealt with
by the municipality, along with their location
and estimated date of completion.

printed from the embedded receipt printer, prepared with hyper-local maps for indicating the
exact location of a problem or suggestion, allows submission of this information to the local
authority to be a straightforward task. On request of the local authority, a constantly updated
to-do list of known issues, suggestions, and plans for the immediate locality is made available
in the same manner.

 City Tickets makes the bureaucratic and opaque workings of governance more transparent
and accountable, while redefining the balance of power supporting participatory urban planning and management processes. It allows this existing infrastructure to be reconsidered as a
tool to make cities more responsive to the needs and desires of their inhabitants.

· · · **Mayo Nissen is a designer interested in
applying the methods, approaches, and craft of
interaction design to the unique and complex
context of cities.**

Nissen   City Tickets

FROM SITE TO TERRITORY

LOLA SHEPPARD

Recent discourse and practice in architecture has increasingly sought to ally itself with the fields of urbanism, infrastructure, landscape, and ecology. Yet the space in which each of these disciplines traditionally operates varies in scale, jurisdiction, complexity, and constitution, therefore complicating architecture's agency in such a relationship. Typically, architecture has been consigned to site; urbanism and landscape architecture are defined by context; infrastructure and ecology operate in the territory. If architecture is to engage other spatial disciplines in contemporary terms, it will increasingly need share their protocols; to be resilient, adaptable and responsive to changing environmental conditions. Architecture can no longer define its parameters and responsiveness at the scale of its immediate site, but rather, must operate at the scale of the broader *territory*, a space expanded and thickened with environmental data, competing social and political claims, economic forces, systems of mobility, ecological systems, and urban metabolisms. This new territory is expanded as each of these influences brings its own spatialization, producing composite, fluid boundaries; and, it is thickened by strata of information which extend from the subsurface depths of geology to aerial resources. In this scenario, territory is understood as a series of nested scales from the local, to the regional to the global.

After Site

In her essay "On Site", from the 1991 publication *Drawing, Building, Text*, Carol Burns untangles recent understandings of site. She suggests two paradigms for apprehending site: the "cleared" and the "constructed." The "cleared site" is based on the assumption that site is neutral ground, devoid of content or meaning, and dependent upon a planimetrically-based mathematicization of land. The "constructed site," Burns argues, emphasizes the visible physicality, morphological qualities, and existing conditions of land, looking at the natural and human forces that have shaped the land. In emphasizing the visual however, what is not directly identifiable is ignored.

Burns tracks the multiple notions and terms historically associated with site—the lot, the plot, location, position—all spatially and visually-based, and quantitatively determined. Burns posits a 'third' way, which proposes to look at the specificity of each site, "to discover its latent qualities or potential."[1] In this situation, an intervention becomes a reading, dialogue and critique of existing conditions, and concludes that site is "a work, a human or social trace."[2] While Burns'

proposal for a new understanding of site is provocative, it remains ultimately rooted in a legacy of the *genius loci*—teasing out the inherent, but unknowable qualities of a site, understood as an exclusively physical host.

Given the complexity of contemporary ecological and urban systems, and the increasing marginalization of architecture within an expanded discourse regarding spatial networks, this earlier conceptualization of architecture's relationship to site is, twenty years onward, too limited in scope. As we accept the notion that we have entered an Anthropocene era, one in which no region of the globe is left untouched—whether directly or indirectly—by humankind's impact,[3] every site must be understood as a palimpsest of forces. While systems such as ecology, mobility and technology manifest themselves in spatially tangible ways, others, such as political and economic forces, operate often unseen and by spatially remote means. Each, however, is central in shaping aspects of the built environment, whether financing, site selection, program, or construction methods. Traditional conceptions of site do not explicitly acknowledge the more intricate and often invisible forces at work on the environment. Territory has become the necessary scale required to register and engage the complexity of networks and information at play in a given physical environment. For architecture to think at the scale of territory does not require an amplification in size, but rather, a conceptual shift; it demands that architecture, regardless of its actual scale or extents, engage its extrinsic environment.

It is useful to acknowledge the root meanings of both site and territory to attempt to arrive at new definitions or interpretations. Site, which comes from the root of *sinere* meaning "let, leave alone or permit," is defined as "place or position occupied by something."[4] Territory, on the other hand, has more contested roots. *Terra* means land, earth, nourishment, sustenance; but the root verb *terrere* means to frighten, to terrorize. Territory is land occupied by violence.[5] In French, there exists the distinction of the *terroir*, and a *territoire*. A *terroir* designates a geographic area homogenous in terms resources and production—often related to agricultural production—and tied to distinct cultural communities. A *territoire*, on the other hand, is understood in two categories: a political or jurisdictional region, often defined by a border, and natural territories, defined by more ambiguous ecological delimitations.

The notion of territory becomes more complex when considering the condition of globalization—the spaces of information exchange, of international trade and retail, or

1. Carol Burns, "On Site: Architectural Pre-occupations," in *Drawing, Building, Text*, ed. Andrea Kahn (NY: Princeton Architectural Press 1991), 155.

2. Ibid.,164.

3. For further discussion of the Anthropocene era, see Jan Zalasiewicz, Mark Williams, "Are we now living in the Anthropocene?" *GSA Today*, v.18, no.2 (Feb 2008), http://www.see.ed.ac.uk/~shs/Climate%20change/Geo-politics/Anthropocene%202.pdf (accessed September 20, 2011).

4. Etymology of *site*, http://www.etymonline.com/index.php?allowed_in_frame=0&search=site&searchmode=none (accessed September 15, 2011).

5. David Delaney, *Territory: A Short Introduction* (Malden, MA: Blackwell Publishing, 2005),14.

of military occupation. How, for instance, can we define the site of Walmart, a military base, or a displacement camp? In these scenarios, individual sites or nodes are so integrated and dependent on larger economic or technological networks, or the by-product of geopolitical negotiations, that node and network merge into ambiguously delimited boundaries; sub-sites are nested within sites, operating at multiple scales. One might equally ask, what are the limits of a site when engaging questions of ecology? What are a site's boundaries with respect to hydrology, toxicity, or species migration? Ecosystems are increasingly understood as dynamic, subject to the influence of larger-scale flows of materials and energies.[6] Others envision ecosystems as sequences of scalar relationships, where sites display variable levels of stability and dynamism according to their size.[7]

New Cartographies: Representing Territory

Given the extent and often fluid nature of territories, cartographic representation becomes a primary method for apprehending the complexity and mutability of forces at work, but equally, in projecting potential futures. In some sense, the cartographic act becomes both the synthesis of information and the initial registration of a potential (territorial) site. Not surprisingly, Burns' understanding of site also depends upon its representation: the planimetrically-driven cleared site versus the sectionally-understood constructed site. Implicitly and explicitly, Burns acknowledges: "landscape and survey inform ways of seeing because they are forms of knowledge. Like architecture, they frame information or content; they control by establishing principles that make the world comprehensible."[8]

In the ensuing twenty years, our capacity to apprehend the complexity of territory has been amplified by the ever-increasing amount of data available. Access to environmental reports, ecological studies, economic analyses, and seasonal data, for example, offers an opportunity for the architect to acquire this knowledge, but also the need to sort, arrange, and prioritize this information in order to then find productive points of intersection.

Anthropologist Gregory Bateson, from his essay "Form, Substance and Difference" in *Steps to an Ecology of Mind* (1972), elucidates the essential impossibility of knowing what constitutes the territory, given that any understanding of it is based on some form of representation. Bateson posits that "the map is different from the territory. But what is the territory? What is on the paper map is a representation; and as you push back, what you find is an infinite regress, an infinite series of maps. The territory never gets in at all."[9] Bateson points out that the usefulness of a map (a representation of reality) is not necessarily a matter of its literal truthfulness, but in its having a structure analogous to the territory.[10] The cartographic act, in this sense, becomes the code-work for comprehending the territory. However the code-work can be re-scripted to construct new understandings of the territory, forming a feedback mechanism of information collection and production.

Architect and inventor Buckminster Fuller understood the capacity of maps to oscillate and shape our reading of the territory. In his essay "Fluid Geographies" from *Ideas and Integrities* (1963), Fuller sets up the dichotomy of sea and land to describe the dymaxion map he first published in 1927. The dymaxion representational system was the substrate by which to understand territorial relations and networks—energy, resources, migration patterns—anew. He presented two versions of the map: one that prioritized the relationships of land masses as a nearly continuous chain (in which all projective error is massaged into the oceans); and the other prioritizing the oceans as continuous. Fuller's recognition that our reading of territory can oscillate is fruitful in embracing a more complex, "softer" reading of the term. The implication of Fuller's maps is that geography can be understood as dynamic, and that the cartographic act should incite new modalities for documenting and apprehending complex territories.

Embracing the need for an expanded and more fluid understanding of context, and as a counterpart to Burns' distinctions of site twenty year ago, I would offer two conceptions of territory that have driven our contemporary understanding of context—the "layered territory" and the "networked territory." These two models correspond both to methods of analyzing and representing, but equally, to ways of conceptualizing territories.

Layered Territory

The layered territory stratifies its environment into a series of individuated layers and systems. It enables an in-depth examination of the systems—physical and natural—at work within a site, but with little focus on the interconnection or potential overlaps of these systems. Landscape architect and planner Ian McHarg brought this methodology to its apotheosis in his seminal book, *Design with Nature* (1969), which provided strategies for disaggregating a territory into its multiple uses. Such methodology focused primarily on patterns of land use and human settlements, and formed a precursor to the Geographic Information Systems (GIS), which decades later remains a powerful tool for the analysis of layers of information that can be spatially cross-referenced.

McHarg is widely credited with a revolution in the field of landscape architecture, shifting it from garden design to multi-disciplinary territorial design engaging ecology, geology, and anthropology. However, McHarg's stance throughout *Design with Nature* is largely anti-urban. While recognizing the inevitability of the built environment, his interest is in restoring the centrality of nature and ecology as the systems that determine territorial organization.

6. For a further discussion of site ecology as set of dynamic processes, see Kristina Hill, "Shifting Sites," *Site Matters: Design Concepts, Histories, and Strategies*. eds. Carol J. Burns and Andrea Kahn (New York: Routledge, 2005), 131-152.

7. For a more detailed discussion of the relationship of time, space, scale and ecological stability, see Richard T. T. Forman, *Land Mosaics; The Ecology of Landscapes and Regions* (Cambridge: Cambridge University Press, 2005), 7-14.

8. Burns, *Drawing, Building, Text*, 161.

9. Gregory Bateson, "Form, Substance and Difference," *Steps to an Ecology of Mind* (Chicago: University of Chicago Press, 1972), 460.

10. Ibid., 460.

∧ **Staten Island Study: Existing Land Use; Existing Vegetation; Tidal Inundation. (Image courtesy of Ian L. McHarg Collection, The Architectural Archives, University of Pennsylvania)**

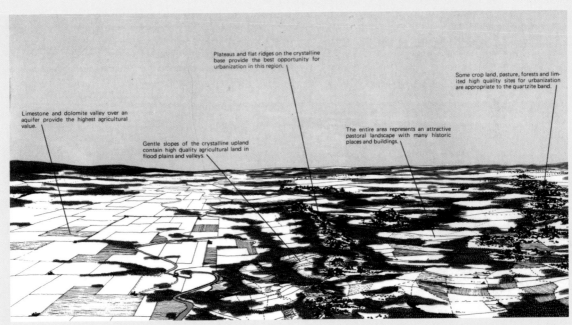

Plateaus and flat ridges on the crystalline base provide the best opportunity for urbanization in this region.

Some crop land, pasture, forests and limited high quality sites for urbanization are appropriate to the quartzite band.

Limestone and dolomite valley over an aquifer provide the highest agricultural value.

Gentle slopes of the crystalline upland contain high quality agricultural land in flood plains and valleys.

The entire area represents an attractive pastoral landscape with many historic places and buildings.

∧ **Potomac River Basin Valley Study. (Image courtesy of Ian L. McHarg Collection, The Architectural Archives, University of Pennsylvania)**

In his 1966 proposal for Staten Island, as in many of his other studies, McHarg documents—through maps, charts, and geological sections—climate, physiography, soil, geology, hydrology, vegetation, wildlife, and land uses. Within categories, gradients are further articulated, from most to least suitable use, in order to prioritize with more refinement the location of development and nature preservation. The maps expose intricate calibrations of uses, which result from "asking the land to display discrete attributes which, when superimposed, reveal great complexity."[11] Design, in this scenario, is determined by a system of prioritization rather than negotiation. Systems are allowed to coexist, but never does McHarg envision overtly hybrid conditions.

The legacy of McHarg's approach is evident in the dominance of this representational system in many large-scale urban and landscape projects today. Often, however, these analytic diagrams read as due diligence rather than a productive strategy for the reconceptualization of a site. To understand the land as a series of separate strata suggests the possibility that such forces can be understood as operating independently, when in fact, they exist in mutually interdependent states. McHarg's most projective drawings, in a sense, are annotated perspectives and geological sections, in which the layers of the landscape are resynthesized into more complex drawings. They suggest tools and possibilities for conceiving of overlaps and transformation of the original layers.

Our built and natural environments have become increasingly intertwined since McHarg authored *Design with Nature*. Urbanization in various mutant forms has spread algorithmically across the territory, leaving very little of the

11. Ian McHarg, *Design with Nature* (Garden City, NY: Doubleday/Natural History Press, 1969), 115.

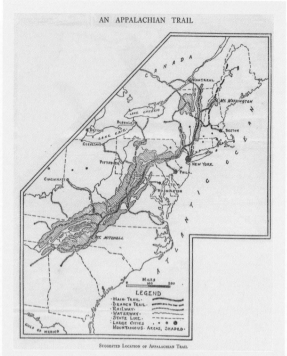

Plan for Appalachian Trail, organizing mobility systems, waterways and metropolitan centre. Image courtesy of Dartmouth College Library.

natural world untouched. Increasingly, the need to recognize and conceive of hybrid systems seems essential. What might a layer merging infrastructure and ecology resemble? To which layer does one allocate green roofs, or mechanized agricultural, or water networks which are both manipulations of hydrology and infrastructure? Current GIS software equally encourages a model of layering and isolating distinct conditions. Perhaps the future of GIS lies in users being able to join categories of information, to produce new layers, new terminology, and new spatial formats. For it is in these synthesized layers that new urban forms, building typologies, and landscapes organizations will materialize that are capable of responding to today's complex physical and environmental conditions.

Networked Territory

Networked territories, in counterpoint to layered territories, conceive of context as the subject and product of multiple intersecting networks of human and natural ecologies. The networked territory understands sites as hubs or pieces within much larger territories—the juncture of multiple forces—political, economic, social and ecological—whose source and destination are often far from the site itself. On the one hand, the hyper-networked territory produces a *deterritorialization*; a fluid space in which globalizing forces move, independent of cultural or political borders.[12] Manuel Castells, Saskia

Sassen, and Michael Hardt and Antonio Negri, amongst others, describe the physical and social implications of global economic and political networks. On the other hand, understanding territory as part of complex terrestrial ecosystems might be understood to produce a *reterritorilization*—an anchoring of territory into locally specific, if dynamic, physical and ecological networks.[13]

Benton Mackaye, an early twentieth-century American regional planner, was an early advocate for comprehensive thinking about territorial networks and what he termed "liquid planning"—an organizational armature capable of negotiating and accommodating infrastructures and environments in flux. Liquid planning consisted of two essential spatial protocols: "watersheds" and "waysides." Watersheds were territories whose boundaries could be elastic or porous. Waysides were large strips of public land running adjacent to highways, conceived of as "critical conduit between towns and wilderness or recreation."[14] MacKaye understood these protocols as ways to structure not just land and water bodies, but also electricity, mobility, distribution of urban centres and population migrations, allowing for the organization of large territories in more fluid ways. It also enabled him to envision the built and natural environment at multiple, nested scales, calling for global environmental organizations, continental treaties, and regional networks.

MacKaye is perhaps best known for the conceptualization and design of the Appalachian Trail, developed during the 1910s through 1920s, as a terrestrial infrastructure network that sustained ecological, cultural and economic ambitions. MacKaye's plan consisted of a footpath running along the entire length of the mountain ridge crest, which connected to rail and road networks, linking cities and economies. The proposal, which placed the footpath as the spine of the system, represented an inversion of traditional planning hierarchies that would typically place rail and highways as the primary order of mobility and trails as secondary. The territory is understood and organized as a reservoir of natural resources—recreation, minerals, forests and hydro-electricity that need to be managed and organized. MacKaye proposed "no master plan, but rather an ordering principle for a new economy… a new mechanism for the migration of populations, as well as the economies of production and distribution."[15]

MacKaye described his field of work as *geotechnics*, or "the applied science of making the earth more habitable,"[16] with respect to physical, economic and social systems. This new science suggests that the land, at a territorial and often continental scale, had to be planned, and it acknowledged that the design of territory extended beyond the dialectic of natural and man-made spaces. Although MacKaye envisioned complex relationships of territorial networks, it is unclear how these might have manifested themselves at a more localized scale. For instance, MacKaye's proposal for "townless

12. For a more extended discussion of empire as a de-territorializing force, see Antonio Hardt and Michael Negri, *Empire* (Cambridge: Harvard University Press: 2000), xi-xvii.

13. See Hill, *Site Matters* and Richard T. T. Forman, *Land Mosaics*.

14. Keller Easterling, *Organizational Space: Landscapes, Highways and Houses in America* (Cambridge: MIT Press, 1999), 57.

15. Ibid., 25.

16. Benton MacKaye, *From Geography to Geotechnics*, ed. Paul T. Bryant (Urbana: University of Illinois Press, 1968), 110-111.

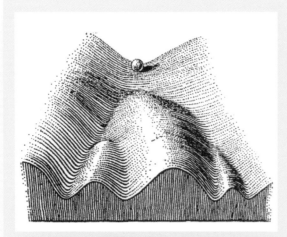

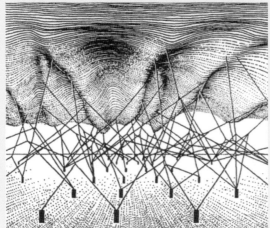

^ **Epigenetic Landscape, seen from above and below. Conrad Waddington, 1957. (Image courtesy of Edinburgh University Libraries, Special Collections Department)**

highways" and "highwayless towns" deliberately separated mobility networks, settlements and green spaces, refuting the idea that systems might intersect or cross-breed, as his large-scale visions and rhetoric suggest.

Epigenetic Territory

If the layered territory acknowledges the vertical stratification of sites, and the networked territory envisions a horizontal intersection of systems and boundaries, the question emerges: does there exist a conceptual model that envisions a three-dimensional field of forces feeding back on each other? And if so, what might be the spatial implications?

Sanford Kwinter, in his 1993 essay "Soft Systems," co-opts biologist Conrad Waddinton's model of "epigenesis" to describe how differentiated form emerges from a formless or homogenous environment. Waddington's diagram of the epigenetic surface attempts to visualize how genes act as anchors or triggers in a complex, dynamic system of non-linear interrelationships. The ball or blastula (the sphere of cells formed during the early stage of embryonic development), is kept moving along the topological surface, in a general trajectory of evolution, but one continuously recalibrating to external forces.

Waddington's epigenetic landscape offers a potentially fruitful diagram by which to imagine a new model of territory.

The network of anchors below the "landscape" suggest the forces at work on a site—not producing literal topological manipulations, but rather conceptual transformations of use, occupancy, and operations. It is worth noting that the anchors in Waddington's diagram are tethered no only to the surface above, but to each other, suggesting a territory thickened by forces, which are dynamic, responsive, and networked to each other. Any change in parameters is relayed throughout the system and in turn recalibrates the surface. The "epigenetic territory" is one in which forces, data and information are continuously scripting its performance. How that information is understood and how it informs a design response offers a way of thinking about architecture operating in an expanded territory.

The question then emerges, do there exist models for such practice? The Dutch firm MVRDV has defined their career leveraging the role of data and information—visualized and spatialized—as a tool for urban and territorial planning. They have been unique in recognizing the potential design agency of the complex forces at work in a territory—economics, population distributions, zoning, land use, infrastructural networks, etc. Information directly impacts program and reconfigures site. MVRDV represents perhaps the first generation of architects attempting to give form, though somewhat literally, to the epigenetic territory.

In their sequence of projects that form part of *NL Stadt* (1997-2004), MVRDV analyze the Netherlands across a host of criteria, acknowledging the country's tendency to organize and manipulate its territory. In the face of increasing bureaucracy, they propose to streamline hierarchies and conceive of the entire country as a single city or territory. They divide and analyze the territory into a coast zone, energy zone, forest zone, airport zone, port zone and so forth, and propose a series of urban speculations in relation to each of these programs. While they engage a range of complex forces in the overall *NL Stadt* project—they isolate each force or layer of information to form the basis of independent investigations, both for testing purposes but equally, to produce more hyperbolic proposals. One of many investigations in *NL Stadt* includes Glass or Greenhouse Zone. Here, MVRDV tests new distributions for Holland's notorious fields of greenhouses, and in the Zuidplaspolder, propose their redistribution into ribbons along highways, freeing up land, serving as noise buffers to housing and capitalizing on less desirable real estate. *NL Stadt* consists of dozens of such speculations, which together form a composite vision for alternative models of urban development in Holland. Despite, or perhaps because of the unrelenting rigour of approach, MVRDV's design system results in a rather literal use of data to produce urban patterns and architectural form, yet they openly recognize such projects are speculations and provocations. These datascapes suggest that traditional architectural design plays a very limited role; it is society in all its complexities that shapes the territory in the most detailed way. Less design than the spatialization of data, MVRDV's speculative work probes the limit states of the forces acting on the epigenetic territory.

A young generation of architects and landscape architects are testing a more evolved understanding of the epigenetic territory, as evidenced in the pages of this issue of

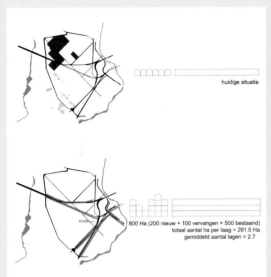 

huidige situatie

800 Ha (200 nieuw + 100 vervangen + 500 bestaand)
totaal aantal ha per laag = 291.5 Ha
gemiddeld aantal lagen = 2.7

∧   **Glasszone, reorganizing the greenhouses of the region into linear corridors. Image courtesy of MVRDV.**

Bracket. From reformatting urban snow collection and river dredge material, to the harvesting of wind power and the processing of ocean water, from the subversion of national sovereignty through soft landscape strategies to the co-option of the military as ecological agent, the question of the architect's role within a site, a boundary, and a territory are provocatively tested in this edition of *Bracket*. In each case design confronts a seemingly impassable constraint—geo-political limits, air rights, ecological thresholds—and it is in these moments that the architect becomes active agent not only in operating in the epigenetic territory, but in designing it; extending its boundaries and performance. To represent the territory is to understand it, is to operate within it, is to (re)design it.

If architecture is to engage the spatial and operational complexities of urbanism, infrastructure, landscape, ecology, and industry, amongst others, it must take on an expanded role, capable of reading the composite territories of a project, negotiating contingencies, and scripting alternative outcomes. The architect in this scenario is less form-maker than spatial 'programmer' capable of negotiating the thickened territory of a project. Architecture must envision spatial formats and processes capable of relinquishing control and responding to their wider environment. Then, architecture will be able to reorganize the epigenetic territory, acting as the registration and interface with larger forces, with the intent of producing new spatial systems, building typologies, and public realms.

contingency/
resilience

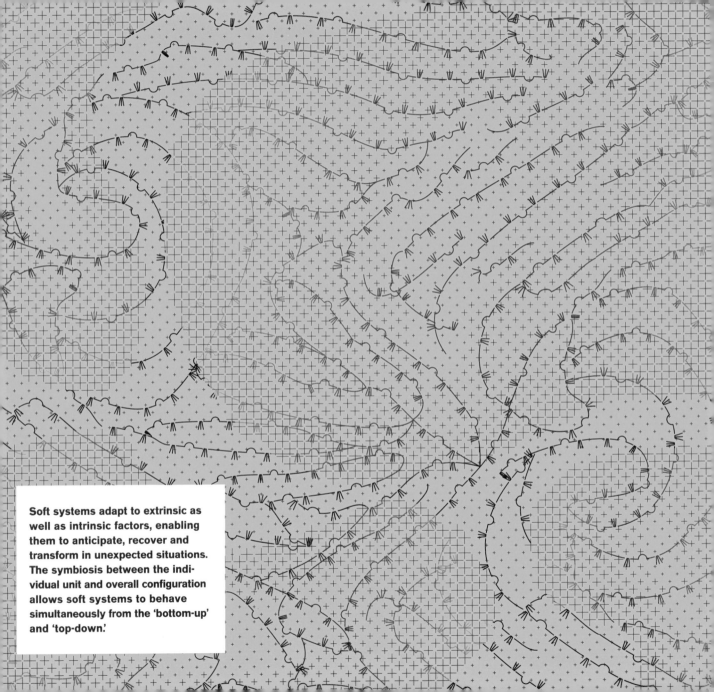

Soft systems adapt to extrinsic as well as intrinsic factors, enabling them to anticipate, recover and transform in unexpected situations. The symbiosis between the individual unit and overall configuration allows soft systems to behave simultaneously from the 'bottom-up' and 'top-down.'

SOFT CULTURE MACHINES
EWAN BRANDA

In the 1960s, the architectural avant-garde had a fascination with information technology. To many, computers and networks contained in their very structures the libertarian ideals of freedom, play, and non-hierarchical organization necessary to realize utopian social reform. Architecture, by adopting the forms and structures of information technology, seemed poised to reclaim its role as one of Western culture's privileged instruments of social organization. Among the small number of built projects that emerged from these techno-utopian discourses, the Centre Beaubourg—later renamed the Centre Georges Pompidou—in Paris seemed the most promising. The brief for the international competition held between 1970 and 1971 announced from the start that "the entire Centre has been inspired by an original perspective, that of constantly renewing information."[1] It went on to describe a complex institution whose metabolism was fueled by information exchange. This institution's ambition was to deploy contemporary discourses in which information systems had the power to transgress boundaries between social groups, expert disciplines, and geographic spaces. The brief argued that the building would need to be permeable to information flows *to* and *from* its environment. This would be achieved by various means such as visual transparency, electronic screens, exhibitions, television broadcasts, publications, and a remotely accessible electronic library catalog, which would extend the Center's reach to the whole of France and beyond. In short, the building was to be a vast information-processing machine, both in metaphor and in actual performance.

The winning entry by Renzo Piano, Richard Rogers, Gianni Franchini, and Ove Arup—a "live center of information" consisting largely of a steel framework covered with information displays, antennae, and satellite dishes—was the only scheme that in the jury's view successfully translated the philosophy of the Centre into an architectural proposal. The presentation was punctuated with aphoristic diagrams of information networks showing Beaubourg at their hub.[2] Peter Rice later described their scheme as a "large, loose-fit frame where anything could happen... loosely based on Archigram, Price, Littlewood... an information machine with movable floors, like the Fun Palace."[3] At the time Rogers said, "[w]e are after a rich, flexible matrix. And we hope that people will understand, learn how to use it. In all this we want to mix as many modern gadgets as possible. Electronic gadgetry is not just a fad.... We see communication, information, as vital."[4] So when the winning scheme was announced, it seemed to many that the wait was over—that the plug-in architecture of the Archigram Group, the cybernetic schemes of Cedric Price, and the indeterminate

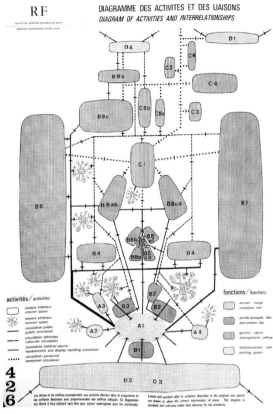

^ Program diagram from the competition brief.

megastructures of Yona Friedman might finally be realized, and in the historic center of Paris no less.

But when Dennis Crompton, a member of the Archigram group, visited the newly opened "live center of information" in 1977, he had expected to see "an intensity of information which [was] not only real and useful, but also gratuitous and entertaining."[5] Instead, he responded, "well, where is it?" All that remained of the media screens and other information-age hardware was their bare supporting frame. Crompton wasn't naive, and recognized that to ask "where is it?" was in many respects a mark of success because, as he put it, "information is only perceptible when it is in the process of being transmitted. It really is not a load of hardware hanging from the ceiling, flashing out of capsules or sprouting off pylons; these are only symbols, which we use on drawings, of a transient activity." Despite this concession, he concluded that the elimination of the apparatus shown in the competition scheme was a missed opportunity. Crompton's equivocation was symptomatic of architecture's changing relationship to information technology.

1. Concours international d'idées à un degré (competition brief) (Paris: Ministère d'état chargé des affaires culturelles, 1970).

2. Concours international pour la réalisation du Centre Beaubourg (rapport du jury)

(Paris: Établissement public du Centre Beaubourg, 1971).

3. Peter Rice, *An Engineer Imagines* (London: Artemis, 1994), 25.

4. Quoted in Peter Rawstorne, "Piano &

Rogers: Centre Beaubourg," *Architectural Design* 42, no. 7 (1972): 407.

5. Dennis Crompton, "Centre Pompidou: A Live Centre of Information," *Architectural Design* 47, no. 2 (1977): 100-127.

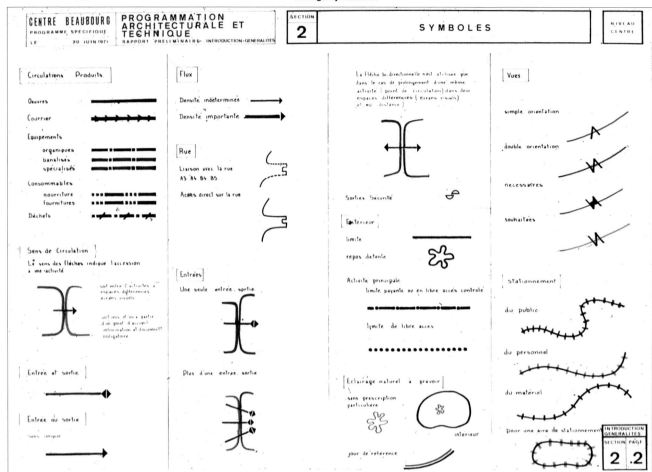

∧   **Programme spécifique: Legend of symbols**
for representing flows and interfaces.

Optimistic experiments in the socially transformative capacity of information technology, so characteristic of the experimental architecture of the 1960s, seemed, by mid-1970s, to have been entirely abandoned. Indeed, the Beaubourg competition entries by Friedman, Maymont, and Archigram seem like mere traces of a period of experimentation that was long ago exhausted.[6] Why did these experiments into the imagery and forms of the information age come to such an abrupt end, at precisely the moment when the information society was starting to fully materialize? Beaubourg was born into a moment of transition in the emergence of the information society, one in which machine-age computer hardware was gradually ceding to the intangibility and invisibility of software and networks. This condition demanded new modes of architectural response and new kinds of technical expertise.

To prepare the competition brief, Pompidou put together a team of skilled technocrats to ensure that his project would not simply languish in the domain of demagoguery, as had André Malraux's Musée du XXe siècle. Heading the planning team was François Lombard, an unknown 30-year-old, Berkeley-educated civil engineer working for the Ministry of Culture's Direction d'architecture on programming methodologies for the planning of the Villes nouvelles around Paris. In late 1969, Lombard recruited Patrick O'Byrne, a friend who was working for a small engineering firm in Montréal, l'Institut de Recherches et de Normalisations Économiques et Scientifiques, one of a group of firms supported between 1963 and 1976 by the Ford Foundation's Educational Facilities Laboratory.[7] The Ford research applied methods of programming introduced by American firms in the late 1950s to the development of flexible, open-plan public schools that paved the way for what became known as the 'performance concept'.[8] The practice of programming that was emerging in postwar research was much more than a list of functions and areas: it merged behavioral psychology and analytical methods

6. Both Reyner Banham and, more recently, Larry Busbea, use the Centre Pompidou prominently in their closing chapters as a marker of the end of 1960s experimentation. (Reyner Banham, *Megastructure: Urban Futures of the Recent Past* (New York: Harper and Row, 1976); Larry Busbea,

Topologies: The Urban Utopia in France, 1960-1970 (Cambridge: MIT Press, 2007).)
7. Interviews with Claude Mollard and Patrick O'Byrne, Paris, 2007-8.
8. G.A. Corriveau, "School Construction and Normalization. RAS Project: Research in Educational Facilities. A Report.," 1968,

ERIC. Little has been written on this influential Ford program.

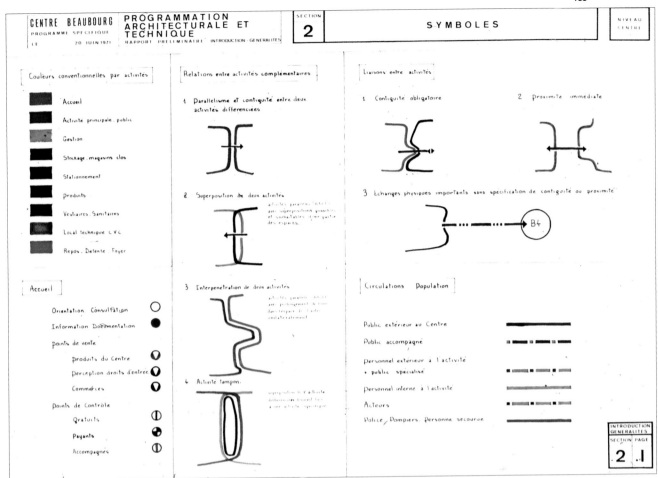

CENTRE BEAUBOURG
PROGRAMME SPÉCIFIQUE
LE   20 JUIN 1971

PROGRAMMATION
ARCHITECTURALE ET
TECHNIQUE
RAPPORT PRELIMINAIRE INTRODUCTION - GENERALITES

SECTION
2

SYMBOLES

NIVEAU
CENTRE

∧   **Programme spécifique: Legend of symbols**
for representing flows and interfaces.

of systems design into a set of techniques for controlling all aspects of a building's performance.[9] Programming specified a total system, with which the avant-garde utopianists of the 1960s would have sympathized, yet it offered no corresponding totality of an architectural solution. As a species of systems engineering, it specified desired performance while leaving the possible set of solutions as open as possible. Lombard saw that the programming methods developed in the Ford research, until then limited to anonymous, industrialized building types, were applicable to Pompidou's prestigious, one-off cultural center, and so he persuaded O'Byrne to return to Paris with him.

In preparing the brief, the programming team developed a formal method in which the institutional department was interpreted as a set of social functions, which Lombard later described, in characteristic fashion, as an "ensemble mathématique."[10] The first task of the programmer was the identification of the set of subsystems and relationships comprising this ensemble and the modes of exchange by which they cohered. The programmer identified a particular class of exchange (such as

document reference, or viewing artwork), followed by the beneficiary of the exchange (researcher, museum visitor), the object of exchange (document, painting), the manner in which the exchange was to be transacted (consultation with computer terminal, walking through an exhibition), the necessary personnel to support the exchange (librarian, docent), and the spatial context of the exchange (reading room, gallery). The architectural program conceived in this way went far beyond the description of floor areas and the correct juxtaposition of functions to describe a complex system of interactions.

This approach challenged available modes of architectural representation. In response, Lombard's team developed a diagramming method that offered a unified language for the representation of people, spaces, objects, documents, and flows. It was difficult to imagine a mode of representation that did not bring with it a host of prior solutions, and in the brief, even seemingly banal terms such as "library," "civic center," or even "city" were considered risky because they imposed prejudice and bias on positivist problem-solving. Lombard accordingly warned architects that they should avoid interpreting

9. The seminal paper on programming is William M. Peña and William W. Caudill, "Architectural analysis: Prelude to good design," *Architectural Record* (1959). See also Clarence Herbert Wheeler, *Emerging Techniques of Architectural Practice* (American Institute of Architects, 1966).

10. François Lombard, "Principe de la programmation," (1973). Archives Centre Georges Pompidou.

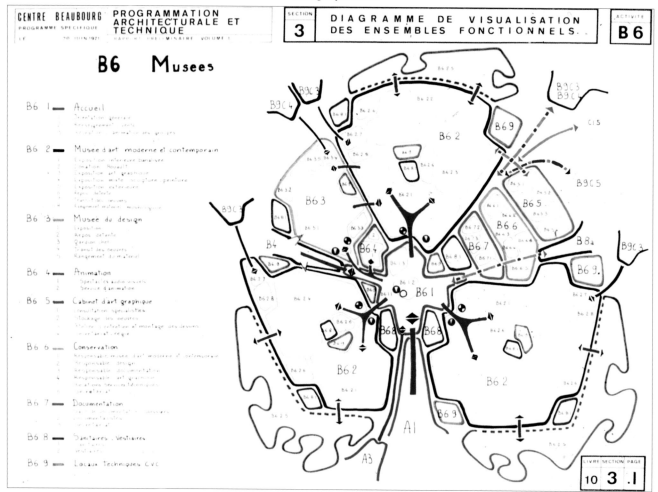

B6 Musees

B6 1 — Accueil

B6 2 — Musee d'art moderne et contemporain

B6 3 — Musee du design

B6 4 — Animation

B6 5 — Cabinet d'art graphique

B6 6 — Conservation

B6 7 — Documentation

B6 8 — Sanitaires, Vestiaires

B6 9 — Locaux Techniques C.V.C

LIVRE | SECTION | PAGE
10 | **3** | .1

∧ Programme spécifique: Diagram of functional clusters for access and reception areas.

such architectural terms as "library" or "hall" as spatial types and instead treat them as scenarios constituted by precisely defined performance criteria. The design of a complex system could only be achieved "by developing an entirely new taxonomy of problem formulation."[11] At Beaubourg, programmers attacked this problem by defining a taxonomy of interactions such as desirable and undesirable views, flows of people, goods, and documents, sound isolation, etc. They then analyzed each activity, identifying the interfaces and flows by which it cohered. Once each activity was sufficiently well defined, the programming team described interfaces between one activity and another through a graphic system for mapping the flow of objects and information between activities.

The resulting diagrams borrowed heavily from graph theory and interaction matrices, which allowed system designers to visualize complex relationships between components.[12] In a 1970 article in *Architectural Design*, Jean Cousin referred to the application of graph theory to architecture, first practiced by Christopher Alexander a decade earlier, as a "topological" as opposed to "geometrical" approach to spatial organization.[13] In place of the imprecise humanist language of earlier utopians, the topological approach offered a theory of representation for a new positive science of design, free of appeals to intuition and perception. The connected graph described a finite set of nodes (represented by circles, which might symbolize any object in a particular domain) and a finite set of connections between them (represented by lines, which could be labeled with a weight, qualitative or quantitative, and which could be made into arrows in order to indicate the direction of a relationship). The graph made apparent relationships that were much more difficult to identify in tabular representations. First-order

11. Raymond G. Studer, "On Environmental Programming," *Arena* (May 1966): 293.

12. For an overview of the concepts and historical development of Systems Engineering see Herman A. Affel, "System Engineering," *International Science and Technology* (November 1964): 18-26. The graph diagram was important from the start: the first issue of the *Journal of Systems Engineering* (Autumn 1969) named its editorial article "Blocks and Arrows."

13. Jean Cousin, "Topological Organization of Architectural Space," *Architectural Design* (October 1970): 491-493. Originally in Jean Cousin, *Organisation Topologique de L'Espace Architectural* (Montréal: Les Presses de L'Université de Montréal, 1970). This opposition of topology to geometry in architecture was, of course, the subject of Reyner Banham's famous essay of ten years earlier. See Reyner Banham, "The New Brutalism," *The Architectural Review* (December 1955).

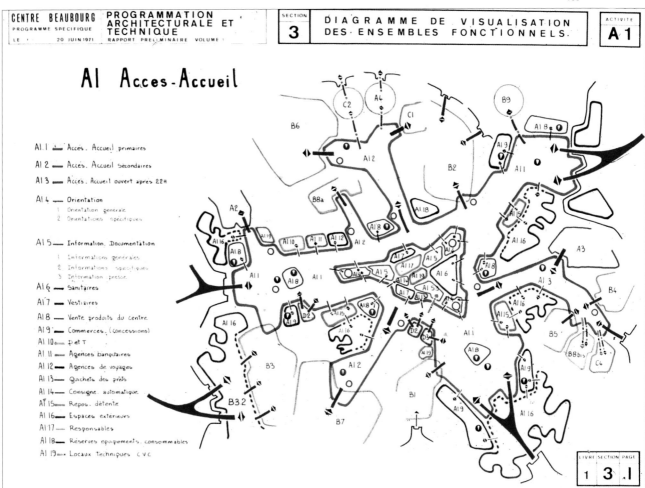

| CENTRE BEAUBOURG | PROGRAMMATION ARCHITECTURALE ET TECHNIQUE | SECTION 3 | DIAGRAMME DE VISUALISATION DES ENSEMBLES FONCTIONNELS. | ACTIVITE A1 |

PROGRAMME SPECIFIQUE
LE · 20 JUIN 1971 · RAPPORT PRELIMINAIRE VOLUME ·

A1 Acces-Accueil

A1.1 — Accés. Accueil primaires
A1.2 — Accés. Accueil Secondaires
A1.3 — Accés. Accueil ouvert aprés 22H
A1.4 — Orientation
  1 Orientation generale
  2 Orientations spécifiques
A1.5 — Information. Documentation
  1 Informations generales
  2 Informations spécifiques
  3 Information presse
A1.6 — Sanitaires
A1.7 — Vestiaires
A1.8 — Vente produits du centre.
A1.9 — Commerces. (concessions)
A1.10 — P et T
A1.11 — Agences banquaires
A1.12 — Agences de voyages
A1.13 — Quichets des prêts
A1.14 — Consigne automatique
A1.15 — Repos. detente
A1.16 — Espaces exterieurs
A1.17 — Responsables
A1.18 — Réserves equipements. consommables
A1.19 — Locaux Techniques C.V.C

LIVRE SECTION PAGE
1 3 .1

∧ **Programme spécifique: Diagram of functional clusters for access and reception areas.**

relationships were obvious enough and could generally be identified by talking to users and other stakeholders, but second-order relationships, for example one in which a department might be related to another within an organization via a "middleman," were much harder to discern since nobody on the ground had a sufficiently elevated viewpoint to apprehend them. At Beaubourg, where interdisciplinarity governed, second and third-order relationships were crucial. Like industrialized systems building, this relational approach elevated the interface between subsystems to a privileged place. While systems building located interface in the invisible contractual space between manufacturers of components, the program diagram located the interface at the shared boundaries between activities. The form and material that made up this boundary was a matter for the architect; indeed, the programming team went to great pains to make it clear that walls were only one way of reifying the boundary surfaces shown on the diagrams. The diagrams could therefore to be understood less as plans than as three-dimensional matrices; a connecting arrow between functional elements might be satisfied by a door, window, corridor, stair, or elevator.

The visual language of the program diagrams is their most striking feature. This language was only hinted at in the brief, but was fully developed during the initial design phases immediately following the competition.

In drawing them, the programming team consciously avoided rectilinear forms, both so as to not compete with the architects, and in order to assert the autonomy of their disciplinary contribution. In response to Banham's challenge that architects run with technology or be left behind, these curvilinear forms were altogether different from the curves and bubbles of 1960s techno-utopianism. They were neither an index of a computational process nor the formal representation of the liberation of form (and by extension of material existence) brought about by information technology. Here, curvilinear forms are merely an outcome of a technique whose computational logic is intermediary and invisible, its relationship to architectural form is indeterminate since both rectilinearity and curvilinearity are viable formal outcomes of the graph's topological logic. Positioned halfway between topological and geometric approaches, the diagrams assert a disjunction between their particular visual language and the resulting architectural forms, and it is herein that their intelligence lies.

Programming at Beaubourg operated in this gap between political intention and architectural form. Many of programming's inherent paradoxes, such the need for top-down control within a system whose *raison d'être* was to engender freedom and accident, echoed those of the project's political context, a paradox that Richard Rogers pointed out in his infamous critique of *Programmation*

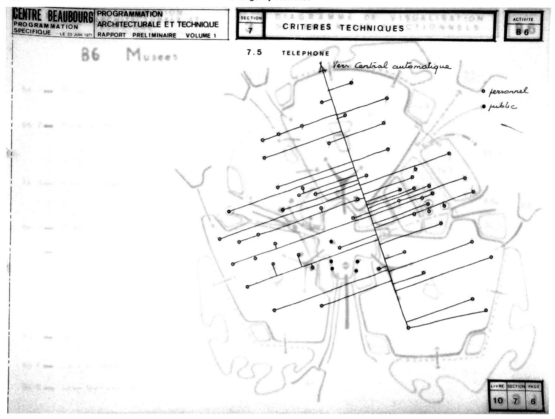

∧   **Programme spécifique: Diagram of
functional clusters for museum with overlay of
telecommunications systems.**

delivered during a working meeting with Lombard's team. No amount of flexibility could mitigate the irredeemable openness of the system that the program was trying to control. By 1973, Horst Rittel and Melvin Webber had observed that complex systems—and particularly social and environmental systems of the type described by Lombard—were inherently undecidable.[14] In the end, Programmation remained suspicious of activities at the edges of the closed system, such as the non-programmed events and happenings so close to the hearts of the architects. Fifty years earlier, the French management theorist Henri Fayol characterized the complex organization as an abstract legal entity based on rational rules and structures of authority: while Taylor had focused at level of the individual, Fayol was concerned primarily with reorganization at the top, a view of organizational reform echoed by Beaubourg's sponsors.[15] The programming team thus faced an aporia: a Fayolist approach to critical reorganization entailed the reinforcement of departmental identity and therefore of boundaries, while the new humanist religion of interdisciplinarity demanded their erasure. Techo-utopians of the 1960s had by-and-large sidestepped this problem, since their libertarian theories for the most part refused all organizational categories larger than the individual or family. But for administrators at Beaubourg, the "department" was integral to the discourse of organizational reform: at

issue was not the elimination of departments and other organizational categories but rather, in what ways might new relationships between them be put into play.

If Piano and Rogers' winning scheme perfectly translated the informational aims of the brief, it did so with only one foot in the 1960s. Indeed, while visiting the new building, both Price and the members of Archigram found it "too static and consistent."[16] Compared to the more conventional megastructures submitted by several other competitors, the winning design was a minimalist black-box in which any activity could unfold. Unlike the utopian schemes of the 1960s, it neither mimicked in its organization the topologies of networks or computing machinery, nor treated architecture as an ever-receding backdrop to a new technological environment. Both of these earlier positions assumed a distinction between hardware and software, that was typical of postwar paradigms in which information was stuff that flowed through a complex hardware of pipes and gates. Put simply, in Banham's megastructure, the static structural framework could be understood as hardware while its everyday modes of inhabitation were the software. In this way, the winning scheme provided a loose-fit frame inside which Lombard, who was an influential member of the jury as head of the technical committee, could implement his methods.

14. Horst W. J. Rittel and Melvin M. Webber, "Dilemmas in a General Theory of Planning," *Policy Sciences*, no. 4 (1973): 155-169.

15. Claude S. George, *The History of Management Thought* (Englewood Cliffs, NJ: Prentice-Hall, 1972), 114.

16. Tattooist International Ltd and Arts Council of Great Britain, Beaubourg Four Films by Denis Postle (Arts Council, 1980).

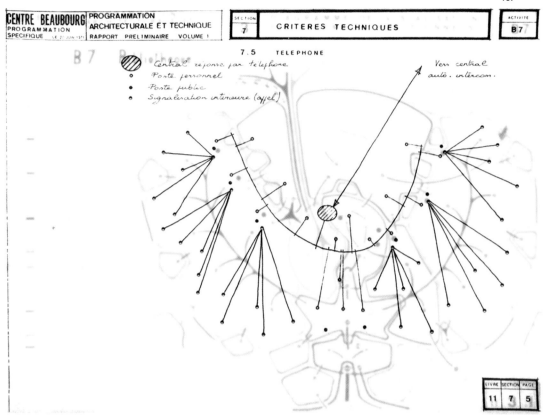

7.5 TELEPHONE

∧ **Programme spécifique: Diagram of functional clusters for library with overlay of telecommunications systems.**

Ultimately, programming challenged the megastructure model. In 1978, Simon Nora and Alain Minc's *L'informatisation de la Société*—a government report that became an unlikely bestseller in France—argued that such unhelpful dichotomies as "hard" and "soft" were being made obsolete by what they called *télématique*—the convergence of computers and telecommunications technologies that emerged in the mid-1960s. According to Nora and Minc, *télématique* would soon "alter the entire nervous system of social organization."[17] They observed that over the preceding decade in France, American corporations (among which IBM had acquired a mythical status) had encroached on the traditional cultural roles of the state. The challenge, as they saw it, lay in finding a new role for government that would involve all possible levels of state action, from top-down decree, to looser practices of regulation, to complete laissez-faire withdrawal. Unlike the postwar computing machinery analogized in the architectural forms of the 1960s, both the hardware and software of telematic systems were virtual, the logic of their operation hidden in new kinds of invisible and diffuse architectures. Programming at Beaubourg was thus a response to the problem of building a live center of information at a moment when, in the words of Nora and

Minc, "the seemingly natural boundary between hardware and software begins to fade away."

Photos of building are by author. All diagrams from the Programme spécifique are courtesy of Hélène Dano-Vanneyre and Patrick O'Byrne, architects and programmers in charge of the original programming for the Centre Georges Pompidou under the direction of François Lombard.

Note: I would like to thank Hélène Dano-Vanneyre and Patrick O'Byrne of the original programming team for their generosity in sharing both their experiences with the Beaubourg project and the images shown above.

⋯ **Ewan Branda is a Los Angeles-based architect, software designer, and professor of architecture at Woodbury University.**

17. Simon Nora and Alain Minc, *The Computerization of Society: A Report to the President of France*, trans. Daniel Bell (Cambridge: MIT Press, 1980), 10. Originally published as Simon Nora and Alain Minc, *L'informatisation de la société* (Paris: Seuil, 1978).

SCAFFOLDING CITY: ARCHITECTURAL UTOPIA OF THE FUTURE PAST

EDWARD DODDINGTON

∧ *Scaffolding City*, perspective view.

In an increasingly volatile world, a model of architecture and urbanism based on planning, authority, and permanence has less and less ability to respond to today's fluctuating economic and environmental conditions. In its place, a system of construction that has speed, flexibility and responsiveness is required to nimbly address complex social and economic issues.

This is not the first time that an architectural solution of speed, lightness and flexibility has been proposed to solve our most challenging urban problems. In the 1950s and 60s, architects in Europe and North America such as Cedric Price, Buckminster Fuller, Peter Cook and Yona Friedman, proposed radical visions for flexible and mobile architecture and urbanism.[1] Yet the mega-structuralist project failed to deliver its promises of freedom and democracy. It sought to upend social and economic hierarchies through architectural design, only to find itself complicit in these hierarchical structures.

Nonetheless, urban models which aspire to infinite flexibility, quickness of construction, lightness of materials and "plug and play" techniques borrowed from Fuller and Freidman are required once again. However this time, they must be wedded to a vision of vernacular building methods and a greater understanding of ecological and biological models of growth and development.

The Starn Brothers have, in the last few years, constructed massive flexible bamboo structures as installations for temporary occupation. The structures are never fully complete and instead exist in a state of constant change and motion. Not only is there a perpetual cycle of construction occurring in the works, but the elastic properties of bamboo allow for a subtle movement and flow throughout the structure.

This type of locally specific/globally complex system can be seen in a variety of other biological systems. The mechanical parts also allow for a remarkable degree

1. In the late 1950s Friedman theorized a "Mobile Architecture." His *Spatial City* of 1958 is the manifestation of this theory which demonstrates this mobility by establishing a three dimensional space-frame over a zone (city, farm, highway) providing an infinitely flexible space for the inhabitants.

2. Van der Levy, Sabrina, and Markus Richter, *Megastructure Reloaded* (Berlin: Hatje Cantz Verlag, Ostfildern, 2008) 29-31.

< "...locally specific / globally complex system can be seen in a variety of other biological systems at an equally diverse range of scales..." Big Bambu. (Image copyright, D+M Starn, 2011)

of flexibility within the system—it can be moved, used, and reused in multiple locations. The method of construction (lashing branches) is locally simple and globally complex, that is to say, specific, simple construction techniques that produce a complex, dynamic global arrangements. While not typically characterized as an "efficient system" it is defined by the new three "R's"— redundancy, repetition and resilience.

Scaffolding City is an architectural system that responds quickly and flexibly to internal and external pressures, be they urban, economic, or ecological. As such, it cannot exist on its own, it must rely upon our solid urban structures. Faced with these

scenarios, it becomes a second, complimentary system of urban habitation—a system of disaster—preparedness, of thickening urban edges, of redundant habitation and easily accessible construction materials.

Much like the work of those avant-garde architects nearly fifty years ago, *Scaffolding City* attempts to reposition architecture as a flexible strategy of urban habitation, and not as a prescriptive solution to an unknowable problem. It will come to more closely resemble a type of semi-living system characterized by real-time change and adaptability found in flexible construction techniques.

Scaffolding City is a place where citizens hold the potential to reshape their cities and

where the built landscape becomes collectively more active, agile and soft. It is a radically heterogeneous city—part superstructure, part favela, part bird-nest and part tree house—where many different urban animals can roost, camp, and live. It is, at times, a parasitic or a symbiotic structure, latching on to other structures or borrowing resources for a short amount of time. In return, *Scaffolding City* capitalizes on underutilized spaces and generates micro-economies of alternative resources. This city has never been seen before but might look strangely familiar. It is a city from the future past.

3. Tate, Melissa L. Knothe, "Wither Flows the Fluid in Bone?," *Journal of Biomechanics*. Volume 36, Issue 10, October 2003: 1409-1424.

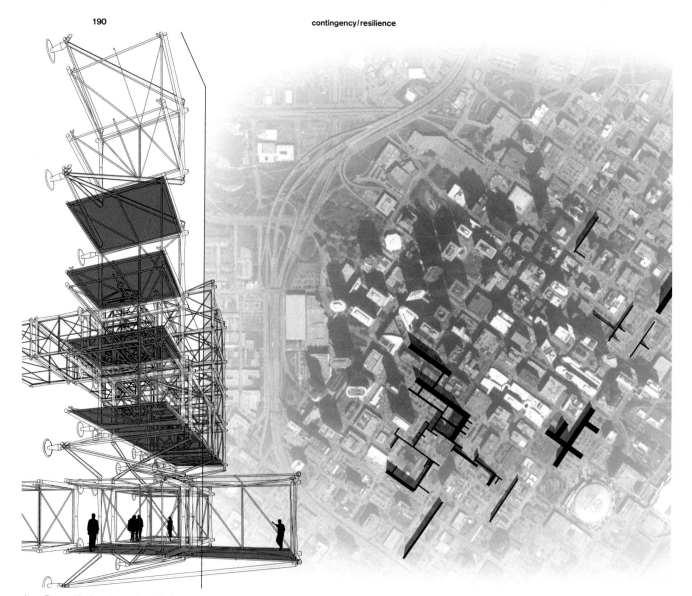

∧   **Perspectival section and aerial of deployment.**

Scaffolding City sets up six principles:

The Need for Speed
Our current model of architecture is too slow to react to global ecological and economic crises. A faster system is required, that can quickly adapt, bend, and rebuild.

Redundancy
The new ethos is for designers to embrace change and flexibility, in order to respond to unknowns. To design for potential failure is more realistic than an 'impervious' or materially efficient design.

Network the System
City planning will rely not on a strict plan but on access and proximity to resources, local economic conditions and ecology. This will be a dynamic system of planning, free to move from location to location.

Open to Economy
Incentivize use. Keep material costs low and the system will generate innovative uses and techniques. People will re-interpret materials, re-invent uses and develop secondary and tertiary economies surrounding the transfer and transformation of materials.

Democratize the Construction Process
Lower the level of specialized construction knowledge such that each citizen can become a contractor, and thereby contribute to the growing system.

Open to Ecology
The new architectural city will be easily accessible and amenable to other animals for habitation. Its openness will take advantage of ecological assets, getting stronger as it is incorporated into a living thicket of trees or gathering thicker as populations of birds and animals make it their homes.

· · · **Edward Doddington is a Houston-based artist, designer, and entrepreneur.**

THE BLADDERS

JONATHAN WALKER

∧   **The Bladders Project Triptych.**

The Bladders is a vision for a future municipal water retention and treatment infrastructure sited across the 2012 Olympic Park, within London's Lower Lea Valley. Giant inflated water bladders and anaerobic digester stomachs are the key elements of an architecture that returns a segment of the Lea Valley into a 'backyard' for Londoners to explore. The project is inspired by the behavior of natural membranes, the construction methods of tensile structures, and drawings from Cedric Price's *City of the Future*.

The *City of the Future* was a hyper-infrastructural city and an architectural manifesto. One drawing from the series advocates that air and water will become major structural elements—sheltering, supporting and positioning. This potential of pneumatic networks and formats was one of Price's ideas for a future metropolis and plays an eminent part in establishing a spatially performative architecture within *The Bladders* project.

The project responds to the classification of London as a city of 'serious water stress'[1] and offers a new infrastructure for the city's ailing water cisterns. The proposal looks to 2031 when London's reservoir cistern is predicted to reach capacity, and when projected shifts in climate will bring hotter, drier summers and a greater risk of water shortages. The Lea Valley already contains one fifth of the capital's water reserves, and is a void that divides East London from the city. It has always been a place where the city's utilities are hidden away and where Londoners can escape the confines of the city streets. *The Bladders*

takes on a symbiotic role of recreational landscape and utilitarian infrastructure, a relationship recalling the 'steam islands' of 19th century Germany. When steam power was first introduced to Germany from Great Britain in the nineteenth century, the estates of *Glienicke* and *Sanssouci* near Potsdam became testing sites for this new technology. These 'islands' were steam-powered industrial parks and models of a new technological sublime; they consisted of embellished temples as engine houses powering monumental waterfalls and fountains that visitors could explore. *The Bladders* project similarly integrates a utilitarian infrastructure with an architectural landscape that is an artificial performance for visitors.

The water filled bladders lie bloated and endlessly reshaping; they are responsive to the flows of water around the site's pneumatic network, causing the membrane structures to sag, fold and swell. They are sustained by a set of instruments performing specific operations across the site, some of which are skeletal and gangling and built from re-invented remnants from the Olympic Games, such as the stadiums removable plastic seats and the outer stadium wraps. The instruments' watery bodies present a bizarre architecture where, alongside utilitarian function, performance and recreation can be sought.

· · · **Jon Walker is a designer, artist, and part**
II architect based in London.

1. The Environment Agency, from *The Mayor's Draft Water Strategy*, Greater London Authority (2009).

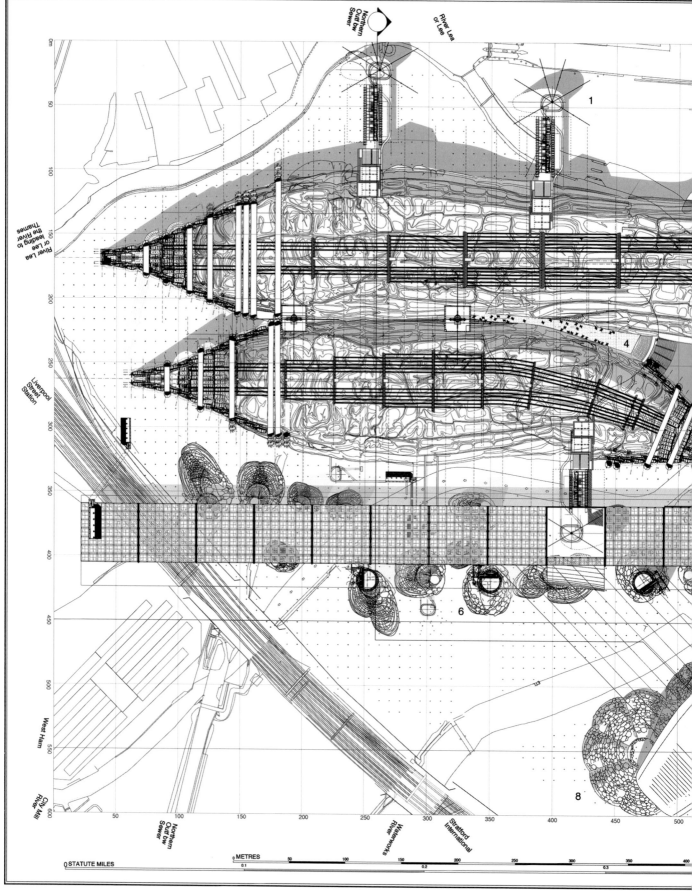

∧   OS Landranger *The Bladders*, Lower Lea Valley.

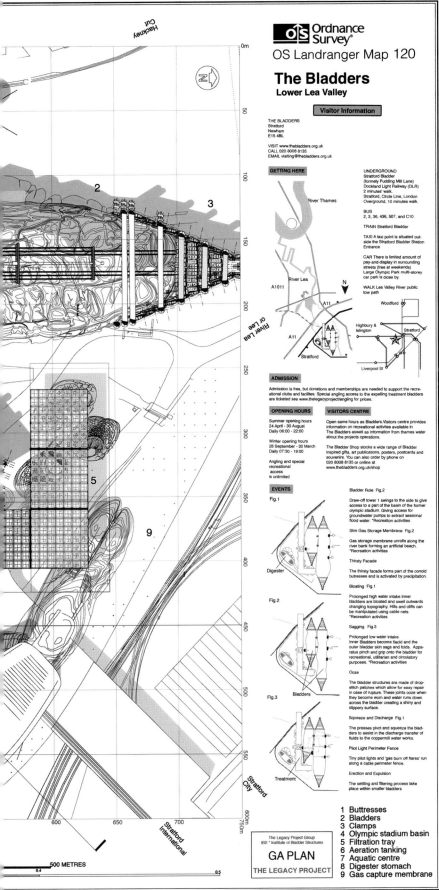

Hackney Cut

0m
50
100
150
200
250
300
350
400
450
500
550
600m
750m

2

3

5

9

Stratford City

Stratford International

600 650 700

500 METRES

0.4 0.5

N

Ordnance Survey®
OS Landranger Map 120

The Bladders
Lower Lea Valley

Visitor Information

THE BLADDERS
Stratford
Newham
E15 4BL

VISIT www.thebladders.org.uk
CALL 020 8008 8135
EMAIL visiting@thebladders.org.uk

GETTING HERE

River Thames

River Lea

A1011

River Lea or Lee

A11

A11

N

Stratford

Woodford

Highbury &
Islington
Stratford

Liverpool St

UNDERGROUND
Stratford Bladder
(formerly Pudding Mill Lane)
Dockland Light Railway (DLR)
2 minutes' walk.
Stratford, Circle Line, London
Overground, 10 minutes walk.

BUS
2, 3, 36, 436, 507, and C10

TRAIN Stratford Bladder

TAXI A taxi point is situated outside the Stratford Bladder Station
Entrance

CAR There is limited amount of
pay-and-display in surrounding
streets (free at weekends)
Large Olympic Park multi-storey
car park is close by.

WALK Lea Valley River public
tow path

ADMISSION

Admission is free, but donations and memberships are needed to support the recreational clubs and facilites. Special angling access to the expelling treatment bladders
are ticketed see www.thelegacyproject/angling for prices.

OPENING HOURS

Summer opening hours
24 April - 30 August
Daily 06:00 - 22:00

Winter opening hours
28 September - 30 March
Daily 07:30 - 19:00

Angling and special
recreational
access
is unlimited

VISITORS CENTRE

Open same hours as Bladders.Visitors centre provides
information on recreational activites available in
The Bladders aswell as information from thames water
about the projects operations.

The Bladder Shop stocks a wide range of Bladder
inspired gifts, art publications, posters, postcards and
souvenirs. You can also order by phone on
020 8008 8135 or online at
www.thebladders.org.uk/shop

EVENTS

Fig.1

Digester

Fig.2

Bladders

Fig.3

Treatment

Bladder Role Fig.2

Draw-off tower 1 swings to the side to give
access to a part of the basin of the former
olympic stadium. Giving access for
groundwater pumps to extract seasonal
flood water. *Recreation activities

Slim Gas Storage Membrane Fig.2

Gas storage membrane unrolls along the
river bank forming an artificial beach.
*Recreation activites

Thirsty Facade

The thirsty facade forms part of the conoid
butresses and is activated by precipitation.

Bloating Fig.1

Prolonged high water intake.Inner
bladders are bloated and swell outwards
changing topography. Hills and cliffs can
be manipulated using cable nets.
*Recreation activities

Sagging Fig.3

Prolonged low water intake.
Inner Bladders become flacid and the
outer bladder skin sags and folds. Apparatus pinch and grip onto the bladder for
recreational, utilitarian and circulatory
purposes. *Recreation activities

Ooze

The bladder structures are made of drop-
stitch patches which allow for easy repair
in case of rupture. These joints ooze when
they become worn and water runs down
across the bladder creating a shiny and
slippery surface.

Squeeze and Discharge Fig.1

The presses pivot and squeeze the bladders to assist in the discharge transfer of
fluids to the coppermill water works.

Pilot Light Perimeter Fence

Tiny pilot lights and 'gas burn off flares' run
along a cable perimeter fence.

Erection and Expulsion

The settling and filtering process take
place within smaller bladders

1 Buttresses
2 Bladders
3 Clamps
4 Olympic stadium basin
5 Filtration tray
6 Aeration tanking
7 Aquatic centre
8 Digester stomach
9 Gas capture membrane

The Legacy Project Group
IBS * Institute of Bladder Structures

GA PLAN

THE LEGACY PROJECT

2018

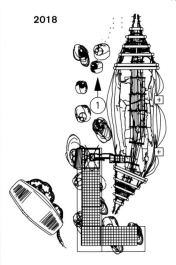

1

+

2021

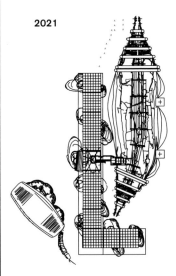

+

2031

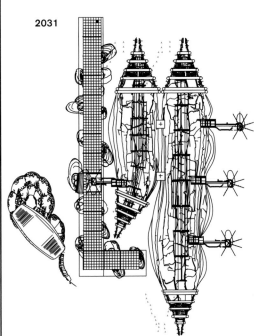

+

∧ **Olympic Park transformation.**

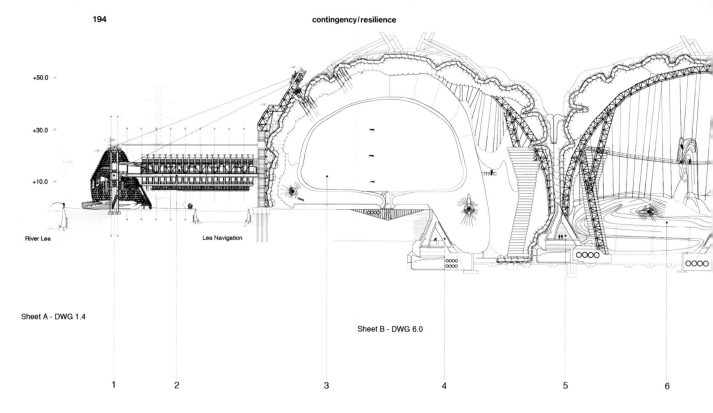

+50.0

+30.0

+10.0

River Lea

Lea Navigation

Sheet A - DWG 1.4

Sheet B - DWG 6.0

1   2   3   4   5   6

∧   **GA Section with model.**

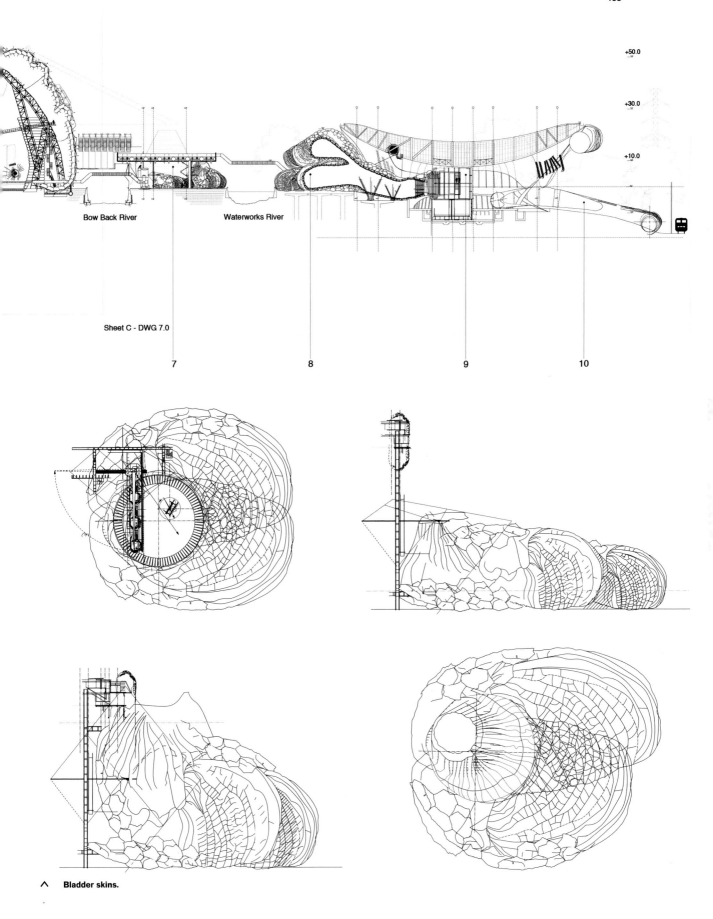

+50.0

+30.0

+10.0

Bow Back River   Waterworks River

Sheet C - DWG 7.0

7   8   9   10

∧   **Bladder skins.**

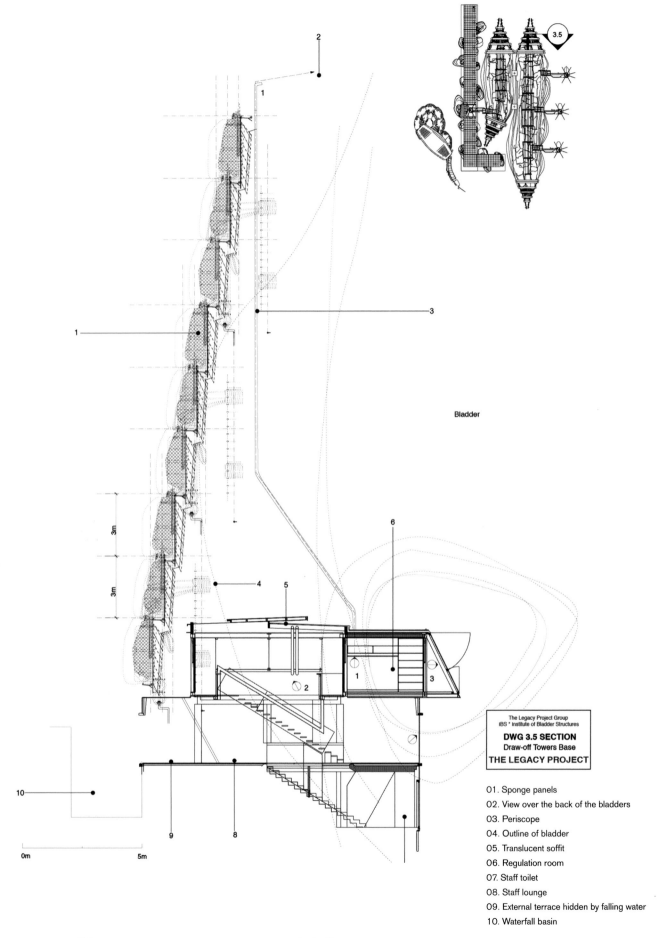

3.5

Bladder

3m

3m

The Legacy Project Group
IBS * Institute of Bladder Structures

DWG 3.5 SECTION
Draw-off Towers Base

THE LEGACY PROJECT

01. Sponge panels

02. View over the back of the bladders

03. Periscope

04. Outline of bladder

05. Translucent soffit

06. Regulation room

07. Staff toilet

08. Staff lounge

09. External terrace hidden by falling water

10. Waterfall basin

0m   5m

Walker   The Bladders

∧　Instrument No.5—Dilators—allows access
between the soft bladder folds.

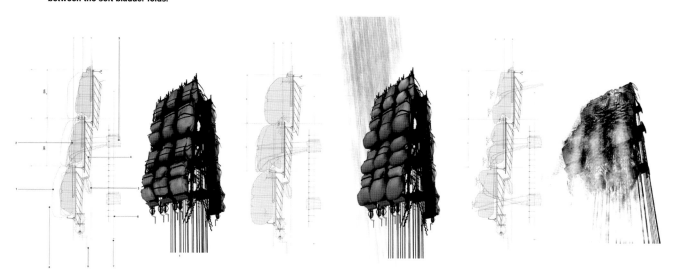

∧　Draw-off towers and bladder sections.

∧   **Instrument No. 2—Thirsty Walls—hard
shell performative water collection.**
⟩   **Instrument No.7—Clamps: Draw-off towers
—controlled draw off of water from soft bladder
system. Clamps avoid over-topping and maintain
structural stability of the bladders.**

Walker   The Bladders

THE BLADDERS

SWAMP THING
ALL THAT IS SOLID

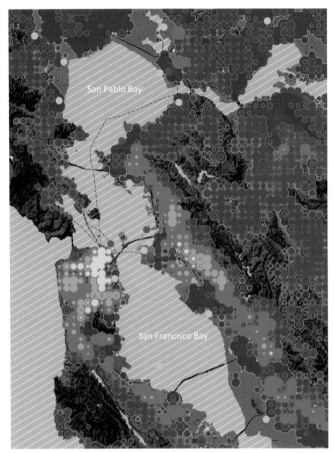

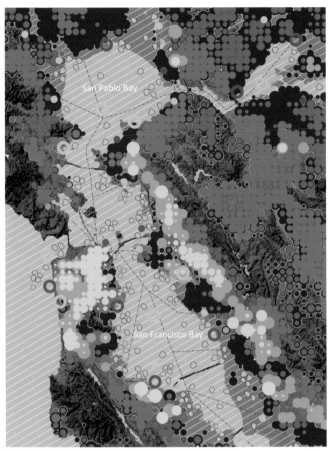

∧   +0 Year San Francisco Bay Estuary.
**The San Francisco Bay is home to the port of
Oakland, one of the busiest ports in the U.S.
Dredging to maintain the shipping channels in the
bay is economically critical; however, dumping
dredged silt into the Estuary destroys habitat
and biodiversity.**

∧   +100 Year San Francisco Bay Estuary.
Swamp Thing **re-appropriates three to seven million
cubic yards of dredged silt and over 700,000 un-
used shipping containers languishing in ports across
the U.S. to an amphibious urban edge. This offers a
heterogeneous mix of zoning, transportation, and
recreational scenarios from which new socioeco-
nomic, cultural, and bionomic relations emerge.**

In the famous Marvel comic, *Swamp Thing*, scientist Alex Olsen is genetically transformed by scientific blowback, marking Nature's reaction against efforts to control it through experimentation. This parable finds parallels in the current crisis of rising water levels, as global warming progressively wreaks havoc on the urban infrastructure of coastal cities across the globe. Despite a collective desire to solve these problems, we must accept that a first generation of disasters may have already fallen upon us. We have witnessed tidal waves in the seas of south China, levee failures in New Orleans, and sinking coastlines. *Swamp Thing* accepts

disaster as a founding principle, and assumes that only in response to crises can political will conjure the creative forces of human action and design.

The twentieth century gave rise to iconic public works projects that revolutionized the American landscape. Natural disasters, technological innovation, and federal initiatives provided important mandates for the U.S. Army Corps of Engineers (USACE). Under the culmination of the Flood Control Act of 1936, the USACE, with its enormous centralization of research and funding, began to re-sculpt much of the riparian landscapes with intricate levee and dam systems. Prior to World

War II, cooperative interests in hydroelectric generation, New Deal labor relief, and disaster mitigation produced a federal top-down effort at scales never witnessed before. However, as early as 1852, engineers such as Charles Ellet, Jr. had sensitively understood the fallibility of a catch-all levee system and instead believed in a complex site-specific system of levees, wetlands, and tributary relief systems.[1] Unfortunately, other voices dominated and an aggressive strategy of levee and damming was implemented. Growing urbanization and populations forced settlements to spread directly up to the waters' edge.

1. Joseph L Arnold, *The Evolution of the 1936 Flood Control Act* (Fort Belvoir, Va.: Office of History, U.S. Army Corps of Engineers, 1988), 7.

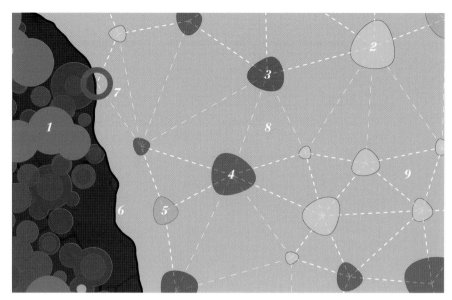

‹ **Initial Deployment Strategy.** Based on reclaimed marshland and local population demands (1), a proper ratio is determined that strives initially to restore 20% of lost marshland. These wetland islands (2) also act as buffers from fluctuating sea levels. Recreational islands (3) are introduced as flagship eco-tourist industries over the following years while farming (4) and aquaculture (5) islands provide food sources closer to the urban edge (6). Future ports (7) are opened near dense urban centers. Dredging depth and island proximities allow for vessel clearances ranging from post Panamax ocean vessels (8) to dredging boats and cruise vessels (9).

Swamp Thing examines the San Francisco estuary watershed which covers roughly sixty thousand square miles or nearly forty percent of the surface area of California. As the largest estuary in the northern hemisphere, the San Francisco water system is also home to the main valve for the world's largest manipulation of hydrological systems, composed of dams, reservoirs, channels, and aqueducts, which move water from the Sacramento San Joaquin River Delta to local farmlands and beyond to Southern California. This mega-artery provides drinking water to two thirds of California and irrigates 4.5 million acres of farmland annually. However, population growth, volatile climate patterns, and leveraged state budgets continue to compound, threatening the water infrastructure with potential stress and failure.

Swamp Thing is a *peri*structure, an alternative to the top-down approach where infrastructure does not seek to be the dominant and totalizing system. Instead, its efficiency emerges from nuanced and selective insertion of a softer system of cellular buoys cast into the watershed that grows intensively. This attenuated web absorbs the flux of weather patterns and tidal movement. Rather than suppressing and, ultimately, repressing natural forces, the peristructural strategy leverages the feedback loops resonant in healthy hydrographies in order to exponentially restore ecologies while maintaining urban complexities. The project envisions an incremental, cellular network of artificial islands that will grow over decades, streaming into our consciousness and watershed. These tethered buoys hold soft absorptive bionomic material, which will facilitate the emergence of natural systems along the edges where ecologies, both natural and artificial, sit on the verge of collapse. The simplicity of the unit belies the abundant complexity that will eventually graft onto peristructure.

The San Francisco Bay serves as a test site. The significance of the San Francisco watershed is indisputable. It is an ecology upon which the entire state's economy, culture and livelihood depends. Over the last two hundred years, urban development and re-sculpting of the San Francisco watershed has reduced the delta from five hundred square miles to ninety square miles. Of the three hundred square miles of brackish and salt marshes along the fringes of the Bay, roughly two thirds remain in the form of tidal marsh and salt ponds while twenty percent has been modified as diked marshland. Seventy-five percent of the original watershed has been taken over by direct or indirect agricultural and industrial uses. *Swamp Thing* seeks to repeal this environmental impact. Reintroducing marshland in the form of floating ecologies, the compartmentalization of land, water, and city can be mitigated. *Swamp Thing* proposes the transformation of the modern landscape and its orthogonal binaries of coastal/inland and urban/suburban. This mutation will create zones of rich and complex landscapes where urbanism can be more intensively experienced by degrees of "wetness." Over the course of the next hundred years, as tides rise, this system has the potential to restore the wetlands back to their original state of two hundred years ago.

The buoyant islands and their 'soft centers' are designed with a variety of programs and bio-materials. Along urban coasts, the initial release of floating farms and fish hatchery islands can serve consumers and also shorten the chain of food distribution. Elsewhere, the gradual accumulation of marsh islands will piggy-back off existing dredging channels placing fill inside the buoys as absorptive matter, increasing biodiversity and subduing storm surges. This network will work as passive levees or flood tanks to store, capture and reuse water. The islands will be equipped with sustainable, passive technologies that include hydroelectric power and self-irrigation. Local constituents will guide the placement and programming of islands creating ownership and fostering the stewardship of local habitat.

Emergent micro-ecologies embedded in natural systems provide more diverse, adaptable and responsive alternatives than mechanized responses in handling water levels. *Swamp Thing* proposes a fundamentally altered vision of the city in which a heterogeneous mixture of built and natural environments will produce a new landscape of the picturesque. *Swamp Thing*, like the *Man-Thing* scenario, argues that human development and survival is contingent upon its ability to reconcile itself to natural forces.

Project Credits: ALL THAT IS SOLID—Alex Chew, Max Kuo, Danielle Wagner; Project Assistant—Heather McGinn

• • • **ALL THAT IS SOLID is a collaborative architectural design and research practice investigating material and strategic ecologies and the novel sensations they produce.**

ISLAND TYPE	ISLAND PROGRAM	ISLAND FUNDING		

01 TIDAL MARSH

 Wildlife Reserve

 Research & Conservation

 Utilize Dredged Silt

 Construction Recycled Mat

02 FARM LAND

 Agricultural Food Production

 Production Of Goods

Corporate Sponsorship

 Construction Recycled Mat

03 FISH HATCHERY

 Sustainable Fishing

 Production Of Goods

 Corporate Sponsorship

 Construction Recycled Mat

04 URBAN INFILL

 Ecotourism

 Travel Destination

Corporate Sponsorship

 Construction Recycled Mat

05 TIMED-RELEASE PROGRAM

 Dining   Urban Markets   Concerts & Event Space   Sports & Recreation   Urban Water sports

01 TIDAL MARSH

By reintroducing marshland in the form of floating islands, we have the ability to manipulate its density, location, and hydrographic nature. These tethered islands will concentrate in areas in need of protection from storm surges and tidal fluctuations.

02 FARM LAND

Producing foodstuffs and local crop is an essential feature of Swamp Thing. Along with other overland local distributors and farmers markets, this will shorten the distribution chains that are currently subsidized by cheap petrol.

03 FISH HATCHER

Certain islands will be donuts where a bottomless center is filled with farmed fish hatche Along with farmland, this firs phase deployment is a step towards replacing unsustaina fishing practices.

03

∧   **Island types, deployment, and economic strategy.**

ISLAND FUNCTION

Ecological
Water Consumption

Ballast
Submersion

Erratic
Storm Buffer

Hydroelectric
Wave Energy

Water
Filtration System

Erratic
Storm Buffer

Hydroelectric
Wave Energy

Ballast
Submersion

Erratic
Storm Buffer

Hydroelectric
Wave Energy

Ecological
Water Consumption

Erratic
Storm Buffer

Hydroelectric
Wave Energy

ISLAND DEPLOYMENT

Clustered To
Form Buffer Zones

Clustered Near
Dense Urban Edge

Clustered Near
Industrial Edge

Clustered Near
Dense Urban Edge

Camping

Aviaries

Game Fishing

Hunting &
Outdoorsmanship

Co-op

05

04   URBAN INFILL

The urban grid will be under-
mined by shifting wet sedimentation. New coastlines will require
synergistic relations between
overland and oversea travel, new
shoreline views, and hard/soft-
scaping.

05   TIMED-RELEASE

In a projective cellular time-
release, Swamp Thing will deploy
with careful coordination
between the region's multitude of
stakeholders and inhabitants,
increasing its programmatic
diversity over time.

04

02

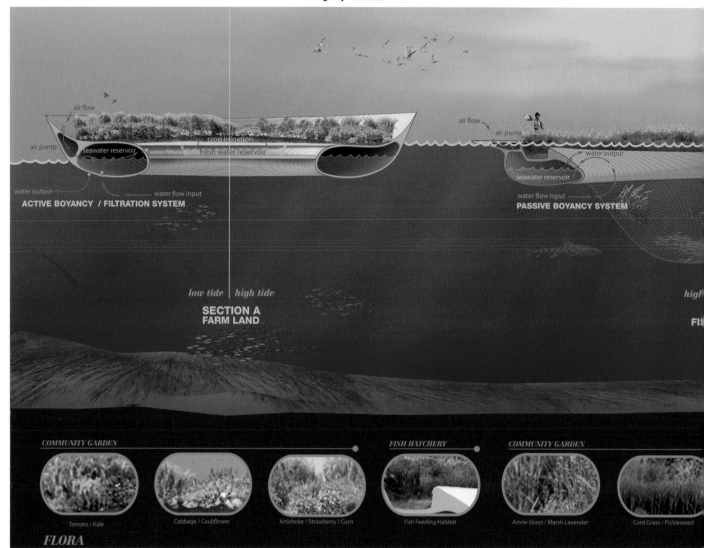

air flow
air pump
seawater reservoir   water filtration   **fresh water reservoir**
crop irrigation

air flow
air pump
water output
seawater reservoir

water output   water flow input
ACTIVE BOYANCY / FILTRATION SYSTEM

water flow input
PASSIVE BOYANCY SYSTEM

low tide | high tide

SECTION A
FARM LAND

high

FIS

COMMUNITY GARDEN   *FISH HATCHERY*   *COMMUNITY GARDEN*

Tomato / Kale   Cabbage / Cauliflower   Artichoke / Strawberry / Corn   Fish Feeding Habitat   Arrow Grass / Marsh Lavender   Cord Grass / Pickleweed

FLORA

∧   **Sections through farm, fish, and marsh**
island types.

TIDAL MARSH - FLOATING

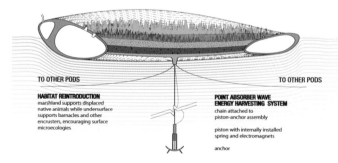

TO OTHER PODS   TO OTHER PODS

HABITAT REINTRODUCTION
marshland supports displaced
native animals while undersurface
supports barnacles and other
encrusters, encouraging surface
microecologies

POINT ABSORBER WAVE
ENERGY HARVESTING SYSTEM
chain attached to
piston-anchor assembly

piston with internally installed
spring and electromagnets

anchor

HYDROPHYTIC VEGETATION
emergent vegetation on edges
floating vegetation as it gets deeper
submergent vegetation in the middle

HYDRIC SOIL
top layer of organic soil (can be shifted from
other already established wetlands)
bottom layer of dredged silt

LONG TERM WATER MANAGEMENT
shallow marshland utilizes and dissipates water while
photosynthesis introduces clean air into ecosystem

wetland plants act as natural filtration
for water management

TIDAL MARSH - SUBMERGED

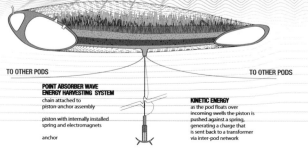

ORIGINAL OPEN WATER LEVEL
ORIGINAL TIDAL SWELL
swell keeps growing as a result of
compounding unobstructed forces

NEW OPEN WATER LEVEL
NEW TIDAL SWELL
force of current diminishes as it
hits submerged peri-structure

REPLENISH
marshes replenish themselves
with water during tidal surges and
high tide through a process of
artificial submersion

the concave curvature froms a
crucible of water/silt retention

BUOYANCY CONTROL
pumps fill and empty
ballast tanks as needed
much like a submarine
to control buoyancy
and capture water

CAPTURED WATER
unaffected by swell

reintroduced as
swell subsides

TO OTHER PODS   TO OTHER PODS

POINT ABSORBER WAVE
ENERGY HARVESTING SYSTEM
chain attached to
piston-anchor assembly

piston with internally installed
spring and electromagnets

anchor

KINETIC ENERGY
as the pod floats over
incoming swells the piston is
pushed against a spring,
generating a charge that
is sent back to a transformer
via inter-pod network

All That Is Solid   Swamp Thing

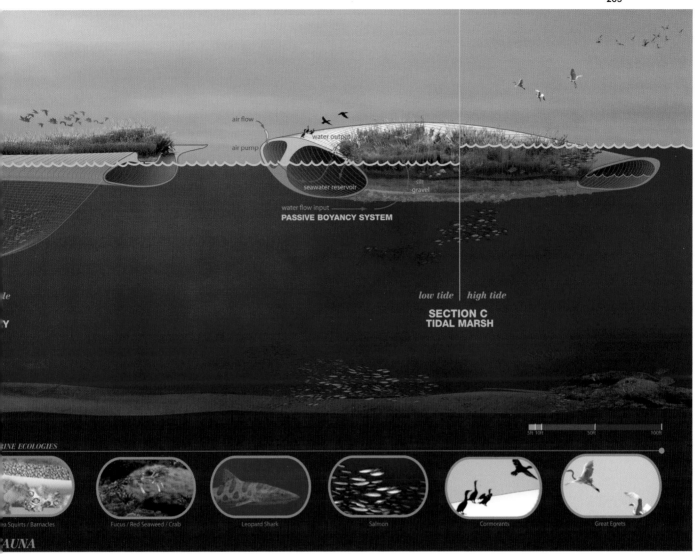

air flow

water output

air pump

seawater reservoir

silt
gravel

water flow input
PASSIVE BOYANCY SYSTEM

low tide | *high tide*

**SECTION C
TIDAL MARSH**

RINE ECOLOGIES

a Squirts / Barnacles

Fucus / Red Seaweed / Crab

Leopard Shark

Salmon

Cormorants

Great Egrets

AUNA

FISH HATCHERY

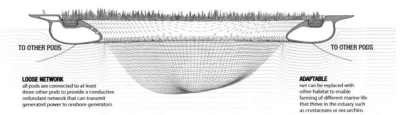

HYDROPHYTIC VEGETATION
marsh ring around feeding area to grow
plankton, krill and algae

SELF SUSTAINING
periodically submerges to feed fish and
replenish water supply thus requiring
less on site monitoring of aquaculture

TO OTHER PODS

TO OTHER PODS

LOOSE NETWORK
all pods are connected to at least
three other pods to provide a conductive
redundant network that can transmit
generated power to onshore generators

ADAPTABLE
net can be replaced with
other habitat to enable
farming of different marine life
that thrive in the estuary such
as crustaceans or sea urchins

COMMUNITY GARDEN

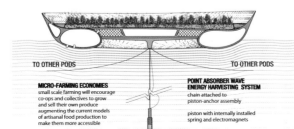

DEW COLLECTION
tall sloped walls with foil surface
for dew collection and protection
from salt water

collection tray sends water through
osmosis chamber en route to
fresh water storage tank

CYCLING CROPS
in order to maintain soil richness
crop cycles that are symbiotic with
one another will be planted

TO OTHER PODS

TO OTHER PODS

DRIP IRRIGATION
embedded drip irrigation system
waters plants automatically requiring
less monitoring

EFFICIENCY
deployed close to urban areas
the garden pods will offer a truly
local food source

MICRO-FARMING ECONOMIES
small scale farming will encourage
co-ops and collectives to grow
and sell their own produce
augmenting the current models
of artisanal food production to
make them more accessible

**POINT ABSORBER WAVE
ENERGY HARVESTING SYSTEM**
chain attached to
piston-anchor assembly

piston with internally installed
spring and electromagnets

anchor

REVERSE OSMOSIS WATER FILTRATION
utilizing buoyancy pumps to push
water through the reverse osmosis
chamber into clean water tanks

reduces the stress on existing
farmlands and water systems
while anticipating for exponential
population growth in the future

floating land mass is an alternative
to urban gardens where the value
of land might be prohibitive

∧ **Marsh islands.**

∧ **Farm islands.**

AQUA_DERMIS
MARIELA DE FELIX

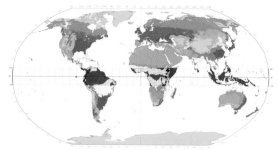

∧ **Zones of greatest humidity and heat in the Equatorial Belt.**

Climate defines the way we eat, work, and even sleep. It affects not only our daily life, but also the way we behave as a civilization. As an inherently powerful physical force, our relationship with climate will eventually determine our potential survival as a society. The alarming rate of change in world temperatures demands new performative models of occupation that react and adapt to environmental change. Inspired by the body's capacity for thermo-regulation, *Aqua_Dermis* is speculative prototype for desalination and cooling. The project explores how specific conditions found in hot and humid equatorial zones provide a unique opportunity for alternative cooling systems, which can fully adapt to climatic demands.

Aqua_Dermis is a hybrid prototype for residing in the tropical zone, comprised of a desalination facility and fresh water storage facility embedded into an occupiable living surface. Its porous, yet highly reflective surface becomes the connection between solar heat and cool deep ocean water, producing fresh water through a low-energy evaporative process. Mainly composed of rubber, a local material in many tropical regions, the system is supported by an internal steel mesh similar to the structural composition of a domestic water hose. This material allows for unidirectional flexibility while providing inherent rigidity, especially when filled with water. In order to become buoyant and stable on the water, a layer of recycled foam is embedded in between the rubber and the steel mesh.

The extensive variety of sensorial environments created above and within this surface become part of an occupiable homeostatic skin that provides a conditioned environment for its inhabitants. During the hot seasons, the surface takes advantage of the abundant sun to activate evaporation of the cool ocean water below. Working similarly to the *Watercone* (a marketed passive solar desalination unit), the desalination cell produces fresh water through condensation. The structure of each 'cell' diverts this water into filtering and storage pockets on the sides. The project integrates existing low-cost desalination and sand-filtration techniques, to create a water bank for future use, both locally and regionally. *Aqua_Dermis* responds directly to its climatic conditions, creating a misting, cooling surface for inhabitation during the hot season, and collecting fresh water during the rainy season.

Three different case studies are presented to demonstrate the flexibility of the system and its adaptation to

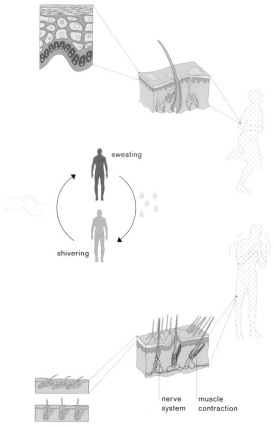

∧ **How does our body regulate its own temperature?**

different economic conditions and programmatic situations commonly found in the equatorial belt. The first site is a fishing village where the system is simple and economical. In this case, the surface serves mainly as a cooling storage facility for fish and produces fresh water for the subsistence of nearby settlements. The second site is a coastal agricultural village where the system is mainly used to store produce and provide fresh water to coastal settlements. The third site proposes a system of leisure for offshore marinas where fresh water supply is limited and beaches are not accessible. In this proposal the system acts as an artificial beach with cooling surfaces and fresh water supply for visiting boats. In all three case studies, the system responds to local conditions of resources, program and economies while embedded within a territorial discussion of how soft surfaces can inhabit the equatorial belt.

• • • **Originally from Puerto Rico, Mariela has always been interested in alternative cooling strategies, especially in the humid tropical zone. After completing her Master's in Architecture from the University of Toronto, she has continued her research on how ocean water can be a vital part of creating sustainable environmental comfort in hot regions.**

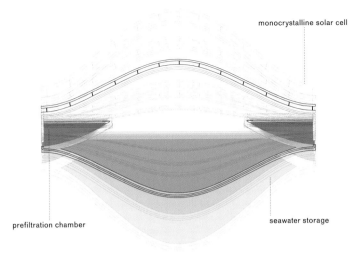

monocrystalline solar cell

prefiltration chamber

seawater storage

DESALINATION UNIT
with Solar Panel and Transfer Pocket

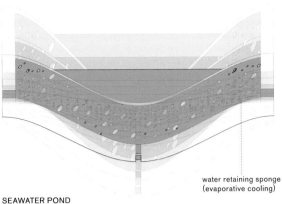

water retaining sponge
(evaporative cooling)

SEAWATER POND
with Water Flow Control System

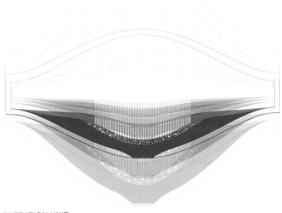

FILTRATION UNIT
with UV and Sponge Filter

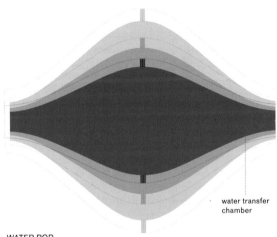

water transfer
chamber

WATER POD
with Water Flow Control Systems

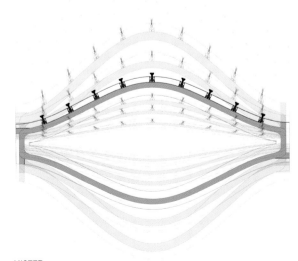

MISTER
with Seawater Channel

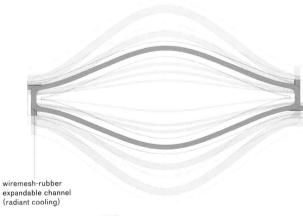

wiremesh-rubber
expandable channel
(radiant cooling)

WATER WALL CHAMBER
with Water Flow Control System

 Cell typologies.

∧ **Comprehensive section.**

∧ **Offshore marina.**

de Felix   Aqua_Dermis

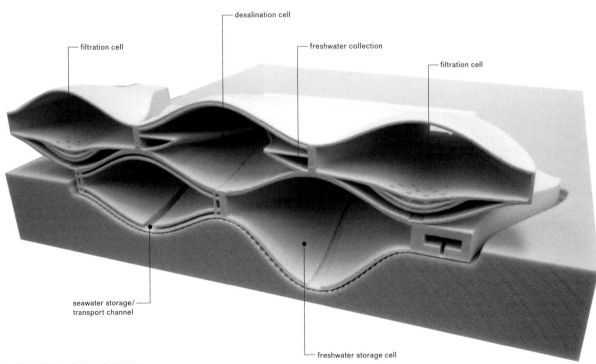

filtration cell

desalination cell

freshwater collection

filtration cell

seawater storage/
transport channel

freshwater storage cell

∧ **Desalination diagram/prototype.**

GOES SOFT

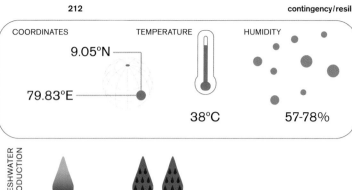

COORDINATES   TEMPERATURE   HUMIDITY

9.05°N

79.83°E

38°C   57-78%

FRESHWATER PRODUCTION

FRESHWATER USAGE

COOLING

SOLAR ENERGY

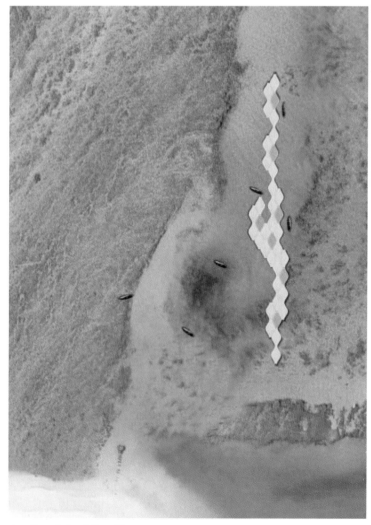

∧   **Case study—fishing village.**

de Felix   Aqua_Dermis

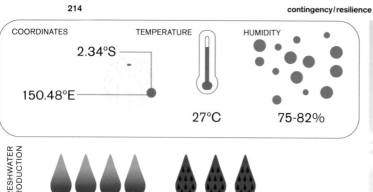

COORDINATES

2.34°S

150.48°E

TEMPERATURE

27°C

HUMIDITY

75-82%

FRESHWATER PRODUCTION

FRESHWATER USAGE

COOLING

SOLAR ENERGY

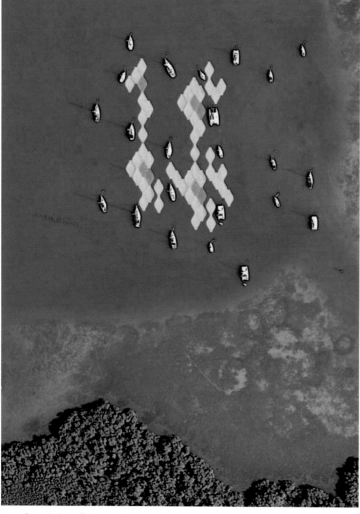

∧   **Case study—offshore marina.**

de Felix   Aqua_Dermis

RESILIENT INFRASTRUCTURES

NEERAJ BHATIA

Throughout the history of architecture, the role of the Architect has been to determine lines that ordered the world. In the past two centuries, however, as cities have rapidly expanded into vast urban territories that are organized through the negotiation of politics, economics, ecosystems, and cultural values, the ability to determine such lines has become progressively more complex and suspect. Such suspicion stems in part from the fact that architecture traditionally deals with determinacy, permanence and form—characteristics that are increasingly difficult to reconcile with the rapidly transforming metropolis. On the one hand, this has sparked a disciplinary identity crisis characterized by a yearning for architecture's opposite—flexibility, dynamism, immateriality and indeterminacy, in response to such emergent variegations. Moreover, the transformative nature of these systems acts as a fundamental disturbance to architecture, which traditionally thrives in stasis. If resilience is defined as the ability to return to an original state after a disturbance, this is typically achieved in architecture by neutralizing difference or accounting for extremes. Architecture could, however, gain renewed agency by adopting a soft resilience into its very structure—evolving and transforming with the contemporary metropolis.

To understand how architecture and urbanism can operate with a soft resilience, it is useful to begin by framing architecture as oscillating between *ecological* poles. The definition of ecology is *both* an organism's relationship to other organisms—the *'human ecology'* (i.e. our political, economic and social spheres); as well as an organism's relationship to its environment—the *'natural ecology'* (including the design of landscape, infrastructures, urban form, as well as the impact of environmental conditions such as geology, weather and ecosystems, to name a few). Architecture has always been a negotiation between the 'human' and 'natural' spheres, collecting resources and responding (often hermetically) to the external environment, while also requiring political will, social approval and economic support to reify. But such a negotiation has usually privileged one sphere over another, rather than seek a symbiosis between these spheres to create a true ecological project that operates through feedback and resilience.

i. Human Ecology—The Dialectic of Pluralism

As a decisive factor on how we approach the issue of economics, social integration, the environment and their associated spatial formats, the political sphere acts as a critical hinge in the reconciliation of the ecological project. Two patterns that have become realities over the past three decades include the increasing urbanization of the globe[1] and its simultaneously

∧ **City Square, Giacometti (1948)—A collective platform of distinct individuals.**

expanded interconnectivity.[2] Although these patterns are no longer shocking, they have brought to the surface the question of multiculturalism, diversity, and pluralism in the globalized city. While pluralism is typically understood as meaning diverse, different or divergent, it is in fact much more complex and political in nature. Political theorist Hannah Arendt has one of the most refined definitions of pluralism, calling it the dialectic of our 'distinct-equality' and positioning it at the core of the public sphere:

> Human plurality, the basic condition of both action and speech, has the twofold character of *equality* and *distinction*. If men were not equal, they could neither understand each other and those who came before them nor plan for the future and foresee the needs of those who will come after them. If men were not distinct, each human being distinguished from any other who is, was, or will every be, they would need neither speech nor action to make themselves understood.[3]

Arendt's characterization of this complex and seemingly contradictory public sphere is perhaps best summarized through her analogy of a group of people sitting around a table. For Arendt, the table is the common world—it simultaneously connects and bonds those around it while preventing them from falling over each other and assimilating belief systems. The disappearance of the table would leave strangers in a space that lacked a common bond—this would be the fall of the public realm and its associated reality and stability.[4]

1. UNFPA, "Urbanization: A Majority in Cities", http://www.unfpa.org/pds/urbanization.htm

2. Thomas Friedman, *The World is Flat* (New York: Farrar, Straus and Giroux Publishers, 2005).

3. Hannah Arendt, *The Human Condition* (Chicago, IL: University of Chicago Press, 1958), 175-176. [emphasis added]

4. Ibid., 52.

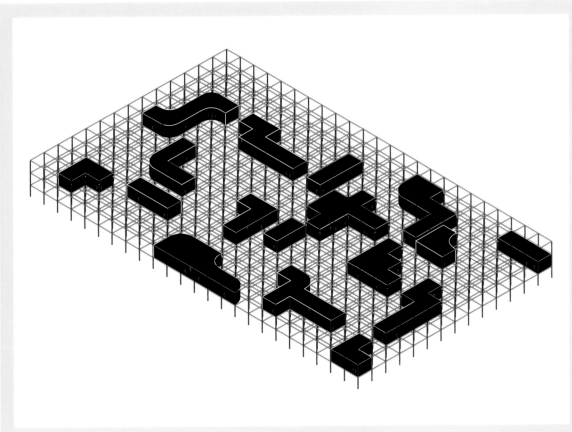

∧ *Ville Spatiale*, Yona Friedman (1959–)—A collective framework containing individual, flexible and mobile pods.
(Drawing by Alicia Hergenroeder)

In essence, the metaphor of Arendt's pluralism is embodied within Giacometti's *City Square*, wherein distinct individuals are tied together on a common platform. Extrapolating from Arendt, the political project of the city is to reconcile the collective (*equality*) and individual (*distinction*). Surely, Arendt is not alone in this quest—think about the tension and similarities on various philosophical and design debates over the past two centuries: objective vs. subjective (*Enlightenment vs. Romanticism*)[5]; collective vs. individual (*CIAM*)[6]; exterior vs. interior (*Team X's Doorstep Analogy*)[7]; control vs. choice (*Archigram*)[8]; frame vs. pod (*megastructure*)[9]; determinacy vs. indeterminacy (*hard vs. soft systems*)[10]; etc. None of these debates, however, was able to mediate such a dialectic that is at the core of a politically empowered metropolis. Increasingly comprised of a grouping of various constituencies, a scan through the current metropolis provokes the ultimate question of *where the common object of collectivity presently exists*? The issue of diversity[11] is even more pronounced today, with more than half the population of some cities consisting of visible 'minorities'. This growing situation prompts a design interrogation of how one can provide unity in diversity, reconcile the individual and collective, and accommodate distinction and equality. It is a political ecology rooted in pluralism that can produce a collective agency, capable of restructuring our economic and socio-cultural territory and its relationship to the natural environment.

Form and the Emergence of Soft

An attempt to reconcile such issues reached a fatalistic apogee in the typology of the megastructure. Le Corbusier, who repeatedly stressed the importance of the individual and collective in the C.I.A.M Athens Charter, planted the seed for the megastructure in his *Plan Obus* (1933) in Algiers. In his project, a continuous linear form merged architecture, infrastructure and topography, while subdividing into multiple dwelling units. Within such a framework, Corbusier left the dwellings "open"

5. Isaiah Berlin, "The Counter-Enlightenment" in *The Proper Study of Mankind*. ed. Hardy, Henry (New York: Farrar, Strauss and Giroux, 1997), 243-268.

6. Le Corbusier, "The City and Its Region" and "Conclusion—Main Points of Doctrine." in *The Athens Charter* (New York: Grossman Publishers, 1973), 43-49 and 91-105.

7. Van Eyck, Aldo, "Is Architecture Going to Reconcile Basic Values?" in *Documents of Modern Architecture: CIAM '59 in Otterlo*, ed. Jürgen Joedicke (New York: Universe Books Inc., 1961), 26-35.

8. Archigram, "Control and Choice" in *Archigram*, ed. Peter Cook and Michael Webb (New York: Princeton Architectural Press, 1999), 68.

9. Hadas Steiner, "Within the Big Structure" in *Megastructure Reloaded*, ed. Sabrina van der Ley and Markus Richter (Berlin, Hatje Cantz, 2008), 136-152.

10. Archigram, "Open Ends: Editorial from Archigram 8" in *Archigram: A Guide to Archigram 1961-74* (Taiwan, Garden City Publishing, 2003), 216-227.

11. As opposed to political concept of pluralism.

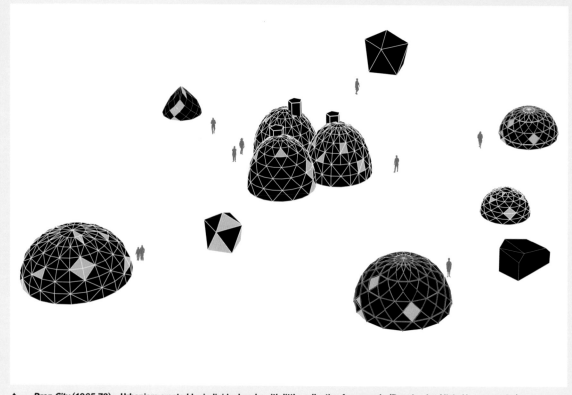

∧   **Drop City (1965-73)—Urbanism created by individual pods with little collective framework. (Drawing by Alicia Hergenroeder)**

to be designed by their individual occupants and revealed the diversity that he envisioned through his sketches. Thirty years later, in the 1960s, the megastructure had fully bloomed and its basic characteristics were exemplified in Yona Friedman's *Ville Spatiale* (1958). The *Ville Spatiale* was organized by a universal frame of infrastructure descended from Enlightenment values—it was permanent, deterministic, and provided order to the collective. Within this frame, a series of indeterminate, mobile and flexible pods were to empower the individual. The megastructure oscillated between control and choice and was eventually critiqued for being a mere illusion of choice disguised behind controlled variations. Emerging as a reaction to the heavily deterministic and hard projects of C.I.A.M and the New Monumentality (not to mention WWII), the megastructure was attempting to shed the 'hard' and such criticism resonated with its primary proponents. For instance, Archigram's acknowledgement of this contradiction shifted their own discourse in favor of "choice", stating in the editorial of Issue 7 an attempt to go "beyond architecture" (the title of the issue) and forecasting that Issue 8 might not have any buildings at all.[12] The editorial of Issue 8, "Open Ends", stated in regards to design: "It is less a question of total idea and total consistency,"[13]

revealing the abandonment of the hegemonic framework and a refocusing of efforts on the individualistic counterculture projects of the soft pod. Soft material constructions, such as inflatables, were viewed as a democratic alternative, allowing for continuous change and portability.[14] Soft was deemed to provide differentiation to an increasingly heterogeneous society comprised of individual subjectivities through characteristics such as flexibility, responsiveness, and adaptability,[15] and no longer required a collective frame.

With such a focus on the soft *unit*, few examples of urban projects stemming from the pod exist from this era. Archigram's *Instant City* (1968-72) is often cited as an emblematic soft urban project. In *Instant City*, a temporary, nomadic, event metropolis (which also happens to be an airship—the largest soft pod of all) plugs into an existing city, utilizing it as hardware. The dependence on the existing city's framework revealed the difficulty in providing overall coherence, which is required of infrastructural integration at the scale of urbanism. Archigram intelligently avoids this issue by solely focusing on the software as a parasite to allow for the purity of the pod(s). *Drop City* (1965-1973) serves as another example of a settlement constructed solely of soft

12. Simon Sadler, "Beyond Architecture: Indeterminacy, Systems and the Dissolution of Buildings" in *Archigram: Architecture without Architecture* (Cambridge: MIT Press, 2005), 90-93.

13. Archigram, "Open Ends: Editorial from Archigram 8" in *Archigram: A Guide to Archigram 1961-74* (Taiwan, Garden City

Publishing, 2003), 216-227.

14. Hadas Stiener, "The Forces of Matter" in *The Journal of Architecture*, 10 (2005), 91-109.

15. For more in depth discussion of the 'soft pod' project in the Viennese context, see: Jon Cummings, "Of Pop and Prosthesis: Vienna, 1965-72" in this almanac.

pods. Formed as an artist community established from the bottom-up in Southern Colorado, *Drop City* epitomized the counter-culture hippie movement of rural communal living. It was comprised of a series of Fuller-inspired geodesic domes assembled by residents from found materials. There was no 'city plan' but rather a collection of pods that alluded to the impermanence of a camp. The collective process of building held the socio-political ecology of the community together, as described by a resident:

> The hardest time in a commune, particularly *Drop City*, is the time after the building gets done. While everyone is working together on actual construction the energy is centered, there is fantastic high spirit, everyone knows what he is doing all the time. But after the building is done comes a time of dissolution. There's no focus for the group energy…"[16]

The dissolution felt by residents was the lack of collective goal once a project was completed, as the focus and origin of the city was built from the scale of the individual with little collective framework. As *Drop City* gained attention and grew in size (to approximately thirty residents), internal conflicts between residents lead to its very demise. To characterize *Drop City* in Arendt's terms would suggest that the city was a grouping of individuals existing within a tenuous collective framework, ultimately inciting the breakdown of its public sphere. While the abandonment of the universal collective frame seemed like an innocent move for Archigram and other megastructuralists, its disappearance eroded the frail dialectic of pluralism as well as the city as a collective political form.

A crucial lesson from the megastructure and soft-pod projects is the necessity for feedback between the collective and individual to allow each to influence and transform the system.[17] This is critical because it allows disturbance to be absorbed by the units, which can reconfigure the framework, or by the frame itself, forecasting an alteration to the organization of the units. Soft resilience can therefore be achieved through a distributed, differentiated and networked system that can respond at a multiplicity of scales. In this sense, the system is simultaneously 'bottom-up' and 'top-down'. Perhaps even more important than feedback is the need for a communal goal, which serves as the impetus for the collective. While this goal may evolve in time, it continually links the individual and collective and makes the city more than a mere grouping of buildings.

ii. The Natural Ecology—Soft Infrastructures

The photograph *Earthrise*[18] taken by the Apollo space shuttle framed the globe as a unified, yet differentiated object and provided an image for a new global collective in a moment of increasing socio-political fragmentation. In the current era of environmental crisis, the natural environment is perhaps the only issue that effects all of humanity equally and requires the

∧ **Earthrise (December 24, 1968)—The first image of the globe depicted a new collective as well as the feedback between various scales and systems. (Image NASA/Apollo 8)**

formation of a new collective to be addressed. This emphasis on the collective natural environment repositions the role of *infrastructure* as the foundational spatial format, as it allows for the interconnection between the human and environmental spheres—constantly negotiating the boundary between landscape, urbanism and architecture. As the notion of the 'public' continues to parcel into various niche groups, infrastructure, as one of the few spatial categories that is funded and utilized by the entire public, remains the last vestige of publicness in the contemporary metropolis.

Equally important to the framing of a collective, *Earthrise* depicted the globe as a vast and complex series of dynamic systems and made it apparent that the globe's stability was rooted in such dynamism. These systems could be characterized as 'soft' in their complex negotiation through feedback of the XS and XL scales. The renewed soft project stemming from such understanding has evolved beyond materiality to a *system* of organization. Infrastructure is implicated here once again as it oscillates between the local and global as well as the natural and artificial. Typically emerging from the top-down, infrastructure traditionally operates in the framework of resistance instead of resilience. In essence, infrastructure has been deployed as a machine over the larger landscape, which thrives from its subcomponents conforming to its logic. While sub-networks of infrastructural systems offer a form of contingency, the essential conception and deployment has been to mitigate and eliminate disturbance. Although infrastructure supports almost all aspects of our daily lives—water, waste, mobility, energy, food, etc.—it has rarely been

16. Bill Voyd, "Funk Architecture" in *Shelter and Society*, ed. Paul Oliver (London: Barrie & Jenkins Publishers, 1976), 156.

17. For larger discussion on complex feedback processes, see: Nicholas Negroponte,

"Responsive Architecture" in *Soft Architecture Machines* (Cambridge: MIT Press, 1975), 135-137.

18. Further discussion of *Earthrise* and its relation to the soft project can be found in:

Sanford Kwinter, "Soft Systems" in *Culture Lab*, ed. Brian Boigon (New York: Princeton Architectural Press, 1992), 207-227.

Bhatia

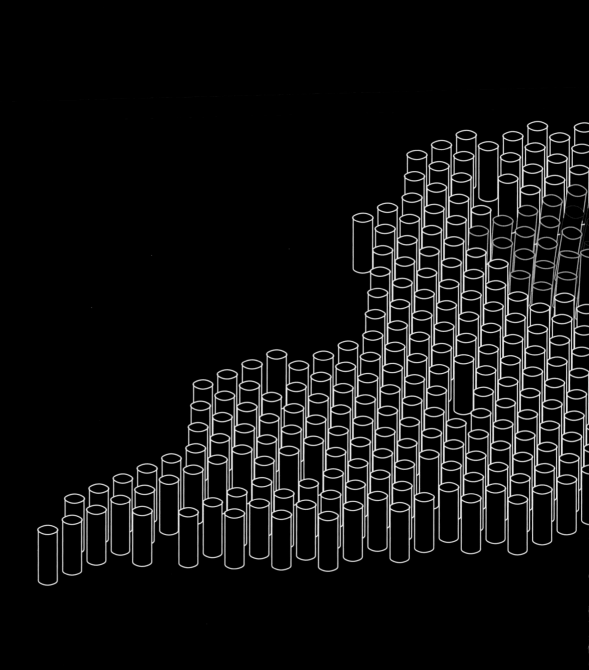

∧ *Magic Carpet and Brunhilda's Magic Ring of Fire*, Michael Webb (1968)—soft field of air tubes that suppresses the notion of the collective framework. (Drawing by Alicia Hergenroeder)

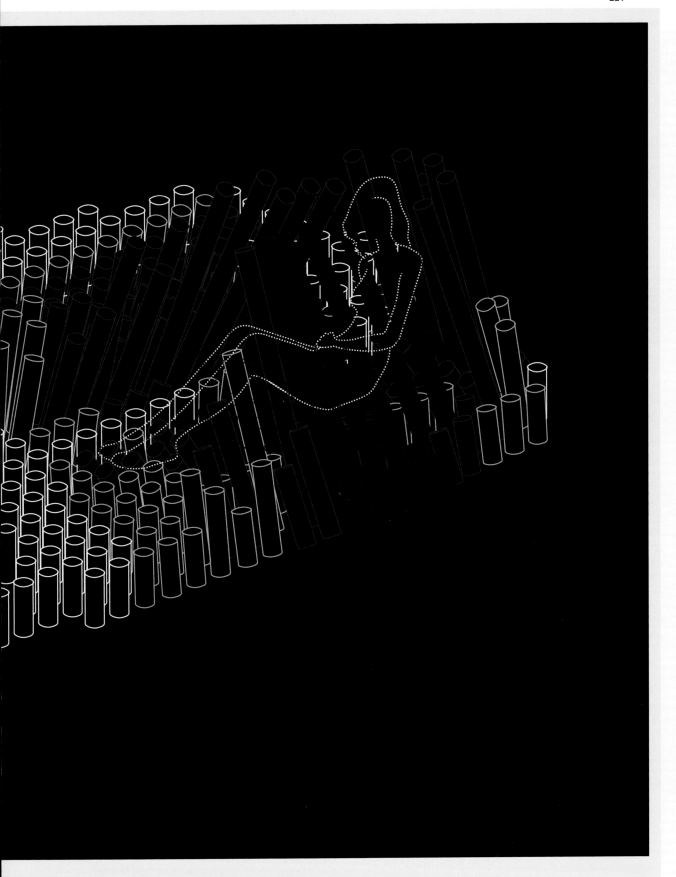

thought of holistically or symbiotically. The critical project that this new collective must undertake is a paradigmatic shift in the role and deployment of infrastructure, such that it operates symbiotically between the human and natural spheres as a soft system that provides resilience through the continual negotiation of 'top down' and 'bottom up' organizations within the ecological poles.

Soft Fields and Frameworks

While the soft pods of the 1960s and 70s typically operated at the limits of material properties and were therefore scaled to the individual, there are some examples that provide cues on how infrastructure could be deployed or conceived with systemic symbiosis or offer resilience. A project that differentiates itself from the typical inflatable bubble is Michael Webb's *Magic Carpet and Brunhilda's Magic Ring of Fire* (1968). In Webb's speculative project, a field of air tubes function as a reverse hovercraft, which can adapt to the transforming positions of the body. What makes Webb's project unique from earlier experiments such as *Cushicle* (1966) or *Suitaloon* (1967) was the abandonment of a singular pod envelope for a field condition of air jets. Blowing air at varying pressures, the tubes are in constant renegotiation to support the body in different positions. As a distributed, non-hierarchical network of individual components, the 'enclosure' is able to actively respond to its user's local circumstances while also having overall continuity from the gridded matrix. While it is conceivable that a framework would need to exist to hold the field in place and host the mechanical equipment, Webb completely omits this information from the drawings. Representing the tubes as emerging from the landscape, and suppressing the notion of the framework, Webb's project examines the limits of dematerializing the frame while still providing collective unity to the field. His '*mini*-structure' depicts how a field that privileges its unit and their local relationships can, on the one hand, reconcile the individual and collective, and on the other, absorb and adapt to disturbance.

This frail line between the individual and collective also finds a form of reconciliation at the scale of urbanism in Black Rock City (BRC). Conceived as a temporary settlement, BRC is organized on the ancient lakebed in the Black Rock Desert for the eight-day annual event, Burning Man. With modest beginnings of twenty friends in 1986, the event has grown to host over fifty thousand participants. The current urban plan, which formalized a spontaneous organization, was put into place for safety, municipal, and social reasons. The planner of BRC, Rod Garrett, stated that before the plan was instituted:

> We got to a point where I saw people becoming irrationally
> angry with each other and with the city… It occurred to me that
> this might be an effect of overpopulation, and that we'd hit some
> tipping point where people were no longer comfortable.[19]

Garrett had noticed that the collective was dissolving as the populace overtook the city's framework and lost its coherence and organization. Yet, the notion of a 'top-down' planning regime was antithetical to the concept of the festival, which revolved around the symbolic burning of "the man." Within such a seeming paradox, Garrett explored the notion of a soft framework to organize the public and harness collectivity without suppressing individual expression or identity. Garrett's plan is based on a radial grid that is etched into the desert landscape. These concentric rings are centered on the "burning man," a legible orientation device (as well as symbolic icon) that unites the collective. The grid is cut transversely into roughly Manhattan sized blocks, with streets occurring every 7.5 degrees. Not only do these streets all orient to the burning man, they are spaced to align with hands on a conceptual clock (located every fifteen minutes). Main promenades are thirty feet wide and occur on the 3:00/9:00 and 6:00/12:00 axes. Secondary streets at 7:30 and 4:30 widen as they reach the playa to provide nodes for art installations. The concentric streets are ordered alphabetically, with their names changing each year depending on the theme of the event. The one hundred and sixty blocks (and growing) are zoned to host both art installations and residences in the form of trailers, tents, and other temporary shelters. The horseshoe plan was purposely not enclosed into a circle, as Garrett had witnessed through empirical study that the circle lacked overall directionality, disorienting participants into fragmented groups and shattering the notion of collectivity. Garrett's soft framework links legibility and collectivity—materializing through symbolic markers, mental mapping, and territorial organization—allowing the individual to continually understand their relationship, and thereby participate in the collective.

Black Rock City is an experiment in the coupling of an unplanned bottom-up organization within a top-down framework. This presents a form of 'mega-*soft*ure', wherein the framework itself can adapt to needs of the unit and vice versa.[20] This allows the system to evolve in the event of disturbance, providing for resilience that operates at the intersection of the individual and collective. This soft framework has proved remarkably resilient to growth; for instance, in 2010 a record population of 51,525 participants attended Burning Man, instigating the fabrication of two concentric streets during the middle of the week.[21] The same conceptual plan, which accommodated nine thousand participants in 1998, now hosts over fifty thousand inhabitants. Each year the plan is updated based on observation, allowing for feedback into the framework's organization, as stated by Garrett:

> As our plan has grown, we have learned how to differentiate and
> separate various specialized, and potentially conflicting uses. This
> involved an empirical study of our social needs as they've naturally emerged from an increasingly sophisticated social reality.[22]

19. Nate Berg, "Burning Man and the Metropolis", *The Design Observer/Places Magazine*, http://places.designobserver.com/feature/burning-man-and-the-metropolis/23848/

20. For further discussion on the relationship of platform and application, see: Scott Colman, "Soft Progressivism in a Wasteland of Urban Code" in this almanac.

21. Will Chase, "Afterburn Report 2010", *Burning Man*, http://afterburn.burningman.com/10/

22. Rod Garrett, "Designing Black Rock City", *Burning Man*, http://www.burningman.com/whatisburningman/about_burningman/brc_growth.html

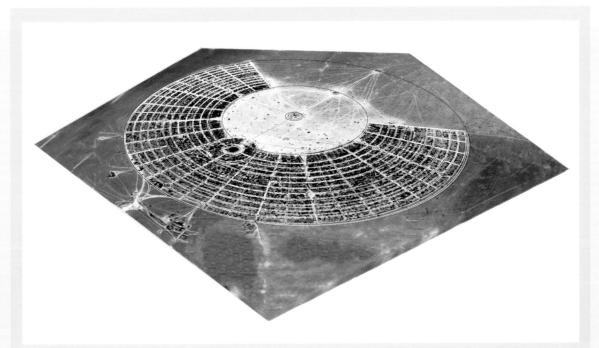

∧ **Black Rock City, Rod Garrett—a soft collective framework organizes without suppressing individual identities.**
(Drawing by Alicia Hergenroeder)

∧ **Informal aggregations in Black Rock City, organized by a soft frame. (Image from Flickr user Tobo, Creative Commons)**

The informal (individual) and formal (collective) dialectic in BRC has reached a balance that allows both scales and forms of colonization to function, and through feedback, affect each other. While the soft framework operates through organization, hierarchy, legibility, and centralization, it also allows utmost flexibility for self-generated occupation. As stated by Garrett, "Our city is dynamic, adaptive and reactive."[23]

While Black Rock City provides clues on how a soft organizational framework ('road' layouts, planning guidelines, and occupational zoning) can be deployed to create resilience, its collective is essentially generated before the event. The curated interests that bond its residents is not the case in the contemporary metropolis, but the notion of how soft fields and frameworks are conceived and organized in these two projects, provide a template for infrastructural deployment that accounts for and reacts to disturbance.

Resilient Ecologies

Feedback, non-linearity, scalar indifference, resilience—these characteristics, adopted from natural ecosystems are critical to understanding how to reconcile the dialectics of pluralism if applied to the human ecology. This understanding aligns itself with Félix Guattari's *The Three Ecologies*,[24] wherein Guattari merges the human and environmental sphere into the concept of "ecosophy." Guattari's three ecological registers—environment, social relations, and human subjectivities—could be re-characterized as the *natural world* and *human political world* (comprised of both the *collective* or 'social relations' and *individual* or 'human subjectivities'). The collective platform, if we recall Giacometti's *City Square*, could thus be reframed as the external environment (the natural ecology) and the socio-political environment (the human ecology). The figures embody the distinct individuality of our subjectivities. The spatial format that reconciles such symbiosis is infrastructure as it oscillates between the natural and artificial and requires collective support yet enables individual actions. Constantly negotiating between the socio-political (both individual and collective) and environmental spheres, soft infrastructures can operate as ecologies that are highly resilient.

Fabricating resilience—to allow and adapt to disturbance—is perhaps the only way to gain agency in a metropolis that is increasingly divergent, crisis-ridden, contradictory, and formed by the complex negotiation of politics, economics, culture and the environment, amongst other factors. Disturbance from natural and human factors is increasingly not the exception but the norm. By seeking symbiosis and feedback between these divergent spheres, we can reframe the city as an eco-political project that finds holistic unity while allowing for distinct localism.

. . . .

23. Ibid.

24. Félix Guattari, *The Three Ecologies*
(London and New Brunswick, NJ: Athlone
Press, 2000), 28.

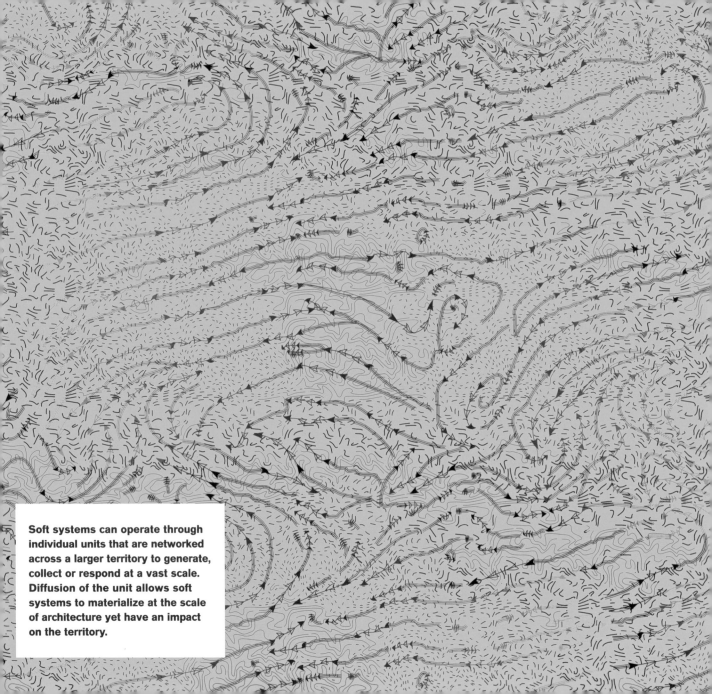

Soft systems can operate through individual units that are networked across a larger territory to generate, collect or respond at a vast scale. Diffusion of the unit allows soft systems to materialize at the scale of architecture yet have an impact on the territory.

SOFT ENERGY CONTROVERSY

RANIA GHOSN

In October 1976, Amory Lovins, a consultant physicist and British representative of Friends of the Earth, published the article "Soft Energy Paths: The Road Not Taken." Lovins' paper outlined an alternative "soft path" to conventional energy policy,[1] announcing that sustaining energy growth was not the answer. The hard path technologies—high-energy nuclear and centralized electric energy—resulted in excessive waste of resources, which could not continue given rising costs, adverse environmental impacts, safety concerns, and the proliferation of weapons. A significant social change, Lovins reasoned, was necessary to transition from the hard to soft energy path. The goal was to shift industrial societies to lower-energy, fission-free, and decentralized sources that would match energy supply and quality to user demands.

The "Soft Energy Paths" article brought a storm of controversy that culminated with a congressional hearing of Lovins and his critics in December 1976.[2] Beyond its historical significance in contemporary policy circles, the debate on the hard and soft paths has had an important legacy in the discourse on renewables and social change. This essay traces some of the contributions and limitations of Lovins' argument to frame a critical discourse on energy. On one hand, it acknowledges the significance of Lovins' position in highlighting how our energy choices are socially and politically grounded, particularly when bringing their costs, benefits and risks into public discussion. On the other hand, it questions the appropriateness of the hard-soft binary which abstracts the social relations it proposes to anchor itself in, and what alternative worlds it promises to deliver.

The Soft as a Critique of the Fossil Fuel Energy System

In the words of Dr. Pickering, one of Lovins' critics and a professor of social ethics, Lovins deserves "our critical attention because he is trying to generate a sense of alternatives, and because he does pose, however backhandedly, the problems of social change which are necessarily entailed in any serious discussion of the future of our energy needs or the future of democratic institutions."[3] On a basic level, Lovins proposes to expand the narrow disciplinary framing of Energy, and by extension the grounds from which to engage choice. In his response to a memorandum from the Energy Research and Development Administration, which framed "energy supply as primarily the domain of the engineering disciplines and demand as in the domain of the economics," he states that a tendency to narrow the energy debate into the exclusive domain of economics and engineering ignores other and perhaps more important perspectives.[4] In contrast to energy modelers who view energy decisions as governed by the number of kilowatt hours delivered per dollar invested, Lovins views energy choices as fundamentally social, political, and institutional in nature.

In the gestalt of the early 1970s, Lovins proposes to dissociate energy consumption and economic development, which typically centered on growth and cost. In his view, the energy problem was closely tied to the society that used it, and in particular to the underlying assumption that "the more energy we use the better off we are."[5] Indeed, environmental historians have elaborated how the carbon regime was propelled by the belief that energy consumption is an essential facet of social progress, or development *tout cours*.[6] By equating the rate of energy consumption with progress, development indicators have contributed to the exponential increase in oil sales. Lovins instead shifts the discussion towards an examination of the different energy uses. If the hard path rests on the belief that the more energy we use, the better off we are; in the soft path, how much energy we use is considered a measure our failure. Wilhelm Ostwald, a chemist and Nobel-prize laureate, had already preached as early as 1900 that the stature of a civilization should not be measured by its level of coal consumption but by the quality of its exploitation of energy. The soft path espouses end-use orientation to determine how the volume and kind of energy needed for a given task, and then supplying the required kind of energy.

Along with a critique of growth, the convergence of the environmental movement and the energy crisis suggested an alternative worldview that took into account the finite nature of the world's resources and of its geographic space to critique the historically cheap price of energy. "'Cheap' energy," Lovins argued, "is actually very expensive; we pay for it by structural distortions everywhere else in the economy."[7] In the United States, the "tacit identification of the rate of growth of primary energy use with the level of well-being," has lead to the subsidization of energy supply.[8] Myriad direct and indirect public subsidies have kept the price of oil artificially cheap and not indicative of its full economic cost to society. In particular, the historic

1. Amory Lovins, "Soft Energy Paths: The Road Not Taken," *Foreign Affairs* 55 (1976), 65-96.

2. U.S. Senate, Select Committee on Small Business and Committee on Interior and Insular Affairs, *Alternative Long-Range Energy Strategies* (Washington D.C.: GPO, 1977). A selection of Lovins' critics and his responses are published in Hugh Nash, ed. *The Energy Controversy: Soft Path Questions & Answers*

(San Francisco: Friends of the Earth, 1979).

3. Hugh Nash, ed. *The Energy Controversy: Soft Path Questions & Answers* (San Francisco: Friends of the Earth, 1979), 237.

4. Ibid., 36.

5. Amory Lovins, *Soft Energy Paths: Towards a Durable Peace* (Cambridge: Friends of the Earth, 1977), 4.

6. Martin Melosi, "Energy and Environment in the United States: The Era of Fossil

Fuels," *Environmental Review* 11.3 (1987): 167-188.

7. Hugh Nash, ed. *The Energy Controversy: Soft Path Questions & Answers* (San Francisco: Friends of the Earth, 1979), 60.

8. Amory Lovins, "Soft Energy Technologies," in *Annual Review of Energy* (1978): 477-517, 477.

∧   Yellow Brick Road. (Rania Ghosn and
Khaled Malas. Photomontage, 2005)

price of the "hard path" has not accounted for pollution, health hazards and damages to the environment and communities, which have been treated as "external" to the economics of energy. Furthermore, the centralized organization of the hard system has "allocated benefits to suburbanites and social costs to politically weaker rural agrarians... in an increasingly divisive and wasteful form of centrifugal politics."[9] The hard path, Lovins adds, entails serious environmental risks, "many of which are poorly understood and some of which have probably not yet been thought of."[10] He advocates that the market prices of all forms of energy—"hard" or "soft"—should not be distorted by subsidies or regulation and should include environmental and other external costs, without however addressing the challenge of whether and how to quantify them.[11]

The Soft is not an Alternative Energy System

Although Lovins sets out to convince us of the soft, the compelling aspect of his argument is inherently limited by its binary structure. Dr. Pickering shares that it required an effort on his part to "divest [his] mind of the sexual imagery suggested by such terms as 'hard,' and 'soft,'" and to understand why one is better than the other.[12] Lovins' reply does not defend the choice of the term soft. His

response is at best apologetic; that he was unable to find a more satisfactory term, "that any term is bound to have unsatisfactory connotations, and that in retrospect he should have perhaps have made up a nonsense word—if he could find one with no affective content."[13] Whatever the second arm of the binary is, "soft" or another congenial term for that matter, the asymmetrical structure is essential to the construction of the argument.

The hard-soft duality rests on a set of associations that dismisses the former in favor of the latter. On one hand, the hard path is one whose polity is dominated by such structural problems as centrism, autarchy, and technocracy. In particular, Lovins hones the "vulnerability" of the hard path to promote decentralized energy technologies. He argues that the XL scale increases incentive for "sabotage and disruption, including war, and so reducing national security."[14] In a later book, *Brittle Power: Energy Strategy for National Security*, he documents a wide array of accidents, malicious attacks, and near misses on U.S. energy systems, identifying the infrastructures for electricity, natural gas, oil, and nuclear power as "disasters waiting to happen."[15] Throughout, his discourse is neither critical of the concepts of "energy risk" and "energy security" nor of their historical deployment to legitimatize choices of war

9. Amory Lovins, *Soft Energy Paths: Towards a Durable Peace* (Cambridge: Friends of the Earth, 1977), 92.

10. Ibid., 88.

11. Hugh Nash, ed. *The Energy Controversy: Soft Path Questions & Answers* (San Francisco: Friends of the Earth, 1979), 48.

12. Hugh Nash, ed. *The Energy Controversy: Soft Path Questions & Answers* (San Francisco: Friends of the Earth, 1979), 236.

13. Ibid.

14. Amory Lovins, "Soft Energy Technologies," in *Annual Review of Energy* (1978): 488.

15. Amory Lovins and Hunter Lovins, *Brittle Power: Energy Strategy for National Security* (Andover: Brick House, 1982), 10.

and federal budgeting in domestic and foreign policies. He overlooks that discussions of energy are ineluctably part of the larger constructions of geopolitics, and as such need to engage with the deconstruction of particular geographies of "vulnerability," "threat," and "insecurity."

On the other hand, the soft alternative is supported by a set of "universal" values—such as freedom, a high quality of life, and increased equity. It promises to be more democratic, less militarized, less hazardous, more flexible, and more efficient in its uses of energy and capital. Such ideological embrace of the soft rests on other supporting binaries—such as the local/global, populist/elite, small/big. In particular, Schumacher's *Small is Beautiful*[16] haunts the soft path, although Lovins at moments distances himself from the soft-small associations. In a response to his critics, Lovins emphasizes that he did not begin "with a preconceived attachment to a particular ideology about energy or technology, such as the "small is beautiful philosophy that some have tried to read into my results." He reaffirms, "I do not think Schumacher makes sense."[17] At the end of the day however, the soft path favors decentralized neighborhood-scale technologies. Whereas hard technology is "an alien, remote, and perhaps humiliatingly uncontrollable technology run by a faraway, bureaucratized, technical elite," soft technology Lovins argues, is an "understandable neighborhood technology."[18] Soft technologies "can often be made locally from local materials and do not require a technical elite to maintain them; they resist technological dependence and commercial monopoly."[19] In support of soft technologies, Lovins associates positive values to the neighborhood—less coercive, more participatory, and equitable.

His argument however, abstracts political relations at the scale of the locality while simultaneously isolating individual technologies from the larger technological systems in which they are embedded. As opponents of "community-participation" and "new urbanism" have well observed, the neighborhood or locality is enmeshed in political and economic relations that are operative over broader spatial scales. If soft technologies are commercially viable—and hence mass-produced, they will become absorbed in a web of commercial corporations competing in the manufacture, distribution, marketing, and servicing of them. Furthermore, the scale of an individual technology does not determine the sociopolitical structure of the energy system. An important aspect of Thomas Hughes's seminal *Networks of Power*[20] is to overcome the customary focus on the light bulb as harbinger of social change

and argue that such artifact was just one among many interrelated elements within a geographically extended system for the supply and transport of electricity.[21] It is not only the fixity, the durability, and the enormous capital? costs of energy infrastructures that make them highly path dependent, but as well the interests of, and interactions among various social groups which have invested financial, labor, and research resources in the planning and functioning of a specific system. By linking many interests, the large technological system develops a considerable momentum towards inertia, resisting the flexibility suggested by soft systems.

Lovins briefly mentions that a hard energy path is consistent with the interests of a few powerful American institutions, and that it is important to remove subsidies to conventional fuels and vigorously enforce anti-trust laws.[22] He compellingly argues that the mismatch between the scale of centralized energy system components (large) and the scale of most power consumption (small) is at the core of the energy predicament. The massive technological fixes that have historically been the response to previous energy crises will further exacerbate the problem. However, his argument omits that the mismatch is, in fact, *by design*. Instead, his proposal to rectify the vulnerabilities of the hard path by increasing energy efficiency overlooks the reality that the "energy problem" of the twentieth century has been how to design for abundance rather than to procure for shortage. Energy abundance was essential for the economy of incessant growth. Through a series of tax breaks, including the oil depletion allowance, as well as easy access to public lands and international concessions, government promotion has allowed for fossil fuels to be artificially cheap. Organized around a regulatory regime favorable to a state-backed, debt-financed consumption order, the "American way of life" was predicated upon cheap and abundant petroleum. The postwar urban process was supported by generous government-financing programs, including federal funds for national interstate highways, the financing of millions of suburban homes by the Federal Housing Authority, and large government subsidies for agribusiness. In such a political and economic context, the challenge of the oil industry was to deliver fossil fuels in ever-increasing quantities while ensuring that abundance does not drive price down. To eliminate competition and stabilize prices, major oil companies deployed a spatial and legal infrastructure, which strove to achieve monopolies on supply by instituting concession areas, exclusive transport channels, and a vertically integrated oil industry.

16. E.F. Schumacher, *Small is Beautiful: Economics as if People Mattered* (New York: Harper & Row, 1975, c1973). First published during the 1973 energy crisis, *Small is Beautiful* critiques growth and advances that the modern economy is unsustainable. Coinciding with the rise of ecological awareness, the book is often used to champion small, appropriate technologies that are believed to empower people more.

17. Amory Lovins, *Soft Energy Paths: Towards a Durable Peace* (Cambridge: Friends of the Earth, 1977), 12.

18. Ibid., 92.

19. Ibid., 89.

20. Thomas Hughes, *Networks of Power: Electrification in Western Society, 1880–1930* (Baltimore: Johns Hopkins University Press, 1983). Hughes' most significant contribution to the history of technology, the book locates electrical technologies in context analyzing how both human and technological elements were bound together in large scale "systems." Hughes characterizes systems as fundamentally constituted not only of interconnected technological artifacts (such as generators, couplers, relays, lamps) but also local, regional, and national political structures, perceived (and constructed) societal need, geographical features, etc.

21. Thomas Hughes, *Networks of Power: Electrification in Western Society, 1880–1930* (Baltimore: Johns Hopkins University Press, 1983).

22. Hugh Nash, ed. *The Energy Controversy: Soft Path Questions & Answers* (San Francisco: Friends of the Earth, 1979), 29-30.

The expansion of the industrial corporation and of its infrastructure to the scale of the globe was thus central to the carbon regime. Lovins does briefly mention the prohibitive actual and environmental costs of offshore and arctic operations, coal stripping, and the plutonium economy. The crux of his argument rests however on the fact that the hard path is economically unworkable, as it relies on capital-intensive and vulnerable systems. The soft path on the contrary is more flexible; it distributes and minimizes the economic risks to capital. His later books, *Small is Profitable* and *Natural Capitalism*, make evident how the accounting for human and environmental costs serves to power a new industrial revolution through the invisible green hand of the market. *Small is Profitable* proposes that the global economy can serve a sustainability interest if the 'raison de market' wins the energy policy debate. Thus, it suggests that society can turn "more profit with less carbon," by "harnessing corporate power to heal the planet."[23]

Lovins' initial promise to move beyond the narrow grounds of engineering and economics eventually confines the energy question to market-initiated techno-centric solutions. The soft path espouses the rhetoric of autonomous progress, comparing the coming industrial revolution to a train about to depart the station, leaving behind all those who fail to board.[24] Such technological fetishism ignores the geometries of power, the long history of governmental subsidies, and the underlying questions of social justice associated to alternative paths. More importantly, the soft path does not recognize Energy as a situated historical concept of human existence over the last two centuries. The critique he advances operates *from within* the nineteenth century thermodynamic concept of Energy as the ability "to make nature do work."[25] As such, it perpetuates many modern industrial practices of controlling nature and favors the appearance of the ecocrat, whose analogies and management tools fit nature into his domain.[26] It borrows key concepts from ecology such as "resilience" which are then designed into energy systems to include a modular structure, redundancy and adaptability, diversity, and the possibility of decoupling, and dispersion.[27] The ecological caché leaves the costs and risks of the soft path itself unaddressed. Lovins trusts that "soft technologies give everyone the costs and benefits of the energy system he chooses,"[28] and that by minimizing all fossil-fuel combustion, their "environmental impacts are relatively small, tractable and reversible."[29] The Soft somehow shies away from a critical engagement with its premises and promises.

Deessentializing the Hard-Soft Binary

Four decades later, the controversy over the strategies addressed by Lovins and his critics carries the significant legacy of critically examining Energy. The Soft initiates the crucial task of deconstructing Energy into its constitutive end-use elements and questions the necessity of expanding supplies to meet the extrapolated demands of the economy. In a more modest way, it hints as well to the costs of our energy choices, the social relations underlying both paths, while keeping open opportunities to engage the structures, worldviews, and costs of different energy alternatives. To the architecture of energy, one of Soft Energy's most significant contributions is that it highlights the scales of energy production which spur a broad range of design responses, from the detail to the megaregional. In recent years, the Soft Energy project has opened up opportunities to design material and shape their properties and appearance, a potential mobilized by designers such as Sheila Kennedy and Sean Lally amongst others. Furthermore, by identifying the reliance of urbanization on resources often far from sites of consumption, the Soft has also drawn attention to the systemic and territorial attributes of the distribution and transportation of energy, whether the spatio-political adequacy between the ordering of space and forms of political regulation, or the forms of territorialities produced by such systems. Rather than obliterating the significance of infrastructure in favor of decentralized off-grid movements, the Soft path has highlighted the significance of the network and the large-scale as sites for energy imaginaries. Informed by the critiques advances by the soft path, contemporary energy proposal such as AMO's Roadmap 2050 have sought to recuperate the promises of the network by dissociating the form from associated negative ecological connotations all while reaffirming its political potential to integrate geographies. Drawing on Fuller's World Grid, AMO's proposal capitalizes on Europe's geographic diversity through an E.U. network of hydropower, geothermal, biomass, and solar power, which helps to unify the territory it serves and reinforce its economic position. The technology (solar for example) is thus expanded beyond the locality through the grid distribution system. Such hybridization of technologies and scales deessentializes the hard-soft binary leaving the door wide open to questions concerning the broader political significance of "renewable" forms of energy.

· · · · Rania Ghosn is an architect, geographer, and founding editor of the journal *New Geographies*.

23. Amory Lovins, "More Profit with Less Carbon," *Scientific American* (September 2005): 74-83; Amory Lovins and Hunter Lovins, "Harnessing Corporate Power to Heal the Planet," *The World and I* (Washington: Washington Times Corporation, 2000).

24. Paul Hawken, Amory Lovins, and Hunter Lovins, *Natural Capitalism: Creating the Next Industrial Revolution* (Boston: Little, Brown and Company, 1999), xiii.

25. Ivan Illich, "The Social Construction of Energy," in *New Geographies #2: Landscapes of Energy*, Rania Ghosn ed. (Cambridge: Harvard GSD, 2010), 11-19; 13.

26. Ibid., 18.

27. Amory Lovins and Hunter Lovins, *Brittle Power: Energy Strategy for National Security* (Andover: Brick House, 1982), 23, 179-82.

28. Amory Lovins, *Soft Energy Paths: Towards a Durable Peace* (Cambridge: Friends of the Earth, 1977), 92.

29. Ibid., 88.

KINETIC BACKBONE
LEIGH SALEM

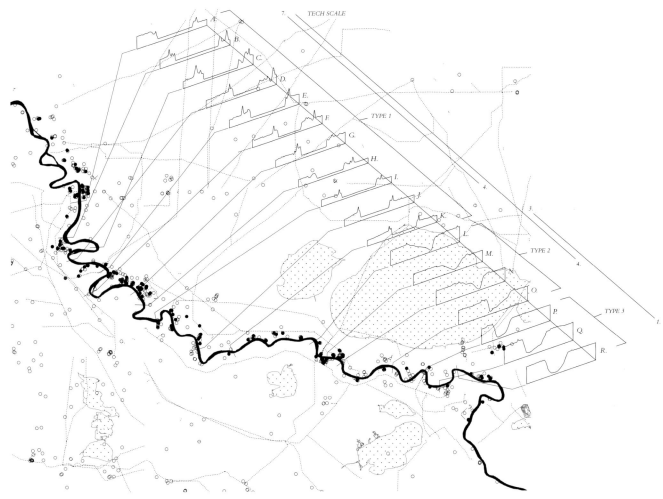

^   Map and sectional profiles of Mississippi River.

The Mississippi River corridor and in particular the region stretching between New Orleans and Baton Rouge, has assumed the role of America's petrochemical headquarters. The industries on the river process, refine, and manufacture products ranging from concentrated plastic pellets to derivative fertilizers. Although the industry initially bolstered the state's economy, the over reliance on the oil and natural gas market has encouraged limited economic diversification and in turn entrenched the energy sector deeply in the political realm. Ironically, the state's abundance in oil rich resources have drastically hindered the economic development of the region and further allowed for state sanctioned environmental damage.

Louisiana and the Mississippi corridor do not suffer only economic woes. While the industries prosper, the surrounding dependent communities suffer from low standards of life. According to Steven Mufson of the Washington Post, the state has the second lowest life expectancy, ranks forty-sixth in percentage of population over twenty-five years holding college degrees, and second in population living below the poverty line. As Mufson writes, "Oil riches didn't create these problems, of course, but it is striking that they didn't ameliorate them." Oliver Houck, an environmental law professor at Tulane University further states, "What oil and gas did is replace the agricultural plantation culture with an oil and gas plantation culture."[1] The plantation culture is founded

^   Cycle of private and public investment.

1. Steven Mufson, "Oil Spills. Poverty. Corruption. Why Louisiana is America's Petro-State," The Washington Post, July 18, 2010. www.washingtonpost.com/wp-dyn/content/article/2010/07/16/AR2010071602721_pf.html

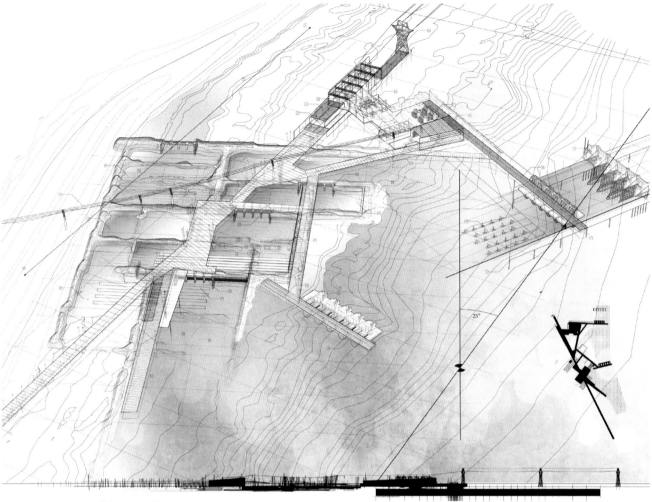

∧   **Axonometric view of the river and bank connection.**

on the severe concentration of economic resources and lack of distribution to the outside communities. The omnipresent ghost of the plantation system haunts the state, but nowhere more apparent than on the shores of the lower Mississippi River itself.

Through a common tradition of exploitation, the Mississippi river has grown to signify a passive resource—a body that can be molded and shifted for the benefit of centralized players. It is a vehicle for transportation, dilution, and waste reception. Consequently, the shadow of the petrochemical industry enshrouds the shores, barring external interaction and recreation. Pipes of natural gas weave through the fields and marshes, merging degrading ecosystems and manufactured landscapes.

As manufacturing and labor-intensive processes continue to be outsourced to nations outside of the US, inevitably the petroleum industry of the corridor will shift away from Louisiana's banks. The industry will leave a network of looming sepulchers, the skeletons of dependency, and the communities will bear the true burden. In order to

secure a choice in the future, there must be a decentralization of economic hegemony. This can only be achieved through a conscious restructuring of local infrastructure, regional dynamics, and resource policy surrounding the waterway.

Louisiana and specifically the "Cancer-Alley" stretch of the Mississippi between Baton Rouge and New Orleans must begin to view the river as a potential positive energy source. The development of a hydrokinetic spine along the river corridor would allow for active participation in the crafting of a national super-grid and the re-positioning of Louisiana in domestic policy. While offshore wind-farms are constructed in the Atlantic, the hydrokinetic backbone would offer a new mode of clean energy creation and distribution throughout the Midwest. Collaboration with existing corporations through subsidization tools and statewide regulatory enhancement will strengthen the industrial ecology of the corridor while providing resource efficiency and in-situ remediation. A new ecology will predominate: a network

of forward-moving policy, research, and economic vehicles.

Kinetic Backbone examines the Mississippi's potential for energy development and the consequential re-distribution of resources on both a local and regional network. Through analysis of water dynamics and electrical transmission frameworks, the project facilitates efficient energy generation and new modes of community use. Although the Mississippi flow rates are quite low when compared with the typical water speed of large-scale hydroelectric infrastructures, by utilizing new small-scale river technologies, the energy may be captured and efficiently transported. The technology channels regional high voltage DC transmission, local low voltage AC networks, allowing for individualized consumption through small and frequently located battery platforms. In addition, the energy infrastructure offers an opportunity for water filtration and public interaction on the shore. The landscape acts as an adaptation of the petrochemical industry's own mechanical water filtration systems, taking in the slow moving water,

∧　In river turbine technology and pedestrian walkway.

cleaning, and removing the ever-constant sedimentation. While the power substations require hard construction types (concrete and steel pilings) the public paths can be built through soft techniques such as live staking and branch packing. The permanent concrete structures of the power stations turn into gabion walls while the wood pilings transform into tree growth and soft solutions.

The sites for construction are chosen according to three factors. The first concerns the water speed along the outside banks and the sectional potential across the river. While new turbine technologies have the capability to exploit low-flows, constant high speeds are ideal and tend to be associated on outside bends where the sectional profile is more severe. Second, the onshore power stations are sited according to their role in distribution. Three types of stations are proposed, each catering to different end-users: existing manufacturing centers, local residential communities, and long-distance transportation to the national grid. Lastly, site selection depends on the potential for reintroducing recreation along the corridor. In order to

increase visibility and transparency in the energy sector, the platforms will allow for pedestrian access and community outreach. Thus, the sites must have direct connection with the existing settlements.

At the human scale, the infrastructural proposals allow for the community's reconnection with the once legendary and honored water source. In approaching the river as a potential for energy creation, it begins to restore the legacy of the waterway and its image in the American psyche. Instead of a dirty, ignored, and problematic throughway, a renewed Mississippi ties together and defines the region through its symbolic unbridled power, true to the visions described by Mark Twain and the American writers of the past. The constant flow of the water is translated directly into an agent and tool for redistribution of economic resources. The river's path will reflect new settlement strategies. The backbone will locate Louisiana in the forefront of hydrokinetic research, targeting investment and young tech start-ups. New businesses focused on environmental technology will surround the corridor attracting attention on

a global scale. As the *Kinetic Backbone* grows and matures, reallocation of businesses, manufacturing, and economic opportunities will be based on the relative proximities to the river's bends, the source of creation and community. Consequently, at a regional level, the settlement of the river corridor will be founded on the conservation of the original natural resource rather than on an industry dependent on the river's exploitation and destruction.

• • • **Leigh Salem is New York-based designer and MArch Candidate at Columbia University GSAPP.**

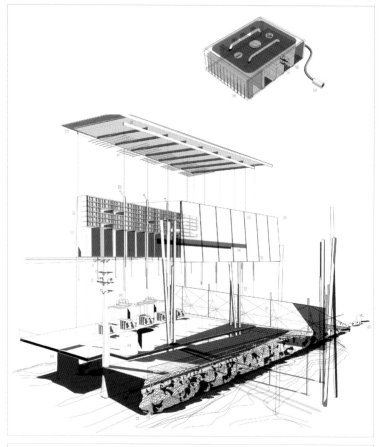

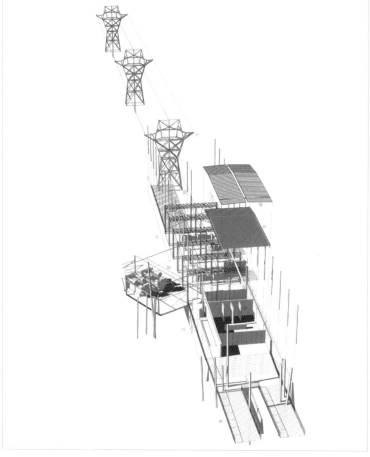

∧   **Electricity platforms and battery houses for
local distribution.**

Salem   Kinetic Backbone

∧   **Sedimentation pools for water remediation
with pedestrian walkways.**

Remediation Process
1. Sediment piping from pool 1
2. Weir 2 to filtration pool
3. Shared pilings for boardwalk
4. Gabion mesh railing
5. Recycled timber planking
6. Live staking sleeve
7. Sedimentation pool overflow
8. Rubble wall

Construction Types
A. Steel pilings/precast wall system
B. Wood pile/concrete low wall
C. Tree packing/gabionwall
D. Loose rubble/brush

GOES SOFT

bracket—

∧   **River floor generation.**

〉   **Following pages: Resettlement of
the river corridor.**

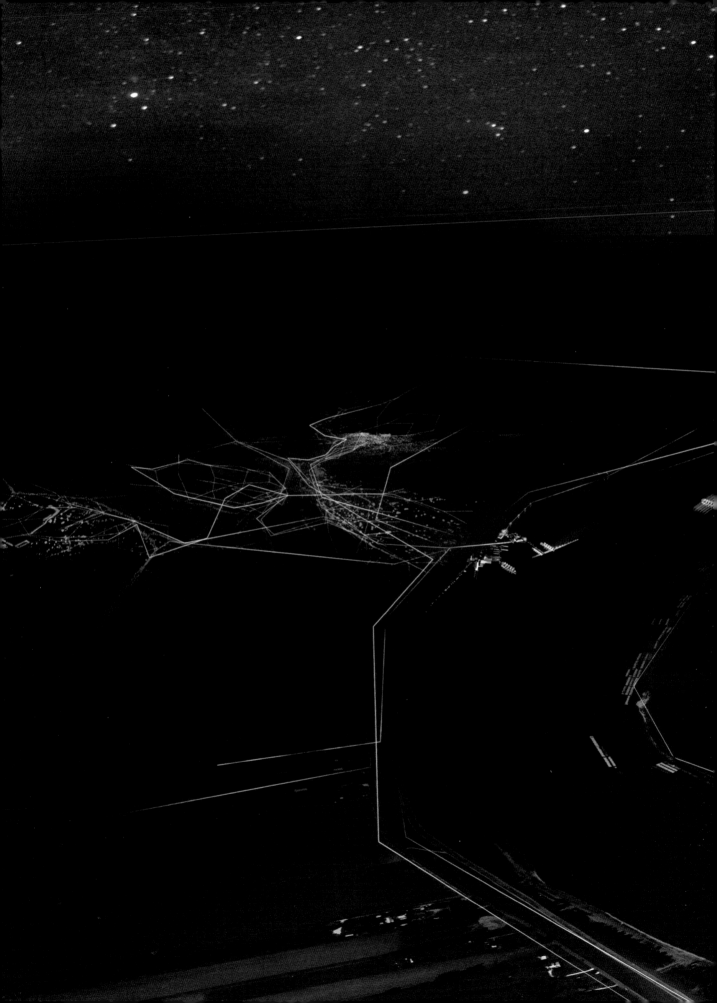

KINETIC BACKBONE

50 FATHOMS UNDER THE SEA

MARIANNA DE COLA

Resettlement Growth Centers, 1954-1975

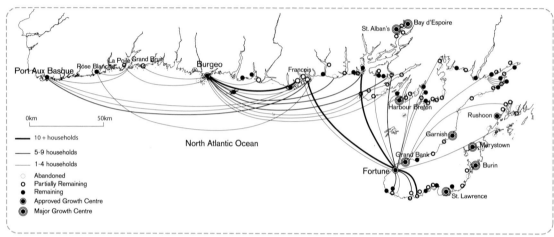

Resettlement Pattern in Southern Newfoundland, 1954-1975

∧ **The 1950s to the 1970s were decades of mass movement within the province. Approximately three hundred communities were abandoned (amounting to close to 30,000 people) and many more depopulated. The people on the move received government assistance to relocate to the designated "growth centres". A complete reorganization of the province was the consequence. A close up on the southern coast displays Burgeo, Port Aux Basques, and Fortune as popular destination towns.**

"When blinding storm gusts fret thy shore, And wild waves lash thy strand, Thro' spindrift swirl and tempest roar, We love thee, wind-swept land."
—Ode to Newfoundland

At 6:00pm on July 7th, 2010 the south coast ferry unleashed itself from Grand Bruit's dock for the very last time. Full of the final remnants that filled each of the homes, the stern of the boat sunk low. The wake in the harbor slowly calmed as the ferry headed westward for the final time along that southern crossing.

The history of Newfoundland is intimately tied to its relationship with the sea. Not only has its status as an island created cultural isolation, it has also initiated reliance on the fishing and oil industry. Newfoundland's history is one of tides—of prosperity and loss, migration and resettlement, occupation and erasure. The stories of the sea and movement outline the historic spatialization of Newfoundland's population, infrastructures, and economies. Further, they simultaneously depict the social and economic deficiencies of modern approaches to developing the island.

This investigation examines the nature of mutable landscapes—shifting settlements, resources and infrastructures—revealing the diversity in type and supply of different communities. More specifically, it asks how can the spatialization of contemporary energy infrastructure link the ecological, political, cultural, and historical constituents in atomized communities? Such a dynamic system forces a presence in the everyday lives of the cultural habitat. Situated off the southern coast of Newfoundland, a mobile, water-based energy, research, and cultural infrastructure is proposed that engages both the coast and the seas. Divided into three zones: onshore, nearshore and offshore, the new infrastructure seeks to link ecology, economy, and the populations along the coast.

Centered on wave energy and monitoring systems, the design exists within three realms. The first realm territorializes the sea, and consists of an offshore network

∧ Loading belongings on board.
(Photograph by author, Grand Bruit, 2010)

∧ Rusted equipment in the landwash.
(Photograph by author, Isle Aux Morts, 2010)

∧ Exterior of storage silos.
(Photograph by author, Isle Aux Morts, 2010)

∧ A resident struggling to move his deep
freezer. (Photograph by author, Grand Bruit, 2010)

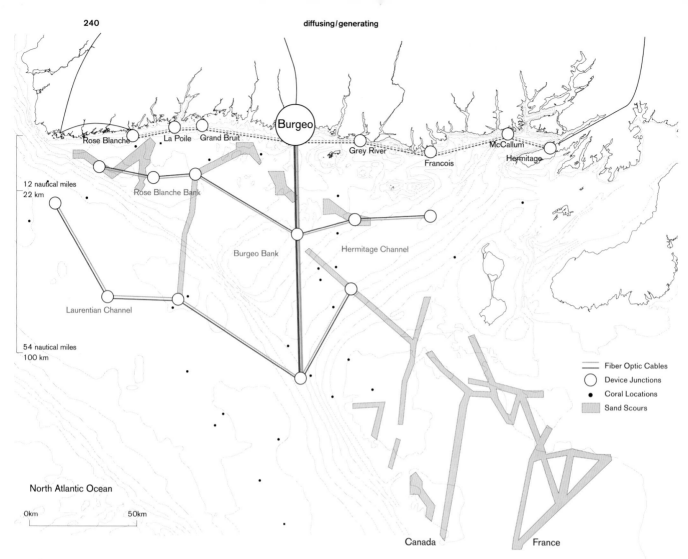

**∧　South coast monitoring and energy network
with Burgeo hosting the main onshore station.**

that provides wave energy generation, points of monitoring, and the possibility of occupying the sea to varying degrees. The second realm anchors to the land, and is a proposal for the main monitoring building located in the more stable town of Burgeo. The third realm is an outport intervention, including a temporary monitoring building that is a model for all of the outports on the southern coast. This realm responds to the fluctuating ecologic and economic tides of the region.

Without attempting to tame, resolve, or control the sea, *50 Fathoms* utilizes mutable forces as instigators and organizational devices in design. The sea is always itself, ordered by its own cycles of tides, currents and ecologies. One can only synchronize the relationships between land and sea by recognizing these differing and dynamic forces.

·　·　·　**Marianna de Cola is a Toronto-based
designer. She is a graduate of the University
of Waterloo School of Architecture.**

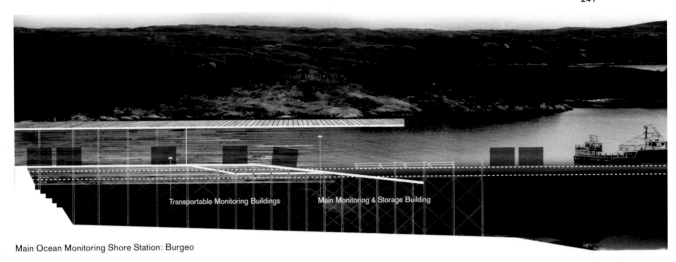

Transportable Monitoring Buildings   Main Monitoring & Storage Building

Main Ocean Monitoring Shore Station: Burgeo

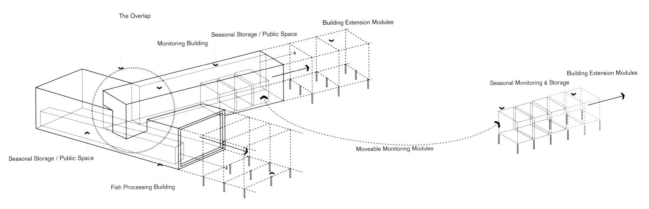

High Tide

Low Tide

Transportable Monitoring Buildings   Inshore Monitoring Devices   Outport Monitoring & Storage Buildings

Subsidiary Ocean Monitoring Shore Station: Grand Bruit

∧   **Modular building transportation from Burgeo to Grand Bruit. The flexibility allows for the expansion, contraction, and abandonment of monitoring in any outport community.**

The Overlap

Monitoring Building

Seasonal Storage / Public Space

Building Extension Modules

Building Extension Modules

Seasonal Monitoring & Storage

Seasonal Storage / Public Space

Moveable Monitoring Modules

Fish Processing Building

Building Extension Modules

∧   **Building diagrams of the main shore station located in Burgeo and all other outport portable buildings. The intervention in Burgeo hosts fish processing, ocean monitoring, and watercraft storage. Designed with the ability to expand or contract to respond to economic and ecological conditions as well as alternate program throughout the different seasons. The outport interventions are flexible and modular monitoring buildings (found within the Burgeo shore station) that convert into storage units for the platforms and monitoring devices in the winter.**

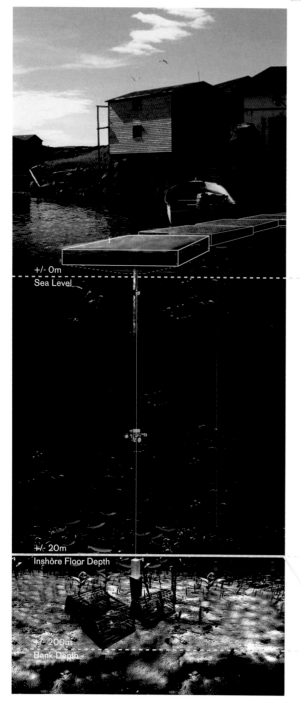

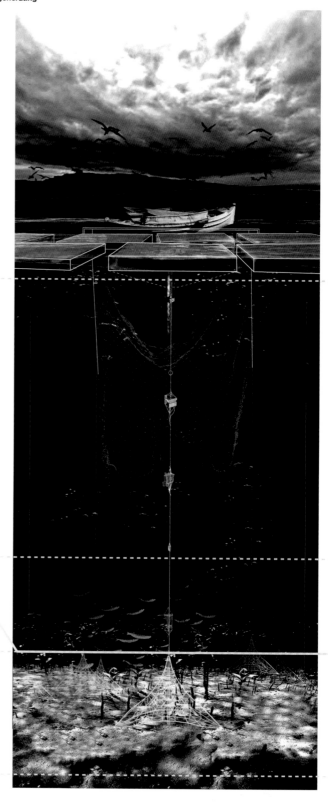

+/- 0m
Sea Level

+/- 20m
Inshore Floor Depth

+/- 200m
Bank Depth

+/- 400m
Channel Depth

∧   Device elevation breakdown based on
depth of deployment. The buoyant element on the
upper portion aids in the harvest of wave energy.
Along the anchoring line, monitoring units are
suspended to collect data within the network.

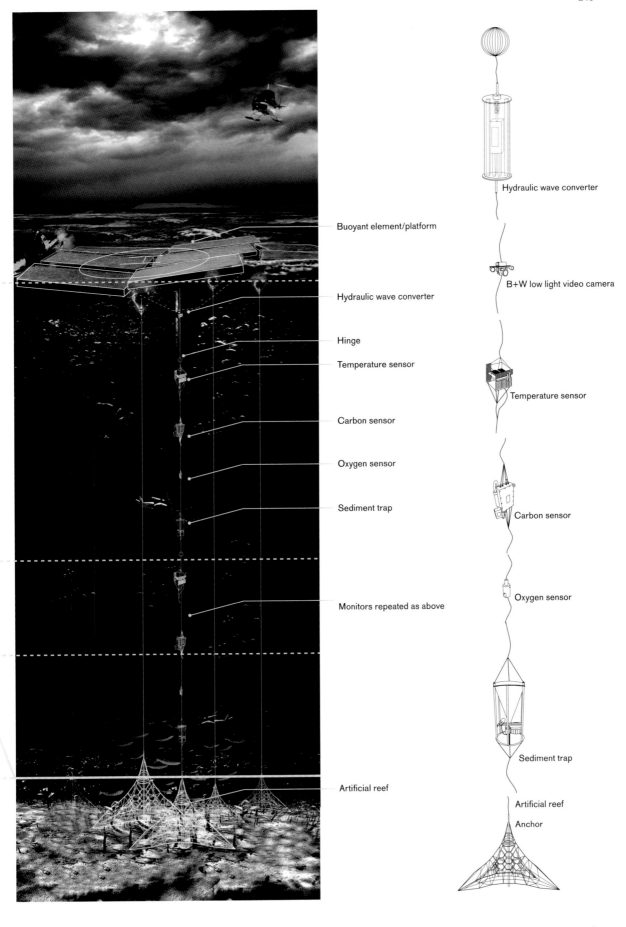

Buoyant element/platform

Hydraulic wave converter

Hinge

Temperature sensor

Carbon sensor

Oxygen sensor

Sediment trap

Monitors repeated as above

Artificial reef

Hydraulic wave converter

B+W low light video camera

Temperature sensor

Carbon sensor

Oxygen sensor

Sediment trap

Artificial reef

Anchor

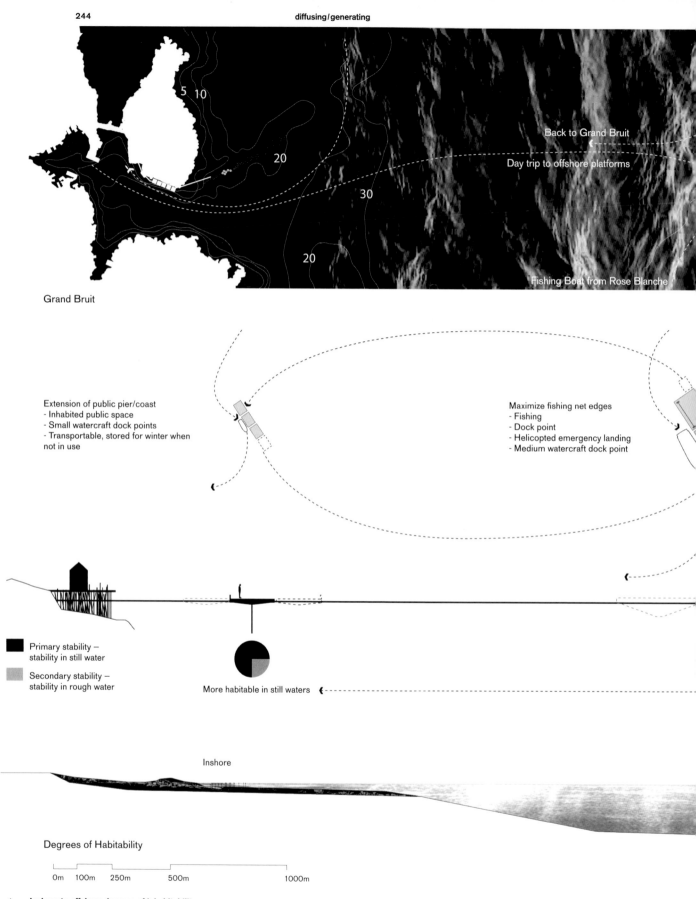

Grand Bruit

Extension of public pier/coast
- Inhabited public space
- Small watercraft dock points
- Transportable, stored for winter when not in use

Maximize fishing net edges
- Fishing
- Dock point
- Helicopted emergency landing
- Medium watercraft dock point

Back to Grand Bruit

Day trip to offshore platforms

Fishing Boat from Rose Blanche

■ Primary stability —
stability in still water

■ Secondary stability —
stability in rough water

More habitable in still waters

Inshore

Degrees of Habitability

0m   100m   250m   500m   1000m

∧   **Inshore to offshore degrees of inhabitability.**
Platform design is based on distance to shore
and sea conditions.

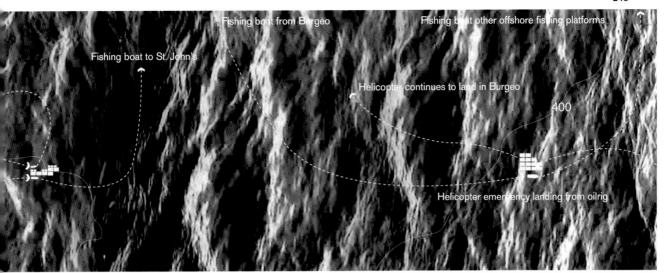

Fishing boat from Burgeo

Fishing boat other offshore fishing platforms

Fishing boat to St. John's

Helicopter continues to land in Burgeo

400

Helicopter emergency landing from oilrig

Maximize flat surface
- Helicopter emergency landing
- Coast guard dock point
- Large watercraft dock point

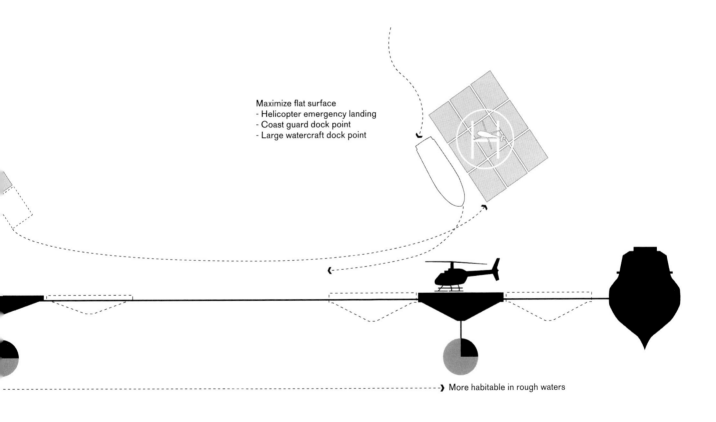

More habitable in rough waters

Banks

Offshore

+/- 0m sea level
+/- 20m inshore floor depth
+/- 200m bank depth
+/- 400m channel depth

GOES SOFT

bracket—

SKY_NET: A HIGH POWER MIGRATION NETWORK

JARED WINCHESTER

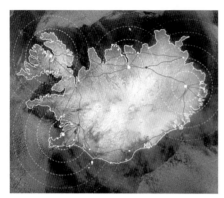

∧ **The National Power Migration Network of Iceland: This map indicates a proposal for a new power loop encircling the island and reaching all populated areas, which are mostly located along the periphery. Geothermal power plants feed the network while in transit power production feeds into the grid along the way. Local landlines will remain around some towns to minimize the impact of the new infrastructure. Over time these linkages could be relocated underground or be serviced by new power migration lines.**

Any sufficiently advanced technology is indistinguishable from magic.
—Arthur C. Clark

∧ **Many experimental high-altitude wind turbines currently under development offer the potential to generate power and facilitate its transmission with a much lighter presence upon the landscape. (Image courtesy of Sky WindPower)**

Design Ideology for Remote Area Power Transmission

This project re-imagines the electric infrastructure of Iceland by integrating multiple technologies, which are only now becoming viable, into a singular symbiotic network. *Sky_Net* resolves an ongoing conflict in Iceland, between the need for transmitting power supply to towns across great distances of pristine landscape and the desire to preserve the appearance of its landscape, by reimagining the electrical grid as an ethereal infrastructure held aloft high-up in the sky. Across vast, remote regions of the country this new electrical transmission landscape will be suspended midair by a network of high altitude wind turbines, riding the consistently strong air currents like a kite. In this way, wind energy becomes a supplemental power source that feeds into and enhances the grid, while at the same time acting as the infrastructure to support the transmission lines themselves. While geothermal energy is a seemingly renewable resource that Iceland is progressively tapping into, it is

not without its own environmental impacts and it is speculated that some of Iceland's thermal reservoirs could become depleted within the next fifty years. This new infrastructure will allow for a transition from power sourced from the earth to one sourced from the sky.

Transmission Distance = Power Generation Opportunity

Both the wind turbine modules and high voltage power lines coexist in an interconnected fabric of power generation and transmission. These float at an altitude that renders invisible their presence at ground level. The strength and constant force of wind in the high altitude air stream will keep the modules operating, generating power and producing lift for the transmission lines. To keep *Sky_Net* aloft during low-speed winds, power is pulled directly from the electro-magnetic field to increase turbine speeds for additional lift. The network requires periodic tethering to the ground with high strength cable stays, in order to maintain its approximate

course through the sky. Where these cable-stayed structures anchor to the ground near inhabited areas, power line tethering points will also contain a substation. Power can be carried underground from this point for local distribution—eliminating the need for any new transmission line towers.

Environmental Impact

Sky_Net allows for bird migration below its altitude range, and avoids commercial airline flight paths above it. Low energy LED lighting alerts aircraft at night, and will be faintly visible from the ground. The *Sky_Net* floats along the edges of urban areas, supplying power and keeping people a safe distance from its electro-magnetic field. The new power line infrastructure flies like a kite: adapting to wind and weather patterns. Because of the flexibility and scale of *Sky_Net*, its changing shape and position in the sky will act as like a weathervane for wind and weather recognition. In time, the infrastructure might be enhanced through new technologies such as carbon dioxide harvesters and ozone

∧　The presence of the new power infrastructure will at times be nearly invisible.

detectors—thus allowing the system to grow and evolve its intelligence with each new phase of Icelandic innovation.

Adaptability and Implementation
The availability of consistent high altitude wind speeds, the desire to limit infrastructure's impact on remote wildernesses, and the need to avoid conflict with air traffic, make this infrastructure best suited for implementation in the far northern and southern hemispheres. One could imagine variations of this infrastructure in extreme, remote locations such as base camps in Antarctica, where the network would function as an entirely closed loop system. As climate change unlocks both potentials and challenges for the polar territories, *Sky_Net* could become a favorable power strategy for emerging development industries within the Arctic as well.

・・・**Jared Winchester is a designer based in Albuquerque, New Mexico. He is founder of the architectural studio, Entropic Industries.**

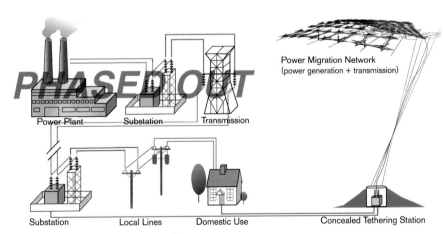

∧　A new power distribution + generation paradigm.

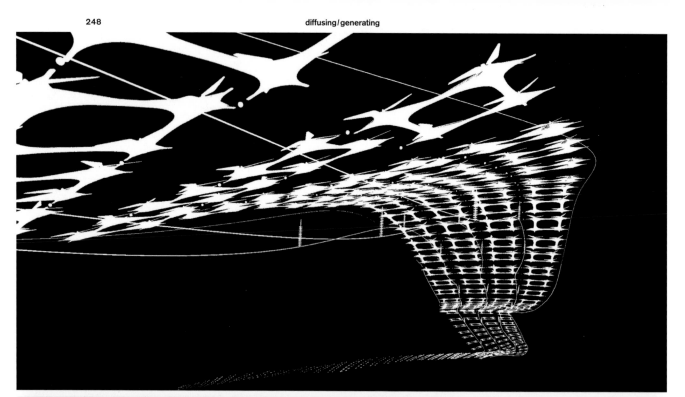

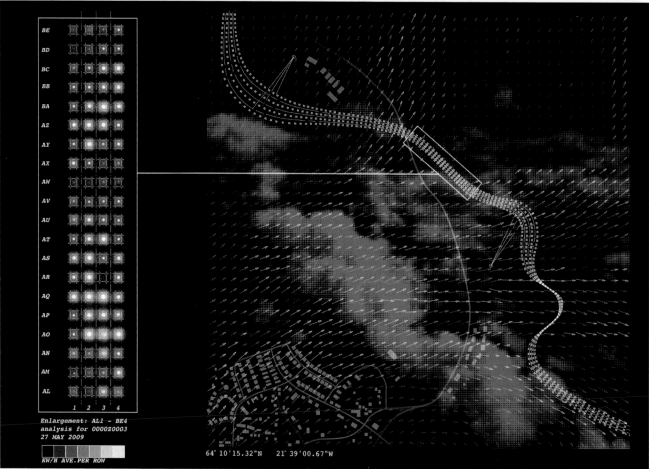

Enlargement: AL1 - BE4
analysis for 0000Z0003
27 MAY 2009

KW/H AVE.PER ROW

64° 10'15.32"N   21° 39'00.67"W

∧   **Monitoring stations will split the power loop down into smaller sections for analysis and power mapping. This could range from an inventory of regional power production to the specific efficiency output of an individual module. Technological enhancement to the modules could provide opportunities to monitor other meteorological data in the future.**

Winchester   Sky_Net

∧   The power migration lines position themselves at an altitude of consistent wind velocity above various regions in Iceland. Adjustments in altitude can be made to optimize performance, stay clear of cruising intercontinental aircraft, and stay above migration routes of most bird species. Individual turbine units may be switched to manual operation, detached from the *Sky_Net* grid, and flown down to ground as a remote controlled aircraft for maintenance purposes.

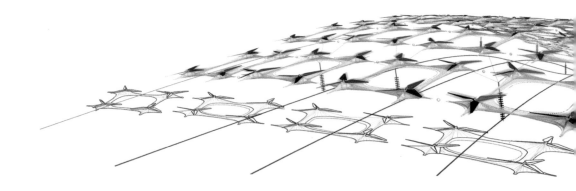

∧   A vast panoramic view in rural Iceland
reveals a power migration linkage hovering
in and out of sight. Its degree of visibility
and location within the sky relative to outly-
ing communities will constantly change with
the prevailing wind and weather conditions.
>   Following page: Power migration
intertwined with the aurora borealis in the
winter months

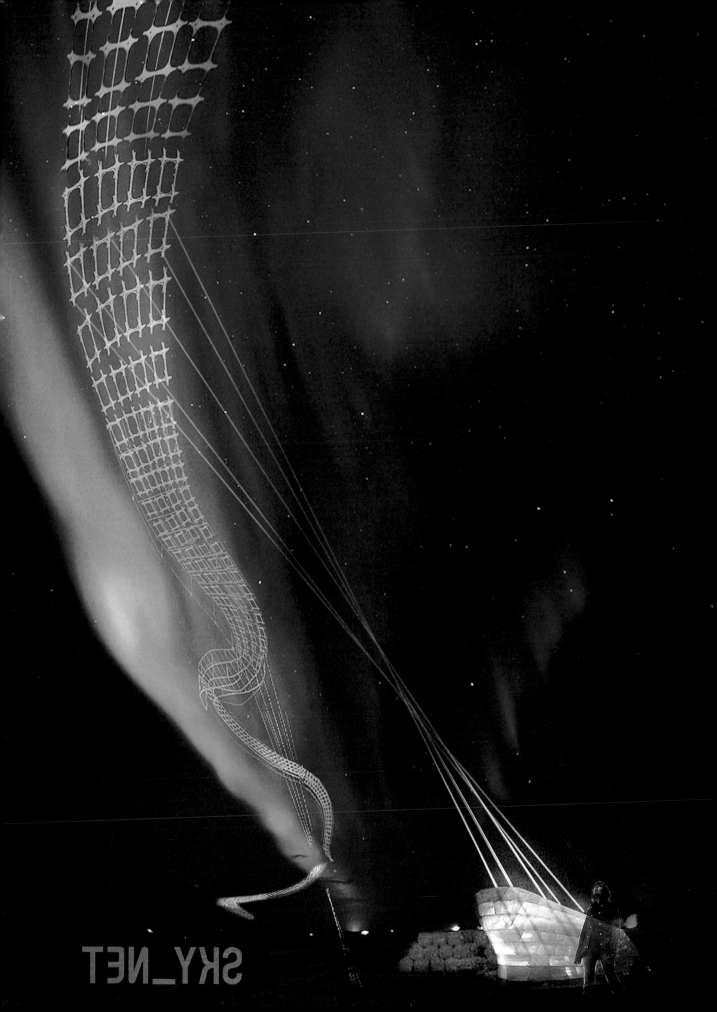

KNOWLEDGE CULTIVATION

NICHOLAS MUSSER

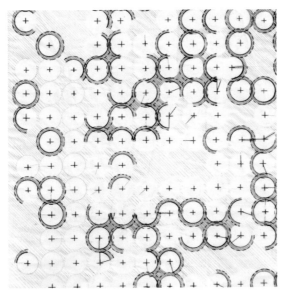 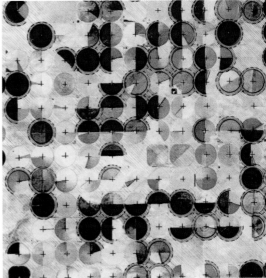

∧   Initial study of crop circle patterns in the
Midwest, testing the potential of the voids.

Patterns

This project began by looking at agricultural methods
and their impact across the United States, and by reacting to the configurations of these immensely scaled
interventions. In America, the radial irrigation methodology was quickly found to be an efficient system that
subsequently cast its pattern almost effortlessly across
the agrarian landscape. Unfortunately, this method of
farming interrupts biodiversity and natural ecosystems.
This technological crutch limits farming practices,
and distances humans from the land as fewer and fewer
people continue to farm.

Traces

The "traces" in this story depict a conversation between
two brothers, one a Master Builder and the other a Master
Cultivator. The brothers tend the land and are stewards
of the Earth. Although they occupy the site for many seasons, they do not own the land. In their eyes land cannot
be owned. Their first act on site is to refocus the technological crutch that is the irrigation arm, in an effort
to inscribe local knowledge into the land. They design a
paddock (two hundred feet by two hundred feet) that can
be pulled by the irrigation arm. Each day the arm pulls the
paddock and cattle to fresh pasture. Chickens follow three
days later in a similar paddock and are part of symbiotic
relationship with the cattle. The inscription that is left
behind is meant to be a guide for future generations of
Cultivators and Builders, and hopes to renew an interest
in working the land.

Seasonal Shifts

The Builder finds protection beneath the silo datum for
the first winter, spending much of their time milling
wood from the site to construct a windbreak for the cattle.
When the spring rains fill the well, they emerge from
their underground shelter and head back to the city for
the warmer months. The rains activate life on the farm,
and as the well fills with water, the silo datum floats to
the observation posture. During the summer months, the
farm is in full growth. The Builder and Cultivator work
together during the fall to collect the irrigation arms and
utter triggers as they prepare the land for the resting season. As the dormant season arrives, the Builder returns to
the protective well beneath the silo. They continue to mill
wood and store their bounty on the drying rack that they
built the previous winter. As winter fades to spring, the
Builder recalibrates the drawing sled for the next season,
and after two seasons the drawing sled and irrigation arm
migrate to a new site to begin drawing again.

• • • Nicholas Musser was raised in the
agrarian landscape of Pennsylvania. He studied architecture as an undergrad and is now
working in Philadelphia.

∧   **Spring: The drawing sled deposits a mound
of soil every two hundred feet.**

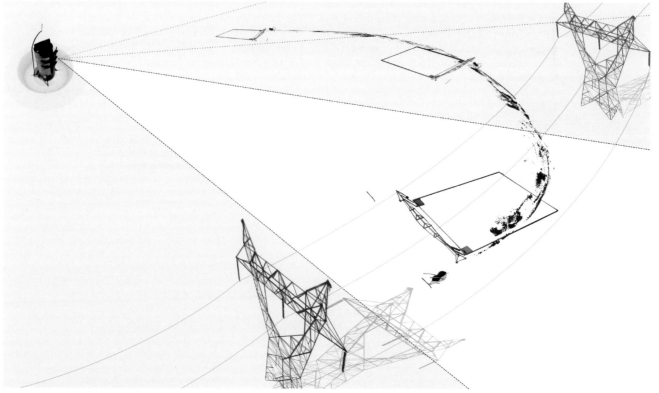

>   **Diagram of the cultivator observing the
Paddocks as they pass beneath the high tension
lines.**

> The initial conversation between the culti-
vator and the builder. Each day the irrigation arm
pulls the paddock to fresh pasture.

⋀⋀ **Summer: A rare lightning strike bursts**   ⋀   **Fall: The power lines emit such a powerful**   lines glow until the first frost shorts them out,
the network of frost lamps to life and they pulse   electromagnetic field that fluorescent tubes glow   reminding the cultivator that the season has
slowly until their collected energy dissipates.   beneath them without an external power source.   come to an end.
                                                       The frost lamps that are in close proximity to the

bracket—

DREDGE LOCKED
ALEX YUEN

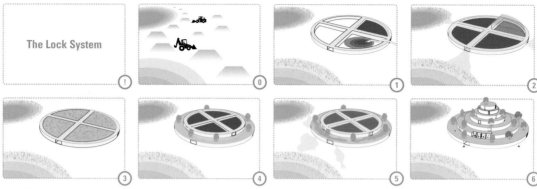

∧ The proposed system addresses the treatment of dredged material and the process of remediation, to foreground water treatment and topography in Houston.

Unnoticed by many, Houston's shipping channel, like many commercial waterways, is subject to a continual process of dredging in order to maintain the breadth and depth required to accommodate the vessels that enter and leave the city's port. However, this material is seldom regarded as anything other than waste, and is deposited and contained either within the channel or onshore, taking up space and spreading harmful petrochemical bi-products, which are released by local facilities and find their way into the channel. Up to this point, such actions have rarely been scrutinized and this system of isolating and hiding the contaminated material, even at such a massive scale, continues. Yet in a new era of environmental awareness and accountability, significant opportunities are lost by simply sweeping these materials under the rug.

As *The International Association of Dredging Companies* notes, "the need for confined disposal facilities for dredged material is greatest near coastal areas, precisely the regions where the competition for other land uses such as housing, recreation, and nature reserves is greatest."[1] *Dredge Locked* proposes to capitalize on dredging containment, as a means of opening up alternative urban uses. The project is a system of containment and remediation of dredged materials. While deployed in Houston, the system has applicability to any number of regions where dredging occurs. The project is based on cycles of remediation, in order to remove the contaminated water that makes up a large portion of what is dredged from the channel. Before any dredging is dumped on site, parcels of land are excavated and wetlands are established within them. These wetlands serve as the primary zones of phytoremediation, where plant life, algae, and bacteria absorb or breakdown toxins present in the effluent from the initial dredging dumps.

Once these wetlands are established, a re-engineered form of the dikes, currently used to contain dredged material, is put into place. These locks, which are circular and quadrisected by two tubes, play a number of roles over time. Initially, they serve to contain dredged material that is pumped directly on land from boats in the channel. Once the slurry begins to separate, with sediment dropping to the bottom and water heading to the top, the quadrisecting tubes act as filters to direct leaching liquid into the wetlands. When the dredged contents have dried, plant life and vegetation can be grown above the lock, establishing another zone of phytoremediation to account for the runoff produced by placing another, smaller, lock on top of the original. What results is a long-term system of storage and remediation, which over years will cleanse the contained material of its contaminants while creating layers of greenery and plant life.

Once the lock's remediation responsibilities are over, it begins to accommodate human habitation within its poché and the drying of the dredged material allows housing to slowly colonize the accumulating mounds. The continued implementation of the system gradually transforms the site from disposal facility to inhabited community where residents, attracted by the rare possibility of topography in Houston, witness the landscape emerge and grow around them. Situated between infrastructure and architecture, container and housing, disposal facility and oversize planter, the functional flexibility of the lock defines a unit that can be configured and stacked to form a productive landscape that is continually indexing the economy. Over time, the system gives rise to a region that fluctuates between industrial site, urban wetland, residential community, and constructed topography.

• • • Alex Yuen is an undergraduate student at Rice University where he is a candidate to receive his Bachelor of Architecture degree in 2014.

1. International Association of Dredging Companies, "Facts About Confined Disposal Facilities, An Information Update from the IADC," Number 1, 2010. www.iadc-dredging.com/index.php?option=com_content&task=view&id=140&Itemid=330.

The site accomodates 1,000,000 cubic yards of sediment every 3-4 years

YEAR 0   **YEAR 4**   **YEAR 8**   **YEAR 15**   **YEAR 23**

The system creates a constantly evolving landscape

Humans can occupy a lock once its dredge has dried

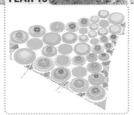

The project will reach its capacity after about 30 years...

∧   The process plays out over years, creating a dynamic landscape of dredging, cleansing, and housing.

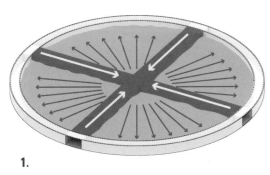

1.

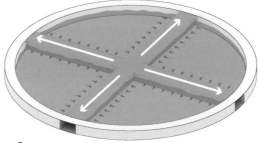

2.

1. The primary function of the structure is to lock and contain dredged material. In order for the walls to become hollowed out, tubes dissect the circle providing rigidity and an element to counteract the forces that result from filling the structure with dredging.

2. Once the dredging has been placed into the container and the sediment and liquid have begun to separate, water must be removed from the container. Due to a slightly porous nature, the tubes begin to allow that water to be absorbed and channelled out of the lock.

3. The partitioning of the wall is done in a manner that compensates for the weaknesses that result from the opening in the wall from the tubes. Thus, the closer to an opening in the wall, the higher the rate of partitioning. This effect also creates a slight diversity in spaces to accommodate the needs of different occupancy groups.

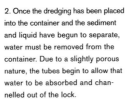

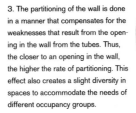

3.

4.

4. Once the enlaced dredge has been dried and the structure is ready for inhabitation, the tubes serve as internal circulation across the current level, as well as forming connections to the above and below levels through a vertical core located at the center.

5. Finally, the poché can also be used to allow for automobile circulation up and down the structures allowing for certain mounds to accommodate parking.

5.

∧   A new hybrid infrastructure serves as a container for dredged material, a filter for contaminated liquid and housing units or parking structures, becoming the main building block for a new ecology and urbanity.

Yuen   Dredge Locked

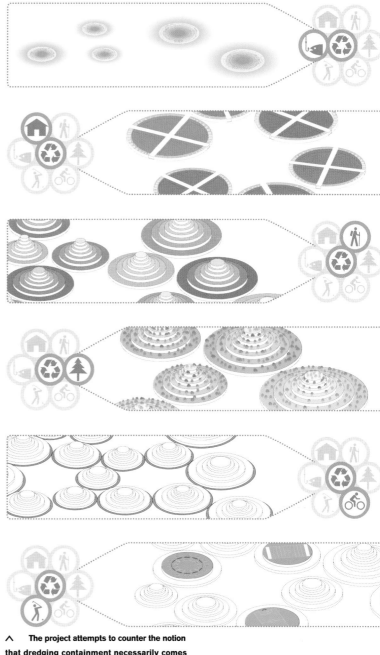

∧ View of wetlands/locks—continually in construction/remediation.

< Located just east of the I-610 belt, the site of the proposal finds itself at the confluence of the urban, the suburban, and the industrial. Continually growing towers of remediation make up the new development. Vegetation covers the earthy material held within the lock, a new type of containment in an area already very familiar with petrochemical storage.

∧ The project attempts to counter the notion that dredging containment necessarily comes at the cost of other natural or recreational experiences.

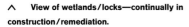

goes soft——editorial board

Neeraj Bhatia is an architect and urban designer focused on the intersection of politics, infrastructure and new urban environments. He received his Masters of Architecture + Urban Design from MIT and his B.Arch from the University of Waterloo. He has worked for Eisenman Architects, Coop Himmelblau, Bruce Mau Design, OMA, ORG, and Lateral Office. He has taught at the University of Waterloo, the University of Toronto and is currently the visiting Wortham Teaching Fellow at Rice University. Neeraj is a co-director of InfraNet Lab, a non-profit research collective probing the spatial byproducts of contemporary resource logistics, and founder of The Open Workshop, a design office examining the project of plurality. He is co-author of *Pamphlet Architecture 30* (Princeton Architectural Press, 2010), and co-editor of *Arium: Weather + Architecture* (with Jürgen Mayer H., Hatje Cantz Publishing, 2009).

Benjamin H. Bratton is a sociological, media, and design theorist. He is Associate Professor of Visual Arts at the University of California, San Diego and Director of the Design Policy Program at the California Institute of Telecommunications and Information Technology. Benjamin is the former Director of the Advanced Strategies Group at Yahoo! and taught at UCLA and SCI_Arc for several years. His work sits at the intersections of contemporary social and political theory, computational media and infrastructure, and architectural and urban design problems and methodologies.

Julia Czerniak is an Associate Professor of Architecture at Syracuse University and the inaugural Director of UPSTATE. She is also a registered landscape architect and founder of CLEAR, an interdisciplinary design practice. Czerniak's design work focuses on urban landscapes in Rust-Belt cities, and it has been recognized with numerous awards. Most recently, her collaborations have won the Syracuse Connective Corridor competition, the artNET Public Art competition in Toledo, Ohio; and the Pittsburgh Charm Bracelet competition. Her work as designer is complemented by a body of writing. Czerniak is editor of two books, *Large Parks* (Princeton Architectural Press, 2007) and *Case: Downsview Park Toronto* (Prestel and Harvard Design School, 2001), that focus on contemporary design approaches to public parks and the relationship between landscape and cities. Other writings include essays in *Landscape Alchemy: The Work of Hargreaves Associates* (2009); *Fertilizers: Olin Eisenman* (2006); *Landscape Urbanism* (2006); and *Assemblage 34* (1998).

Jeffrey Inaba is the founder of INABA, an architecture firm in Los Angeles and New York that is currently working on projects in Europe, Asia and the United States. INABA's work has been exhibited at the Whitney Biennial, New Museum, Walker Art Center, Storefront for Art and Architecture, and Fondazione Sandretto Re Rebaudengo. He directs C-Lab, a research unit at Columbia University's Graduate School of Architecture, Planning, and Preservation that investigates urban and architecture issues of public consequence. C-Lab co-edits *Volume* magazine, an independent quarterly where Inaba is the features editor. He is the author of other publications, including the book, *World of Giving* (Lars Müller Publishers, 2010). Previously, Rem Koolhaas and Inaba led the Harvard Project on the City, a research program that explored contemporary urbanism, and before starting INABA he was a principal of AMO. Inaba received a Master of Architecture with Distinction and Master in the Philosophy of Architecture degrees from Harvard University and an AB from The University of California, Berkeley.

Geoff Manaugh is the author of BLDGBLOG (bldgblog.blogspot.com) and *The BLDGBLOG Book* (Chronicle Books, 2009), former senior editor of *Dwell* magazine and a contributing editor at *Wired UK*. Along with Nicola Twilley, he organized and co-curated "Landscapes of Quarantine," a design studio and group exhibition at New York's Storefront for Art and Architecture (2010), and he is solo curator of an exhibition at the Nevada Museum of Art entitled "Landscape Futures: Instruments, Devices and Architectural Inventions" (2011). In addition to lecturing on a broad range of architectural topics at museums and design schools worldwide, Manaugh has taught at Columbia University, USC, the Pratt Institute, and the University of Technology, Sydney. In 2011, he became co-director of Studio-X New York, an off-campus event space and urban futures think tank run by Columbia University's GSAPP.

Charles Renfro is a practicing architect and partner of Diller Scofidio + Renfro (DS+R), based in New York City. Renfro was an associate at Smith-Miller+Hawkinson Architects and Ralph Appelbaum Associates, and a founding partner of the Department of Design before joining Diller + Scofidio in 1997. He has served as Project Leader on the Brasserie, Eyebeam, the BAM master plan (with OMA), Blur, and the Boston Institute of Contemporary Art. Recently, Renfro has served as a Design Principal for the redesign and expansion of The Juilliard School, Alice Tully Hall, Public Spaces at Lincoln Center for the Performing Arts, High Line, and the Museum of Image and Sound in Rio de Janiero, among other projects. Prior to joining DS+R, his work has been exhibited in several galleries including the Storefront for Art and Architecture in New York. In 2009, Renfro joined the board for the Storefront for Art and Architecture. His writing has been published in *Bomb* and *A+U* magazine. He lectures frequently both in the United States and abroad. Renfro is a graduate of Rice University and holds a Master's degree from Columbia University's GSAPP. He has been on the faculty of Columbia since 2000 and was the Cullinan Visiting Professor at Rice University in 2006. Since 2009, Renfro has served as Visiting Scholar at the Friends Seminary and Visiting Professor at Parsons New School for Design.

Lola Sheppard is an architect based in Toronto. She received her B.Arch from McGill University and her M.Arch from Harvard Graduate School of Design. She is currently Assistant Professor at the University of Waterloo, School of Architecture in Canada. She is a founding partner of Lateral Office (2003) with Mason White, a firm dedicated to the productive overlap of architecture, landscape, infrastructure and urbanism. She is also a co-director of InfraNet Lab (2008), a research laboratory dedicated to probing the spatial by-products of contemporary resource logistics. Lateral Office and InfraNet Lab were awarded *Pamphlet Architecture 30*, published by Princeton Architectural Press (2011). Lateral was awarded the Emerging Voices Award (2011) and the Young Architects Forum (2005) from the Architectural League of New York and the Canadian Prix de Rome (2010).

Philippe Rahm was born in 1967 and studied at the Federal Polytechnic Schools of Lausanne and Zurich. In 2002, he was chosen to represent Switzerland at the 8th Architecture Biennale in Venice and is one of the 20 manifesto's architects of the Aaron Betsky's Architectural Venice Biennale (2008). He was a nominee for the Ordos Prize in China (2009) and was in the top ten ranking of the International Chernikov prize in Moscow (2008). He has participated in a number of exhibitions worldwide (Archilab 2000, SF-MoMA 2001, Centre Pompidou, Beaubourg 2003-2006 and 2007, Canadian Centre for Architecture 2007, Louisiana Museum 2009). He was Head-Master of Diploma Unit 13 at the AA School in London in 2005-2006, Visiting professor in Mendrisio Academy of Architecture in Switzerland in 2004 and 2005, at the ETH Lausanne in 2006-2007 and he is currently visiting lecturer at Princeton University's School of Architecture. He is working on several private and public projects in France, Italy, Germany and Taiwan.

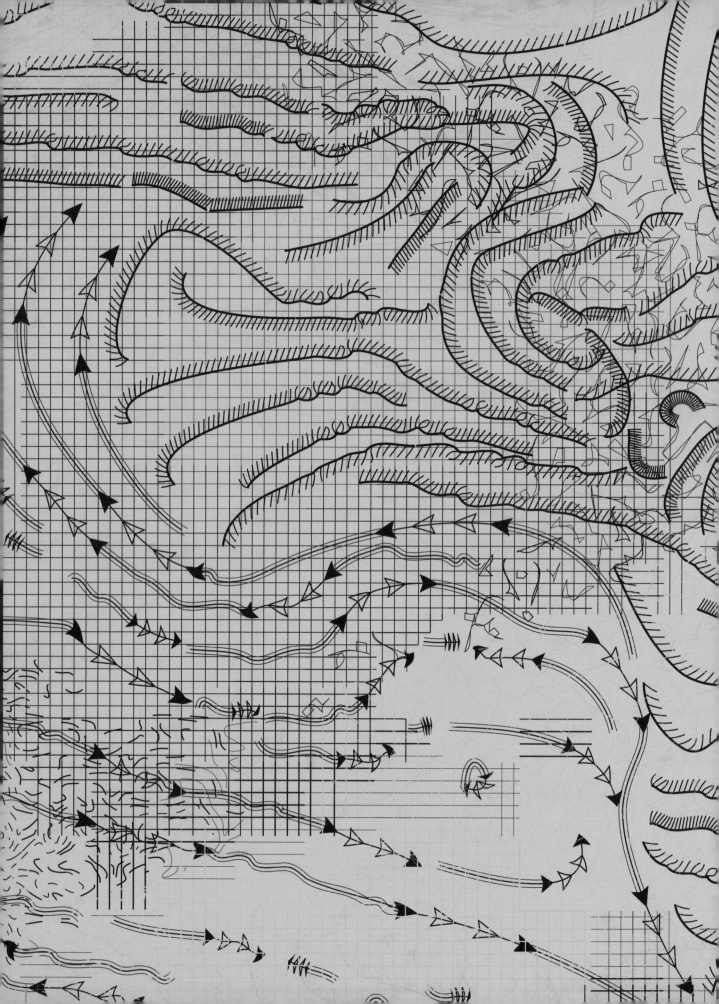

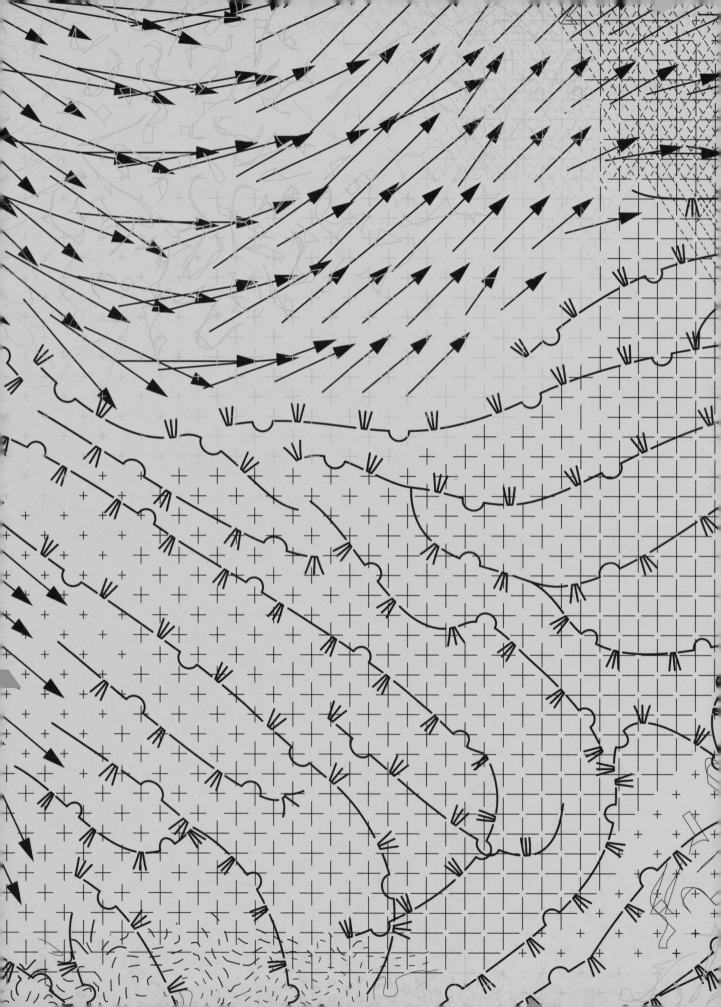

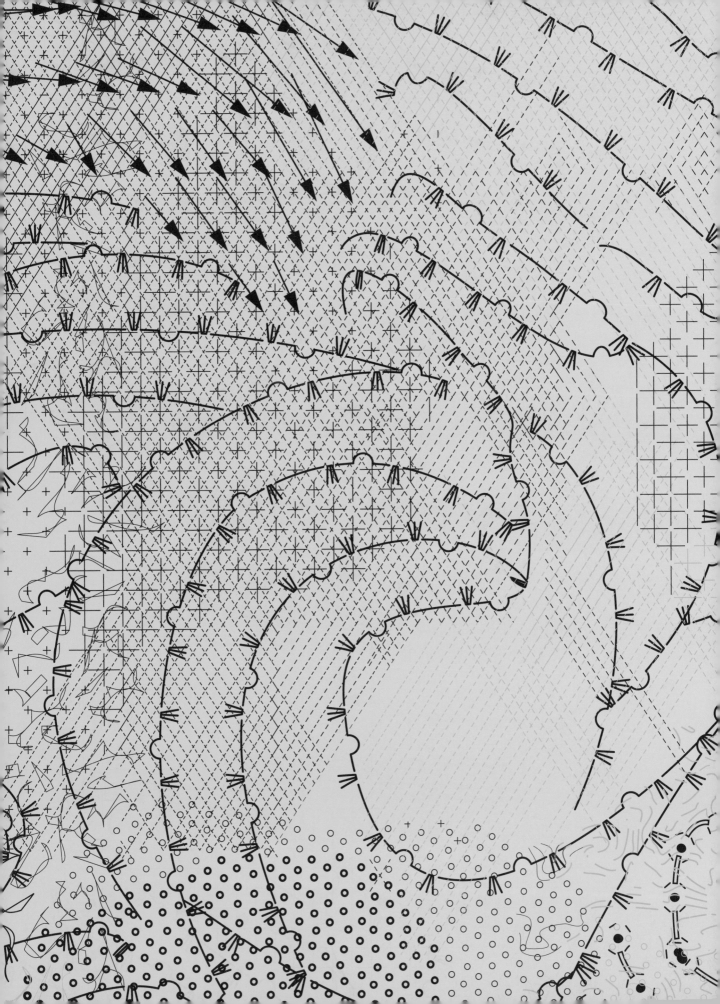

bracket —— at extremes —— almanac 3

editors ——
Maya Przybylski and
Lola Sheppard

editorial board ——
Julien De Smedt
Keller Easterling
Michael Hensel
Alessandra Ponte
François Roche
Hashim Sarkis
Mark Wigley

call for entries ——

Bracket 3 invites the submission of critical articles and un-published design projects that investigate the architectural potentials when situations extend beyond norms—into the extremities. What are the limits of wilderness and control, of the natural and artificial, the real and the virtual?

Bracket [at Extremes] will examine architecture, infra-structure and technology as they operate in conditions of excess or scarcity, negotiate tipping points and test limit states. In situations of imbalance, the status quo is no longer possible; systems must extend performance and accommodate unpredictability. As new protocols emerge, new opportunities present themselves. Bracket 3 will explore architecture's response to the operational and performative implications of extreme states, in relation to themes of environment, scale, and technology.

Please visit www.brkt.org for further information and schedule.

Bracket is an annual almanac of architecture, environment, and digital culture founded by InfraNet Lab and Archinect.